INTEGRATING ENGLISH

DEVELOPING ENGLISH LANGUAGE AND LITERACY IN THE MULTILINGUAL CLASSROOM

D. SCOTT ENRIGHT
MARY LOU McCLOSKEY

Georgia State University

SANDRA J. SAVIGNON
Consulting Editor

 ADDISON-WESLEY PUBLISHING COMPANY

Reading, Massachusetts • Menlo Park, California • New York
Don Mills, Ontario • Wokingham, England • Amsterdam • Sydney
Bonn • Singapore • Tokyo • Madrid • San Juan

Library of Congress Cataloging-in-Publication Data

Enright, D. Scott.

Integrating English: developing English language and literacy in the multilingual classroom/D. Scott Enright, Mary Lou McCloskey; Sandra J. Savignon,
consulting editor.

    p.   cm.

Bibliography: p.

Includes index.

ISBN 1-201-11554-9

1. English language—Study and teaching—Foreign speakers. 2. Education,
Bilingual. I. McCloskey, Mary Lou. II. Savignon, Sandra J. III. Title.

PE1128.A2E6   1988   428'.00724—dc19   87-26345

                                                  CIP

ISBN 0-201-11554-9

10-CRS-97 96 95 94

Contents

To Posy
A Teacher

Introduction

This book describes a language teaching model that can be used by any teacher who is working with school-age students learning English in addition to their native language. We call this model the "Integrated Language Teaching Model" (ILT) because of its emphasis on bringing together many already existing instructional and professional resources in order to better use what we currently know about second language development in the classroom and thus to better serve the needs of second language learners. Since today teachers seem to be asked to *teach everything* to the students they are given, this book is about how to *integrate* what is taught and how it is taught in order to serve in that effort. The forms of integration that are discussed in the book include, among others, integrating English language learning with content and subject-matter learning; integrating the English language processes of reading, writing, listening, and speaking; and integrating students' home language and learning experiences with their school language and learning experiences.

We have developed the integrated language teaching model, along with the many instructional activities and recommendations that are proposed in relation to it, through our own work as classroom teachers in bilingual, English as a Second Language (ESL), and grade-level classroom settings; as curriculum developers; as teacher educators; and as students learning more about language teaching and learning (i.e., as researchers). Our colleagues who are performing these same professional roles make up our intended audience. The ideas in *Integrating English* are directed to *all* teachers whose students are learning ESL, although we shall make some distinctions throughout our discussions to take into account the varied circumstances under which bilingual, ESL, and grade-level classroom teachers work. We also hope that the ideas we present will be of use to all those individuals —teacher educators, curriculum developers, researchers, and others—who are dedicated to supporting teachers in their performance of the language teaching task. Given the limited resources available for schooling our ESL students today, it is only through the well-conceived and concerted efforts of all these educators working together that our major educational goals for our young language learners will be realized. In this hopeful spirit of integration, as well, we title this book *Integrating English*.

THE PLAN OF THIS BOOK

In Part I of *Integrating English* we provide the theoretical framework for the Integrated Language Model and apply the model to the major components of the multilingual classroom. In Chapter 1, we develop a rationale for the integrated model by reviewing the current status of second language education and the recent first and second language acquisition literature. Chapter 1 also outlines the major theoretical assumptions of the integrated model and presents seven instructional criteria which can be used to apply the model in the classroom. Chapter 2 discusses the need for integrating ESL and subject-matter instruction and for integrating the language processes of listening, reading, speaking and writing together within the curriculum. Chapter 3 deals with arranging the classroom social environment to support the various kinds of activities and collaboration necessary to implement the integrated curriculum. Chapter 4 does the same for the classroom physical environment. The difficult task of integrating children's previous language and ways with words with the new language and ways with words of the school is dealt with in Chapters 5, 6, and 7, which all treat the teacher's multiple roles in the integrated classroom. Chapter 5 offers specific suggestions for providing useful, "real" oral discourse to second language students in order to support their oral second language development. Chapter 6 offers specific suggestions for providing real written discourse to second language students to further extend their meaning-making capacities in English. Chapter 7 offers suggestions for integrating students in various stages of second language development in order to facilitate their further language and literacy development through the formation of a pluralistic classroom literacy community. The last kind of integration implied by our seventh criterion and our entire instructional model is dealt with in Chapter 8, "Developing Ties with the School, Home, and Community."

Acknowledgements

Many individuals—more than we can ever thank—have given inspiration, help and support for this project.

Through their creative and dedicated work both inside and outside the classroom the teachers at the Garden Hills International Summer School have helped us to develop this model of second language teaching and many of the ideas and activities for implementing it. We wish to thank Safa Abdur-Rahman, Betty Bolander, Barbara Borgman, Karen Breazeale, Amelia Brown, Diana Davidson, Linda Williams Dorage, Cindy First, Mary Fisher, Annette Gibson, Alma Grubbs, Florence Ngoc Halloran, Cary Duncan Holt, Regina Hughes, Myrtle Joyner, Myrna Lehman, Rosamond Lombard, Alice Martin, Stella Matherne, Rabbi Lawrence Meltzer, Karl Michel, Rena Morano, Mary Jane Nations, Irma Nesby, Kay Nielsen, Barbara Phillips, Tom Phillips, Knox Porter, Susan Putzell, Susan Rawlston, Barbara Rohal, Roberta Rosenberg, Betty Sampson, Marianne Dunlap Sansom, April Schaps, Clara Segars, Vicki Shanahan, Mildred Simms, Carol Skaggs, Frances Smith, Marsha Taylor, Patricia Thornton, Patricia Truslow, Janice Utterback and Margaret Levitt Wynne. In addition, the leadership and counsel of principal Peggy Geren and head teacher Sally Lovein helped to make the summer program flourish and to make this project possible.

Our thanks to Sarah Hudelson for providing us with the direction and integration needed to develop the major ideas in the book and to Janet Ramsay for helping to anchor many of those ideas in the current educational context.

Jean Handscombe's careful review of the manuscript and cogent suggestions for improving it were much appreciated and are gratefully acknowledged here.

We thank Elaine Persons and Cheryl Eidex who entered revision after revision of the copy with unfailing good humor. Thanks also to Cary Buzzelli and Patricia Emerson for their photographic contributions.

Finally, we offer our thanks to Joel Reed, Tom Reed, Sean O'Brien and Kevin O'Brien for their belief and support which made it possible to begin this undertaking and for their patience and humor which were necessary for its completion, and to Nadine Watson for her faith, her wisdom and her carefully placed and lovingly delivered kicks to the posterior.

POETRY ACKNOWLEDGMENTS

Part I

The Integrated Language
Teaching Model

Chapter 1

Rationale

Anonymous

I know a poem of six lines that no one knows
who wrote, except
               that the poet was Chinese and lived
centuries before the birth of
Christ. I said it aloud
               once to some children, and when I reached
the last line suddenly they
understood and together all went—
                              "Ooo!"
imagine that poem, written
                    by a poet truly
who is Anonymous, since
                    in the strict corporeal sense
he hasn't existed for thousands of years—imagine his little
                                        poem traveling
without gas or even a single grease job
across centuries of space and a million
miles of time
          to me, who spoke it
softly aloud to a group of children who heard
and suddenly all together
                    cried "Ooo!"

—Martin Steingesser

3

1.1 INTRODUCTION

The question "What should I do with my students who don't speak English?" is being asked by a growing number of North American teachers today. Projections by the U.S. Department of Education (Oxford et al. 1981) indicate that the number of "limited English-speaking students" (their term) in the U.S. population between the ages of five and fourteen will continue its rapid rise for at least the remainder of this century. In Canada, natural population decreases, combined with "moderate, controlled immigrant population increases throughout the 1980s and 1990s" (Burke 1986) suggest a continued increase in diversity throughout Canadian schools. No longer are these students to be found in relatively few school districts in a few states and provinces; rather, the trend is toward the creation of linguistically different households in a growing number of communities across all regions of North America. The diversity of the students in this population is also astounding, as it increasingly includes not only children from different linguistic groups (e.g., Vietnamese, Spanish, Cantonese), but also students from diverse cultural and socioeconomic backgrounds within these linguistic groups (e.g., Vietnamese physicians' children and Vietnamese fishermen's children, Cantonese children from urban areas and Cantonese children from rural areas). Today, multilingualism and multiculturalism are quickly becoming the rule rather than the exception in North American schools.

In the United States, as the linguistic and cultural diversity of the public schools is increasing, educational programs in general are being trimmed. With regard to students with "special needs," including students learning English as a Second Language (ESL), the prevailing federal as well as local philosophy appears to be that these students should be "mainstreamed" (placed in the regular school program with minimal additional support) as soon as possible. Of course, the burdens created by implementing this policy are borne by teachers. Bilingual and other grade-level classroom teachers must try to cope with increasing diversity and greater demands on their limited resources, including instructional time. ESL teachers, while trying to continue to meet the needs of the students they are assigned, must add to their responsibilities plans for supporting and advising their students' other teachers, and they must try to do this in the face of declining resources and support. This text offers some suggestions for coping with these new challenges.

1.2 THE TWO WORLDS OF TEACHING

As if all of these difficulties weren't enough, those who teach in the public schools today also find themselves trying to accomplish their goals in two different and often conflicting educational worlds. One of these, and the one we will discuss first, is the world of education as a scholarly, professional discipline. Here, teachers can find a breathtakingly rich assortment of innovative instructional techniques and materials. They can subscribe to diverse professional journals describing current educational research insights and instructional innovations and ways to utilize them in the classroom. They can (and often must) take further college courses and seek advanced degrees in education. Teachers can also join their colleagues in professional associations to discuss important issues, to conduct research in their classrooms, and to attend conferences at which scholars and fellow teachers present their own studies and thoughts about how children learn and how teachers should teach. In this "ideal" educational arena, two assumptions are made: first, that teachers control what happens in their classrooms, and second, that they therefore accept responsibility for what happens in their classrooms. Thus, professional inquiry is esteemed, and efforts to make instructional innovations that will improve individual teaching performance are encouraged. Bilingual/ESL education is a vibrant and rapidly growing field within the world of education as a professional discipline. As such, it offers a number of fresh perspectives and applications of these perspectives to teachers interested in improving their teaching performance with respect to their second language learners. Many of these ideas will be discussed in this book.

Increasingly, however, the world of education as a scholarly and professional discipline abruptly terminates at the school's front door, where the other world in which teachers operate begins. This is the world of the centralized educational bureaucracy. Here, teachers find an astonishing assortment of files, computer forms, and records that they are required by their employers to complete and maintain, and that have little or nothing to do with their primary job function—teaching. They find a long list of other noninstructional duties that they are required to perform as well—from monitoring cafeteria lines to collecting money. They find a rigid working environment within which they must conduct their day-to-day teaching activities, a place where standards and operating procedures are complex and inviolable and serve the interests of the bureaucracy, not of the classroom. They often find themselves working for a skeptical or downright hostile community and with unfriendly or uncaring colleagues. Contrary to the working assumptions of the ideal world of education, in the "real" world of the centralized bureaucracy, many of the most important decisions about what will happen inside classrooms are made by people outside classrooms. These individuals believe they know more about what is best for students than teachers do, and the factors they use to make the overall decisions that affect the schools (such as political power, public relations, and bureaucratic efficiency) often do not relate to the needs of students and teachers. Although teachers have little control over major decisions about how they will work, they are still the members of the educational bureaucracy who are held responsible when the schools fail to live up to traditional public expectations. When SAT scores sag and dropout rates soar, the accusing headlines in the daily newspapers and on the covers of the weekly news magazines read "Why Teachers Can't Teach," not "Why Legislators Can't Legislate," "Why Administrators Can't Administer" or "Why Test Designers Can't Test."

In this second educational world, the players who control the decision making often seem skeptical about or threatened by the other world of education as a place of ideas, growth, and change. Moreover, they have developed formal and informal mechanisms to fend off teachers' autonomous efforts to innovate and to engage in professional inquiry. Like all well-entrenched institutions, the centralized bureaucracies in place in our public schools generally handle new theoretical perspectives and research ideas that are developed in education as a discipline in two ways, both of which serve to preserve the status quo: they either resist and ignore them, or they reduce and rigidify them into new instruments of external control. One current example of this is the continuing outcry by many teachers and educational theorists against using standardized testing as practically the sole means for labeling and penalizing or rewarding children and teachers, for determining curriculum and instructional processes, and for making many other critical educational policy decisions. In spite of this protest, these centrally administered and bureaucratically efficient production control instruments continue to be the driving force in modern U.S. schools.

Unfortunately, many of the recent developments in the field of children's language acquisition and second language education require just the sort of substantive changes in policy and instruction that the centralized educational bureaucracy resists. Indeed, we will argue that the overall organization of the educational bureaucracy and of the schools and curriculum it supports is based largely on an instructional model that differs dramatically from the one predicated by recent second language acquisition research. Therefore, we will present a language teaching resource book to accomplish three related tasks: (1) to summarize some of the most important concepts from the world of education as a discipline regarding how children learn language (including their first language and their second or additional language); (2) to outline the classroom implications of these concepts; and (3) to make suggestions for how to put these concepts and implications to work in the classroom to assist second language students, while taking into account the limited resources and control that many public school teachers have available to them.

To accomplish our three tasks, we will use a new working assumption about the powers and control of teachers today, one that at least partially synthesizes those assumptions which are held separately by the two worlds we have identified. Our working assumption is that while you—the teacher reading this book—are indeed buffeted by continual external demands on your teaching and are perhaps very low in the power configuration of your own educational bureaucracy, you still maintain a great deal of power and control within your own classroom which can be used to carry out the instructional agendas in which you truly believe. One of our main goals as the authors of this book will be to highlight several areas of instruction (such as the ways in which you organize your furniture and lessons and the ways that you talk with your students) which you as a teacher still do control but may not always exploit for your own teaching purposes. Our illustrations and recommendations will center on second language instruction, since our main focus is the improvement of second language teaching. We strongly believe, however, that a continuing awareness of these areas of teaching control and decision-making can increase your powers in all instructional settings and subject-matter disciplines.

1.3 WHY A MODEL?

In the recent history of public-school second language education in the United States, there has never been a clear consensus within either the educational community or the public at large concerning our goals for our young second language learners, much less concerning the instructional methods and materials that should be used to reach these goals. At present, in government circles, in the popular media, and in the two worlds of education, the debates continue over basic second language education issues such as bilingual education versus ESL education (e.g., Gersten and Woodward 1985, as contrasted with Santiago 1985) and "cultural assimilation" versus "cultural pluralism" (e.g., Rodriguez 1982, as contrasted with Feinberg 1981-1982).

Within these debates and within the formal programs and curricula that have been derived from them, teachers struggle to maintain their own personal teaching goals and methods—which sometimes match those of the programs and curricula imposed upon them and sometimes do not. What happens when teachers' personal goals and teaching styles do not match the goals of these curricula and programs? We think that both the programs and the teachers suffer. This mismatch partly explains why many of the solutions that have been proposed to solve the problems of second language education have neither succeeded nor endured.

As teacher educators and teachers ourselves, we do not believe that the most effective instruction comes from one particular curriculum or program that has been externally designed and then imposed upon teachers. Rather, we believe that it comes from those teachers who have a clear idea of what they want their students to get out of their classrooms (their educational goals), who have a clear theoretical and practical framework for accomplishing their goals (their instructional model), and who constantly strive to develop and improve their knowledge and performance and to grow professionally. These beliefs have guided us in our work with second language teachers and in preparing this book. In the pages that follow, we will first describe our own educational goals for second language learners, and we will then describe the theoretical and practical framework—or *instructional model*—which we have developed to meet these goals, a framework that is based on our own teaching experiences and on current first and second language development research and theory. You may then compare the goals of this model to your own educational goals and use the framework and teaching ideas that are derived from it to enhance your own instruction as you see fit.

We have designed the integrated language teaching (ILT) model as a coherent but flexible framework for thinking about and organizing language instruction, not as a set of instructional "commandments" that must be slavishly followed in order to produce success. In this way, our model is meant to be inclusive rather than exclusive, permitting many instructional materials and strategies to be used within the framework we provide. Only you can finally decide what is really worthwhile and workable for you, given your teaching strengths and weaknesses and your students. On the other hand, the ILT model will *not* offer you a magical remedy or a quick fix for all your educational problems, nor will the instructional criteria, learning activities, and teaching ideas that we present in this book be "quick and easy" to implement. We do not promise you easy ways to meet the educational needs of your second language students, because we don't believe there are any. We do offer you some ways to think about the field of second language education and some ways to think about and organize your teaching, and we believe these ideas and methods will go a long way toward meeting those educational needs. In this way we also hope to add to the satisfaction you receive from teaching second language learners.

1.4 THE GOALS OF THE INTEGRATED MODEL

We state below the educational goals for second language students which we hope to accomplish through the integrated language teaching model. In so doing, we hope to assist you in understanding and evaluating the ideas that follow and in applying them to your own teaching.

1. *Joy.* Before anything else, we would like the students in our classrooms to become excited about and to enjoy learning, including learning a new language. This means that we place a high priority on having fun in our teaching and in our writing about teaching. As the following pages will demonstrate, we believe there are sound empirical and pedagogical grounds for including students' fun and their own goals in the design of any educational program. Even beyond this, our love and

respect for students as growing and changing but already full human beings compel us to set this as a central goal of our teaching.

2. *Community*. We would also like the students in our classrooms to celebrate themselves and to learn how to apply, to the fullest extent possible, their considerable linguistic, social, and cultural resources towards learning a new language and culture. Recognizing that each new group of students presents a new, diverse set of these "natural resources," we commit ourselves to learning as much as we can about our students in order to develop *pluralistic classroom communities*. These are classrooms in which students' diverse backgrounds are recognized, valued, and used to develop new resources for the entire class. We do not believe that organizing instruction for second language students means forcing a choice between the use of their home language and culture at the expense of learning English and North American culture, or vice versa. Our goal is to use each in the service of the other through the creation of integrated classroom communities. The choice is not either/or, but more.

3. *Access*. Our third goal is closely related to the second. We wish to help our students gain access to the educational resources that are or will be available for the remainder of their school and societal experience. Beyond "survival" or "conversational" English for the world or "academic" or "content" English for the classroom, we hope to provide our students with the English communication and interaction skills they need in order to be perceived and treated by teachers and other school personnel as fully functioning students worthy of instruction and attention. We also hope to provide our students with these skills so that they can take full advantage of all the learning opportunities around them, both in and out of school. Thus, within our daily instruction, we labor to ensure that our second language students' accomplishments in learning a new language and new culture are beginnings of learning and not ends. We work to ensure that they develop the interactional and sociocultural competence required to go on receiving opportunities to learn and to display that learning for the rest of their school days.

4. *Literacy*. This fourth goal has as much to do with our students' own goals as with our hopes and dreams for them. We want our students to become fully literate in English. We agree with Frank Smith (1985) and Gordon Wells (1987) that beyond using language for communicating and for transmitting information, literacy also signifies the use of language to transform knowledge and construct new personal worlds of experience. As Wells (1987:114) puts it, "in the fullest sense . . . to become literate is to become able to exploit the full symbolic potential of language, for thinking in either the written or the spoken mode."

Accepting this definition of literacy and making it one of our central educational goals entails a commitment to become aware of our students' own personal, creative, and communicative wants and needs. It means we must become more conscious of the many settings in which the processes of listening, speaking, reading, and writing (and acting, signaling, gesturing, etc.) occur and the many ways in which they can be used to create and share experience. It also entails a commitment to become more conscious of the various media that can be used for meaning-making (from telephones to VCRs to billboards to books), and to continue our own literacy development (e.g., to become "computer literate" so that we can incorporate computers into our second language instruction). And finally, it means offering our students the opportunity to use language in its most profound ways—to write poetry and novels and manifestos as well as employment forms and "friendly letters" and purchase requisitions. Although we cannot hope to accomplish this goal completely with any of our students during our brief time with them, we still accept it as an ideal end, a guide in our day-to-day instructional decisions.

5. *Power.* All of the preceding goals lead inescapably to our final general educational goal, that of empowering our second language learners. To empower students means to give them control of their personal destinies both inside and outside the school—no small ambition for a classroom teacher! Yet without advocating this, we believe we cannot genuinely advocate any of our other goals. We believe that as teachers we only fool ourselves if we think we can teach language skills or literacy without integrating students' own ideas, purposes, and dreams into the teaching program. We also believe that we only fool ourselves if we think that somehow we can control the exact content and amount and direction of our students' learning and still have them truly learn. For us, school success without empowerment is a hollow accomplishment; literacy without empowerment is a debilitating myth.

The educational goals of joy, community, access and literacy lead to the fifth educational goal of empowering students—of giving them control of their personal destinies inside and outside the school.

1.5 THE THEORETICAL FOUNDATION OF THE INTEGRATED MODEL

We have called our instructional model the "integrated" language teaching model for two reasons. The first is the many important kinds of instructional integration that are involved in its application. The second reason is that it is based upon the integration of two overlapping areas of recent educational research, theory, and practice: (1) the recent first and second oral language acquisition literature, and (2) the recent first and second language literacy development literature. In the following section we shall review each of these briefly. If you are already familiar with this work or if you would be content to read the set of theoretical assumptions that we have synthesized from it, you may wish to skip this section and go on to the next one.

The Oral Language Development Literature

Beginning roughly in the late 1960s, researchers studying the oral language development of young first language learners (e.g., Snow 1972; Brown 1973; Clark 1973; Shatz and Gelman 1973; Wells 1974; Cook-Gumperz and Gumperz 1976) and of young second language learners (e.g., Fantini 1976; Wong-Fillmore 1976; Genishi 1976) began to shift the primary focus on their research and discussions from the *products* of language development and syntactic dimensions of those products to the *processes* of language development and the semantic and social/contextual dimensions of those processes. One-dimensional studies of samples of children's speech collected largely in experimental settings began to be supplemented by multidimensional studies of children's discourse and communicative behavior collected in naturally occurring language settings both in the home and at school. This shift in the focus of child language research was accompanied by a reconceptualization of how children (and perhaps all language learners) approach the language-learning task. Earlier theories of language development were strongly nativist (i.e., children acquire language through mere exposure and through the activation of an innate "language acquisition device") or behaviorist (i.e., children develop language by having their verbal behavior conditioned and shaped by parents and other adult speakers). The evidence from these new naturalistic studies of children's communication, when added to the previous research, suggests that children's cognitive and language development (both first and second language) is a strongly interactive process that relies not only on specific (and perhaps innate) linguistic and cognitive mechanisms, but also on children's participation in a rich linguistic environment that is attuned to their communicative needs.

This interactive, communicative view of language development is expressed today in several forms, ranging from those (like the social-interactive theories of Snow [1977] and Wells [1981]) which place slightly more emphasis on the language that is provided to children and what they *take from* their linguistic environments and communicative encounters, to those (like the "creative construction" theory of Dulay and Burt [1974]) which place slightly more emphasis on children's cognitive and linguistic mechanisms and on what they *bring to* their linguistic environments and communicative encounters. Particularly within the second language education field, this view of language development has in turn been accompanied by a revision of our whole notion of what children "have" when they have progressed through the oral language development process, with "language proficiency" being replaced by the broader construct of "communicative competence" in second language research and curricula.

Since these early reconceptualizations of the process of first and second language development, researchers have continued to pursue both quantitative and qualitative investigations of children's developing language use and the complex circumstances in which it occurs. In the field of first language development, researchers have paid considerable attention to the language that parents and caretakers provide to young first language learners (e.g., Snow and Ferguson 1977; dePaulo and Bonvillian 1978; Wells and Robinson 1982); to the developing contexts and functions of children's speech (e.g., Cook-Gumperz 1977; Dore, Gearhart, and Newman 1978; Ervin-Tripp and Mitchell-Kernan 1977; Nelson and Gruendel 1981; Tizard and Hughes 1984; French, Lucariello, Seidman, and Nelson 1985); and to the relations between first language learners' developing oral language and beginning uses and concepts of print (e.g., Wells 1981; Y. Goodman 1983, 1986; Olson 1981; Galda and Pellegrini 1984; Teale and Sulzby 1986).

In the field of second language education, investigators have focused on issues such as the similarities between first and second language development (e.g., Spolsky 1979; Dulay, Burt and Krashen 1982; Hatch, 1983); how proficiency in the first language contributes to or impedes acquisition of the second language (e.g., Cummins 1981, 1984; Keller-Cohen 1981); and how different groups and individuals approach the second language development task (e.g., Cathcart, Strong, and Wong-Fillmore 1983; Ventriglia 1982; Strong 1983; Wong-Fillmore 1983; Gomez 1987). Second language oral language theorists and researchers have also paid considerable attention to the language that is provided to second language learners. One of the most influential contributions to this discussion has been the work of Krashen, whose early (1976) theoretical distinction between language *acquisition* ("developing ability in a language by using it in natural, communicative situations") and language *learning* ("having a conscious knowledge about language") brought renewed interest and attention to the nature and role of input, or the language that is provided to both child and adult second language learners.

Many studies of the past decade have also attempted to describe the input that is provided to second language learners, as well as which kinds of input may be the most useful to them in developing their second language oral language capacities (e.g. Gaies 1979; Long 1981, 1983; Wong-Fillmore 1982; Gass and Madden 1985). Krashen himself has embedded the input issue into his overall theory of second language acquisition (1980, 1982) as one of its five central "hypotheses": "the (input) hypothesis states simply that we acquire (not learn) language by understanding input a little beyond our current level of (acquired) competence" (Krashen and Terrell 1983:32). Following this hypothesis and his overall model, Krashen believes that—as in first language development—the best kind of input that second language teachers can provide to their students is "comprehensible input," or language that is communicative in intent and that second language learners can largely understand and use (1982).

At present, researchers continue to conduct both quantitative and qualitative investigations of second language students' exposure to language and developing use of oral language in the many contexts in which the second language occurs both inside and outside the school. These researchers are also taking a new look at the output that second language students create in their various language learning settings and at the interactional processes that may contribute to oral second language learning (e.g., Ellis 1985; Gibbons 1985; Swain 1985; Wong-Fillmore 1985; Long and Porter 1985; Enright 1986; Gomez 1987). At the same time, ethnographers and other researchers are beginning to detail the complexity of the school second language environment and the diverse communication settings and language demands and expectations that second language learners encounter there (e.g., Philips 1972, 1983; Carrasco, Vera, and Cazden 1981; Erickson and Mohatt 1982; Deyhle 1983; Enright 1984; Heath 1985). However, much information remains to be gathered about the various kinds of first and second language experiences that linguistically and culturally different children undergo at home and at school before anything approaching a comprehensive description and explanation of their oral language development can be accomplished.

Several instructional applications of the interactive, meaning-constructing view of oral language development outlined above have been proposed for both adult and child second language learners. These include general recommendations for adapting the classroom environment and overall instruction (e.g., Burt and Dulay 1981; Ventriglia 1982; Saville-Troike 1978; Urzúa 1985; Lindfors 1987) as well as comprehensive approaches and methodologies such as the "Counseling-Learning" or "Community Language Learning" method (Curran 1976), the "Natural Approach" (Terrell 1982; Krashen and Terrell 1983), and the "Communicative" approach (e.g., Brumfit and Johnson 1979; Widdowson 1979; Littlewood 1981). While all these methods and recommendations have certain unique theoretical assumptions and distinctive instructional applications, they share several key theoretical assumptions about oral language learning. These assumptions form one of the main sources of the integrated language teaching model and are summarized later in this chapter.

The Reading and Writing Development Literature

The recent literature dealing with first and second language learners' reading and writing has evolved in much the same way as the oral language acquisition literature. Again, beginning roughly in the late 1960s, reading and writing scholars expanded the focus of their investigations and discussions from the analysis of individual texts/compositions and isolated reading/writing performances to the examination of the complex and evolving processes involved in children's reading and writing development (e.g., K. Goodman 1971, 1973, 1977; Rosenblatt 1969; Smith 1971, 1978; Clay 1972).

In the field of reading development, researchers began to focus on children's developing awareness and concept of print and reading, what young readers bring to the reading event, and what they do during the reading event. Researchers also began to focus on the content and construction (or "readability") of the texts used in the reading event rather than focusing on reading "comprehension" as a one-way, static end product. For example, Y. Goodman and Burke (1972) developed a system for identifying, recording, and analyzing the "slips" or "miscues" made by readers as they construct meaning from their interactions with the printed page. (K. Goodman calls reading a "psycholinguistic guessing game.") This work has culminated in what is referred to today as a *transactive* view of the reading event and the reading development process (Rosenblatt 1969; Burke 1981; K. Goodman 1985), a view that Watson summarizes as "the idea that readers construct meaning as they bring information that is already in their heads to the messages authors have encoded in text. The information readers use has many dimensions, including background experiences, knowledge of language, expectations about the text, perceptions of themselves as readers, and information gained from everyone and everything in the context of the situation in which they are reading" (1985:314).

A similar shift has occurred in the field of composition development, where researchers have begun to conduct naturalistic, longitudinal investigations of young students' writing at home (e.g., Bissex 1980) and at school (e.g., Graves 1983; Calkins 1983). Besides analyzing the compositions themselves, the studies have focused on children's brainstorming, authoring, editing, discussing, and revising of their writing. These researchers and others have also begun to document the various functions that print and writing serve for students (e.g., Britton, Burgess, Martin, McLeod, and Rosen 1975; Dyson 1981) and the various transformations that their writing undergoes as their control over the written word improves (e.g., Applebee 1984; Sulzby 1986). The overall picture of reading and writing development that emerges from the recent literature—as in the oral language development literature—is one of students actively interacting with and using language (in this case, print) to construct meaning for themselves and for others during the course of their ongoing literacy development.

Naturalistic studies of the multidimensional processes of reading and writing development continue to be conducted across home and school settings (e.g., Heath 1983; Taylor 1983; Applebee 1984; Cochran-Smith 1984; Goelman, Oberg, and Smith 1984; Harste, Woodward, and Burke 1984; Doake 1985; Teale and Sulzby 1986). These and many other studies continue to document the creative, social, dynamic, context-sensitive, and highly interwoven nature of the developing literacy processes. They are also beginning to uncover some of the ways in which these meaning-making processes develop out of and interact with oral language processes and how all four of the language processes (listening, speaking, reading, and writing) interact with one another to support general cognitive and linguistic development (e.g., Cook-Gumperz and Gumperz 1981; Emig 1981; King 1984). Today, discussions and investigations of reading and writing and language arts as they contribute to an overall process of literacy development, or "emergent literacy," are common in first language education.

Because young second language learners bring diverse experiences with print to the classroom, just as they bring experiences with speech, second language researchers have also set out to examine and describe these experiences—how they overlap and how they are reconciled with classroom second language literacy expectations and literacy experiences. Recent qualitative and longitudinal studies of linguistically and culturally different students' reading development (e.g., Hodes 1977; Rigg 1977, 1986; Steffenson, Joag-dev and Anderson 1979; Au and Jordan 1981; Devine 1981) and writing development (e.g., Edelsky 1983, 1986; Hudelson 1984, 1986; Heath 1985; Heath and Branscombe 1985; Ferreiro 1986) have indicated that previous conceptualizations of second language children's reading and writing development have significantly under-estimated the importance of the cultural, linguistic, and literacy experiences that they bring to the English literacy development task, while at the same time over-estimating the amount of time that second language learners must spend in their new language environment before they are "ready" to learn about and learn through print. As Hudelson explains in her review of the second language reading and writing development research: "These findings suggest that even children who speak virtually no English read English print in the environment; that ESL learners are able to read English with only limited control over the oral system of the language; that the experiential and cultural background of the ESL reader has a strong effect on reading comprehension; that child ESL learners, early in their development of English, can write English and can do so for various purposes." (1984:221)

As these investigations continue today, researchers are just beginning to detail the extraordinarily complex and interlocking nature of students' second language oral language and literacy experiences as they are added to their first language and literacy experiences and development. Much remains to be done, however, before we will have an adequate understanding of second language literacy and how it is supported by both the diverse first language experiences that students apply to their second language development and by the multiplicity of second language environments in which these students' second language literacy development occurs.

Efforts to apply the literacy development literature described above to the classroom practice have taken place largely in the area of first language (English) literacy development and up until very recently have had the most support (at both the teaching and institutional levels) in English-speaking countries outside the United States. As with the communicative approaches to second language oral language instruction, these instructional approaches appear under several different names and have received the impetus for their development from a variety of sources.

As early as 1963, following the publication of Ashton-Warner's book *Teacher*—the momentous record of her own experiences with literacy instruction in New Zealand—language teachers and specialists in Australia and New Zealand such as Clay (1972, 1975) and Holdaway (1972, 1979) began to examine children's overall literacy development in order to design new literacy instruction curricula and programs and specific instructional techniques to facilitate young children's use of their meaning-making capacities. Holdaway's 1979 book, entitled *The Foundations of Literacy* provides one of the most comprehensive descriptions of these early integrated applications of first and second language literacy development theory. The book includes highly readable descriptions of such literacy instructional strategies as developing a useful classroom literacy environment to facilitate children's first language literacy development; using children's own experiences and vocabulary in their first language literacy development; and using literature in a number of ways (including the "Big Book" or "Shared-Book-Experience" technique) to develop first language literacy. (We will discuss some of these strategies later in this book.)

In Great Britain, a similar surge of new curricula and new literacy instruction programs began in 1975, following the publication of *A Language for Life: Report of the Committee of Inquiry Appointed by the Secretary of State for Education and Science under the chairmanship of Sir Alan Bullock, F.B.A.* (more commonly known as the Bullock Report). The Bullock Commission centered its inquiry on literacy development and cognitive development in Britain's secondary schools, and as Marland, a member of the committee, points out (1977), the results of the report were heavily influenced by the discourse theories and investigations of Britton and Barnes and their colleagues (e.g., Britton 1970; Barnes, Britton, and Rosen 1971; Britton, Burgess, Martin, McLeod, and Rosen 1975; Barnes 1976). The work of these language specialists received considerable new attention following the appearance of the Bullock Report, and contributed to what has come to be known as the "language across the curriculum" movement, a title lifted out of the final report itself.

"Whole-school language policies" (Marland 1977) are a good example of an application of the language across the curriculum movement in Britain. In secondary schools that follow these policies, various subject-matter departments and instructors develop overall curriculum policies and cooperate and communicate in order to avoid the fragmentation and neglect of literacy development that often result from traditional segmented secondary school curricula. Policies similar to those suggested by the Bullock Report have been adopted at the provincial level and at the board of education (school district) level in Canada—for example, in Toronto (Bates 1984).

In the United States, one of the earliest efforts to turn the central tenets of first language literacy development theory and research into practice was undertaken by Moffett and the Houghton Mifflin Company, who in the early 1970s created a commercial language arts curriculum package entitled *Interact*, based largely on Moffett's work in literacy development (e.g., Moffett 1968a, 1968b).[1] Another significant and influential early curriculum effort was Van Allen's "language experience approach" (e.g., Van Allen and Allen, 1976). Since these early efforts, curriculum applications in the United States have occurred largely at the individual classroom and school level but are currently beginning to be adopted in district and state curriculum programs as well. These applications have collectively come to be referred to as the "whole language" approach.

Harste and Burke (1977) used the phrase "whole language" to describe one of the three major "theoretical orientations" regarding reading instruction which they were encountering in their own research in U.S. classrooms. (The other two orientations they identified were a "sound/symbol or decoding orientation" and a "skills orientation.") Later, DeFord (1981) provided detailed descriptions of classrooms using these different orientations and compared them to one another. Edelsky, Draper, and Smith (1983) also described the "whole language orientation" and contrasted it to the other primary classroom literacy orientations in the following manner:

> According to the *whole language* orientation, meaning-making is the central focus of reading and writing. All systems of written language (systems of grapho-phonic, syntactic, semantic, and pragmatic cues) are interactively, interdependently, and simultaneously present in any act of reading and writing. The *whole language* classroom looks different from the *phonics* or *skills* classroom; there are no spelling books, no sets of reading texts with controlled readability, no writing assignments. Instead, the children's writing and authorship are integrated with a reading program of children's literature. Whole, meaningful texts are the instructional materials, not isolated words, sound, or vocabulary-controlled "stories." In a *whole language* classroom, oral and written language must be functional, fulfilling a particular purpose for the language user. . . . Student-teacher and peer interactions are essential to the *whole language* orientation. (1983:259)

More recently, the Australian educator Cambourne (1987) has outlined the various ways that the term "whole language" has been used and misused while providing his own definition of the approach and its teaching applications.

Several conferences and publications sponsored by the National Council of Teachers of English have included the "whole language" approach as one of their themes, and references to the approach are becoming more frequent in the general U.S. literature dealing with school-age literacy instruction (e.g., Newman 1985; K. Goodman 1979, 1986; Clarke 1987). In contrast to the curricular and programmatic innovations in other countries, however, the "whole language" movement in North America remains largely a teacher-led, grass roots effort representing more of a shift in teachers' overall pedagogical orientation than a single program or curriculum (Rich 1985). The key assumptions of the "whole language" approach and its interactional cohorts make up the other main source of the ILT model and appear in the following section.

1.6 THE KEY THEORETICAL ASSUMPTIONS OF THE INTEGRATED MODEL

As we have already mentioned, the integrated language teaching model is meant to be used in planning and organizing instruction across the entire language spectrum (and the entire curriculum!). As such, it is derived from some basic assumptions about how children develop communicative competence and literacy which emanate from the first and second language acquisition literature we have described. Once these assumptions have been identified, we can translate them into specific criteria for organizing second language instruction.

The key theoretical assumptions of the integrated language teaching model are as follows:

1. The whole of language is greater than the sum of its parts. Language is a limitless capacity to make meaning and therefore should not be broken down and "taught" as tiny, discrete "skills" or "habits" or "facts." Language is better viewed as a verb (*using* language) than as a noun (*knowledge* of a language).

2. Students develop language and literacy through using language as a tool for creating and sharing meanings rather than through studying it as different "subjects" (e.g., reading, language arts) in which it is detached from its purposes and the actual circumstances in which it is produced. Students use speech and print to construct both *inner*-personal meanings (i.e., to think) and *inter*-personal meanings (i.e., to communicate).

These students are using hammers as tools to build and share a playhouse as they use language as a tool to build and share meanings.

3. Comprehensible, interesting, and useful classroom language—"real" language (Urzúa 1985)—is most helpful to students in their language and literacy development. Students need multiple opportunities both to take in (i.e., listen and read) and to give out (i.e., speak and write) this real language in order to become successful second language communicators and thinkers.

4. The whole of language development is greater than the sum of its parts. Students develop language and literacy as part of a broader process of semiotic or meaning-making development. They do this through using the processes of listening, speaking, reading, and writing in concert with one another rather than separately. Thus the development of each language process can support the development of the others.

5. Students make use of all of their available resources—linguistic and nonlinguistic, internal (cognitive, affective) and external (social, environmental)—in their second language development. Among the resources that students bring and apply to the second language and literacy development task are a diversity of prior native language cultural, language, and literacy experiences.

6. Full language and literacy development includes the capacity to take into account the diverse contexts in which language is used and the various people with and for whom it is used in creating, sending, and receiving meanings. Students fully develop second language and literacy through using the second language in many different settings, with a wide variety of respondents and audiences (including themselves), and for a wide variety of purposes.

7. Students' language and literacy development is facilitated by a comfortable atmosphere: one that values, encourages and celebrates efforts to use language; that focuses primarily on the meaning and intention of utterances and messages rather than on their form; and that treats "errors" as a normal part of becoming increasingly better thinkers and communicators.

1.7 THE KEY INSTRUCTIONAL CRITERIA OF THE INTEGRATED MODEL

The seven assumptions outlined above represent a specific way of thinking about first language and second language development which is supported by two substantial bodies of theory and research. These assumptions can now be transformed into seven key instructional criteria to be used in thinking about and organizing the curriculum and the classroom to promote second language students' learning. These seven criteria are as follows:

Collaboration

If language is a tool for meaning-making and if communication and thinking are learned through using language to get different things done, then instruction should be organized to facilitate interaction and collaboration. Collaboration signifies two-way classroom experiences in which learning takes place as teachers and students actively work together, as opposed to one-way lessons in which the teacher gives instruction and the students (passively) receive it. These two-way experiences include students working and learning with other students as well as with their adult instructors. (What may be called "cheating" in some classrooms is called "helping" in the integrated language classroom.) Organizing for collaboration also means providing activities that require sharing and communicating. For example, a teacher who incorporated this criterion into an animal unit might have small groups of children discuss and categorize different animal photos and then explain and justify their groupings to the rest of the class, instead of providing only a full-group lecture on mammals and reptiles to "cover" this content. Finally, organizing for collaboration means incorporating students' family members and the wider home and school community into their learning. Students interviewing their parents or grandparents about the schools they attended or fifth grade students preparing storybooks and reading them to kindergartners are examples of these wider forms of collaboration.

Purpose

If students develop their language and literacy capabilities by using real language in real situations to accomplish real goals, then classroom language activities should be planned which have genuine purposes. Language is used in the integrated language classroom to encompass and to develop four overlapping kinds of language purposes. The first purpose is the sheer joy of using language—playing with it, expressing oneself with it, and learning about its possibilities. We call this "fun discourse." Students reading storybooks, writing poems, and singing songs just for the fun of it are all examples of fun discourse. Second, language is used to communicate and to accomplish whatever goal is inherent in a particular activity. We call this "share discourse." Students reading the instructions for assembling a model airplane, writing down the lines they will deliver in their puppet show, and talking to the custodial staff about their work in order to create an article about them for the class newspaper are all examples of share discourse. Third, language is used in the integrated language classroom to provide or to glean new information and content and concepts. We call this "fact discourse." Students reading encyclopedias to do research for a class project, taking notes during a visiting farmworker's presentation to the class, and describing a family pet or a vacation during "show and tell" are all examples of fact discourse. Fourth, language is used to reflect, to imagine, and to organize and retain new ideas. We call this "thought discourse." Students reading about and discussing various theories on the origin of the universe; creating new computer games and programs on the class microcomputer; holding an election staff meeting to lay out a campaign strategy for their student presidential candidate; and writing autobiographies and personal life predictions are all examples of "thought discourse."[2]

It should be noted that the use of the purpose criterion to create all of the authentic and purposeful forms of discourse outlined above does not prohibit the organization of learning activities with adult instructional purposes and objectives embedded in them. However, it does prohibit the organization of learning activities with purposes that are completely extrinsic to the activity itself, such as completing an activity for some other payoff at some other time (e.g., "Do this worksheet because you have to know your math facts to do well in third grade") or completing an activity out of fear of adult authority (e.g.,

"Do this worksheet or I will give you an F"). All of the examples mentioned in this section include adult learning purposes (or "learning objectives") within them, but they are first selected with their intrinsic purposes in mind.

Student Interest

If students develop language and literacy best when the discourse they are provided with and asked to learn is meaningful and interesting, then instruction should be organized with students' interests as well as their needs in mind. It is important to select activities that have real purposes for your second language students, and these purposes must be related to the students' own interests. For example, the purpose criterion might be employed to teach measurement, nutrition, and language by having students prepare a balanced meal in class in addition to filling out measurement worksheets, reading about the four food groups, and memorizing and reciting English food vocabulary. Employing the purpose and interest criteria together in this same activity, the students themselves would choose the dishes for the class meal! To further illustrate, the concepts of legal authority and civic responsibility can be taught by having students read, watch, and discuss current news reports (criterion #2, purpose) and it can also be taught by writing about and discussing the intent and the "fairness" of school and home rules such as the school dress code and home curfews (criteria #2 and #3, purpose and interest).

Previous Experience

If students indeed apply their diverse linguistic, social, and cultural experiences to the second language development enterprise, then these experiences should be incorporated into their learning activities. Instead of expecting second language learners to adapt themselves as best they can to the new classroom cultural environment, it is necessary to adjust that environment to first give students an opportunity to make connections or build "bridges" (Ventriglia 1982) between their lives and experiences outside the classroom and the world within it, and then to facilitate students' continuing integration of these two realms of experience. This necessitates the creation of a *pluralistic classroom community* in which students' home and school experiences are both celebrated, and within which students have opportunities to share their previous experiences with the other members of the community and to use those experiences in their own second language development. Applying this criterion in choosing curriculum materials, cultural symbols from the backgrounds of all students could be used in a unit on symbols, or folktales from each student's native country could be included in class reading groups and in the library corner.

Applying this criterion to homework assignments, homeWORK assignments could be transformed into homeFUN assignments through developing after-school learning activities that involve students in collaborating with family and neighborhood members and that involve the use of home language and cultural resources. Collecting family photos or family trees or other artifacts and interviewing family members are examples of homeFUN assignments. Applying this criterion to the organization of classroom discourse would result in the provision of many different ways for students to take turns and share information during different group activities at different times, in contrast to the provision of only one way to do all these things.

Support

If students become successful second language thinkers and communicators in a pleasant and comfortable atmosphere, then instruction should be organized to create and maintain a supportive classroom environment. Applying this criterion to the classroom entails showing students that their efforts to communicate and to contribute to the classroom community are valued and that these efforts themselves are valued above students' perfect accomplishment. It entails providing multiple opportunities for students to succeed in their language-using efforts and making sure that uncomfortable and potentially harmful situations are avoided through the use of communicative requests that are comfortably within students' current communicative repertoires and cultural styles. For example, at first newly arrived students might only be expected to show that they are paying attention and cooperating as best they can during a daily read-aloud activity. As these students begin to acquire English and to feel comfortable in the classroom, they might be asked to remind the class of what happened in the story during the previous day's reading or to predict what will happen today. Employing the support criterion will result in the creation of opportunities for students to fail in their communicative efforts, too, but to fail comfortably. This can be accomplished by setting up functional language and literacy activities that take into account students' cultural styles but that test their second language capacities to the fullest, and in which their failures (whether grammatical errors or inappropriate or incomprehensible utterances) can be met with prompt feedback, part of whose purpose is to explain that such failures are a natural and necessary part of the learning experience. For example, some students might be able comfortably to clarify their pronunciation as a result of direct feedback from their peers during a speech to the class, while other students might feel more comfortable hearing such feedback from a partner on the other end of a walkie-talkie—but both these scenarios incorporate mistakes and failures as meaningful and natural learning components.

The support criterion also encompasses the use of print. To illustrate, having students edit and add punctuation marks to their letters because their pen pals in a bilingual school in another country will be able to understand them better is an intrinsically useful and supportive way of correcting writing that no amount of red correction marks made on a student's writing assignment can ever produce. Similarly, having pairs or small groups of students meet regularly to listen and comment upon one another's story drafts (Calkins 1986) provides a more purposeful and supportive mechanism for revising and editing than written teacher feedback. Both the author's function (creation) and the editor's function (formatting, mechanics) are utilized and taught in the integrated language classroom, but the latter function is carried out in support of the former and with a real audience in mind for the final writing.

Organizing instruction to provide and maintain a supportive classroom environment enhances students' second language and literacy development.

Variety

If developing language and literacy in the second language involves using real language for diverse purposes in various settings and with various people, and if students bring diverse previous experiences to the second language development task, then clearly variety should be included as a criterion in the overall organization of instruction. This criterion can be employed in combination with each of the criteria that have preceded it; thus, language and literacy activities or sets of activities can be developed which employ a variety of forms of collaboration; activities with different purposes; activities that appeal to different student interests; and activities that draw on a range of familiar and novel student experiences in order to utilize and augment students' previous experiences. The classroom examples in this section are but a few of the many activities that might be found in the integrated language classroom.

Integration

Finally, if the whole of language is greater than the sum of its parts, and if the whole of the process of language learning is also greater than the sum of its parts, then instruction should be organized in a multidimensional, holistic, integrated fashion; that is, the variety of student resources and classroom activities implied by the above criteria should be made to work *together* in the classroom and within the curriculum. This seventh and last criterion encompasses all the others and, as such, gives the overall model its name. The kinds of integration that are mandated by this criterion include integrating content instruction and language instruction; integrating the language processes of reading, writing, listening, and speaking; integrating the various members of the classroom community; and integrating the multiple worlds of second language students' language experience.

1.8 SYNTHESIS

Clearly, the instructional criteria that have been set forth here overlap considerably and depend on one another for their meaning and usefulness. When taken as a group, however, they become the firm theoretical underpinnings and the driving force for a powerful instructional model that can be applied across all the components of the school program to benefit second language learners. In keeping with the model's criteria and with the image of teachers and learners as co-explorers in the language development process which it implies, we present in Figure 1.1 a metaphorical image of the model as a practical, sturdy and fully-outfitted landrover ready to carry its operators (teachers and students) across the fascinating and challenging terrain of the classroom and the curriculum towards the mountaintop goals of instruction.

Figure 1.1:   The Integrated Language Teaching Model

The following lists summarize the key educational goals, theoretical assumptions, and instructional criteria of the integrated language teaching model:

THE GOALS OF THE ILT MODEL

1. *Joy—Children will experience the joy of learning and using language.*
2. *Community—Children will become part of a pluralistic classroom community in which diversity is celebrated and used for developing language and literacy.*
3. *Access—Children will acquire full access to the educational resources provided by the school and surrounding community.*
4. *Literacy—Children will achieve full literacy in English.*
5. *Power—Children will develop control over their own destinies both inside and outside the school.*

THE THEORETICAL ASSUMPTIONS OF THE ILT MODEL

1. *The whole of language is greater than the sum of its parts: language is a verb (doing language), not a noun (knowledge of a language).*
2. *Students learn language best by using it, not by studying it.*
3. *Real (comprehensible, interesting, and useful) language is most useful to students in their language and literacy development.*
4. *The whole of language development is greater than the sum of its parts: students develop their second language listening, speaking, reading, and writing processes together.*
5. *Students use all of their available resources to learn language: linguistic and nonlinguistic, internal and external, and previous cultural, language, and literacy experiences in the first language.*
6. *Students must learn how to take the context and the audience or respondent into account in using speech and print; they do this by using the second language in diverse settings, with a wide variety of people (including themselves), and for a wide variety of purposes.*
7. *A comfortable atmosphere, one that values efforts to use language and that focuses on meaning before form, best facilitates language and literacy development.*

THE INSTRUCTIONAL CRITERIA OF THE ILT MODEL

Organize for:

1. *Collaboration*—Students work cooperatively toward mutual goals with peers, teacher, family, and community members.

2. *Purpose*—The learning activities in which students engage have authentic goals and purposes, and students have an authentic investment in those purposes.

3. *Student Interest*—Instruction both promotes and follows student interests.

4. *Previous Experience*—Instruction incorporates and builds on students' previous linguistic, social, and cultural experiences.

5. *Support*—The environment is comfortable, and it supports students' involvement and risk-taking within the language and literacy development task.

6. *Variety*—Students have diverse opportunities to learn language through different topics, settings, materials, modes of interaction, and modes of learning.

7. *Integration*—Instructional resources are holistic and multidimensional; language and content, the four language processes, the worlds of students' language experience, and the students themselves all work together to facilitate language and literacy development.

1.9 A FEW WORDS ABOUT LABELS

Before turning to curriculum development with the ILT model, we would like to explain the labels that we use throughout this book.

In his best-selling book entitled *Love*, Leo Buscaglia reminisces:

> I was born in Los Angeles, and my parents were Italian immigrants. A big family. Mama and Papa were obviously great lovers! They came from a tiny village at the base of the Italian Swiss Alps where everyone knew everyone. Everyone knew the names of the dogs, and the village priest came out and danced in the streets at the fiestas and got as drunk as everybody else. It was the most beautiful scene in the world and a pleasure to be raised by these people in this old way. But when I was taken, at five, to a public school, tested by some very official-looking person, the next thing I knew I was in a class for the mentally retarded! It didn't matter that I was able to speak Italian and an Italian dialect. I also spoke some French and Spanish—but I didn't speak English too well and so I was mentally retarded. I think the

term now is "culturally disadvantaged." I was put into this class for the mentally retarded and I never had a more exciting educational experience in my life! Talk about a warm, pulsating, loving teacher. Her name was Miss Hunt, and I'm sure she was the only one in the school who would teach those "dumb" kids. She was a great bulbous woman. She liked me even if I smelled of garlic. I remember when she used to come and lean over me, how I used to cuddle! I did all kinds of learning for this woman because I really loved her. Then one day I made a tremendous mistake. I wrote a newspaper as if I were a Roman. I described how the gladiators would perform and so on. The next thing I knew I was being retested and was transferred to a regular classroom after which I was bored for the rest of my educational career. (1972:28–29)

Happily, we have come a long way in the U.S. schools from the days when many of the students who, like Buscaglia, "didn't speak English too well" were automatically placed in programs for the mentally handicapped when they arrived at school. But we educators continue to love labels (Harris 1976). One of the reasons for this is that we need jargon as a sort of shorthand to aid as in our daily dealings with extremely complicated issues. But another reason for the educational labeling phenomenon may have to do with the way that schools are organized and students are viewed and treated. In the public schools of today, once students can be labeled as having one kind of learning weakness or strength or another, then they can be placed in programs that can deal with that weakness or strength. It doesn't seem to matter that, as Buscaglia points out, most student characteristics are culturally and contextually bound and it is very difficult to accurately assess these supposed deficits and gifts.

Buscaglia's anecdote illustrates another problem with educational labels: they often take on a life of their own. The things they come to stand for are different from the things they were originally meant to stand for, and they come to be used to "distance" (as Buscaglia refers to it) or to separate and "stigmatize" (Goffman 1963) the individuals to whom they are applied. Thus quite often in our schools, labels and programs that were originally invented to help students gain access to education in practice accomplish the opposite end of denying them that access.

In order to communicate our educational ideas clearly in this book, we too must use some kind of shorthand to refer to the different kinds of students and classrooms that we want to discuss. But we are not enthralled by the labels that have been used within U.S. education to refer to students who arrive at school in the same state as Buscaglia did. The most common of these labels are "non-English-speaking" (or "non-English-proficient") and "limited-English-speaking" (or "limited-English-proficient"). The prefixes "non-" and "limited-" in these labels clearly emanate from a deficit perspective regarding these students—they *lack* English, they are *deficient* in some important way. The acronyms for these labels are hardly preferable to the labels themselves. When we hear the term "LEP," we think of colonies of the ostracized and fatally ill;

when we hear "LES," we find it hard not to automatically associate it with inferiority or insufficiency *(less!)*. In addition, these labels put the emphasis on only one of the language processes, that of speaking. The labels "bilingual" and "English as a Second Language" (ESL) are also problematic in that they summon up the political dimensions of the second language education issue in the U.S. and are often used to differentiate between attitudes toward students' native language and its use in the classroom—issues that we do *not* want our labels to represent.

The label "second language" has also been used often within the second language education literature to distinguish between those classrooms and individuals and programs which are involved with a second language and those which are not. Although this label also has its limitations (for example, it is often simply inaccurate when applied to students like Buscaglia who are learning a third or fourth language!), it does avoid many of the confusing and negative connotations of the other common terms. Therefore, from now on we will refer to native-English-speaking students as "first language" students, and we will refer to students who are adding English to their previously developed language(s) as "second language" students. Additionally, in order to make broad distinctions within our discussions between children who are at different points in their language and literacy development in English, we will call new students just beginning their English experiences "beginning second language," students who are well into their English development but who still have a ways to go "mid second language," and students who have more or less completed their English development "full second language."

We are also not enamored of the terms that have come to be used for the classrooms our students attend which are not uniquely concerned with facilitating their language development: "regular" and "mainstream" classrooms. These terms suggest that the second language classroom is somehow irregular or is outside the mainstream in some critical way, thus adding to the stigma placed upon the students who go there. Thus, throughout the book we will refer to those classrooms which have been organized to implement the formal, mandated curriculum but which have no formal second language instructional component or dimension as "grade-level" classrooms. Those classrooms which have *also* been organized to implement the mandated curriculum but which additionally have formal second language, bilingual education staff and resources we will refer to as "bilingual" classrooms. We will refer to those classrooms which have been specifically organized to conduct English as a second language instruction rather than the mandated curriculum as "ESL" classrooms. Finally, when we wish to refer to all classrooms with second language learners in them, we will use the label "second language classrooms." Our labels aren't perfect either, but we hope that they capture the additive and enriching nature of second language education as we conceive it to be, as well as the additive, integrative theme that is the touchstone of this book.

NOTES

1. In a provocative "Editorial Note" entitled, "An Innovation That Failed," the editors of *The National Elementary Principal* (1978) provide a number of possible explanations for why Moffett's materials were never widely used.

2. Our four main purposes of language within the integrated model are syntheses of several other theorists' suggestions. For example, Britton et. al (1975) describe the three major functions that writing served for the children in the classrooms they studied as *transactional* (informational, persuasive writing), *expressive* (personalized, self-revelatory writing), and *poetic/literary*. Rosenblatt (1983) describes the reader's primary purpose or "focus of attention" or "stance" in reading a given selection as lying on a continuum between "efferent" reading (reading for information, reading focused on building up meanings to be taken away *after* the reading) and "aesthetic" reading (reading for enjoyment, reading focused on the actual experience created *during* the reading). Wells (1987) sets forth a four-level model for describing the ways in which literacy is defined and used in education. At the lowest level is "performative literacy," which emphasizes "the code as code" and teaches the mechanics of reading and writing. At the second level is "functional literacy," which emphasizes interpersonal communication and "survival" reading and writing skills. At the third level is "informational literacy," which emphasizes the transmission of knowledge, especially subject-matter or content knowledge. At the fourth or highest level is "epistemic literacy," which emphasizes the use of speech and print to conceptualize and to "transform knowledge and experience". Wells finds very few instances of educators either proposing or using this highest form of literacy.

ACTIVITIES AND DISCUSSION

1. Review your recent professional reading and inservice/coursework experiences as well as your work in schools and find three or four instances of *direct conflict* between what the former suggest that you do and what the latter requires you to do. Then develop a list of two or three strategies for resolving each conflict through compromise and accommodation. (Example: you would like to grow a class garden outside your classroom but your school administration does not permit digging up the soil around the school. So you collect pie tins or other containers and have a "window box" garden with one kind of plant in each container along your windowsill.)

2. Develop a list of *your* educational goals for your second language students. Use the list to review your teaching to see if you are meeting these goals or if you need to adjust your teaching to reach them.

3. Find a school's or program's statement of purpose or set of instruction goals. (Use those of your own program if possible). Compare your personal goals to what you find to see if the two sets are compatible. If they are not, think of some ways to achieve your goals within the school's or program's goals and/or develop some strategies for *integrating* the two sets and meeting both. You can also do this activity with a teaching colleague.

4. Examine the theoretical assumptions of the integrated model and decide which ones you share and which ones you don't share, and your reasons for these decisions. Use this information as you read the book.

5. Jot down the labels that you hear used to refer to students and to different sub-groups and characteristics of students (e.g. "wheelchair kids," "behavior problems," "hyperactive students," "low readers," etc.). Listen and observe for a day or two or at a school for uses of these or other labels by the school staff and administration. How do the sets of labels overlap? How are they different?

6. Examine each of the labels that you wrote down for Number Five above and look for the hidden messages and judgments and categorizations that are embedded in them. Decide whether or not these labels accurately capture the characteristics and categories that you want them to chapter. If need be, replace your old labels with new ones which better capture your intended meanings.

FURTHER READING

Britton, J. T., Burgess, N., Martin, A. L., McLeod, A., and Rosen, H. 1975. *The development of writing abilities 11–18.* London: Macmillan Education. The final report of the authors' extensive investigation of 11–18 year old students' writing development. One of the most important products of the study is a taxonomy of types of writing based on its function and its audience.

Calkins, L. 1983. *Lessons from a child.* Exeter, NH.: Heinemann Educational Books. A refreshing and thought-provoking account of one child's growth in writing and the classroom conditions and teaching strategies which supported it.

Dulay, H., Burt, M., and Krashen, S. 1982. *Language two.* Oxford, England: Oxford University Press. A summary of the authors' second language acquisition theories and research and related studies.

Hakuta, K. 1986. *Mirror of language: The debate on bilingualism.* New York: Basic Books, Incorporated. Careful and articulate critique of the current major issues of bilingualism in the United States, including bilingualism in society, bilingualism and intelligence, how children and adults become bilingual, and bilingual education.

Holdaway, D. 1979. *The foundations of literacy.* Sydney Australia: Ashton Scholastic. Holdaway's discussion of the emergent literacy education programs developed with his colleagues in New Zealand is a consistent balance of theoretical insights and clear instructional recommendations. The Shared Book Experience is one of the practical recommendations.

Hudelson, S. 1984. Kan yu ret an rayt en Ingles: Children become literate in English as a second language. *TESOL Quarterly,* 18(2): 221–38. Hudelson uses extensive samples of second language learners' own writing to illustrate her review of what recent research tells us about how children develop their reading and writing capacities in their second language and the implications of this information for classroom practice.

Krashen, S. D. and Terrell, T. D. 1983. *The natural approach: Language acquisition in the classroom.* Hayward, CA: Alemany Press. A teaching handbook based on the authors' theories of second language acquisition. The book includes a summary of those theories as well as a discussion of ways to organize the curriculum, provide input, develop oral communication and manage the classroom.

Larsen-Freeman, D. 1986. *Techniques and principles in language teaching.* New York: Oxford University Press. This teacher resource book reviews eight major language teaching methods—from the Audio-Lingual method to the Total Physical Response method—by describing classroom scenes of the methods in use and then deriving the principles and techniques of the method from them.

Lindfors, J. W. 1987. *Children's language and learning* (2nd Ed.). Englewood Cliffs, NJ: Prentice-Hall, Incorporated. Excellent, readable textbook on children's language development with one chapter dedicated to how children learn a second language.

Moffett, J. 1968b. *Teaching the universe of discourse.* Boston, MA: Houghton Mifflin Company. Moffett's classic statement of his naturalistic, meaningful, and student-centered approach to English teaching.

Ovando, C. J., and Collier, V. P. 1985. *Bilingual and ESL classrooms: Teaching in multicultural contexts.* New York: McGraw-Hill Book Company. A broad review of current second language teaching issues and methods, including teaching oral language, culture in the classroom, content areas in the second language curriculum, assessment, and politics and community involvement.

Richards, J. C., and Rodgers, T. S. 1986. *Approaches and methods in language teaching.* Cambridge, England. A review of the current major language approaches, providing the historical background, the theory of language and language learning, the course design and objectives, and the activities and techniques of each approach.

Rigg, P. and Enright, D. S. 1986. *Children and ESL: Integrating perspectives.* Washington, DC: Teachers of English to Speakers of Other Languages. Among the perspectives used in this collection to address children's second language development are those of a teacher educator, a reading researcher, a writing researcher, an oral language researcher, a community and teacher educator, and a collaborative researcher.

Ventriglia, L. 1982. *Conversations of Miguel and Mariá: How children learn a second language.* Reading, MA: Addison-Wesley Publishing Company. Ventriglia describes the set of the cognitive and socio-affective strategies children use to develop a second language and classroom implications of each strategy. Based on Ventriglia's own work as well as on the general research literature.

Wong-Fillmore, L. 1986. "Teaching bilingual learners." In M. C. Wittrock (Ed.) *Handbook of research on teaching* (3rd Ed.) (pp. 648–85). New York: Macmillan Publishing Company. Thorough review of the major recent bilingual education research.

Chapter 2

The Integrated Curriculum

Take a Word Like Cat

Take a word like cat
And build around it;
A fur room over here
A long meow
Floating from the chimney like a smoke tail.
Draw with words
Balance them like blocks
Carve word furniture
A jar of pussy willows,
Catkins, phlox,
Milk in a dish,
Catnip pillows,
A silver bell,
A plaster bird,
An eaten fish.
When everything is perfect in its place
Step back to view the home
That you have built of words around your word
It is a poem.

—Karla Kuskin

2.1 INTRODUCTION

Three important planning components of instruction can be organized through the use of the ILT model in order to set up the kinds of language and literacy experiences that you want your students to have. These three components are the curriculum (the learning activities), the social environment (the ways in which children will carry out the learning activities), and the physical environment (the places and the materials that the students will use in order to carry out the learning activities). In the integrated model, all three of these components are by definition dynamic in nature and will continually change after you have planned them. Nevertheless, it is important to think about them carefully and to have their overall organization in mind and largely in place when your students arrive.

This chapter deals with the broadest and most important of the three instructional planning components: the integrated curriculum. In the sections of this chapter that follow, we will begin by describing the views of the curriculum and of teachers and students which the ILT model implies and contrast them with the views that are presently operating in the public schools. Then we will outline and exemplify an integrated curriculum development process that is based directly on these views and on the integrated model's seven key instructional criteria.

2.2 CONTRASTING VIEWS OF LEARNERS, TEACHERS, AND THE CURRICULUM

As outlined in Chapter 1, the child language development research of the past two decades or so has resulted in a much more interactive, or two-way view of the first and second language development process, as well as a view of the child learner as an active participant within that process. This in turn has led to revised conceptualizations of the roles of the teacher and the curriculum as formal aids to students' second language development. However, as many critics of the modern American schools have pointed out, (e.g., Toffler 1970; Goodlad 1984; Karp, 1986), the centralized bureaucracies that operate in our school systems and that control our public schools have not undergone a similar alteration. Instead, they continue today to employ the one-way, behaviorist learning theories and production-oriented conceptualizations of learners, teachers, and curriculum that were originally used to create the public schools during the time of the country's emergence as an industrial nation. In his book *The Hurried Child,* David Elkind sums it up this way:

> The industrialization of the school is not surprising, for universal schooling in America was introduced, in part, to prepare children for new ways of

living and working that were a consequence of industrialization. What is surprising about our schools today is that they have reached full industrialization just at a time when factory work, as it was once known, is becoming as obsolete as the farmer with a horse-pulled plow. (1981:48)

The Transmission of Knowledge View

What is the view of learners, teachers, and curriculum that emanates from the "industrialized" model of schooling to which Elkind refers, and which is still largely in place in the public schools today? In developing his thesis that today's children are "hurried" into adult roles and are robbed of many of the essential experiences of childhood, Elkind provides us with a vivid depiction of these views:

> Schools today hurry children because administrators are under stress to produce better products. This blinds them to what we know about children and leads them to treat children like empty bottles on an assembly line getting a little fuller at each grade level. When the bottles don't get full enough, management puts pressure on the operator (the teacher, who is now held accountable for filling his or her share of the bottles) and on quality control (making sure the information is valid and that the bottle is not defective). This factory emphasis hurries children because it ignores individual differences in mental abilities and learning rates. The child who cannot keep up in this system, even if only temporarily, is often regarded as a defective vessel and is labeled learning disabled or minimally brain damaged or hyperactive. Yet these same children can easily demonstrate how much knowledge they acquire from television and how quickly they can acquire the skills needed to operate electronic games. (1981:48)

In the factory model of schooling Elkind describes here, students are passive recipients of knowledge (see also Goodlad 1984). They are empty vessels waiting to be filled, and merely "go along for the ride" on the assembly line of schooling. As the factory workers in this assembly line model, teachers are also regarded as passive components. They merely receive the "knowledge" —already determined by others—that they are to add to their students, and their job is simply to pass that knowledge along. So-called "teacher-proof" educational packages are illustrative of this part of the model.

Curriculum in the factory model of schooling is the "stuff" (knowledge in its noun form) with which the students are to be filled by their teachers. It is a concrete substance (quantified and measurable); it is made up of various ingredients, each added separately and sequentially to the bottles/students (it can be broken down and incrementally and sequentially taught as different "content areas," "facts," "habits," or "skills"); it is the same for every bottle/student (it is standardized); it is developed outside the assembly line before production begins (it is a priori); and the factory workers/teachers have no say over its composition or distribution (it is externally controlled).

Barth (1972) provides us with a graphic depiction of this traditional industrial model of schooling, which he calls the "transmission of knowledge" model:

$$K \rightarrow C \rightarrow A \rightarrow S$$

In Barth's diagram, K stands for our "accumulated body of knowledge"; C stands for the curriculum, or the "parts of K that school boards, superintendents, and principals consider most crucial and appropriate for children of different ages to 'know;'" A stands for an agent, "usually a teacher, but it might also be a written program, TV set, tape recorder, movie, or computer," who transmits the curriculum to the students; and S stands for the students (1972:61–62). Barth's diagram visually captures the relations among the various components of schooling, as well as the one-way direction in which instruction is supposed to take place within the industrial transmission model, with teachers acting as the "middle-men" in the process, transmitting the static and atomistic curriculum onward to students. Notice that there are no arrows going outward from the students in Barth's diagram. Students are at the end point of the transmission conduit and have no role at all to play in the transmission process except as receivers. Henceforth we will refer to this model and its components as the *transmission* model.

It is distressing but hardly surprising that most of today's major public school language teaching curricula—whether intended primarily for first language students (e.g., basal reading series, basal spelling series) or for second language students (e.g., basal ESL series, basal "foreign language" series)—are designed to follow the conceptualization of curriculum that appears in the transmission model just described. That is, they treat language as a subject that can be broken down into discrete "habits" or "skills." These habits or skills can then be defined in behavioral terms as objectives; arranged sequentially and hierarchically in order of difficulty and importance; and taught (drilled and practiced) until full "mastery" or "fluency" in reading or speaking is reached. Until recently, the major debate among U.S. language curriculum developers has been about *which* skills and habits to teach (e.g., phonics skills or sight word skills, grammatical habits or discourse habits), not about whether such a conceptualization of language and language curriculum is accurate or justified. The work cited in the previous chapter in establishing the theoretical base for the integrated language teaching model suggests that the conceptualization is neither accurate nor justified.

The Integrated Model View

While the integrated model view of learners, teachers, and curriculum is derived largely from recent first language and second language development research, it too has its roots in long-standing epistemological and pedagogical traditions, including but not limited to the work of Froebel, Pestalozzi, Montessori, Piaget, and Dewey; the twentieth-century progressive education and open education movements in North America; and the infant schools work in Great Britain. If this view were to be represented in a two-dimensional diagram, it might look like the following (Enright 1983):

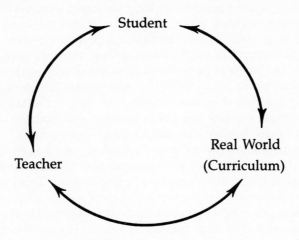

The theoretical assumptions of the ILT model posit a view of students, teachers, and curriculum as equal contributors to the language development process. This is represented by their circular arrangement within the diagram and by the double-headed arrows that represent their relations. The double-headed arrows also denote the collaboration that is necessary for successful language development, and the circular arrangement also denotes the continuous and integrated nature of the language development process—one that makes constant connections between previous language experiences and new ones, or as Dewey explains it in describing a "learning experience":

> . . . a backward and forward connection between what we do to things and what we enjoy or suffer from things in consequence. Under such conditions, doing becomes trying, an experiment with the world to find out what it is like; the undergoing becomes instruction—discovery of the connection of things . . . the perception of relationships or continuities to which it leads up. (1916:140)

In the integrated model of language instruction, students are viewed as willing, active, and intentional participants who both affect and are affected by their teacher and their learning environment. To borrow from Lindfors (1983), the image of second language learners that emanates from this view is one of students as language "explorers," interacting with and testing out their environment and their position and skills with respect to that environment (thus the landrover operators in Figure 1.1), in contrast to the transmission image of learners as empty bottles waiting to be filled. Similarly, teachers in the integrated model are viewed as active, vigilant, and inventive "decision-makers" and "instructional dilemma managers" (Lampert 1985) who are constantly aware of and responsive to their children's progress in their second language exploration. They are able to use this awareness to sustain their children's learning, both through initiating appropriate second language instructional activities and through following their students' own instructional leads. Far from the image of passive and mindless factory workers or transmitters of curriculum which is implied by the transmission model, in the integrated model teachers are viewed as senior partners in the second language development process, both creating the conditions for and directly and indirectly participating in their children's second language development.

Finally, curriculum in the integrated model is viewed as the materials and activities that the teacher organizes to encourage, facilitate, and sustain students' language learning experiences, or "explorations." This curriculum also creates the optimal conditions for teacher-student instructional exchanges and relations to occur as a critical part of students' language explorations (see Figure 1.1 and Chapter 6). Just as language in the integrated model is viewed as a verb (meaning-making) rather than as a noun (a set of facts or skills), curriculum in the integrated model is viewed as the *means* for practicing and developing second language meaning-making rather than as the *end* of instruction.

In the integrated model, any part of the "real world" of the students' experience—past, present, and future—that has the potential for involving them in productive language and literacy learning relations can reasonably become a part of the curriculum, including books and texts and computer software, but also including pancakes and puppets and poison ivy. In contrast to the view of curriculum offered by the transmission model, curriculum in the integrated model is unbounded (it is difficult to pin down and measure); it is holistic (it cannot be reduced to a "subject," made up of even tinier "facts" and "skills"); it is dynamic (it is ever developing and ever changing); it is responsive (it provides for diverse students' needs and interests and changes as these needs and interests change); and it is cooperatively constructed and controlled by teachers and students as they work together throughout the school year. Integrated curriculum is developed as teachers plan flexible learning experiences for their students which grow out of their own instructional agenda and their knowledge of their students' needs and interests, and these experiences involve students' active participation.

In the integrated model, any part of the "real world" that helps children acquire language can become a part of the curriculum—even blowing bubbles!

We suspect that one reason the transmission view of curriculum has been so popular and durable is that it mandates a tidy, sequential, step-by-step, easy to control, and easy to follow curriculum and curriculum development process. In contrast, the integrated view of the curriculum as holistic, multifaceted, and interactive by definition precludes most of these bureaucratically and industrially desirable elements. However, it is possible to develop curriculum within the integrated model and even to convert many of the curriculum packages and products that have emanated from the transmission view to suit the views and purposes of the integrated model. The process that we have developed for doing this is outlined in the rest of this chapter.

2.3 CONVERTING THE
TRANSMISSION VIEW: UPSIDE
DOWN AND INSIDE OUT

Curriculum developers within the transmission model begin with a given subject (e.g., history) or language process (e.g., composition) and the discrete facts or skills or habits of which it is supposedly composed. They then develop activities (often drill and practice) to "reinforce" these discrete items in the belief that this will eventually result in "mastery" of the entire subject or language process. In the integrated model, this process is turned "upside down" so that curriculum developers begin with the overall processes of meaning-making that comprise language and literacy as a whole and *then* look for places to embed direct presentation and practice (or "direct instruction") of various facts and skills within these integrated curriculum activities, both in terms of planning and actually conducting them.

Turning the transmission curriculum upside down does not mean abandoning direct, didactic presentation of facts or instruction in specific skills, but it does mean making sure that those facts and skills are meaningfully taught as interesting and useful components of students' overall language explorations and drive toward second language literacy as we have defined it. Turning the transmission curriculum upside down will ensure that your students can use and display the particular subject matter and language items that are a part of the transmission curriculum (and for which you are held accountable) while at the same time ensuring that the wider goals of literacy, access, community, joy, and power—the touchstones of the integrated model—are also addressed.

Within the transmission view of curriculum, adult knowledge and competence are at the heart of planning, with students placed well outside the planning process as the eventual recipients of the already developed curriculum. In the integrated model, this arrangement is turned "inside out" so that students are at the heart of the development process (Yalden 1983) and are directly involved in both planning the curriculum (e.g., as topic selectors and task setters and rule makers) and in implementing it (e.g., as group leaders, questioners, researchers, and actors).

Turning the transmission curriculum inside out does not mean turning the classroom over to the children and simply responding to their whims. As Bussis and Chittendon (1970) point out, a teaching role that consists of acting as a kind of "unobtrusive valet" for students in the classroom is just as passive as one that consists of being a transmitter of curriculum. It does mean constructing the curriculum *with* students and putting their developing abilities, interests, and needs first in carrying out your instructional role and responsibilities. It also means making instructional decisions both in preparing activities for students and in working with students within the activities to ensure that *both* your educational goals and your students' goals are met. As Kierstead (1986) has noted, the traditional distinction between "direct" (i.e., teacher-controlled) and "experiential" (i.e., student-controlled) curricula is a false one—effective instruction consists of anchoring the direct instruction of "basic skills" as well as long-term learning objectives within student-owned and student-operated learning activities. Thus, turning the curriculum inside out will enable you to exercise your leadership and control as the senior partner in the second language development process. At the same time, it will simultaneously allow your students to take their place as active partners in that undertaking and to develop the communication processes and cognitive processes they will need in order to take over their own meaning-making and learning as full members of society (Toffler 1970; Goodlad 1984; Heath 1985; Morin 1986).

2.4 THE INTEGRATED CURRICULUM

How can you apply the seven instructional criteria of the integrated model —organizing for collaboration, purpose, student interest, previous experience, support, variety, and integration—to develop an integrated curriculum in your classroom? How can you turn your present curriculum upside down and inside out? The single best means that we have discovered is through using *thematic* or *integrated curriculum units*. Other first language curriculum developers (e.g., Corwin, Hein, and Levin 1976; Kohl 1976; Moss 1984) and second language curriculum developers (e.g., Brumfit 1984; Edelsky 1986; McCloskey 1987; McCloskey and Nations 1987) have described this method as well. In an integrated curriculum unit, teachers choose themes or topics that are of interest both to students and themselves (e.g., rivers, myths and legends, pirates, newspapers); then, around a central theme, the teacher designs a series of learning activities across many content areas and across all the language processes of speaking, listening, reading, and writing. In the following section, we will outline the stages you might go through in developing an integrated curriculum unit, using the seven instructional criteria of the integrated model.

The Integrated Unit Development Process

The process for developing integrated units, like all curriculum, will differ according to your specific needs, materials, and thinking style. However, in this section we would like to describe the overall "flow" of the planning process as we and our colleagues have used it. We will illustrate each of the general steps in the unit development process by describing a sample integrated curriculum unit—Heroes and Superheroes—as we go along. This unit is presented in full in Part II of this book.

In an integrated unit on plants, students learn language and content together by playing the roles of sun, plant, animal, water, and nutrients in a dramatization of the plant life cycle.

Stage One: Selecting a Theme

"Where do we begin?" is a question we have asked ourselves and other teachers who have successfully developed and used integrated thematic units. Most of us have answered with some variation of instructional criterion #3: "Interests." We often begin with interests that have been demonstrated or expressed by our students; for example, fossils brought in on a Monday morning; discussions about a current event on the evening news or in the neighborhood; a student's antecdote about a camping trip; the sharing of books taken out of the library about whales or pirates or rain making applesauce (see Part II). We also often begin with our own interests, with the confidence that if we are excited about a particular theme, we will be able to design tantalizing activities that will extend that interest to our students. What is most important in a unit's theme is not who originally thought of it but whether the unit and the activities that stem from it have the potential for operationalizing our instructional criteria. We begin with our interest and student interest in choosing and developing the theme, and then plan the actual unit activities, keeping in mind these interests and the other integrated model criteria. Thus, besides its interest to students and to you, the only other beginning requirement for an integrated unit theme is that it must be general enough to permit the applications and integration called for by the criteria, including application in a variety of subject-matter disciplines (e.g., math activities, social studies activities); application for a variety of students with a variety of learning resources and learning needs; and application across the four language processes.

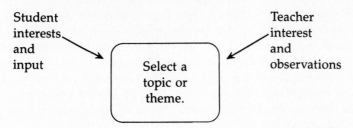

Figure 2.1: Stage One

Of course, many of the textbooks and basal series and other prescribed curricula that you have in hand can aid you in selecting a theme or subtheme and activities for your integrated unit. Unfortunately for students, many of today's prepared curricula take quite wonderful and exciting themes and topics for learning explorations and transform them into dull and meaningless drill and practice activities. If you are a bilingual or grade-level teacher, you can use the seven criteria to transform these materials back into exciting and meaningful learning experiences. For example, a grade-level science textbook chapter on plants and the things they need to grow can create the framework for a unit on gardens and plants! The textbook itself can then become another handy reference for the unit activities. Similarly, if you are an ESL teacher, you can find out what textbooks and basals your students' grade-level teachers are using and incorporate the topics and concepts and language from these materials into your units. If you and your second language students are excited about growing plants and gazing at the stars, but as a teacher you know that these students' grade-level science text is covering the former, plan a garden unit instead of an astronomy unit, or save the astronomy unit for later. Just remember that in this selection process, student interest comes first and the required curriculum comes second.

Selection of the Heroes and Superheroes Theme

The theme for our sample unit originated in a middle elementary school class discussion about television shows students watched after school and on Saturday mornings. The class included a majority of second language students and about 25 percent native English-speaking language students. The children spent a great deal of their daily conversation time in this class discussing the adventures of She-Ra, the Hulk, GI Joe (and such unique characters as Quick Kick, Alpine, and Lady J), as well as the classic comic book characters Wonder Woman, Superman, Falcon, Spiderman, and Captain America. Several students were collectors of superhero figures (which appeared in class at various times). A few others read and collected *Marvel* and *D.C.* comics.

The Heroes and Superheroes topic combined these student interests and previous experiences. It also had the potential to incorporate the interests that the teacher of this class (we'll call her Ms. Kay) held in exploring the lives of mythical, historical, and personal heroes. It seemed to have the potential to incorporate several of Ms. Kay's school-district and state curriculum objectives. It was broad enough to have the potential to fulfill all seven instructional criteria as well. In other words, it was a natural theme for an integrated unit! We'll see how Ms. Kay proceeded with this theme.

Stage Two: Brainstorming and Creating "Webs"

The next stage in developing an integrated language unit is enjoyable, but it demands creative, divergent thinking. Find a relaxed moment and try to "brainstorm" (Gordon 1981) subtopics and activities that might be included in a unit based on your theme. This stage in the planning process is the free, generative one, so go ahead and write down anything and everything that occurs to you as you think of it. We have found Kohl's (1976) planning practice of making web diagrams during this brainstorming stage to be quite helpful. Whereas a list helps you to think in a linear, hierarchical fashion, connecting your ideas in a web diagram helps you to expand thoughts in several directions simultaneously, and enables you to establish interrelationships within and across subtopics as you brainstorm. Figure 2.3 demonstrates the brainstorming process, and gives you an idea of what a thematic unit web might look like.

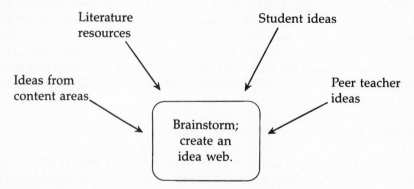

Figure 2.2:   Stage Two

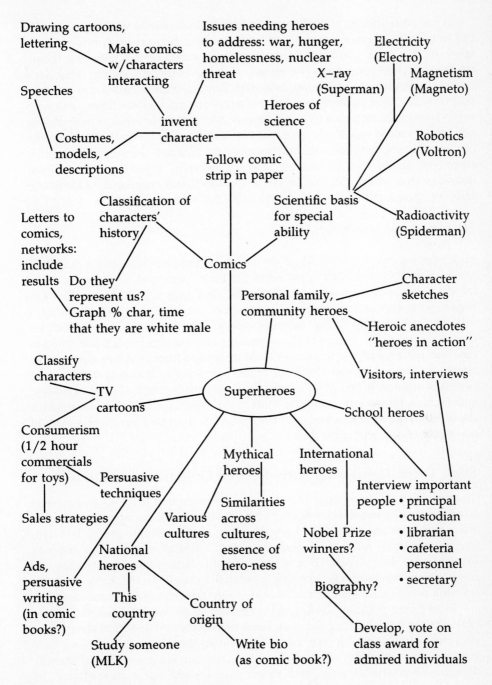

Figure 2.3:   Unit Development Web

It's often helpful to consult peers and students as you do your web. A group can frequently be more creative than an individual, because one person's ideas spark another's. It's also helpful to have some new experiences with your theme in order to get your "creative juices" flowing before or during your web making—flipping through some newspapers when brainstorming a newspaper unit or watching a pirate movie before brainstorming a pirate theme will help make your thematic web a rich and diverse one. Remember that your final web will contain many more subtopics and curriculum areas for exploring than you can possibly use for your unit, but the more possibilities you create during this stage, the greater the opportunity for subsequently planning a set of unit activities that will fulfill the seven ILT instructional criteria, in addition to fulfilling your goals and your school's goals for your students.

The Heroes and Superheroes Web

In developing her unit web, Ms. Kay used the brainstorming activity described above. She also consulted with peers for their ideas and with students for information about their avenues of interest. As Figure 2.2 illustrates, Ms. Kay began with the central theme, Superheroes, and then branched off into subtopics falling into many different subject-matter areas. These subtopics included comics; TV; heroes in the mythology of various cultures represented in the class; national heroes from the United States and from students' countries of origin; international heroes; school heroes; personal community heroes; and heroes of science. When Ms. Kay was finished with her web, she had a diverse and exciting network of potential content and language learning ideas which she could use to structure and plan the actual activities that her students would do as part of her unit. And then . . .

Stage Three: Developing Activities and Objectives/Potentials

The next stage in developing an integrated thematic unit involves two interrelated tasks: selecting and developing activities from the ideas appearing in your web, and selecting and developing learning objectives (we prefer the term *learning potentials*) for these various activities. Since all of your activities will involve using both language and concepts, this latter task requires that you think about the language learning potential as well as the subject matter learning potential of your activities—in reality they can never separated!

In our own planning during this selection stage, we have found that we typically begin by thinking about all kinds of exciting activities that we are sure students would love to do in order to learn about the theme. But once we have three or four possible activities in mind, we quickly move on to specific thoughts about the learning needs of our students and our goals for them; the curriculum that we are required to teach by the state and the school district; and

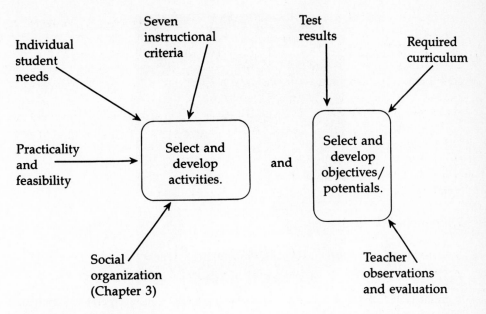

Figure 2.4: Stage Three

issues of feasibility and practicality. From then on, these areas of thinking overlap and interact as the unit takes shape.

Here are some suggestions for how you might handle this important stage of the unit planning process. As you did in selecting the overall unit topic, start with the instructional criterion of interest and then use the other criteria of the integrated model to begin to come up with some unit activities. Your aim is eventually to have a set of learning activities that allow your students to explore different subject matter areas using different thinking processes and language processes (*integration*); activities that are exciting and enjoyable for students to do (*interest*); activities that are meaningful and important to students and which have authentic goals (*purpose*); activities that build on students' previous cultural and linguistic experiences (*previous experience*); activities that involve students working cooperatively toward mutual goals with peers, with you, and even with their families and community members (*collaboration*); and activities that provide success to students at many levels while using mistakes as an accepted, integral part of their organization (*support*). If you can come up with a set of activities from your web which meet all of the above criteria, you'll probably already have plenty of *variety* in your unit as well, but you can review the overall unit with this criterion in mind at the end of this stage of unit planning just to be sure. Use the seven instructional criteria to think about and evaluate your overall unit as it emerges rather than to evaluate each separate activity.

In an integrated unit, one activity, such as baking a cake, can incorporate a variety of language and content area purposes.

Begin also to think about the kinds of learning that could take place within each activity and about the specific learning needs of your children. Developing a pre-instructional awareness of what you think students could and should learn within a given activity increases the likelihood that your students *will* learn it. This awareness is the original reason for doing lesson plans! Again, for your second language students, this attention should focus on both their language learning potential and their subject-matter learning potential. For example, reading political heroes' speeches and then preparing a speech on a political issue and reading it to the class offers the potential to teach a lot more than history and social studies. This one subset of unit activities involves using all four of the language processes; understanding and using very specific and patterned forms of written and oral discourse; and using share discourse, fact discourse, thought discourse, and fun discourse as well!

At this point, it will also be helpful to think about the social organization of your activities—how you will group students and how you will have them interact and use speech and print to carry out the activities. This dimension is dealt with in detail in the next chapter.

Next, you can deliberately embed the external curriculum objectives and competencies that you are responsible for teaching into your unit activities. Having reviewed the texts and other materials on hand, and being familiar with the required curriculum of your state and/or school district and/or school, you've probably already done this to a great degree, but this is the place where you should explicitly do this embedding, both to ensure that these objectives are included in the students' experiences (and within your thinking and teaching!) and to enable you to justify your integrated curriculum to administrators, and parents and other concerned adults by being able to point out the places in *your* curriculum where the required curriculum is being "covered." It should be noted, however, that this last embedding activity takes place *after* you have made your major decisions about what students will do and how they will do it on the basis of your own goals and the criteria of the integrated model, which is why we refer to this process as turning the transmission curriculum "upside down."

Finally, as you continue to think of the assortment of activities that will make up your unit, you will have to address the issues of feasibility and practicality regarding the activities while you are organizing them. Is there enough time for putting them together and for actually doing them? Enough space? Are the materials and human resources needed to do the activities readily available? Are they reasonably acceptable to your administrators and to the rest of the school? Obviously, you will have to consider these and similar questions as you plan your unit, although we suspect that to adequately fulfill the seven criteria, you may have to push the bounds of feasibility, practicality, and convenience further than you have in the past.

The Heroes and Superheroes Unit Activities and Objectives/Potentials

Figure 2.5 presents a summary list of the activities that Ms. Kay designed for her Heroes and Superheroes unit. These activities are more fully detailed in the presentation of the Heroes and Superheroes unit in Part II of this book.

Introduction
Part A. Superheroes
   Activities:
      1. A Visit from Spidey
         a. Before the Visit
         b. During the Visit
         c. After the Visit
      2. Legendary Superheroes
         a. Collecting Legends and Myths
         b. Assessment/Evaluation
         c. Extensions
      3. Tallying Cartoon Heroes' Speech and Characteristics
         a. From Tally to Graph
         b. Assessment/Evaluation
         c. Extensions

4. Individual Superheroes and Group Adventures
   a. Developing Individual Superheroes
   b. Group Adventures
   c. Assessment/Evaluation
   d. Extensions

Part B. Heroes
   Activities:
   5. Homefun: Family/Community heroes
      a. Sunshine Outline
      b. Assessment/Evaluation
      c. Extensions
   6. In-School Field Trips: School Heroes
      a. Before the Trip
      b. During the Trip
      c. After the trip
      d. Assessment/Evaluation
      e. Extensions
   7. A Civil Rights Hero: Martin Luther King, Jr.
      a. A Real-Life hero
      b. Assessment/Evaluation
      c. Extensions
   8. I Have a Dream: A Hero's Speeches
      a. Listening to Speeches
      b. Writing and Delivering Speeches
      c. Assessment/Evaluation
      d. Extensions
   9. Homefun: Heroes from Native Cultures
      a. Heroes from Home
      b. Assessment/Evaluation
      c. Extensions
   10. Heroes and Superheroes Learning Center
       a. Where Is Spidey?: Communication Game
       b. Sequencing Heroic Adventures
       c. Listening to Speeches
       d. Interpreting Supergraphs
       e. Designing a Supervehicle

Part C. Supercelebration
   Activities
   11. Refreshments: Hero Sandwiches, Superhero Cake
       a. Cooking Terms and Tools
       b. Assessment/Evaluation
       c. Extensions

12. Program: Speeches, Biographical Sketches, Comic Display
    a. Preparing to be Hosts/Hostesses
    b. Assessment/Evaluation
    c. Extensions

Suggested Resources for Heroes and Superheroes

*For the sake of clarity and simplicity, we use the terms *hero* and *superhero* to refer to both males and females throughout this unit.

Figure 2.5: Heroes and Superheroes—Outline of Unit Activities

As we have described, Ms. Kay followed her students' interests and leads in choosing the original theme (Stage 1) and some of the most important subtopics (Stage 2) for her unit. Then, in order to begin developing unit activities (Stage 3), she added in her own interests, her current knowledge about her students, and teaching goals based on that knowledge. Ms. Kay had specific second language and literacy development areas in mind as she began to plan her unit, such as her second language students' needs for using standard language patterns correctly (including past and present tenses of verbs) and for learning to participate in peer conferencing in small groups to develop oral language and to improve writing through the use of revision strategies. In the social and content areas, Ms. Kay saw the need for students to expand their understanding of one another's cultures through the exploration of cultural universals, and she saw a need for them to review information they had learned in a previous unit about simple machines, and to apply this information to a new situation.

Ms. Kay also used her knowledge of individual children's needs and progress to design her unit. For example, she knew that Mami, a beginning second language student, was not yet feeling that she was a full, valued member of the class and needed activities that would make her feel welcomed in the class and that would give her a chance to contribute directly to it. She knew that Mami would benefit from references to familiar classical heroic characters from her home country, Japan. Ms. Kay had also observed that Eutiquio's oral English was becoming quite fluent and grammatically accurate but that teachers and students who didn't know him well had trouble understanding him because of his pronunciation. She also knew that Eutiquio, as one of her full second language students, was ready to focus on pronunciation and would benefit from a semistructured opportunity to give a speech either to her, to peers, or into a tape recorder. Ms. Kay had further observed that Tran, a recently arrived Southeast Asian refugee, was quite a capable illustrator but had had little time or opportunity for play during the last several years of her life. This student, Ms. Kay felt, would benefit from opportunities to use her artistic talent in situations that required her to imagine and to distinguish fact from fiction. These and many other observations and evaluations of her students helped Ms. Kay to select and organize the activities for Superheroes.

Language:	1. A Visit from Spidey	2. Legendary Superheroes	3. Tallying Cartoon Heroes	4. Superheroes' Adventures	5. Family/Community Heroes	6. In-School Field Trips	7. Civil Rights Hero	8. A Hero's Speech	9. Heroes from Native Cultures	10a. Where Is Spidey?	10b. Sequencing Heroic Adventures	10c. Listening to Speeches	10d. Interpreting Supergraphs	10e. Designing a Supervehicle	11. Refreshments	12. Program
1. Follows directions	•	•	•	•	•	•	•	•	•	•	•			•	•	
2. Recalls main ideas and some supporting details of information presented orally	•	•		•	•	•	•	•	•		•			•		•
3. Listens to and summarizes oral reports		•		•	•	•	•	•			•			•		
4. Summarizes information presented orally	•	•	•	•	•	•	•	•			•			•		•
5. Presents oral reports		•		•	•	•	•	•								
6. Conducts and reports interviews	•			•	•			•								
7. Demonstrates understanding of specialized vocabularies related to subject areas	•	•	•	•	•	•	•	•	•	•	•	•	•	•	•	•
8. Uses conventional language patterns	•	•	•	•	•	•	•	•	•	•	•	•	•	•	•	•
9. Selects appropriate word usage	•	•	•	•	•	•	•	•	•	•	•	•			•	•
10. Enunciates words clearly	•	•	•	•	•	•	•	•	•	•	•	•	•	•	•	•
11. Reads aloud with expression and fluency	•		•	•	•	•	•	•	•						•	•
12. Interprets nonliteral meanings of words	•		•		•			•					•			
13. Selects and uses reference sources: dictionary/thesaurus, index, table of contents, telephone book, maps/diagrams and other sources	•	•	•						•							
14. Uses study strategies	•	•	•	•				•					•			
15. Makes generalizations, draws conclusions	•	•	•	•				•			•	•				
16. Uses a card catalog, atlas, almanac, encyclopedia to locate information	•	•	•				•						•	•		•
17. Shares and discusses ideas gained from reading done independently	•	•			•	•	•					•				
18. Reads and interprets different types of material: books, directories, forms, catalogs, newspaper, etc.	•	•	•	•		•		•				•	•			•
19. Distinguishes between fact, opinion, fiction, nonfiction	•	•	•	•	•			•				•				
20. Reads and interprets maps, charts, graphs, tables	•		‹					•	•							
21. Interprets basic instructions and labeling information	•	•	•	•	•		•			•	•	•				
22. Demonstrates an interest in literature by choosing appropriate books	•					•	•				•					
23. Reads for a variety of purposes in a variety of sources; obtains directions, information	•	•	•	•	•	•	•	•	•	•	•	•	•	•	•	•
24. Uses creative arts to interpret literature				•												•
25. Prepares reports with correct word usage, capitalization, punctuation and spelling		•	•	•	•		•	•								

Figure 2.6:　Objectives for Heroes and Superheroes. [page 1]

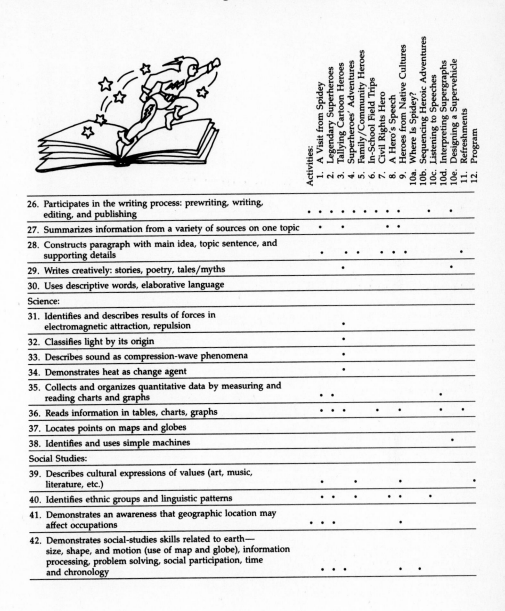

Objective	1. A Visit from Spidey	2. Legendary Superheroes	3. Tallying Cartoon Heroes	4. Superheroes' Adventures	5. Family/Community Heroes	6. In-School Field Trips	7. Civil Rights Hero	8. A Hero's Speech	9. Heroes from Native Cultures	10a. Where Is Spidey?	10b. Sequencing Heroic Adventures	10c. Listening to Speeches	10d. Interpreting Supergraphs	10e. Designing a Supervehicle	11. Refreshments	12. Program
26. Participates in the writing process: prewriting, writing, editing, and publishing	•	•	•	•	•	•	•	•				•	•			•
27. Summarizes information from a variety of sources on one topic	•	•							•	•						
28. Constructs paragraph with main idea, topic sentence, and supporting details	•		•	•		•	•	•					•			
29. Writes creatively: stories, poetry, tales/myths			•											•		
30. Uses descriptive words, elaborative language																
Science:																
31. Identifies and describes results of forces in electromagnetic attraction, repulsion			•													
32. Classifies light by its origin			•													
33. Describes sound as compression-wave phenomena			•													
34. Demonstrates heat as change agent			•													
35. Collects and organizes quantitative data by measuring and reading charts and graphs	•	•											•			
36. Reads information in tables, charts, graphs	•	•	•			•		•						•	•	
37. Locates points on maps and globes																
38. Identifies and uses simple machines													•			
Social Studies:																
39. Describes cultural expressions of values (art, music, literature, etc.)	•			•			•									•
40. Identifies ethnic groups and linguistic patterns	•	•		•			•	•			•					
41. Demonstrates an awareness that geographic location may affect occupations	•	•	•					•								
42. Demonstrates social-studies skills related to earth— size, shape, and motion (use of map and globe), information processing, problem solving, social participation, time and chronology	•	•	•					•	•							

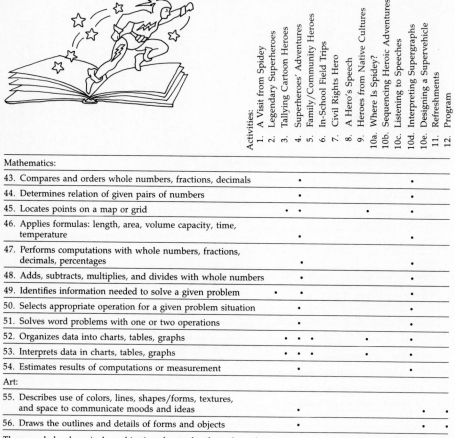

	1. A Visit from Spidey	2. Legendary Superheroes	3. Tallying Cartoon Heroes	4. Superheroes' Adventures	5. Family/Community Heroes	6. In-School Field Trips	7. Civil Rights Hero	8. A Hero's Speech	9. Heroes from Native Cultures	10a. Where Is Spidey?	10b. Sequencing Heroic Adventures	10c. Listening to Speeches	10d. Interpreting Supergraphs	10e. Designing a Supervehicle	11. Refreshments	12. Program
Mathematics:																
43. Compares and orders whole numbers, fractions, decimals				•							•					
44. Determines relation of given pairs of numbers				•							•					
45. Locates points on a map or grid			•	•						•	•					
46. Applies formulas: length, area, volume capacity, time, temperature				•							•					
47. Performs computations with whole numbers, fractions, decimals, percentages				•							•					
48. Adds, subtracts, multiplies, and divides with whole numbers				•							•					
49. Identifies information needed to solve a given problem	•			•							•					
50. Selects appropriate operation for a given problem situation				•							•					
51. Solves word problems with one or two operations				•							•					
52. Organizes data into charts, tables, graphs	•		•	•						•	•					
53. Interprets data in charts, tables, graphs	•		•	•						•	•					
54. Estimates results of computations or measurement				•							•					
Art:																
55. Describes use of colors, lines, shapes/forms, textures, and space to communicate moods and ideas				•										•		•
56. Draws the outlines and details of forms and objects				•										•		•

These grade level curriculum objectives for grades three through six were taken from *Basic Curriculum Content for Georgia Public Schools* (Georgia Department of Education, 1985).

Figure 2.6:   Objectives for Heroes and Superheroes [page 3]

As Ms. Kay developed a wide assortment of activities that met the seven criteria of the integrated model and that had the potential to address her students' specific needs, she also kept in mind the external academic expectations for her students. She recalled her students' performance on the standardized tests given in her school at the beginning of the year, in which spelling, puncutation, reading comprehension, and the use of reference materials had posed the most difficulty. She made sure that her unit included work in these broad areas and that she was aware of places in the unit where opportunities existed for students' authentic use of these skills. She also kept in mind the existence of these skill areas as part of the students' future test experiences. At this point in her planning, Ms. Kay also began to consult the curriculum guidelines and objectives that she was responsible for covering in her classroom (in her case, the *Basic Curriculum Content for Georgia's Public Schools*, Georgia Department of Education, 1985), and she embedded these objectives in her activities as well. Figure 2.6 presents a summary list of the Georgia curriculum objectives that Ms. Kay included in her unit.

Ms. Kay was able to incorporate a large number of required objectives from a variety of content areas into her integrated unit. For example, she planned an activity in which students did tallies of comic book heroes' attributes and exploits across a number of categories, turned this information into fractions and percentages, and displayed the results in graphs. This one activity met state math area objectives for fractions, percentages, and graphing. An activity in which students each created a hero with a small group of peers and wrote and illustrated a comic book about an adventure incorporating all of the students' characters fulfilled state language and art area objectives. By having a review of previous lessons on simple machines and follow-up activity in which students made "supervehicles," Ms. Kay fulfilled state science area objectives. Social studies area objectives for community study and language objectives for conducting interviews were embedded in the activity in which students interviewed family and community "heroes" and invited them to class. By helping students write letters to comic book publishers and/or television networks telling the results of their research on how well media superheroes represent our multicultural society and by helping students plan and conduct interviews with important people in the school concerning changes students would like to see, Ms. Kay also included ways to help students use the writing process while they simultaneously learned to understand how decisions are made which concern them. As these examples illustrate, the set of activities in Ms. Kay's final unit fulfilled the *same* curriculum objectives as the drill and practice activities that were being used in other middle elementary classrooms, but the Heroes and Superheroes activities also fulfilled the instructional criteria of the ILT model.

In making the final decisions about the activities she hoped to utilize in the Heroes and Superheroes unit, Ms. Kay considered their practicality and feasibility. For example, even though the idea had lots of learning potential, she decided not to take the class to a showing of the movie *Star Trek IV* because of the expense involved and because of the state educational policy severely limiting the number of field trips that public school classes are allowed to take each year. She decided that she would allow children to design superhero vehicles but that she would not have them launch an actual Superhero rocket, because there was no good space around her urban classroom where such a launch could easily and safely take place. She added baking a Superman cake to her unit activities when a supervisor who had heard about the unit offered her a wonderful Superman cake tin to use. The cake was then served at a comic book publication party. Thus, Ms. Kay's final unit was a product of what she knew she could reasonably accomplish as well as what she wished she could accomplish.

As Ms. Kay continued to build her unit on the basis of the seven criteria, her knowledge of her students' needs, and the dictates of the required curriculum, she also saw new directions and new ways of organizing already established activities. As a result, she went back and revised her activities and objectives/

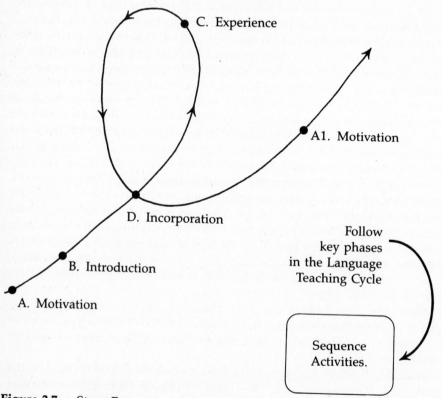

Figure 2.7:   Stage Four

potentials as she went along, continuing to consult peers and students whenever possible. The Heroes and Superheroes unit is but one example of the complex, overlapping, and cyclical process that is involved in curriculum planning within the integrated language instruction model.

Stage 4: Sequencing Activities Using the Language Teaching Cycle

We have said that the language learning process is not a linear one in which content (a) must be learned before content (b), content (b) before (c), and so on. We do need some organizing principles for sequencing activities in an integrated unit once we have chosen them, however. We outline here a cyclical model that will assist you in getting your activities "roughly tuned" (Krashen and Terrell 1983; Long 1983) to your students' linguistic, cognitive, social, and affective needs using the seven criteria and the view of curriculum, learners, and teachers presented by the integrated model.

We ask you to think about the process of teaching new language and content within the integrated unit format as fitting into a general *teaching cycle*. As with our general conception of curriculum within the integrated model, this process is presented as cyclical rather than linear because there is no specific beginning or end of teaching or learning language in your classroom and because a cycle captures the "backward and forward" connecting and hypothesis forming and testing that children engage in as they learn a new language. Our cycle begins with engaging students' interest and attention on the material of the unit. It then goes on to provide a general overview of that material, and continues by providing opportunities for different students to make the different kinds of language connections they need and to use the unit language and concepts in an increasingly autonomous and creative manner, depending on their own abilities and needs.

You can use the language teaching cycle to help you decide which of the activities in your unit should come earlier and which should come later, and to make sure that your final unit is cohesive and comprehensive. The cycle will also help you ensure that your overall unit provides all of your students with the range of experiences with the unit material that is needed to learn it and use it effectively. The four phases of the language teaching cycle are presented in Figure 2.7 and are described below.

Phase A: Motivation

The first phase in the language teaching cycle which you should consider in sequencing your unit activities is motivation. In this phase, you engage your students' interest and attention on your unit theme and topics and create the learning context for all of the activities that are to follow. The activities that you place in this first phase of the unit should create many more questions than answers. Activities involving "real world" interactions are quite effective for this phase of the language learning cycle, such as activities involving real objects (e.g., looking at a model of the moon with students and letting them ask questions about it) or classroom visitors (e.g., planning a visit from a friendly clown at the beginning of a circus unit) or field trips (e.g., taking a walk around the school grounds, using all five of the human senses before plunging into activities centering on each one). Alternatively, the activities that you place at the beginning of your unit could create vicarious motivation through discussions (e.g., asking the children what makes them children and you an adult and then listing their explanations) or through story reading (see the "Rain Makes Applesauce" unit in Part II of this book) or through the use of other media materials (e.g., watching a film about different kinds of families).

Sometimes, the first "activity" in your unit is provided *for* you and you simply take advantage of it and follow up on it—this is one major way of following students' leads and interests. A unit on electricity might begin with a power outage at your school; a unit on birds might begin with a bird flying through your window (Hawkins 1973); or a unit on earthquakes and on crisis assistance might begin with students' excited reactions to reports of a real earthquake somewhere in the world (Rigg and Enright 1986). Of course, you can also *plan* surprising and exciting events to lead off your unit; for example, one teacher we know introduced her children to the class mascot, a stuffed pink panther, by pasting pink paw prints on the classroom window and on the floor leading over to a closet, where the pink panther patiently waited for the children to discover him!

The activities that you choose for phase A of your unit should either make direct use of already existing student interest and curiosity about your unit theme or should create new student interest in your theme. These initial activities should then focus and engage that student interest on the language and content that is to come. If, in reviewing your unit activities at this point, you find that none of them fits this description of phase A activities, then you might want to think about whether you have sufficiently addressed the criteria of student interest and purpose in your planning thus far. If you conclude that you have not, you can add new activities.

Heroes and Superheroes Motivation. Beginning a week or so before the introduction of the Heroes and Superheroes unit, Ms. Kay focused her students' ongoing fascination with superheroes and comic books by leaving mysterious "alien messages," pictographs, and objects for the students on the blackboard and around the room when the students weren't there; for example, she left the messages "Spidey is coming," "Where will you be on the Ides of October?" and "Who is Spiderwoman?" on the blackboard; she drew a large web on a bulletin board; and she left a "magic" decoder ring on the bookcase. When students inquired about these strange artifacts, Ms. Kay pretended to be as baffled as they were and encouraged them to ask questions and develop hypotheses about the origins and meaning of these items.

Phase B: Introduction

The second general phase in the language teaching cycle which you should consider in deciding the overall order of your unit activities is the introduction of the new content and language area. Introductory activities should give students an overview of the language and concepts that will be contained in the unit and should provide them with an initial framework or "advance organizer" (Ausubel 1963) for dealing with that new material. Thus, the activities that you choose to place in this phase of the language teaching cycle should be your broadest ones, providing a rationale(s) for studying the topic, many sensory aids (e.g., pictures, photos, tapes, real objects), and written aids (e.g., books, handouts, posters) to be used as references throughout the unit. These activities should also provide an initial exposure to the key concepts, vocabulary, and discourse of the unit. Quite often the activities in Phase A—the motivation phase—also provide a good introduction to your unit, as, for example, the reading and discussion of the book *Rain Makes Applesauce* (Scheer and Bileck 1964) that lead off the unit of that title in Part II of this book. At other times, separate activities can serve as the introductory phase of your unit, such as having students watch an earthquake report on TV and then discuss and plan class activities to help the quake victims as a follow-up to their initial excited sharing of what they heard at home about the catastrophe. As with Phase A of the teaching cycle, if upon looking over your set of unit activities you find that you don't have any that provide a broad overview of the unit, you may want to add an activity or two to accomplish this introductory task.

Heroes and Superheroes Introduction. For the introduction phase of Heroes and Superheroes, Ms. Kay invited "Spiderwoman" (a costumed friend and accomplice) to the class and asked the children to find out as much about her as they could, including why she was there and what made her a superhero. Ms. Kay explained to the class that Spiderwoman would answer any questions the students could come up with about her life, background, and adventures, or about how she happened to be in the class on that day, but, of course, since she couldn't talk (no mouth), all questions had to be answerable by a nod of yes or no. The information elicited in this manner was written on the blackboard. After the visitor left, Ms. Kay used a "concept formation" teaching strategy (Joyce and Weil 1972) to have the students place the pieces of information that they had elicited into groups and categorize them. By the time the activity was over, the class had produced a list of the major qualities and characteristics shared by all superheroes (e.g., costume, description, place of origin, special ability, special enemy(ies), secret or special identity) which would be used throughout the unit.

Phase C: Experience

The third general phase in the language teaching cycle is experience. This phase comprises the main body of your unit activities, and it is this phase that most of your learning objectives/potentials will be fulfilled. The activities that you place in the experience phase of your unit should provide a range of opportunities for students to practice and use the language and content that you introduce in your unit within a wide variety of contexts and in diverse ways. These activities should also be organized to permit you to provide different kinds of language instructional input to students at different stages of second language development and with different amounts and kinds of previous experience with the content of your unit.

An optimal set of learning activities for Phase C will include activities with potentials ranging from very focused and structured use of relevant unit material within a specific context (e.g., learning the names of the various layers of the earth's crust in preparing a model of an earthquake) to very creative and free use of the material in general (e.g., sharing the earthquake model with another group of students or writing a descriptive poem about the way an earthquake develops). By developing such a set of activities, you will be creating an opportunity for all of your students to use the unit language and content in more and more diverse and independent ways, even if every student does not complete or even participate in every unit activity. You will also be creating the opportunity for yourself to support and assist each and every one of your students in their second language development at various points in the unit.

Heroes and Superheroes Experiences. Ms. Kay found ways to incorporate a range of uses and contexts for her key Superhero language and content across the activities she used in this phase of her unit, and even within some of these activities. As an example of how she created this range across activities, in one activity she had students create their own Superhero identities, using very explicit guidelines (e.g., they had to come up with a word or a phrase for each of several specified categories), and she circulated and provided individualized instruction, input, and assistance as needed. Later in this same activity, the children came together in small groups to develop original comic adventures involving all of their group's characters, with only minimal procedural guidelines (e.g., length), and Ms. Kay acted as a participant within the various groups to get them going and to keep them going as needed. As an example of how she created a range of language uses within a single activity, Ms. Kay used her cake-baking session to have her small groups rapidly repeat and practice the names of all the ingredients and implements that were present—within a very concrete and teacher-dominated context where parents served as the teachers. She also had students explain what they were doing as they individually used the ingredients and implements to follow the cake recipe (and later to frost the cake) in response to her elicitations. Students volunteered their ideas about other uses of the ingredients and implements as the group went to the cafeteria to put the cake in the oven. Later, during a comic-book publication party at which the cake was devoured, the group had free conversation and sharing in English.

Phase D: Incorporation

The last phase of the language teaching cycle really involves what you do with your unit's material after the activities have been completed. As we've said, development and mastery of particular language and content are complete when that material is able to be utilized successfully for all sorts of purposes and in all sorts of contexts. That's why it is so important to have a wide range of activities in the experience phase of your unit. This same diversity can be extended even further if you incorporate the content and language of your unit into subsequent units and instruction—one more of the important kinds of integration involved in implementing the integrated model! Thus, in the incorporation phase of the language teaching cycle, even though your unit is over, you keep the theme and the concepts and the language in mind in planning and implementing subsequent units, and you refer to the material from previous units and have your children refer to what they learned from those units in your instruction throughout the rest of the school year.

Heroes and Superheroes Incorporation. Within her Heroes and Superheroes unit, Ms. Kay incorporated concepts and language from a previous unit on simple machines into her new unit's "supervehicle" activity. When she moved on to her next thematic integrated unit, "Rain Makes Applesauce" (see Part II), she included the American folk hero Johnny Appleseed. She invoked her Heroes and Superheroes concepts and language in the discussion of this legendary hero's life and in the discussion of the concept of folk heroes as compared to the concept of superheroes. Thus the language teaching cycle just continues to "roll on" from unit to unit to unit!

Now that we've described the cycle for you to use in deciding how to sequence your unit activities, let's go back to our flowchart and examine the final stage in planning and executing an integrated curriculum unit.

Stage 5: Implementing the Unit

The planning of your integrated unit should not end when the first activity begins but should continue throughout the unit as you work with your students to fulfill the learning potential you have created for each activity. As you implement your unit and participate in the unit activities that you have planned, continue to observe your students as they use language and carry out their learning tasks, and continue to evaluate their progress. Use the insights you gain from observing, evaluating, and participating with your students to make any necessary revisions in the range or the requirements of your activities as the unit continues. Follow students' leads from day to day in carrying out each succeeding unit activity, whether this means adjusting activities according to new student interest or lack of interest in a given topic, or adjusting activities according to students' rapid progress or slow progress in learning the unit's language and content. Unit implementation and revision may lead you to develop whole new activities and objectives/potentials and to eliminate others that you had originally planned to use. Most important, grab "teachable moments" and spontaneous language teaching opportunities when they occur within your activities, even if doing so means departing briefly from your overall plan.

As the senior partner with your second language learners in their English development, you are first responsible for knowing your students' needs and for creating the appropriate opportunities and conditions for them to develop language (this is the "senior" component). You are then responsible for working with students within the opportunities and activities that you have created to provide them with the ongoing interaction, instruction, and support they need for developing language (this is the "partner" component). So that you will meet these responsibilities, the planning that goes into your integrated unit should be both thorough and flexible. It must be thorough so that you will know what is needed and what is to happen in your activities so well that you can focus your attention during them on observing and interacting with your children instead of being preoccupied with surface essentials. Your planning must also be flexible, however, so that even though you have an extremely clear idea of what is to take place and how it is to take place within a given activity, you can still easily adjust these things as they actually occur, according to the needs and responses of your junior partners within the activity—your students. Thus, a final consideration in planning an integrated unit might be that no activity in it should be so complicated that while it takes place, you will have to devote most of your attention to the materials and procedures of the activity itself (to "getting it done") rather than to observing, instructing, and interacting with your students.

Implementing Heroes and Superheroes

As Ms. Kay had anticipated, her students (both first language and second language!) were extremely enthusiastic about the Heroes and Superheroes unit, and many of the activities took more time than she had thought they would. As a result, the time allotted to the unit, which originally had been two weeks, was extended to three weeks, and several of the unit activities were explained in class and completed at home as homeFUN or extra credit assignments.

When, during one activity, several students had difficulty in distinguishing fictional powers and abilities from real ones, Ms. Kay stopped the activity to

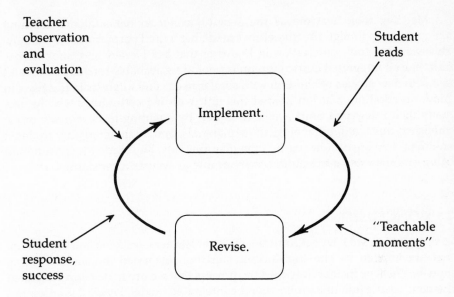

Figure 2.8: Stage Five

define and contrast these concepts, and she elicited attributes and positive and negative examples of each category. The students were amazed to find out that even Ms. Kay wasn't sure about which category some of their heroes' abilities (such as extrasensory perception) belonged in! Similarly, when several students had difficulty in writing in complete sentences for their superhero speeches, Ms. Kay set up a special small group time for them during which they helped her edit a speech she had written which included a number of incomplete sentences. Ms. Kay also found out that Afroud, a mid-second-language student from Afghanistan, knew a song about a heroic warrior and leader of his people, so she helped him write it down and translate it into English, after which he taught the song to the entire class. Jorge, a beginning second language student from Cuba, worked with Afroud to develop a guitar accompaniment.

The class's interest in Dr. Martin Luther King led to adding in new unit activities that centered on the U.S. civil rights movement and its many heroes. In one of these activities, students interviewed their parents about civil rights in their native countries. In another activity, students read about the years before and during the civil rights movement, and compared life at those times to the way things are today. Having written their own speeches, students were also interested in Dr. King's abilities as an orator, and they studied several recordings of his speeches, then applied what they had learned to writing their own civil rights speeches. Later in the year these speeches were incorporated into an all-school program celebrating Dr. King's birthday.

Ms. Kay took her role as the senior partner in her students' learning seriously, even though this sometimes made her a tired partner with her family! However, she took satisfaction in knowing that her Heroes and Superheroes unit, like all integrated curriculum units, would be available for adaptation and use with new groups of children with similar needs and interests in the years to come. In addition, Ms. Kay shared this unit with her colleagues, who in turn made their integrated units available to her. By adapting teacher-made units, published units, and other curriculum materials, and by involving her students and their own ideas in her curriculum planning, Ms. Kay made the transition to using an integrated curriculum a manageable as well as a satisfying one.

2.5 CONCLUSION

In this chapter, we have set forth the views of learners, teachers and curriculum that are implied by the transmission and the integrated language teaching models. We have further described the process that we use to develop integrated thematic curriculum units following the integrated model. Figure 2.9 presents a flowchart summarizing the unit development process as we have described it. It

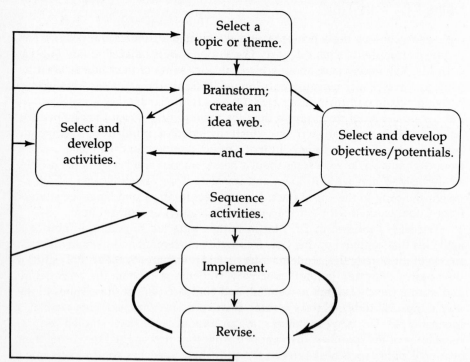

Figure 2.9:   Flowchart for Planning an Integrated Unit

is important to state again here that no linear description or figure can display all of the complexities that go into planning an integrated curriculum unit. However, this chart captures the general "flow" of the planning process and the general order, relations and interactions among its components. Remember that this planning process is meant to be thought-provoking rather than prescriptive. We encourage you to try out our guidelines and our units and learning activities. Our real goal, however, is that you develop your own ways for planning a curriculum which will maximally facilitate your second language students' language and literacy development.

ACTIVITIES AND DISCUSSION

1. Review your school/program organization or a selected school/program organization to see how it compares with the assembly line, transmission educational model summarized by Elkind. What image of the teacher does it use? What image of students? Of curriculum? In what ways do these images fit the model? In what way do they not fit it?

2. Interview a group of second language learners to discover topics and questions of interest and relevance to them. Ask the students if they have previously studied any of these topics in their classrooms.

3. Choose one of the topics/questions discussed by the students in activity #2. Then follow the steps in the unit development process to outline a thematic unit appropriate for the students you interviewed.

4. Evaluate your unit with regard to the seven instructional criteria discussed in Chapter 1. To what extent have you organized for collaboration, purpose, student interest, previous experience, support, variety and integration? Have you incorporated your required curriculum objectives as well?

5. Repeat the activities (#3 and #4) for developing and evaluating an integrated unit described above, only this time use a topic or unit from one of your school's content curricula or textbooks (e.g., social studies, literature) as the starting point. Make sure to figure out how and where students' interests can be incorporated into the unit.

6. Observe a second language lesson in a classroom. Evaluate the lesson according to the seven criteria of the integrated model. Write a new plan for the lesson that incorporates any of the criteria left out in the observed lesson.

FURTHER READING

Brumfit, C.. 1984. *Communicative methodology in language teaching: The roles of fluency and accuracy.* Cambridge, England: Cambridge University Press. Precise description of the contrasting roles of fluency and accuracy in language acquisition and of how they may be taught together using integrated methods and materials.

Elkind, D. 1981. *The hurried child: Growing up too fast too soon.* Reading, MA: Addison-Wesley Publishing Company. Strong arguments for reducing pressure on our children to grow up too fast, to achieve too much too soon, and to meet our adult needs.

Glatthorn, A. A. 1987. *Curriculum Renewal.* Alexandria, VA. Association for Supervision and Curriculum Development. A careful how-to manual for developing and renewing curriculum.

Goodlad, J. I. 1984. *A place called school: Prospects for the future.* New York, NY: McGraw Hill Publishing Company. Report on a vast study of schools in the United States including data from over 27,000 individuals. Describes what occurs in classrooms and schools, what is taught, and makes recommendations for improving education in this country.

Hawkins, D. 1973. How to plan for spontaneity. In C. E. Silberman (Ed.) *The Open Classroom Reader* (pp. 486 - 503). New York, NY: Random House.

Kohl, H. R. 1976. *On teaching.* New York, NY: Schocken Books. The author's musings about a number of topics centering on the craft of teaching, including a section on planning the integrated curriculum.

Moffett. 1968a. *A student-centered language arts curriculum grades K-13: A handbook for teachers.* New York, NY: Houghton Mifflin Company. An authoritative statement of Moffett's discourse and curriculum theories along with several recommendations for translating them into practice.

ADDITIONAL RESOURCES

McCloskey, M. L., and Enright, D. S. 1985. *From rainbows to rhythms to runaway cookies: The Garden Hills international summer school curriculum guide, Vol. III.* Atlanta, GA: Georgia State University.

McCloskey, M. L. (Ed.) 1987. *Turn on units: English as a second language content area curriculum for math, science, and computer science.* Atlanta, GA: State of Georgia Board of Education.

McCloskey, M. L. and Nations, M. J. 1987. *English everywhere: An integrated English as a second language curriculum guide.* Atlanta, GA: Educo Press.

Moss, J. F. 1984. *Focus units in literature: A handbook for elementary school teachers.* Urbana, IL: National Council of Teachers of English.

Chapter 3

The Social Environment

Talking

They tell me that I talk too much.
I'm trying not to talk too much.
But, oh, it's hard to take time out
When there's so much to talk about:
How long it took to pull my tooth.
How hard it is to tell the truth.
Why steel is not as nice as trees.
Why Brian has such scabby knees.
Twelve sights I saw in Williamsburg.
The definition of an *erg*.
Why roller skates are not my style.
Six reasons goldfish never smile.
How come I'd rather freeze than roast.
And ten things that I love the most:
The mustache on my father's face.
Fires in the fireplace.
Any book by Judy Blume.
Never cleaning up my room.
Every single valentine
Sent to me by Chris Romine.
Drummers in a marching band.
Ferry rides,
The Redskins,
Poems, and
Talking.

—Judith Viorst

3.1 INTRODUCTION

As you begin to plan your curriculum and learning activities, you can use the ILT criteria to create or adjust your learning environment so that it will support your new curriculum. Each of the criteria can be applied to your classroom social environment (the rules and procedures and ways of interacting that you use within your classroom and within your learning activities) and to your classroom physical environment (the space and furniture and objects and materials that you use for learning both inside and outside your classroom) to facilitate second language development. In this chapter, we will apply the seven ILT criteria to the social environment.

3.2 "NO TALKING"

In Chapter 2, we described the atomistic transmission-of-knowledge curriculum, which contrasts dramatically with the assumptions of the ILT model. In like manner, most public school classroom environments today have been designed to support a one-way, transmission conception of instruction (Cuban 1982; Sirotnik 1983).

A recent U.S. TV commercial illustrates the pervasiveness of this transmission environment in today's classrooms. The commercial was advertising an electronic teaching-aid toy called Speak 'n Math, and Bill Cosby was the company's spokesman.

Now, one would think that the design and development of Speak 'n Math (and its counterpart Speak 'n Spell) were quite thorough, for they appear to be based on two well-grounded cognitive-developmental principles that the ILT model shares: (1) that learning is two-way and interactive, and (2) that concepts and language are best learned in direct combination. Thus, as the child taps out the components of an arithmetic problem on the Speak 'n Math machine, they appear on a tiny screen, accompanied by an electronic voice that names them (e.g., "three," "plus," "two," etc.). The child's answer to the problem is also orally evaluated by the electronic voice ("Correct, very good" "Incorrect, try again").

But now let's review the scenario in which this communicative toy is presented. The commercial opens on Cosby sitting at the rear of an elementary school classroom with his back to the children and the teacher, who are all busily engaged in doing what teachers and children do. The students are all sitting at their own private desks, and the desks are arranged in rows facing the front of the classroom. There, awaiting their undivided attention, is a large blackboard, at which is positioned the teacher. The teacher is a woman, advancing in years, with spectacles and white hair arranged in a bun, and with a pointer and chalk in her hands. What does the teacher do? She commands the continued attention of the students by writing bits of information on the blackboard and by calling on a succession of students with upraised hands, who take turns responding to her questions and other elicitations.

It is in this setting that Cosby begins his hymn to the wonders of Speak 'n Math. In a voice barely louder than a conspiratorial whisper, he explains how the small machine operates and promises that it will make learning math facts easier and more fun. After the commercial cuts away to provide specific product information, the scene returns to Cosby delightedly trying out the toy, pushing the buttons and listening to the electronic voice. Temporarily (and fatally) forgetting his whereabouts, Cosby raises his voice excitedly to urge the viewers to buy this "neat" toy and try it out! The commercial ends with a shot of the stern visage of the teacher, who is poking Cosby's shoulder and firmly intoning (much to the children's merriment and to Cosby's consternation) the sacred injunction of the U.S. public-school classroom: "No talking!"

The extraordinary irony of this "Speak 'n Math" commercial, and the premise on which its humor depends, is that it directly contradicts the essence of the product it champions. In principle, the toy and the classroom share the same goal: to educate. The "joke" is that the classroom is the one place where the use of this educational toy is clearly forbidden!

What makes this contradiction so believable that it can serve as the impetus for a message shown in millions of North American homes? The answer, we think, is that the commercial is a reasonable (if exaggerated) depiction of life in the public schools as it still exists today. In this respect, it is a vivid representation of the conflict between the assumptions and practices of the transmission oriented real world of the educational bureaucracy (symbolized by the classroom scenario) and those of the integrated model, which is based on insights from the world of education as a scholarly discipline (symbolized by the toy). Certainly, most teachers today do not wear their hair in buns, but it is much harder to doubt the typicality of classroom practices depicted in the commercial, especially the materials, the furniture arrangement, and the kind of interaction it portrays.

How does the integrated language classroom contrast with the Speak 'n Math, transmission classroom? Well, first, the integrated classroom *looks* different. It is filled with pictures and posters and interesting junk (otherwise known in the field as "realia" and "concrete referents"). It is filled with an abundance of print, from signs and labels to books of all levels and all sorts to displays of children's own writing. It is filled with movement, as children engage in a number of meaning-making tasks with a number of different groups. The integrated language classroom often *smells* different from the transmission classroom—when, for example, a tasty cookie-baking experiment or a sulfurous science experiment have just been completed! Above all, the integrated language classroom *sounds* different—sometimes reverberating with many different discussions and recitations and conversations, at other times echoing with the sound of all the voices combined into one single voice. These images of the integrated classroom make good sense if we recall that, as teachers of second language students, our goal is to "use everything"—every inch of classroom space and every kind of interaction and learning opportunity that arises during the time that our students are with us—for the purpose of promoting language and literacy development. Let's look at how the seven instructional criteria we have outlined might be applied to do this, within the classroom social environment.

3.3 ORGANIZING THE SOCIAL ENVIRONMENT

As teachers, we tend to think about and organize our social environments at two levels, both of which we will need to review and adjust in order to meet the ILT criteria. Let's start with the highest (and broadest) level: general classroom rules.

General Classroom Rules

All teachers have a set of rules and expectations which they use to structure classroom interaction in general. Sarason (1982) calls these rules the "classroom constitution." They are usually determined before the children come to school and are then adjusted slightly during the first few days of the school year in order to take into account any unique group characteristics. Often, they are stated explicitly (sometimes even posted) at the beginning of the year, but in some classrooms they remain implicit. In either case, these general rules are quickly internalized by students and become tacit regulators of their behavior (and their teacher's behavior) for the rest of the year. Thus, the classroom constitution exerts a subtle but powerful influence over the kinds of interactions and language experiences that children have there, and it can either support or impede children's language and literacy development.

In the transmission classroom represented by the Speak 'n Math commercial, the main rule governing interaction is "No talking." But if you wish to apply the ILT model to your classroom, just the opposite primary rule must be adopted: *"Yes,* talking," or, in the terminology of the instructional criteria, "Yes, collaborating." It won't suffice to *permit* talking and other forms of collaborating in your classroom; if the ILT model is to be applied, you must dynamically encourage and demand collaboration in daily classroom life. Through imposing a general classroom rule mandating collaboration as a behavior, you will make significant progress toward the goal of making the classroom a useful place for second language students to develop language and literacy.

Integrated, "Yes talking" classrooms encourage and demand collaboration in daily classroom activities.

This advice does not mean that we think there is no place in the integrated language classroom for individualized work and for silent activities: *all* talking would probably be as problematic for second language students as *no* talking. We also do not mean to suggest that a magic set of rules for governing interaction across all classrooms will lead to maximal second language and literacy development while achieving all other instructional goals. Rather, you must develop rules that best suit the needs of your particular students and curriculum and your own interactive style. If the ILT model is to operate effectively in your classroom, you must examine your implicit interactive expectations as they are expressed in your classroom rules and then adjust them where necessary, using the organizational criteria that we have provided.

Two Types of Rules

Many of the rules in your classroom constitution are already working to create the kind of social environment needed to promote second language development. We are concerned here with the rules that *block* second language development and the full implementation of your integrated curriculum. There are two types of these problem rules, each requiring a different response in order to be brought into line with the integrated model.

Problem rules of the first type are those which in their original intention do not violate any of the criteria of the integrated model, but which in their actual application do violate them. These rules can be adapted so that they preserve their original purpose but also support children's language learning. For example, a teacher might create the rule "Don't get out of your seat" to avoid disruptions of teaching or of children's learning, but the actual effects of that rule might be to stifle *all* student interactions, productive and disruptive. A better rule would be, for example, "Respect the needs of others." This rule would include respecting other students' privacy and need to concentrate, but it would also permit children to interact when it was helpful and not disruptive, thereby fulfilling the criteria of collaboration, interest, and support.

The new rules will differ from the ones they replace in two important respects. First, the students themselves will often be involved in the formulation and interpretation of the rules. For example, requiring students to "respect the needs of others" means that students must constantly make judgments: when to interrupt another student, and when not to; when to help another student, and when not to; and so on. On the other hand, "Don't get out of your seat" requires—indeed, mandates—one correct behavior, and it is a behavior that you directly enforce. Second, your new rules will also be much more context- and situation-dependent than your old rules: "Don't get out of your seat" is a blanket commandment with no exceptions, whereas "Respect the needs of others" is a rule with multiple applications, depending on the task and the individuals involved. Thus, for your new rules to be as useful and as powerful as the ones they replace, they will have to be carefully explained and practiced (more on this later on). Once this is done, however, they will facilitate your students' language and literacy development as well as enabling you to manage effectively.

Problem rules of the second type are those which, for whatever reason, block second language development in both their intention and their application. "No talking" is one example. These rules are even tougher to deal with than the first type because the only way to "adapt" them is to change them completely, which may also mean changing or giving up some of your deeply held teaching values or preferences. For example, there are many possible reasons that teachers employ the "No talking" rule. They may want to teach the values of self-control and good manners. They may feel most comfortable in a quiet teaching atmosphere. They may find it difficult to manage children if they give them multiple opportunities to interact. Or they may feel pressured by their principal and fellow teachers to keep their children quiet as an ostensible sign of "good teaching."

If these teachers were to decide to use the integrated language teaching model to improve conditions for their second language students, they would not only have to change their "No talking" rule to "Yes, talking," but they would also have to find ways to deal with the original impetus for their "No talking" rule. For instance, they might decide to teach good manners *and* collaboration; they might choose to get used to more noise and activity; they might seek new management and discipline strategies; or they might choose to meet with their principals and colleagues to explain the rationale behind their "noisy" classrooms. Other common examples of the second type of problem rules are: "Don't answer a question unless you are sure you know the correct answer," and "Don't make a mess." It would be very difficult in the integrated language classroom simultaneously to have error-free discourse and a supportive social environment, or constant tidiness and an interesting, purposeful, holistic learning environment. It would be impossible in the integrated language classroom to forbid students to use oral language and still have a rich and fruitful language development environment. Setting up classroom rules means setting up classroom values. Some values will have to take precedence over others.

Changing Your Rules

Many of the rules and procedures in your classroom will automatically change when you change your curriculum. However, we have found that teachers are more likely to succeed with their new curriculum and learning activities if they deliberately prepare the way for them. You can do this by first adapting your overall social environment—your overall rules. Here is a set of steps which we have found to be helpful in this process.

As with any substantial change in routine, you will be more effective if you change your rules slowly, one at a time, instead of attempting to make over your classroom in a day. But before attempting any changes in your rules, you will first need to make explicit those classroom rules you presently use which may be implicit. Take some time to reflect on how behavior, both verbal (talking) and nonverbal (moving around, taking turns, determining where and how to work, etc.), is structured in your classroom. Then write out a list of the rules you presently use to govern interaction in your classroom. To do this, you may wish to review your lesson plans or to keep a log for a few days to track what happens in class and how you act in your classroom. Pay special attention to times when things seem to be going unusually badly, and see if you can decide which of your rules were causing these highs and lows. Remember, you should be concentrating on determining all of your rules, whether they are directly related to speech (e.g., "No one may talk to the teacher when the teacher is with a reading group") or related to something else (e.g., "Only one student may go to the restroom at a time").

Once you have determined to your satisfaction the rules you currently use in your classroom, you are ready for the second and third steps in the adaptation process. The second step involves using the seven instructional criteria and the two types of problem rules described above to evaluate all your rules. Do you have rules that already encourage integrated language and literacy development? If so, they can be left alone. Do any of your rules partially conflict with one or more of the instructional criteria? These can be adjusted. Do any of them directly conflict with the ILT model in their intention and application? If so, these rules might have to be completely changed. Can you envision creating new rules that would facilitate your students' use of language? If so, these rules can be added. Once you have made this review, you are ready for the third step. Try to write out a new rule (or rules) for each old rule that is in conflict with the seven criteria and add in any new rules that you think might support the criteria even further. Make sure that the new rules you write are clear and that they fit together as a set. Also make sure to take into account your students, your own personality and teaching style, and your teaching situation as you develop your new rules. Some rules (like "Yes, talking") will probably be important and appropriate for any teaching situation, but the applicability of others will vary with the setting. For example, if you are a bilingual education teacher, you probably need rules that explain how, where, and when students are permitted to use each of the two classroom languages. If you are a pullout ESL teacher with groups of students from various classrooms joining you throughout the day, you may need rules that govern how students are to get started in class without your telling them, how they should join an activity that is already in progress, or how they can get help without interrupting. To assist you in reviewing and revising your classroom rules, examples of one teacher's old and new rules are presented in Figure 3.1.

Next, in keeping with our original caution to go slowly, the fourth step in the rules adaptation process is to reorder your new rules. Begin with the ones you'd have the least trouble adopting and move on to those you'd find the most difficult to adopt. Then, in the fifth and final step, begin replacing your old rules with your new ones, one at a time. Remember that you will have to introduce the new rules to your students and explicitly practice them. It will take a few "violations" and "reminders" before they are in full effect. But if you persevere, your efforts will be successful, and you will have made your classroom a richer language learning environment.

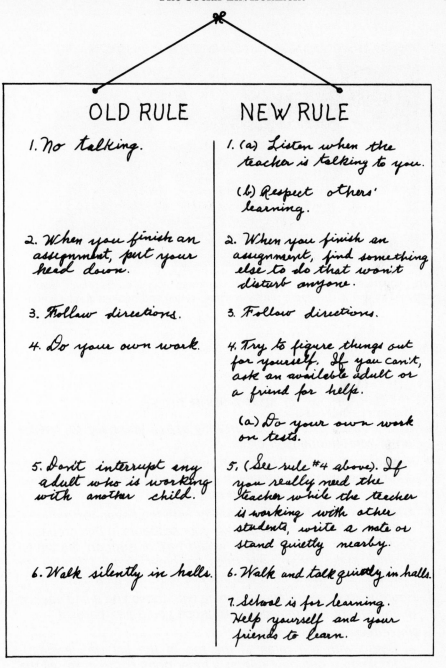

OLD RULE

1. No talking.

2. When you finish an assignment, put your head down.

3. Follow directions.

4. Do your own work.

5. Don't interrupt any adult who is working with another child.

6. Walk silently in halls.

NEW RULE

1. (a) Listen when the teacher is talking to you.

   (b) Respect others' learning.

2. When you finish an assignment, find something else to do that won't disturb anyone.

3. Follow directions.

4. Try to figure things out for yourself. If you can't, ask an available adult or a friend for help.

   (a) Do your own work on tests.

5. (See rule #4 above). If you really need the teacher while the teacher is working with other students, write a note or stand quietly nearby.

6. Walk and talk quietly in halls.

7. School is for learning. Help yourself and your friends to learn.

Figure 3.1: One Teacher's Old and New Rules

Using the integrated model to adapt the classroom social environment involves reviewing and adjusting classroom rules governing verbal and nonverbal interaction.

The following list summarizes the steps we have just described.

HOW TO ADAPT YOUR RULES

1. *Write down the rules you currently use. If you need to, keep a log of what happens in class.*

2. *Evaluate all your rules according to the seven instructional criteria, selecting those which could be expanded or changed to better apply the integrated model.*

3. *Adjust the rules that are in conflict with the seven instructional criteria. (When possible, involve your students in this process.) Develop new rules you think would further support the seven criteria. Make these new rules as clear and as simple as possible, and make sure that they fit together as a set.*

4. *Reorder your new rules, beginning with those you'd find easiest to implement and moving on to those you'd find hardest.*

5. *Implement your new rules:*
   a. *Begin with the rules at the top of the list (the easiest). Implement one new rule at a time; don't try to make all the changes at once.*
   b. *Explicitly teach the rules to your students. Model the new rules, using both positive and negative examples.*

Classroom Activities and Participant Structures

In addition to the set of rules we use for structuring classroom interaction, we as teachers also have a specific set of classroom events or activities that we use to carry out our daily plans. These segments of interaction are generally defined according to their grouping (who is to participate); their content (what students are to learn and what they need to do in order to learn it); their materials (what teachers and students are to use); and their participant structures (how students are to interact). Most teachers begin with the content and materials dimensions of their instruction and then set up a specific set of social activities which they repeatedly use throughout the school year. They give names to these common activities (e.g., "seat work," "reading group," "free time," "class meeting," "morning routine," "greetings time").

In too many classrooms, the activities that are used to organize interaction, like the general rules, are more repressive than helpful. For example, Sirotnik (1983) identifies "teacher explaining, lecturing, and reading aloud" as the most common activity in U.S. public-school classrooms, closely followed by "working on written assignments" and "preparation for assignments/instructions/cleanup." Several investigators (e.g., Bellack et al. 1966; Flanders 1970; Mehan 1979) have also identified the "lesson" as the predominant classroom event. In general, a lesson consists of a teacher lecture, followed by a series of turn-taking sequences involving teacher questions or solicitations, student replies, and teacher evaluations of these replies (e.g., T: "What's the capital of France, Johnny?" J: "Paris?" T: "Right. Paris. Good."). This is the activity that was depicted in the Speak 'n Math commercial. Unfortunately for our second language students, all of the activities described above require an extensive amount of passive student participation, with *small* amounts of collaboration; individualization (including use of students' previous experiences); intrinsic purposes; use of the whole environment; maintenance of student interest; and support. By definition, the use of only one or two activities to organize interaction throughout an entire year violates the seventh organizational criterion of variety. Thus, in deciding how your students will interact within your different learning activities, it is important that you keep in mind your second language students and the seven instructional criteria.

Fortunately, you can manipulate the primary social features of your classroom activities—the groups of participants involved and the ways in which they will interact—in order to meet the seven criteria. That is, you can create new student interest in your activities; new opportunities for children to use the various communication processes integrated into your activities; and new purposes for your activities. You can be aware of individual children's preferred ways of interacting and of their previous experience in your activities, and add these forms of collaboration to your activities. Let's illustrate how this might work for these last two criteria, variety and collaboration.

You could use the *grouping* feature of your activities by having students develop full- or small-group reports, projects, and written assignments in place of individual activities. Placing five students together to write a play will provide opportunities for collaboration (and thus for language learning) that assigning an individual composition will not. Similarly, adding yourself to an activity as one of the participants will often markedly change the communicative requisites and the tenor of the discourse.

The *social task* or the *participant structures* of an activity could also be adapted to require various forms of collaboration. Imagine the language use and collaboration that might occur if low- and mid-second language students were privately taught how to make a holiday art project and then were guided as instructional team leaders to help small groups of classmates complete the project! In like manner, asking the whole class or small groups of students to reach a consensus on the main causes of water pollution and then to write essays on this topic can create a different kind of share discourse and collaboration than having students write individual essays on the same topic. Even the participant structures of routine procedural events could be varied to create different forms of interaction; for example, you could change the usual one-way full-group dismissal ("It's three-thirty. Class is dismissed!") by requiring that each student provide a politeness formula before leaving (e.g., "May I be excused?") or by requiring a response to the same relevant question asked of each student (e.g., "What book did you check out today?" or "What do you want to start with tomorrow?"). You could also increase student responsibility and involvement by assigning a student to lead the dismissal activity. Just think—simply occasionally changing the way you have children carry out routines such as getting in line or going to the restroom can have a positive effect on their language learning! (A variety of participant structures that provide useful language to second language students will be discussed further in Chapter 5, which deals more extensively with oral discourse.)

As mentioned earlier, the major activity dimensions—groupings and participant structures—must be coordinated with planning the content of your activities; that is, within your integrated curriculum. A lesson in the Heroes and Superheroes unit we described in Chapter 2 will serve as an illustration. Once you have decided to bake a Superman cake with the class, choices remain about how to carry out the cake baking. For example, you could have students sit in a circle on the floor, with the ingredients in the middle of the circle, and have individuals come one at a time to the center to measure and add one ingredient. Or you could divide the recipe into halves or thirds and have small groups of students come over to a table to make the cake with you. Or you could be Julia Child, with students sitting in front of you as you explain and demonstrate making the cake. Each of these ways of organizing the same curriculum activity (baking a cake) involves different kinds of language input and language practice. Most of the activities you do in your classroom, both instructional and

Activity	Participant Grouping						Teacher Role				Materials (LIST)	Participant Structure									
	I	D	S	F	C	O	PI	PS	PP	U		QA	L	D	CP	G	P	DM	CM	C	O

Participant

Grouping
I Individual
D Dyad
S Small Group
F Full Group
C Choice
O Other

Teacher Role
PI Present as Instructor
PS Present as Supervisor
PP Present as Partner
U   Unavailable, except for crisis

Materials
list, e.g., text, book, paper/pencil, game, concrete object, media, blackboard, chart, computer, workbook, choice

Participant Structure
QA Question/Answer
L   Lecture/Presentation
D   Discussion
CP Choral Practice
G   Game
P   Project
DM Decision Making
CM Choice from Menu
C   Free Choice
O   Other

Figure 3.2:   Activity Feature Chart

procedural (examples of the latter being dismissal, cleaning up, or going to the restroom) have this same potential for being socially organized to teach many kinds of language and language uses in addition to content and concepts.

Reviewing and Adapting Your Activities

The steps you use to review and adapt your classroom events, taking into account the seven instructional criteria, are quite similar to those you used for your classroom rules. The main difference is that with your rules, you use your general, ongoing classroom schedule and environment as the context for reviewing and changing, but with the social organization of your activities, you use your specific curriculum and units as the context. Here's an exercise that will help you first become more aware of the activities you're currently using and that will then assist you in revising them. A form for doing this exercise is provided in Figure 3.2.

Begin by picking a day within your current teaching schedule to review. If you are planning to do an integrated curriculum unit, you might choose to use a part of this unit instead.

Now, for step 2, make a list of all of the activities you plan to do or that you did with your children during the time frame you selected. Easy ways to capture an individual activity on paper include writing down in your plan book what you usually call the activity (e.g., "silent reading," "math groups") or writing down what the main thing is that children are going to do during the activity (e.g., "choose and read library books," "measure bean plants"). It also helps to write down the times of the activities so that you don't skip any. Remember that in many instances, more than one activity takes place in your classroom at the same time. For example, you may be conducting a small-group reading or a discussion activity while the rest of the class is doing seat work or writing a composition. The first column of Figure 3.3 shows how this list might look for a day in the Heroes and Superheroes unit.

Next, classify each of your activities according to its two major social characteristics of groupings and participant structures/procedures. Use the lists of commonly used features provided on the chart in Figure 3.2 to help you do this. Please note that each list of features in Figure 3.2 includes an "other" designation so that you can write down features you use in your classroom that we haven't thought of! Also, please note that you may check more than one category in each feature list, since more than one grouping, teacher role, or participant structure is often used within a single activity (e.g., an activity beginning with a "lecture" followed by a "question/answer" period). If you haven't decided what to use for a particular activity or feature, leave the space(s) blank.

After you have completed the activity feature chart, you will probably be surprised to see how many different kinds of activities you are already using in

Activity	Participant Grouping						Participant Teacher Role				Materials (List)	Participant Structure									
	I	D	S	F	C	O	PI	PS	PP	U		QA	L	D	CP	G	P	DM	CM	C	O
8:10 Today's News/Free Time	✓								✓		Chart/Marker		✓								
8:30 Attendance/Lunch Count	✓	✓						✓			Cans, Clothespins, Forms		✓			✓					
Share News/Today's Plan	✓	✓									News Chart, Schedule Chart									✓	
8:45 Groups A Superheroes Center											Center Activities										
B Write Comics											Art & Writing Supplies										
C Plans for Trip										✓	Maps, Bus Schedule	✓	✓					✓			
8:45 1-A 2-B 3-C / 9:15 2-A 3-B 1-C / 9:45 3-A 1-B 2-C		✓																			
10:15 Restroom	✓		✓								None	✓									
10:30 PE: Superman Can	✓										Jump Ropes Rhyme Balls, Etc.		✓								
11:15 Lunch: Superfoods	✓								✓		Lunches		✓								
11:45 Break Hero—Name	✓			✓							None	✓									
12:00 SS—MLK Speeches				✓			✓				Tape/Recorder	✓	✓								
12:40 SSR	✓									✓	Books & Magazines										
1:00 Math Supergraphs											Data Collected by Students, Graph Paper						✓				
1:45 Science—Robot Projects		✓							✓		Junk Art Supplies		✓						✓		
2:15 Journals/Share	✓	✓		✓					✓		Journals, Pencils	✓	✓					✓			
2:45 Dismissal																					

Figure 3.3: Activity Feature Chart for Superheroes Unit

a typical day. You will also probably notice that some activities and activity features dominate your chart and that some are not listed at all. In fact, as you do this exercise, you may think of other creative ways to organize your activities. This brings us to the fourth step in reviewing and adapting your learning activities, which is to review your chart to see whether you could adjust any activities so as to fill in blank spaces and increase the variety in your planning. Look for ways to increase your activities' potential for meeting the seven criteria. Have you built a lot of variety into your unit or time frame? Do students have various opportunities to collaborate with different classroom members, using different materials for different language purposes? Do your events use different language processes? Do some of your events integrate various language processes and subject matter and media? Does your chart include activities that incorporate student's previous experiences and learning activities into their organization? If the answer to any of these questions is no, how might you adjust the activities you have planned so that the criterion in question will be satisfied?

You are now ready to change and/or add some new features and activities in order to make your curriculum and social environment even more integrated, communicative, and language rich. Remember that you can change an entire event by altering only one of its features. For instance, you could change the participant structure in our Superheroes cake-making activity. Instead of having the class watch you and listen to you as you make the cake (lecture/ presentation), you could have the class read a rebus recipe next to the table and chorally tell you what to do next (choral practice/decision making). With this change, you would dramatically alter students' collaborative roles as well as the amount of purpose, interest, and integration present in the activity.

After making the necessary adjustments in your planned activities, the next step is to try them out! As you do this, try to keep in mind the changes and additions you made and see how they work in practice. Then use what you have learned to continue to build a better social environment for your second language students' language and literacy development.

The exercise and steps we have outlined here do not provide a magic formula. They will not lead to a set of classroom activities that will meet all the needs of your second language students. Rather, they comprise a set of procedures that, if followed, will lead to an increased awareness on your part of the ways in which you are using your classroom resources and the ways in which you might adapt them to improve the social environment of your classroom. The more you reflect on all aspects of your teaching, the better that teaching will become, and the more likely you will be to "use everything" to help your students develop their meaning-making capacities. Thus, the concluding step of the activities review process involves repeating steps 1 through 5 occasionally to make sure you are continuing to utilize the social dimensions of

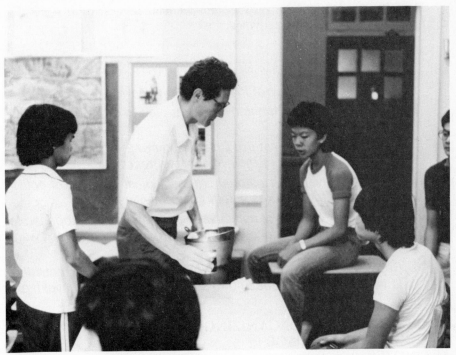

Both the grouping and the social organization (or participant structures) of learning activities can be adjusted to promote second language development.

your curriculum activities, and also to make adjustments in those features as your students' needs change. After completing the Activity Feature Chart (Figure 3.2) a couple of times, you should be able to review your activities in your head; eventually, the process should become automatic. Still, the demands of teaching are so many and so constant that it wouldn't hurt to formally repeat an activities review every so often to keep your awareness level high.

The following list summarizes the steps we have suggested for reviewing and adapting your classroom activities:

HOW TO ADAPT YOUR ACTIVITIES

1. *Select a specific day of instruction to review.*
2. *Make a list of all of the activities you plan to do or that you did within that day.*
3. *Use the Activity Feature Chart (Figure 2) to classify your activities according to their major features.*
4. *Using the seven instructional criteria, adjust your set of activities and/or the features within your activities.*
5. *Try out your new set of activities, then review what happened to see which activities (and changes) were helpful and which were not.*
6. *Repeat steps 1 through 5 occasionally to be sure your activities fit your students' needs and to keep your awareness level high.*

3.4 CHALLENGES IN ORGANIZING INTEGRATED LANGUAGE ACTIVITIES

There are other reasons for the prevalence of large group "lessons" and individualized "seat work" in U.S. classrooms besides their connection to the transmission curriculum. In our own work as teachers and teacher educators, our colleagues have given us many explanations for why they would find it hard or even impossible to replace their full group lessons and individual seat-work activities with a variety of integrated activities designed to accomplish the same learning objectives but also designed to meet the seven criteria of the integrated model and to promote language and literacy development. The three most commonly cited reasons are as follows:

—"There's no way to schedule these kinds of units and activities";

—"Students can't handle that kind of activity"; and

—"Those activities would be too hard and too time-consuming to plan".

These three challenges are examined below.

Scheduling

One of the main reasons for seat work and lessons being so common in U.S. classrooms is class sizes. Classes are often so large that teachers schedule activities in which everyone in the class participates in the same way and at the same time. However, teachers often automatically choose the large group as the "grouping" activity feature when another activity feature could accomplish the same teaching goal with a large class in the same amount of time *while* increasing language and literacy development. All it takes is a little planning and a little imagination! The Heroes and Superheroes unit will serve again to illustrate the point. Let's say that the class has already invented superhero characters and that Ms. Kay now wants the class to use these characters to compose original adventures. One way to do this would be simply to give the class a seat work composition assignment, which might look something like this in the plan book:

PLAN BOOK		
Day	Tuesday	*Independent adventure composition*
Time	1:00–2:00	

Alternatively, Ms. Kay could ask the students as a group to come up with a single class adventure involving their characters. In this scenario, Ms. Kay might possibly act as moderator, and one or more students could act as "scribes." On an integrated unit schedule chart, the activity might look like this:

PLAN BOOK		
Day	Tuesday	*Class adventure Discussion and Development*
Time	1:00–2:00	

Still another way of doing this activity would be to divide the class into groups of four to six children and have them write group adventures involving the characters created by the children in the group. This method is the one we chose to use in planning our version of this unit, which appears as Superheroes unit Activity 4. This is what the activity looked like in Ms. Kay's planning book.

PLAN BOOK		Group A Develop Group Superheroes Adventures	Group B Develop Group Superheroes Adventures	Group C Develop Group Superheroes Adventures
Day	Tuesday			
Time	1:00-2:00			

As you can see, the three ways of doing the activity do not differ in the amount of time they take or in their learning task. They do differ in the kinds of collaboration, thinking, and language use they facilitate, and in the teacher's role within each of them! So why not double the learning potential of your instruction within the same time periods?

Here's another example from the Heroes and Superheroes unit. Ms. Kay had three learning tasks she wanted her students to accomplish during one particular week: (1) to figure out the amounts of speech given to different types of superheroes on a cartoon show; (2) to tell what it was about their real-life hero that makes that person heroic; and (3) to fill in the attributes lists of their personal superheroes. Ms. Kay could have accomplished these three tasks by making them identical seat work activities (with no student collaboration at all) and scheduling them separately, like this:

PLAN BOOK		
Day	*Tuesday*	*Seat work: Videotape "superspeech" math activity*
Time	*1:00–2:00*	
Day	*Wednesday*	*Seat work: Superhero attributes list*
Time	*1:00–2:00*	
Day	*Thursday*	*Seat work: Personal hero qualities list*
Time	*1:00–2:00*	
Day		
Time		
Day		
Time		

Instead, Ms. Kay chose to introduce and schedule three *simultaneous* activities during the three time periods. She organized the superspeech math activity as a small group project (small group, teacher absent, video/papers/pencil, project); the personal hero activity as a teacher-led discussion and writing activity (small group, teacher present as instructor, paper/pencil, discussion + project); and the superhero list activity as an individualized activity for the other children (individual, teacher absent, paper/pencil, independent/teacher task). She then divided the class into thirds and rotated these groups through the activities during the three time periods as follows:

PLAN BOOK

Day	Tuesday	Group A — Superspeech Math Activity	Group B — Teacher Discussion Personal Heroes	Group C — Individual Superheroes List
Time	1:00–2:00			
Day	Wednesday	Group A — Individual Superheroes List	Group B — Superspeech Math Activity	Group C — Teacher Discussion Personal Heroes
Time	1:00–2:00			
Day	Thursday	Group A — Teacher Discussion Personal Heroes	Group B — Individual Superheroes List	Group C — Superspeech Math Activity
Time	1:00–2:00			
Day				
Time				
Day				

This arrangement required the same amount of time, the same curriculum, and the same materials that identical seat work activities would have, scheduled separately and with no student collaboration. But it yielded a variety of opportunities for students to use their listening, speaking, reading, and writing skills to learn content and to develop more English! It also permitted students to work cooperatively toward mutual learning goals and to support one another's learning.

Gail Sheehy (1986) experienced a time and scheduling conundrum similar to the one faced by teachers implementing the integrated curriculum with their second language students when she first met her own adopted Cambodian refugee daughter, Mohm. Here is how Sheehy describes her realization that her initial free time with Mohm, just after her arrival in the United States, was over:

> It was like being yanked out of one kind of time—people time—and locked back into scheduled time. How lovely it had been the past four days, letting myself tune in to sense the tempo Mohm brought with her and trying to adjust city life accordingly. It was natural; that's why it felt so good. People time, which I think of as elastic and responsive to the people around you, also responds to the unpredictable and Mohm's arrival had been nothing if not unpredictable. Yet I had learned well how to function in the straitjacket of scheduled time—compartmentalizing the mind, ignoring others' needs, skipping sleep, and cheating my body with stimulants in order to perform. The tension between the two kinds of time, of course, is the eternal battleground of any career mother's life. (1986:205)

And, we might add, the same tension is likely to occur in the lives of teachers who propose to use the integrated model in their classrooms. Like Sheehy with her beginning second language daughter, "tuning in" to students and making them partners in planning and implementing the curriculum entails going on "people time" rather than on "scheduled time" as much as possible, within the constraints of your own particular educational bureaucracy and teaching situation. Going on people time in your classroom entails frequently stopping a given activity to take advantage of a teachable moment; frequently extending a given activity to allow yourself and your students to follow up on new learning angles and research leads; and frequently throwing out or postponing a given activity or unit and adding in a new one. Switching from scheduled time to people time does not result in "lost" instructional time; rather, it's simply a matter of who is going to be the master—the planned curriculum and the schedule or the students and you! Of course, this means that you will have to constantly seek out ways to accommodate people time to the scheduled time in your own setting and that you will have to work for changes in the schedule that will facilitate the needs of your students rather than the needs of adults and the bureaucracy. If you are in the "pullout" ESL classroom (or closet or hall or corner of the cafeteria), it will probably entail trying to schedule longer and more regular times for working with your students, since doing integrated units and activities tends to require longer periods of time than quick drill sessions with single, isolated facts or skills. If you are in the grade-level classroom, it will probably entail working with the administration and with the specialist teachers your students have (e.g., music, P.E., remedial reading, even ESL!) to create a schedule that allows you to have large blocks of instructional time, uninterrupted by other teaching sessions or other routine activities. Flexibility and responsiveness may be the centerpieces of the integrated curriculum schedule, but they are hardly the centerpieces of the real world of our public schools!

Besides working to maximize the flexibility within your daily schedule and to use people time as much as possible, here is a brief list of other things to consider when you schedule your integrated units and activities:

1. *Units aren't monolithic.* Adopting integrated units in your teaching setting does not mean that all classroom activities must be devoted to unit activities or to a single unit. If, for example, you are having your students write in interactive journals or you are reading a story or a chapter from a book to them each day in your class, these activities shouldn't be abandoned merely because they don't fit into whatever unit you are planning. Similarly, you can have more than one integrated unit running at the same time with your group. One teacher we know likes to introduce three unit topics in the large group setting over a week's time, then has a daily "unit work time" during which the class is divided into thirds and rotates between three activities, each one having to do with one of the three current unit themes.

2. *Divide and conquer.* Before you throw out a given activity because you don't have enough time to do it, try subdividing it into shorter subactivities until it will fit into your overall schedule! Returning to the Heroes and Superheroes cake-baking activity as an example, if you are an ESL teacher and have a group of second language children for thirty minutes at a time, you could take the four phases of the activity that Ms. Kay planned—reading the recipe and learning the names of the ingredients; following the recipe; baking the cake; and eating the cake—and do them at separate times. Monday could be recipe day, Tuesday could be batter day, and Wednesday could be munching day (with you doing the baking without the children on Tuesday). Subdividing activities in this way will preserve the interest, purpose, collaboration, and so on, within your curriculum.

3. *Know your overall goals well.* The better you know what you want your students to learn during their time with you, the easier it will be for you to be flexible within your schedule and curriculum. To illustrate, if you know in the autumn that you want to introduce the concept of

Going on "people time" in your classroom means allowing students as well as the schedule to set the pace of instruction.

multiplication to your class by spring, but in October you are baking a Superman cake with them and they become interested *then* in the notion of doubling or tripling a recipe to increase the number of portions that result, you can grab the occasion to introduce the concept of multiplication at that moment! Even if you decide not to move up your entire multiplication introduction and activities, by knowing your overall goals for your students well, you've freed yourself up to accomplish your own goals and your school's goals for your students while following the students' leads and fulfilling the instructional criteria of the ILT model. Remember: thoroughness goes hand in hand with flexibility.

Capacity of Students

What about the diversity and complexity of integrated language curriculum procedures for second language students who are still struggling to follow what is going on in the classroom? We believe that your students (first *and* second language students) can handle many different kinds of tasks and activities, but only if you take the time to talk about your expectations. Your students will need to be told how you expect them to act in your activities and you will have to work with them to build these new activities and participant structures carefully over time. It is also important that you model new procedures and behaviors, so students can see the right way to handle them. You can't expect students to "know" the procedures for your varied activities after one explanation. It's important to take them step by step through what will be expected of them, and to do this more than once. This includes explaining the content of the activity (e.g., telling students that they must count and tally statements of cartoon heroes and explain the results) and the conduct of the activity (e.g., the group must turn in a single group tally sheet and report; each member of the group must take a turn at being the scribe to record the tally; and the group must agree on a summary and explanation for the results which will be written down by the group leader). It's also important that you carefully select the members of your groups and that you have "experts" assist other members in their groups (e.g., experts in knowledge about the content, experts in drawing, experts in speaking English, experts in writing English). This means that you will also have to spend time teaching your students cooperative ways of interacting in the classroom. In Chapter 7, which is about building the integrated classroom literacy community, we will more fully discuss methods you can use to teach cooperation and cultural respect in order to create a pluralistic classroom community.

Energy

We find it hardest to respond to the third objection to the use of integrated activities in the classroom. We know that it *does* take a lot of your time and energy to plan an integrated language classroom and curriculum. But we believe that the energy you expend outside class in planning exciting, interactive, purposeful activities for your students will be offset by the energy you save during class by not having to continually manage and control children's behavior.

The transmission curriculum centers on developing products—skills, facts, behaviors. It is organized as if students themselves had little or no role to play in the actual process of their development—like bottles of soda pop, they are just the compilation of certain ingredients, having "word-attack skills" and "modal verbs" added to them instead of sugar and carbonation. In contrast, the integrated language curriculum centers on developing human beings—children who are learning and who are expanding the boundaries of their capabilities and powers. It is organized with the participants in learning—children —playing a central role in developing new knowledge and new language and literacy. Whereas soda pop bottles "willingly" sit still for the washing and filling and capping that is their destiny, many children find it quite difficult to sit still for the lecturing and drilling that they are destined to receive in transmission classrooms. Thus, teachers in these classrooms must use considerable energy to manage and control children and to "help" them to sit still and to participate correctly. In integrated language classrooms, this teaching energy is saved. Teachers provide a classroom structure in which they share responsibility for children's behavior and learning with the children themselves. Motivated, responsible, involved children are too busy communicating, following their interests and curiosity, and carrying out their purposes to require much external control and coercion. You can spend energy disciplining or you can spend it planning, structuring, and teaching. It's your choice!

We also believe that the time and energy you spend in preparing an integrated classroom and curriculum is simply better teaching. (If we didn't believe this, we wouldn't have spent considerable amounts of *our* time and energy in writing this book!) And remember—even though the units, materials, and activities that you plan are organized for a specific group of students, those resources can be reshuffled and adapted and reused with new groups of students. Your investment is high, but the dividends are higher, and they will pay off over and over again.

3.5 CONCLUSION

In this chapter, we have discussed the importance and the potential of the social dimension of your classroom learning environment for supporting your integrated curriculum and your second language students' language and literacy development. We have provided you with some exercises for changing your classroom rules and the social organization of your learning activities to meet the criteria of the integrated model, and we have addressed some of the concerns that teachers have raised about trying to accomplish these changes. Once you have established a constitution that is adapted to the framework of the integrated model and have developed activities with groupings and participant structures that facilitate students' oral and written meaning-making, the next step in adjusting the social environment to fit the model is to use this rich and supportive environment to provide students with the kind of oral and written discourse that they require to develop their second language and literacy capacities. This further adaptation in the social environment is discussed in Chapter 5 (on providing oral discourse) and Chapter 6 (on providing written discourse). But first, let's examine some ways for adapting the physical environment.

ACTIVITIES AND DISCUSSION

1. The Speak 'n Math commercial described in this chapter is just one example of the stereotyped images of schooling present in today's media. Keep a log summarizing the instances of school-related themes that you see on television for a week and review each instance for the "hidden" as well as surface messages about education that they convey. This activity can also be done by reviewing issues of a daily newspaper or a popular magazine. Look carefully at the language used and the characters and visual images that are used. Also see if there are different patterns emerging between commercial depictions of schools and "news" and "feature" article depictions of schools.

2. Repeat the above activity, substituting images of linguistically and culturally different people (or "foreigners") in the mass media for images of schools.

3. Make an oral language inventory of your school. List the places in and around the school which are shared by everyone (e.g. the office, the cafeteria, the front of the school, the playground). For each place, record the kinds of interaction you see and hear and try to determine the rules governing interaction in that setting. Do they support students' language learning? Can you derive a probable rationale for the rules?

4. Follow the steps listed in the summary list, "How To Adapt your Rules" (page 78) and adjust your own classroom rules or the rules of a classroom with which you are familiar to support the integrated model.

5. Use the "Activity Feature Chart" (Figure 3.2, page 81) and the steps listed in the summary chart, "How To Adapt your Activities" (page 86) and review and adjust a set of learning activities to support the integrated model.

6. Practice using your class time schedule (or one for a class with which you are familiar) to support the integrated model by taking one or two of the activities that have been planned for the near future and developing at least two *other* ways to get them accomplished within the *same* amount of time.

7. Observe students as they participate in several learning activities. If you can, audiotape the activity. How is oral and written language being used in the activity? How is participation organized? How are different individuals contributing to the activities? Who is doing the talking? What effects do the materials that are present seem to be having on the interaction? Compare your observations and analyses of the different activities.

8. Review some of the textbooks being used in your school/program (or one with which you are familiar) to find out what kinds of learning activities and activity features they contain. Sometimes this information will be explicitly presented; other times it may have to be derived from the instructions to the teacher or from the student materials.

FURTHER READING

Edelsky, C., Draper, K., and Smith, K. 1983. Hookin' 'em in at the start of school in a "whole language" classroom. *Anthropology and Education Quarterly*, 14(4), 257-81. A detailed description of one teacher's use of explicit and tacit rules to communicate her expectations and her goals for the social environment to her students on the first day of school.

Enright, D. S. 1984. The organization of interaction in elementary classrooms. In J. Handscombe, R. A. Orem, and B. P. Taylor (Eds.) *On TESOL '83: The question of control* (pp. 23-38). Washington, D. C.: Teachers of English to Speakers of Other Languages. Characterizations of the classroom interaction hierarchy of rules, events and participant structures, with contrasting examples of each level of interaction taken from a teacher-centered and a student-centered bilingual kindergarten.

Jordan, C. 1985. Translating culture: From ethnographic information to educational program. *Anthropology and Education Quarterly*, 6:105-23. Jordan explains how the Kamehameha Elementary Education Program (KEEP) in Hawaii uses insights gained from the anthropological study of Native Hawaiian students' cultural patterns of language use and interaction to create "culturally compatible" classroom activities.

Philips, S. 1972. Participant structures and communicative competence: Warm Springs children in community and classroom. In C. B. Cazden, V. J. John and D. Hymes (Eds.) *Functions of language in the classroom* (pp. 370-94). New York: Teachers College Press. One of the earliest studies utilizing the concept of participant "mismatch" between minority children's native culture and ways of interacting and the culture and forms of interacting found at school.

Sarason, S. B. 1982. *The culture of the school and the problem of change*. Boston, MA: Allyn and Bacon. Describes various dimensions of the modern American school culture (including "classroom constitutions") that must be understood and taken into account if efforts at changing the schools are to have success.

Sirotnik, K. A. 1983. What you see is what you get: Consistency, persistency, and mediocrity in classrooms. *Harvard Educational Review* 53(1):16-31. A quantitative depiction of the ways that time is spent in elementary and secondary classrooms in the United States, ways that have remained the same throughout the twentieth century. The author laments the *inconsistency* between what educators, parents and students say they want and what the schools actually provide.

Trueba, H. T., Gutherie, G. P., and Au, K. H. (Eds.) 1981. *Culture and the bilingual classroom: Studies in classroom ethnography*. This collection is divided into two sections. The first section offers suggestions for using the tools of ethnographic research to

Integrating English

direct the planning and the maintenance of successful bilingual education programs. The second section offers research reports portraying the various "mismatches" that exist between language minority students' cultural repertoires and the traditional culture of the school and discussion of ways to overcome these mismatches.

Chapter 4

The Physical Environment

The Red Wheelbarrow

so much depends
upon

a red wheel
barrow

glazed with rain
water

beside the white
chickens.

—William Carlos Williams

4.1 INTRODUCTION

As we've suggested, by comparison, classrooms where the integrated language teaching model is being applied look different and contain different resources. These classrooms share four key characteristics: they are functional, flexible, enticing, and student-owned. Figures 4.1 and 4.2 present the physical plans of two such classrooms. We will use these classrooms to give you some ideas for thinking about and adapting your own physical environment to support the ILT model.

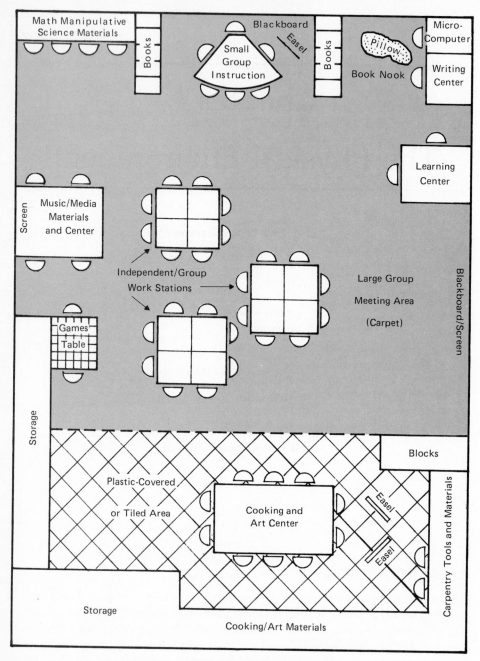

Figure 4.1:   Mr. Nations' Classroom Physical Environment

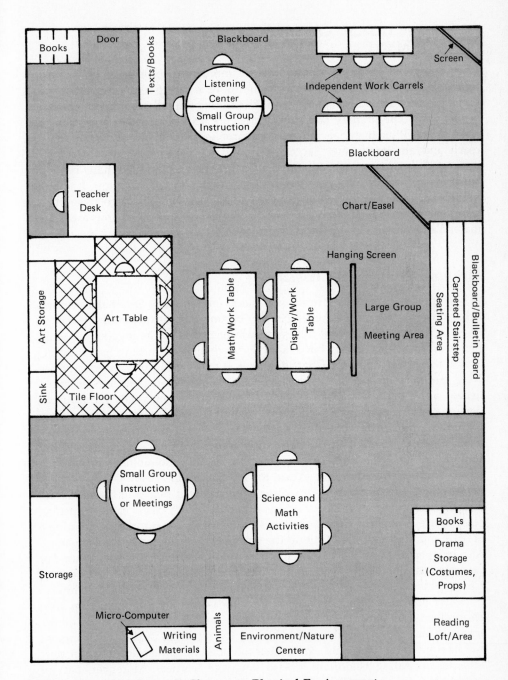

Figure 4.2: Mrs. Gomez's Classroom Physical Environment

4.2 A FUNCTIONAL CLASSROOM ENVIRONMENT

First, integrated language classrooms are more functional than other classrooms. In the transmission classroom the room is set up to accommodate two major kinds of activities: lecturing (and examining the full group) and individual seat work. The primary materials present are textbooks, workbooks, pencils, and paper. Other materials (such as art supplies) are stored out of children's reach and are immediately accessible only to the teacher. In contrast, the integrated classroom environment should be set up to facilitate many types of activities and many kinds of student interaction and collaboration. It should provide easy access to materials that can be used to accomplish a great variety of tasks, and it should communicate the appropriate uses of the various areas and materials to students. Here are some suggestions for accomplishing these aims.

Planning a Functional Classroom

In beginning to plan a more functional classroom, you may find that a map will help you visualize possible changes. Try cutting out scale furniture pieces so that you can try out different classroom arrangements before lugging the actual pieces around! You already have the integrated curriculum flowchart (Chapter 2) and the Activity Feature Chart (Chapter 3) to help you plan your activities. Note that in both sample classrooms, various activity areas have been established, where various sets of activities requiring similar materials and furniture have their own special place. For example, both classrooms have activity areas for reading groups, for whole class meetings, discussions, or teacher presentations, for viewing media presentations or drama, for puppets, for movement, for storytelling, for writing, and so on. Examine the possibilities and decide which of these you might like to add to your classroom. Then work with your model to include them. Remember, many unexpected places in the room and even around the room can be used for activity areas. A closet can be a perfect place to use a filmstrip viewer; the hall is good for paired tutoring or painting a life-size mural; a protected spot on the blacktop is a great place to play games. Also be open to using all possible spaces within the activity areas you plan. For example, learning-center activities could be displayed on a wall or on the side of a file cabinet; a model of the solar system could be mounted on the ceiling.

Once you have decided which activity areas you want to include in your physical environment, plan ways to embed the purposes and rules of the activities for an area into the physical plan. The structure of your environment and its component parts must make their intended functions clear to all of your students, including beginning second language learners. Moreover, part of providing a warm, supportive environment is providing a safe environment. Not only should a classroom environment be physically safe, but students should also be safe from conflicts and criticism that come from their not understanding what is expected of them (criterion no. 5, support.)

Because many second language students don't understand your oral language or English print well enough to be told the rules or to read them, the classroom setup itself can be used to clarify its uses. Various areas can be labeled in pictures and words with activities that occur there. Lots of devices are available for communicating the rules of a particular center. The ever popular art center could have a hat rack with as many painters' caps as the number of students that are allowed to use the center at one time. A student would know just by looking at the hat rack whether there were room for one more. A reading center could also have a sign saying "Quiet, please" and a rebus symbol (perhaps a picture of the "speak no evil" monkey) to indicate that talking was not allowed there.

The storage and display of materials can also be used to communicate their use. Most materials in the classroom should be stored openly and near where they are to be used. For example, supplies of paper, pencils, pens, and binding materials should be placed in the writing area; headphones should be anchored to the listening center table. Materials should be color-coded or labeled with pictures for easy access and putting away. For example, a pegboard could have outlines of different articles, showing where they are to be placed when not in use. Pictures of articles that are kept in a cupboard or drawer or on a shelf could be painted or could be cut out from a magazine or catalog, laminated, and taped on or near the storage place. Written labels, in combination with the pictures, could provide opportunities for practicing reading vocabulary.

A tiled area (or a sheet of heavy plastic taped to the floor) could communicate, "Here's where it's okay to do activities that might get messy." In a classroom meeting area, a taped circle or a drawn-in pattern on the rug could say, "Here's where we have class meetings or circle time." A list of rules with accompanying pictures, as illustrated in Figure 4.3, could communicate what happens during "listening times." These rules could be put on a wall or some other clearly visible surface.

The physical environment of the classroom can also be used to help students understand and follow the new integrated rules you have developed. For example, at first, arts and crafts materials can be introduced to your students in small group activities during which they are taught how to use the art area independently; how to follow instructions for specific activities; how to use materials; how to place materials where they belong; and how to clean up and put away materials. After a while, students can work independently at the center, and newly arrived students can be trained by veterans. A similar procedure can be used to teach students the proper use of equipment in a listening center.

Early in the year, students can be taught how to use the record player and tape recorder and can be issued "operator's licenses" when they demonstrate

Figure 4.3:   Rebus Rules for Listening Time

understanding of the appropriate procedures. Then, as long as one licensed operator is included, groups of students can be assigned to use the listening center independently while other classroom events are taking place.

Once you have embedded the purposes and procedures of your activities into the physical environment, and as your students (including your second language students) become accustomed to that environment, you can begin to extend students' use of speech and print. As the year goes on, the rebus signs and pictures explaining the procedures for the various materials and activity areas can be accompanied or replaced by written procedures. The schedule for the day (see Figure 4.4) can also be posted on the blackboard rather than explained to the students, and class members can be responsible for figuring out what they are to do next, with designated first language and full second language students serving as coordinators to help beginning second language students and new students. Similarly, books from the Book Nook can be checked out for class or home use by a student librarian, and pairs of student gardeners and zoologists can follow the posted procedures to care for the class plants and animals. Children can make a class guest book, and designated hosts can be responsible for welcoming visitors to the classroom, showing them around and answering their questions, and asking them to sign the guest book. Of course, a class job chart listing all of these job titles would be posted (see Figure 4.5) and children's name cards would be frequently changed on the chart so that everyone would have a chance to do different jobs and to read the chart many times in the process!

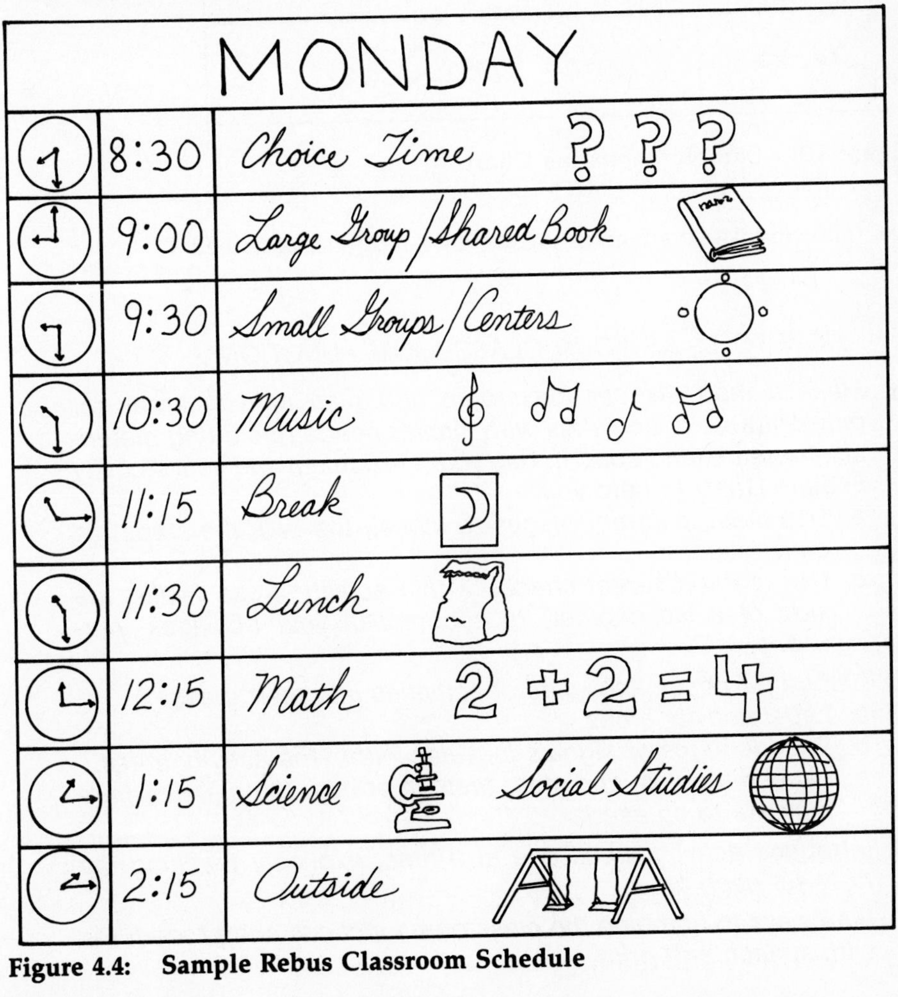

Figure 4.4: **Sample Rebus Classroom Schedule**

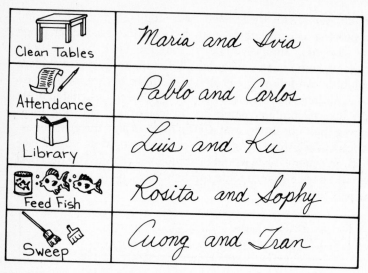

Clean Tables	Maria and Avia
Attendance	Pablo and Carlos
Library	Luis and Ku
Feed Fish	Rosita and Sophy
Sweep	Cuong and Tran

Figure 4.5:   Sample Rebus Job Chart

The following list summarizes the steps we have just described.

HOW TO MAKE YOUR CLASSROOM FUNCTIONAL

1. Make a map of your classroom and plan activity areas for different sets of activities with similar needs (including materials, furniture, and space). Use your curriculum and your Activity Feature Chart to help you.
   a. Use many different places (a closet, the hall, the steps) as activity areas.
   b. Use many different spaces within activity areas (walls, the side of a file cabinet) to accomplish your activities' purposes.
2. Embed purposes and rules of activities into their areas.
   a. Label activity areas.
   b. Provide signs or signals for rules within the activity areas.
   c. Label materials, and store them in or near the places where they are to be used.
3. Introduce activity areas one at a time, explicitly teaching the rules for each area.
4. Find ways to combine the classroom functions and procedures with speech and print.

4.3 A FLEXIBLE CLASSROOM ENVIRONMENT

Integrated language classroom environments are also more flexible than other classrooms, in order to facilitate the dynamic, student-centered curriculum described in Chapter 2. In the transmission classroom, desks are more or less permanently arranged in rows, and the teacher's desk and the blackboard are placed at the front of these rows. This arrangement facilitates the organization of rules and events most commonly applied in the transmission classroom (e.g. lecture and seat work), by focusing students' attention away from one another and toward the teacher or their private seat work. In contrast, integrated language classrooms contain many potential interactive environments within one overall environment. Space and furniture are arranged to create opportunities for a single event to occur or for many events to occur at the same time, in an orderly manner and with a minimum of distraction.

Your physical environment should be designed to permit frequent and easy changes in the arrangement of furniture and materials. This flexibility will facilitate the use of all of those new and diverse learning activities which you have organized to make your social environment and your curriculum more integrated entities! Just as decisions about your thematic integrated units and your curriculum (*what* children will learn and do) largely determine your decisions about your social environment (*how* children will learn and do), so too will your decisions about your curriculum and your social environment largely determine your decisions about your physical environment.

Planning a Flexible Classroom

In the creation of activity areas for your integrated language classroom, keep in mind the requirements of each activity, including the amount of verbal interaction (which will affect the noise level); movement; space; and traffic in and out of the activity (if any). Noisy, busy activities such as drama or blocks should be located as far away as possible from quiet activities such as those which occur in the reading, writing, independent study and listening areas. These quiet areas can be separated to some degree with a bookcase, screen, or other barrier to minimize noise and distraction, and should be located away from the door to keep movement near the area at a minimum.

Furniture that can serve a variety of purposes and that can be easily arranged is helpful in this environment. If you can, choose light tables and/or moveable desks rather than attached desk chairs or other heavy or unwieldy items for your room, and choose stackable chairs that can be put aside to provide space for an active movement event or large group activity where students will be seated in a carpeted area. For example, a set of carpeted stair steps can provide a very successful multipurpose activity area. Students can be seated there for media presentations, because it permits such good vision of the event for everyone. It can be used for class performances and for teacher or visitor demonstrations. If it suits the purposes of the dramatists, the stairs can be used as the stage, with the audience seated on the floor. When the area is not in use for full class meetings, it can be used for small-group games, for small-group dramatic play or rehearsals, or for individual students who want to read.

Like stair steps, much of the furniture in the integrated language classroom can be used by more than one person at the same time, thereby permitting the collaboration that is so necessary for language development. Tables can replace desks to add flexibility, and desks can be shoved together to create group work spaces for the same purpose. Classrooms can have the flexibility to facilitate the activities of the transmission classroom without being organized exclusively for the use of those activities.

In a similar manner, the materials chosen for the integrated language classroom must also be flexible and multipurpose whenever possible, and the classroom rules and expectations should encourage their use in new ways and in many different activities and activity areas. For example, art materials should be given their own prominent area in the classroom, owing to their diversity of potential uses: in addition to being used to create works of art, they can be used to illustrate stories or poems or to create puppet shows (language arts); to make dioramas (social studies); and to make rocket and jet models (science and math). Similarly, display areas lend themselves to multidisciplinary integrated use. A display of fossils and arrowheads can be used for social studies (Native American ways of life); for science (types of rocks and formation of fossils); for language arts (imaginary stories or reports about the physical articles); and for math (counting, weighing, and measuring the articles and graphing results).

Finally, reading and writing materials should be available all around the room for use in conjunction with your multipurpose materials and your general activity areas. A library area and a writing area where quiet prevails are *musts* in an integrated language classroom, but beyond that, writing materials and relevant books should be distributed whenever and wherever they might contribute to students' content and language learning. Puppet-making books and play scripts, for example, could be placed at the art center, along with writing materials for creating original puppet shows. A display of students' rock collections could be accompanied by geology books and books on rock identification, with worksheets for students to write in their guesses as to the types of rocks being displayed. Or small weighing scales could be placed alongside the rocks, and directions and worksheets could be provided for weighing and comparing the various kinds of rocks. One teacher we know even turned his windows (and his children's daydreaming!) into opportunities for language and literacy development by placing books about clouds under the window accompanied by a list of "sky-gazing" suggestions and a large display sheet for recording observations. The point is that the more accessible writing and reading materials are, the more likely it is that children will integrate these materials into their ongoing language- and content-learning activities.

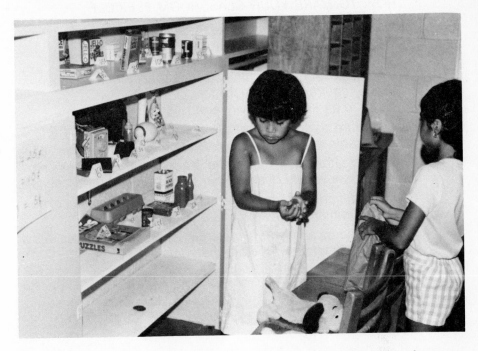

In this flexible and student-owned classroom, objects students bring in from home are used for a "store" center, first with teacher structure and supervision and later as a free-time activity.

The following list summarizes the steps we have suggested for adapting your classroom environment.

HOW TO MAKE YOUR CLASSROOM FLEXIBLE

1. *In your creation of activity areas, keep in mind the following concerns:*
   a. *Noise level of activities (verbal interaction).*
   b. *Movement required in the activities (nonverbal interaction).*
   c. *Space requirements of activities.*
   d. *Traffic in and out of activity areas.*
2. *Use furniture that can be easily rearranged (e.g., light tables and stackable chairs). Beg, borrow, and scrounge!*
3. *Choose furniture that can serve a variety of purposes (e.g., tables and moveable desks rather than attached desk chairs).*
4. *Choose multipurpose materials and encourage their use in new ways and in many activities and activity areas.*
5. *Provide reading and writing materials all around the room, to be used in conjunction with other materials.*

4.4 AN ENTICING CLASSROOM ENVIRONMENT

The third critical attribute of the integrated language physical environment is that it is a rich and enticing place for students to be. In the transmission classroom, the walls tend to be unadorned except for commercial or teacher-made displays. Materials in the transmission classroom are stored in students' desks or in cabinets and closets—in other words, out of students' sight, in order to keep their minds from "wandering." In the integrated classroom, walls and closets and materials are used to create and to maintain student interest, purpose, and collaboration. What might be called "distractions" in the transmission environment are learning starters and learning aids in the integrated classroom. This does not preclude the use of transmission-type activities. Meeting areas still permit teacher exposition or lectures, and independent work stations and work carrels permit student seat work. These two kinds of activities are simply added to the many kinds that can easily be implemented at any moment within the room.

Planning an Enticing Classroom

As the classrooms in both Figures 4.1 and 4.2 illustrate, many of the materials that are to be used in integrated language classrooms are displayed and stored openly in order to suggest their use. If language learning truly involves meaningful communication and reflection, often about concrete and mutual referents, then it is crucial that you have all kinds of different enticing objects for display and use in your classroom, and ones that appeal to all the senses. All kinds of "stuff" relating to a unit of study can be placed on a theme/realia table. One week there may be a rock collection and photographs of geological formations on the theme table, while another week an ant farm, a picnic basket, and a weather chart may be displayed there. Similarly, in a language/music/media theme center, students might find musical instruments, filmstrips, and language games related to a unit on Central Africa. In the integrated classroom, you don't have to limit yourself to materials that are typically associated with school (e.g., books, paper, pencils). You can feel free to add many nontraditional materials (e.g., natural objects, trash, road signs). Not only do "things" give a focus for language, they also focus attention primarily on themselves and on the task rather than on the learners, so that second language students, who feel less self-consciousness and less concerned about making a mistake, are more free to respond (criterion no. 5, support). You can also use objects that are familiar to students in order to introduce unfamiliar concepts and language and ways to use language, thereby bridging the known and the unknown (criterion no. 4, previous experience).

You can also use the walls of your classroom to entice students into using the various kinds of discourse. Walls can be covered with posters and displays of childrens' work; directions for learning centers; signs; and drawings—all of which nicely incorporate the seven criteria of the integrated model. As just one example, you might introduce an upcoming unit by erecting a "wall center" consisting of items such as animal pictures from *Ranger Rick* or *National Geographic World*, with a question under each picture. Answers could be hidden under a flap so that students could check after they'd guessed, or could be revealed at the end of the week. In like manner, there might be a place on a wall of your classroom for the "math problem of the week," or the "riddle of the day," or a stretch of wall or bulletin board formally marked as a place for students to put up writings, art work, memos, and announcements and interesting memorabilia that they want to share with the class.

Your environment and your daily routines hold much potential for enticing literacy activities as well. "Discovery cards" and "curiosity cards" can be tacked up in your activity areas and integrated into your current curriculum theme. For example, during the Superheroes unit, you could place a card at the library center asking students "Can you find information about the following real-life heroes in our library? President Lincoln, Reverend King, Madame Curie? Your favorite hero?" You could also place a card at the art center suggesting: "Make the vehicle or map the routes used by one of these heroic explorers: Marco Polo, Amelia Earhart, Ferdinand Magellan, Neil Armstrong." A class thermometer or that everbeckoning window can serve as the focus for daily observations and weather reports, recorded on a chart and shared at the end of the day or end of the week. School bulletins, lunch menus, and so on, can be displayed on a designated bulletin board, and a class "reporter" can read or summarize them for the rest of the class; students themselves can write or copy notes to parents about class or school activities.

You need not have a graduate degree in interior design to create an attractive, inviting classroom that encourages communication and second language and literacy development. You can use parents, aides, friends, or other teachers with design skills and resources as valuable classroom consultants. To ease the task of year-round room decorations, you can develop a color scheme for the classroom and use backgrounds that needn't be changed with every display. Remember that students will stop "seeing" displays and activity cards after they've been up for a while unless you refer to them or use them in instruction. Design displays with curriculum goals in mind, refer to them often, and change them periodically. Change displays of student work frequently to allow exciting new creations to take their place.

Enticing objects which appeal to all the senses are essential in the integrated classroom. These children have made their own 3-D glasses and are looking at objects in their classroom in a new way.

In summary, to make your classroom an enticing place for students, make sure you have a lot of interesting "stuff" to talk about, to read about, and to write about in your classroom, and then anchor that stuff within thematic units, classroom rules, and activities that efficiently direct the ways in which it is talked, read, and written about! This one strategy will directly assist your second language students with their acquisition of both language and content.

The following list summarizes the preceding key steps.

HOW TO MAKE YOUR CLASSROOM ENTICING

1. *Use materials that students can touch, taste, smell, see, and listen to, and read, write, think about, and talk about!*
2. *Use materials that students can use independently.*
3. *Use a variety of materials, those which are typically associated with school (e.g., books, paper, pencils) and those which are not (e.g., natural objects, trash, road signs).*
4. *Use materials that are familiar to the students in order to introduce them to those which are unfamiliar.*
5. *Organize materials and displays around class themes or units of study (see Chapter 2), and include materials produced by the students themselves.*
6. *Find ways to add activity areas to your units and to add literacy activities to the daily routine and the overall classroom environment.*
7. *Store materials openly.*
8. *Display materials attractively.*
9. *Change materials and displays regularly and refer to them often.*

4.5 A STUDENT-OWNED CLASSROOM ENVIRONMENT

The last critical attribute of the integrated classroom physical environment is that it is student-owned. Transmission classrooms are adult-owned; that is, they are organized with the external, predetermined adult curriculum in mind. They change very little in response to each new group of students, much less to continuing changes within a single group of students. In contrast, integrated classrooms involve students in every way imaginable in creating, planning, and carrying out the language and literacy development enterprise. After all, they are the junior partners in that enterprise!

Planning a Student-Owned Classroom

As we have seen, it is not necessary to sacrifice control in a classroom in order to promote student initiative. Rather, a valuable, indeed essential, part of your exercise of control as the senior partner in your students' education is to involve them in all aspects of daily classroom life, from curriculum planning to tutoring to cleaning up. One way of using the physical environment to do this is to delegate to students various leadership roles and classroom responsibilities, such as attendance keeping; lunch count; room maintenance; supervision of lining up; tutoring; putting up displays; interviewing and escorting visitors; and setting up activities. Anything that students can do that will promote their language learning, growth in self-esteem, and autonomy, they should do. Your task is to prepare them to succeed at these tasks.

As you carefully teach, demonstrate, and model classroom rules, you should also do the same with classroom tasks and procedures. Learning aids can be developed to make these tasks more efficient. A sample procedure for keeping attendance and lunch records can serve as an example: Write each student's name on a clip-type clothespin, and clip the pins around the edge of a large can. Then, as students enter the room in the morning, they can unclip the clothespins and drop their names into labeled cans (milk only, soup lunch, full lunch, etc.). Students keeping attendance can glance at the clothespins not put in the can and know who is absent. They can count the clothespins in each can for the lunch report. At the end of each day, the attendance keeper can pin all the clothespins around the edge of the can again. Alternatively, students can mark their attendance or lunch count on a chart as they walk in the door in the morning, or they can take turns reading and "taking roll" orally.

In the integrated language classroom, students should also be involved whenever possible in classroom planning and in the arrangement of the physical environment. We've already discussed the need for including children in curriculum development; other examples of this strategy in practice might include using students' likes and dislikes to assign small groups for a project or having children make a classroom map to scale in order to figure out where to put the puppet stage that they are building. Also in keeping with this principle, you can see to it that students' work (not just the best students' work, but every student's best work) is prominently and attractively displayed in your class-room. For example, you could laminate a large mat for the work of each student in the class and label it with the student's name. Each week the students could then select their favorite works to display on the mat. As mentioned earlier, you could also provide a permanent free space for children to post and display materials of their own selection. A large cardboard or papier-mâché mailbox for classroom correspondence (see Chapter 7) encourages students to use writing for their own purposes throughout the school year and also gives you an opportunity to provide meaningful responses to their writing. Similarly, a class suggestion box gives students a voice in the business of the classroom, if you read the suggestions openly and try to respond to them (our favorite, from a mid-second language first-grader, is "holkum wey downt gayt a brak fron rooken?" Translation: "How come we don't get a break from working?"). It is also important to place student activities and displays at their eye level rather than at an adult's eye level. This makes it clear that the room and its contents are for the students to use. Besides creating rich opportunities for students to use speech and print and giving them ownership in the classroom, these activities will all promote students' pride in their own creations and will develop their self-evaluative abilities.

Not just the best students' work, but every student's best work is prominently and attractively displayed in the student-owned classroom.

Another strategy for giving students increased ownership is to get them to supply items of their own for the classroom: for example, pictures, stories, objects brought from home, or objects collected on a field trip or found on the school grounds. Many of the displays in the integrated classroom are student-created, in the same way that the curriculum is often student-inspired and that many of the activities in communicative classrooms depend on students' creative and active participation. In the integrated classroom, an interesting insect that was captured by two or three children at recess could easily become the vehicle for science, math, reading, and ESL instruction before being eventually replaced at the nature center by some other fascinating item! Or a wonderful book brought from home may be read to the children, only to become a class favorite to be shared and reshared for several days to come!

The following list summarizes the preceding steps.

HOW TO MAKE YOUR CLASSROOM STUDENT-OWNED

1. *Give students leadership roles and classroom responsibilities.*
2. *Involve students in planning and arranging the classroom.*
3. *Display every student's best work, and change displays often.*
4. *Give students control over classroom spaces and resources (e.g., bulletin boards, a mailbox).*
5. *Use materials and ideas brought in by students to create classroom curriculum, displays, conversation, and texts. Also use students' creations (e.g., a composition, artwork) to create curriculum.*

4.6 PLANNING A NO-CLASSROOM ENVIRONMENT

Some itinerant ESL teachers (specialists who must travel from school to school to work with small groups of second language learners) reading this chapter will say, "Wait a minute! These may be good ideas to use, but I don't have a classroom. I have a closet!" (Or a corner of a classroom or several different borrowed classrooms during the day or a table in the library!) Even "no-classroom" teachers can provide a learning environment that meets the criteria of the integrated model. We aren't going to let *you* off the hook! By adapting many of our suggestions, you can make your traveling learning environment flexible, functional, enticing, and student-owned. Of course, this demands that *you* be flexible—and creative! Here are some suggestions for itinerant teachers.

Making Your No-Classroom Functional

In your no-classroom, you are limited to materials you can store in a small place or carry in the trunk of your car. You, more than other integrated language teachers, must find materials that offer double (or triple or quadruple) potential for use with your students. If an itinerant teacher working with second language Eskimo students and their teachers by flying from village to village in North Alaska can perfect teaching demonstration lessons and conduct in-services out of a backpack (Linse 1985), certainly you can work with a closet! Locate a cart, a giant book bag, or a shelf in a closet of each school where you can keep your basic equipment. Keep essentials packed and ready to travel. Include items that can be used in many ways. A set of basic equipment might include a puppet, several ESL activity books, a tape recorder, chart paper, writing paper, art paper, and labeled resealable plastic bags with such essentials as pens, pencils, markers, scissors, tape and paper clips. Each day, load up special equipment from your storage area (and from anywhere else that occurs to you). Include a few special items such as storybooks that are related to your current theme or an object from the environment that might start an interesting conversation. For example, the box from the toothpaste that you opened this morning might work just fine. You could use it to discuss dental hygiene, advertising, letters and sounds, or lists of ingredients on packages of food products and drugs. Make stand-up "sandwich charts" (folded cardboard display boards) of rules, schedules, and jobs that will move from room to room and be easily set up. Tape a traveling poster or chart on the wall for your lesson. After the lesson, roll it up and roll on to the next class. Most of the ideas we have offered for providing displays and functional print can be transferred to butcher paper or poster board for no-classrooms, too!

Making Your No-Classroom Flexible

A no-classroom *has* to be flexible. Your closet can be any one of the designated learning areas—it just can't be all of them at once. On one day (or during one period of time) it can be a movie-viewing room; on another day it can be a small group meeting area; on another day it can be a learning center; on still another day it can be the kitchen where you prepare an apple pie. *You* control your corner or classroom to the extent that you can change the furniture around, put up and take down displays and posters and other visuals, and, most important-ly, *do* a large variety of activities even within a small space.

Another key to planning a flexible no-classroom environment is making maximal use of the spaces and places outside your closet or corner. These spots are just waiting to be used for rich language and literacy explorations! School grounds offer a treasure trove of "ESL classrooms" and can be used for a number of activities, including walking field trips (see Chapter 8). Also, if you can make friends with other specialists and teachers in the school, your no-classroom space will begin to expand, and will soon include spaces like the cafeteria, the library, and the gymnasium (again, see Chapter 8). You can make plans with the media specialist to have regular "book times" for your various students, and occasionally you can plan ahead to have the media specialist set up a screen in the library for your filmstrip. Similarly, you can arrange with the cafeteria workers to bake your pie in the cafeteria—and perhaps ask them to explain to your students how the oven works! Use stairs or an out-of-the-way hallway as a stage for your play, or use the playground for tie-dyeing or clay sculpture. You'll receive an extra bonus as well from making your no-classroom flexible: as you continue to negotiate more and more access for yourself within your various schools, it is quite likely that your second language students will also begin to acquire better access to school resources and that they will begin to be perceived as full members of the school.

Making Your No-Classroom Enticing

Enticement is a challenge in the no-classroom environment. You can take time to put up a poster or two at the beginning of class, but you cannot set up six learning areas without using up your allotted time with the students before you begin! Remember that *you* are the primary "enticer" and enticement in your no-classroom. Your enthusiasm, your interest, and the interesting things that students have to do when they are with you will make students want to come to your class and want to learn when they get there. Although your room can't be filled with realia, you can bring in a different item or set of items each day. If these items are chosen to be multifunctional (e.g., storybooks and reference books instead of level-one basals), they can be used over and over again between groups and schools. This same principle holds for your organization of your enticing integrated units: try to choose units that allow you to provide authentic language and literacy experiences for beginning as well as full second language students, and for older students as well as younger students. For example, a topic like "The Constitution" might be inappropriate for teaching mixed-grade-level ESL groups from throughout a K-6 school, but "Voting and Elections" might work out fine. Similarly, themes and materials like plants or the solar system or communications or communities all leave plenty of room for using the same high-interest materials to teach many different kinds of students.

Making Your No-Classroom Student-Owned

Although your students may not spend the entire day with you, they can still feel that when they come to you it is *their* class for which they share responsibility. Many of the ideas in section 4.5 concerning a student-owned classroom environment can be adapted for use with your students. In some cases, you can be especially creative. For instance, you can make sure that each student's work is displayed near your no-classroom area—perhaps in the hall outside your door. Try to negotiate for a spot in your students' grade-level classrooms where they can share or display some of their work. When students bring things in, see if you can arrange for them to be shared in the students' grade-level rooms as well.

The integrated language teacher is clearly a resourceful one, and those of you who teach in no-classrooms must be the most resourceful of all. It is said that when a door is closed (a classroom door, in this case), a window is opened somewhere else. If this is so, then itinerant ESL teachers have to open a lot of windows! Perhaps your greatest challenges as a no-classroom itinerant ESL teacher will be to integrate your teaching efforts with those of your students' grade-level teachers, and to integrate your students' learning in your no-classroom with their learning in their grade-level classrooms. These are difficult challenges, and they cannot be met in a week or two, but with perseverance you will succeed.

4.7 CONCLUSION

In this chapter, we have described the physical environment in classrooms using the integrated language teaching model. If any single generalization can be made in contrasting the physical environments of the transmission classroom and the integrated classroom, it is that the former is organized primarily on the basis of adults' interests, goals, and needs, whereas in the latter, the interests, goals, and needs of students are the primary impetus for organization. We believe that if you can turn your classroom social and physical environments "inside out" to support your integrated curriculum, then you will be assisting the education of all your students.

ACTIVITIES AND DISCUSSION

1. Review your classroom's physical environment. (If you don't have your own classroom, choose one and observe in it.) Does the room presently provide areas for small groups, full groups, and independent work? Does it provide for a diversity of activities such as viewing media or dramatic presentations, movement activities, writing, independent reading, listening to records or tapes, art or construction activities, and science displays or experiments? Does it provide for many different kinds of verbal and nonverbal interaction? Make an outline map of the

classroom and cut out scale-sized furniture pieces. Use these items to adjust the classroom arrangement to provide for more activities and forms of interaction as needed. Consider traffic patterns and the internal organization of activities as you plan and adjust.

2. Find a previously unused or little used area in or near the classroom you chose above and/or in the school in which it is located and reorganize it or adapt it to provide a classroom activity function previously unavailable.

3. Evaluate your chosen classroom for effectiveness of storage of materials. Do students have easy access to materials? Are storage places well-labeled so that materials are easy to put away? Does the way areas are arranged communicate their intended uses?

4. Review the classroom constitution (see Chapter 3) and the rules and procedures for each of the major activity areas in your chosen classroom and create posters or rebus charts stating these rules and procedures.

5. Evaluate the materials in your chosen classroom. Are multi-purpose materials, e.g., art materials, manipulatives, old magazines available? Using publishers' catalogues and/or your imagination, select a few additional materials that would provide more flexibility. Negotiate a way to have these materials donated or purchased for the classroom.

6. Visit a classroom that is not your own. Roughly calculate the percentage of classroom and hallway displays that were made and/or designed by students.

7. Walk around a school and look into all the classrooms. Select which classrooms you feel are the most enticing ones. Try to list why this is the case. If you can, select and individually interview a number of students in the school. Ask them to tell you which classrooms in the school they feel are the most attractive and inviting. Ask students to tell you why they like these rooms. Then do the same thing with some students from the rooms you found to be enticing. Select teachers whose names appear on both your list and students' lists of enticing classrooms and interview them. Ask the teachers how they decide what centers/materials/activities to put in the classrooms and how to display them. Review the data you've collected. Are there any patterns concerning what makes a classroom enticing to students? How do the criteria that students use compare with yours? How do the students' criteria compare with the ones used by the teachers you interviewed?

8. As an alternative or addition to the activity in no. 7 above, observe in a school and select student-owned classrooms or functional classrooms

or flexible classrooms. Develop an observational checklist to be used in evaluating classrooms along the four dimensions of integrated class-rooms.

9. Develop a list of materials and supplies for a "no-classroom travel kit" (or actually assemble the kit). Give a rationale for each item you have included.

FURTHER READING

Cohen, E. G. 1986. *Designing groupwork: Strategies for the heterogeneous classroom.* New York: Teachers College Press. Clear explanation of the rationale for cooperative groupwork, ways to plan groupwork and to prepare students for the activities, specific suggestions for bilingual classrooms, and many groupwork activities and cooperative training exercises.

Garvey, C. 1977. *Play.* Cambridge, MA: Harvard University Press. Discussion of the history, importance, nature and development of children's play.

Loughlin, C. E. and Suina, J. H. 1982. *The learning environment: An instructional strategy.* New York: Teachers College Press. Complete text on a conceptual view of environment, organization of space and learning materials, and using the learning environment for special purposes including promoting literacy and supporting children with special needs.

Savignon, S. J. 1983. *Communicative competence: Theory and classroom practice.* Reading, MA: Addison-Wesley Publishing Company. Chapter 4 offers a thoughtful discussion on the selection and use of materials.

Silberman, C. E. (Ed.) *The open classroom reader.* New York: Random House. Part Three, Chapter Two, "How to Manage Time and Space," includes many suggestions for designing and using the physical environment. The entire book is filled with interesting ideas and practical techniques for the student-centered classroom.

ADDITIONAL RESOURCES

Hannah, G. G. 1982. *Classroom spaces and places.* Belmont, CA: Pitman Learning, Incorporated.

Lay-Dopyera, M. and Dopyera, J. 1987. *Becoming a teacher of young children: Third edition.* New York: Random House.

Wendelin, K. H., and Greenlaw, M. J. 1984. *Storybook classrooms: Using children's literature in the learning center.* Atlanta, GA: Humanics Limited.

Zeigler, N., Larson, B., and Byers, J. 1983. *Let the kids do it!* (Books 1 and 2). Belmont, CA: David S. Lake Publishers.

Chapter 5

Providing Real Oral Discourse

A Word

A word is dead
When it is said,
Some say.

I say it just
Begins to live
That day.

—Emily Dickinson

5.1 INTRODUCTION

As you well know, all teachers must fulfill several roles in organizing and conducting instruction and in living up to their professional responsibilities. For teachers of second language students, the number of these roles is even greater! Our focus until now has been on your roles as the planner and creator of your overall curriculum and your classroom social and physical environments. We now turn to examining an essential role that you can fulfill with your second language students once they have arrived: your role as their senior discourse partner in their efforts to develop English language and literacy.

As your students' senior discourse partner, you can provide them with instructional language yourself, and you can arrange opportunities for them to use language by themselves and with others. In this chapter, we will examine some ways in which you can provide students with *oral discourse* as they develop their second language. Chapter 6 describes your role in providing speech-print connections and written discourse to your second language students.

5.2 THE ROLE OF DISCOURSE PARTNER: "THINK LANGUAGE!"

We have described how curriculum developers and teachers using the integrated model turn the transmission-of-knowledge curriculum upside down and inside out in order to promote language and literacy development. But transforming the curriculum isn't enough! In striving to become senior discourse partners to their second language students, integrated classroom teachers also make key transformations in the transmission model's conceptualizations of classroom language and the teacher's responsibilities for using that language. A colleague of ours (we'll call her Molly) summarized the product of these transformations as learning to "think language" in planning and conducting instruction.

What are the transformations involved in learning to think language? Let's examine them by once again contrasting transmission and integrated classrooms.

First, thinking language involves thinking in a different way about what language really is and how people go about acquiring it. These transformations are summarized as the first two theoretical assumptions of the integrated model:

1. The whole of *language* is greater than the sum of its parts. Language is a limitless capacity to make meaning and therefore should not be broken down and "taught" as tiny, discrete "skills" or "habits" or "facts". Language is better viewed as a verb (*using* language) than as a noun (*knowledge* of a language).

2. Students develop language and literacy through using language as a tool for creating and sharing meanings rather than through studying it as different "subjects" (e.g. reading, spelling) in which it is detached from its purposes and the actual circumstances in which it is produced. Students use speech and print to construct both *inner*-personal meanings (i.e. to think) and *inter*-personal meanings (i.e. to communicate).

Teachers in transmission classrooms think of language (speech and print) as instructional ends—as subjects to be taught within a one-way curriculum. A major consequence of this conceptualization is that language is addressed within transmission classrooms only when it happens to be the "subject" being taught—for example, in spelling lessons and ESL lessons and basal reading groups. The many opportunities to teach and use real language as a tool for meaning-making which are available in even the strictest "No talking!" classroom activities are ignored. Instead, transmission teachers plan their learning activities with only two components in mind: the content or subject-matter of the activity (the piece of knowledge or skill or learning objective to be taught) and the management component of the activity (the materials and procedures to be used).

In contrast, teachers in integrated classrooms think of language as the means to many different student meaning-making ends, besides being an intrinsically interesting and fun end in itself. The result of this transformation is that language permeates integrated classroom teachers' thinking and planning of everything that students are to do—from passing out snacks to writing short stories. Teachers in integrated classrooms organize all aspects of their instruction, including their learning activities, with three integrated components in mind: the activity's content, its procedural organization, and its discourse (speech and print). These components are integrated in the sense that it really is impossible to say where one ends and another begins; for example, in making decisions about how you will place students together in an activity (procedures) or what questions you will ask during a group discussion or what kind of product you would like to result from an art activity (content), you are really making language instruction decisions as well! The challenge is to consciously include the language dimension in all of your decisions as you use the ILT criteria to plan your classroom and curriculum. As one mid-second-language boy from India exclaimed after returning with his class from an "English search" for environmental print and speech around the school grounds: "There's English *everywhere!*"

Thinking language also involves thinking in new ways about the *kinds* of language that are being provided to students and how they are to be provided to them. This transformation is summarized as the third theoretical assumption of the integrated model:

3. Comprehensible, interesting and useful classroom language—"real" language (Urzúa, 1985)—is most helpful to students in their language and literacy development. Students need multiple opportunities both to take in (i.e., listen and read) and to give out (i.e., speak and write) this real language in order to become successful second language communicators and thinkers.

Teachers in transmission classrooms do not think of "the language in the environment" of their classrooms as having instructional potential. This lack of attention to real language extends from their *planning* of activities to their actual *conducting* of them. That is, transmission teachers also carry out their daily instruction and interactions with only their curriculum content and procedures in mind, ignoring the actual discourse that is being used and neglecting the opportunities that arise for using that discourse to assist students' language and literacy development. This practice occurs even when the content of the activity is language! One of our favorite speech examples of this is something that occurred when a teacher of eight sixth-grade beginning second language boys was teaching them how to tell time and how to ask for the time. The structure being practiced (the content) was "Do you have the time?" but when one of the boys turned to one of us and asked, "Gotta chick?" the teacher told him to be quiet and had him take his (inevitable) turn repeating the target structure, "Do you have the time?"

In contrast, teachers using the integrated model see the real discourse that is created and used within their curriculum activities as the foundation of their language instruction. That is, integrated classroom teachers not only think about real language in *planning* their instructional activities, but they also consciously think about it while they are *conducting* these activities and while they are interacting with students in general. They do this by combining their knowledge of the language potential in their activities with their knowledge of their students' current stages in their second language development, and then continuously monitoring and adjusting their classroom discourse as it unfolds. As assumption 3 suggests, this monitoring and adjusting involves making sure that students understand and are interested in the discourse they are "taking in." It also involves continually adjusting the language environment and activities as they are taking place in order to provide students with the opportunities that they need to "give out" or to use this discourse, whether in speech or in print. One of our favorite speech examples of this key aspect of thinking language in the integrated classroom came from the teacher of a class of beginning, mid, and full second language kindergartners. As the teacher was bringing the kindergartners inside after an outdoor game, she heard her "line leader" saying to a pushy friend, "I'm in the leader!" This teacher used the rest of the trek into the classroom to playfully and repeatedly move ahead and behind her line leader while proclaiming "*I'm* the leader!" and then letting him resume his rightful place when he used the *real* language, "I'm the leader!" The kind of language instruction that this example represents—taking advantage of authentic, moment-to-moment language-teaching opportunities to provide students with the real language they need to build their meaning-making capacities at the moment that they are ready for it—can occur only when you are actively and continuously thinking language (as well as content and management) amid the tumult of your daily classroom life.

Finally, thinking language within the integrated classroom involves think- ing in new ways about the four language processes and about second language students' previous experiences with these processes. These transformations are summarized as the fourth and fifth theoretical assumptions of the integrated model:

4. The whole of *language development* is greater than the sum of its parts. Students develop language and literacy as part of a broader process of semiotic or meaning-making development. They do this through using the processes of listening, speaking, reading, and writing in concert with one another rather than separately. Thus the development of each language process can support the development of the others.

5. Students make use of all of their available resources—linguistic and nonlinguistic, internal (cognitive, affective) and external (social, environmental)—in their second language development. Among the resources that students bring and apply to the second language and literacy development task are a diversity of prior native language cultural, language, and literacy experiences.

As we've seen, in transmission classrooms language is taught by separating it from its multiple contexts and uses, dividing it up into discrete components and then transmitting it to students as subject matter in the form of lectures and meaningless exercises. A typical part of this process consists of also separating this language-as-content into four *different* new "subjects": Listening, Speaking (a.k.a. "Pronunciation," "Conversation," "Spoken English"), Reading, and Writing (a.k.a. "Composition"). Each of these new sub-subjects comes with its own sets of discrete, sequentially organized (i.e., "Level One," "Level Two") skills and facts, to be given to students at different times and during different lessons. In bilingual classrooms where the transmission model is used to teach two languages, this process simply results in doubling the number of language subjects to be "covered" in class from four to eight: first language Speaking *and* second language Speaking, first language Writing *and* second language Writing, and so on! Thus, in a Spanish/English transmission bilingual classroom, for example, not only is Spanish Writing a different subject from Spanish Listening, it's a different subject from English Writing, too (not to mention History or Algebra or Art Appreciation)! This view of language further dictates that areas of overlap or connections between either the various language processes or between students' first language and second language during a given language lesson are to be avoided, since they would distract students from directly focusing on the new "material" that is being transmitted in the lesson at hand and would "interfere" with students' receipt and mastery of it.

In contrast to transmission teachers' tendency to separate the four language processes and students' first language and second language experiences and learning, teachers in integrated classrooms deliberately seek out ways for each of them to support the development of the others. Knowing that students use their various oral and literate capacities to develop new capacities—Heath (1985) calls this the "tie-in" nature of becoming literate in the second language—integrated classroom teachers constantly build connections between students' oral and literate meaning-making capacities and tie together or integrate the various types and functions of discourse, using speech to teach uses of print and print to teach uses of speech, using one kind of speech to teach another, and so on! Thus, you might find teachers and students in integrated classrooms moving from reading and singing a song from words written on the blackboard to writing new verses for the song. Or you might find them listening to a famous speech (like Dr. Martin Luther King's address in the Heroes and Superheroes unit), taking notes on it, reading its printed version, then writing original speeches and reading and recording them in order to revise them and perform them better. Similarly, knowing that students draw on their first language experiences in approaching the second language and literacy development task—Heath (1985) calls this the "tie-back" nature of becoming literate in the second language—integrated classroom teachers explicitly organize their second language and literacy experiences with these earlier experiences in mind. Thus, you might find teachers and students in integrated classrooms compiling bilingual riddle books or cookbooks with discourse collected from the students' homes and native countries. Or you might find them listening to one of their grandmothers telling stories on Grandmother's Day. Continuously looking for ways to accomplish these two additional forms of integration —allowing students to tie-in and tie-back their various language and literacy experiences—is the last step toward thinking language and becoming a discourse partner to your second language students.

Activities such as collecting and learning jump-rope rhymes give students the opportunity to "tie-in" oral and written discourse and to "tie-back" English to their native language and literacy experiences.

The continuous processes of monitoring, reviewing, adjusting, and refining the curriculum and the ongoing discourse in the classroom are not easy to adopt. Our colleague Molly probably spoke for many of us when she reflected that "thinking language is not automatic or natural. I really need to stop my mental flow to pull up ideas" (Enright 1986). However, as Molly continued to attempt consciously to think language as she planned her activities and interacted with her students in her classroom, she got better and better at it. Eventually, she didn't have to "stop" her mental flow to do it, because it had become an integral part of that mental flow. For grade-level, bilingual education, and ESL teachers alike, practicing thinking language in the ways that we have suggested here until it becomes an automatic part of teaching second language students is a critical, if not *the* critical, component of becoming a discourse partner to these students.

You can fulfill your role as senior partner by directly providing your second language students with real discourse yourself and by indirectly arranging and supervising their use of real discourse by themselves and with other students. Several examples of teachers fulfilling both the direct and indirect dimensions of the discourse partnering role have already appeared in previous chapters. To mention just a few, during the Superheroes unit in Chapter 2, Ms. Kay was directly providing discourse instruction when she baked her Superman cake with small groups of students and when she read legends aloud to the full class; she was indirectly arranging discourse instruction when she organized students' small group comic-book writing and when she assigned and collected students' family/home "hero interviews." Obviously, these two dimensions of the discourse partnering role overlap and operate together; we mention them here to emphasize our belief that you can and should be thinking language and performing your critical role as senior partner even when you aren't around!

The following list summarizes the key components of thinking language in the integrated language classroom:

THINK LANGUAGE IN:

1. *Planning learning activities and everything else that students are to do.*
2. *Conducting instruction, by continuously monitoring and adjusting the ongoing discourse to provide needed language and opportunities to use language.*
3. *Integrating the four language processes and students' first and second language experiences in order for them to tie in and tie back their language and literacy experiences.*

5.3 PROVIDING REAL ORAL DISCOURSE

Talking is at the heart of both ongoing classroom instruction and second language and literacy development. For many of your second language students, your classroom will be the primary place where they will be exposed to oral English that is tailored to their learning needs. Therefore, one of your primary challenges in thinking language will be to find ways to provide your students with enough of the oral language they need to develop their second language abilities.

As we mentioned in Chapter 1, during the past two decades many theorists and researchers have examined the oral language, or input, that is provided to second language learners. Much of this work has centered on describing the adaptations that native and fluent first language speakers (such as language teachers) make in talking to second language learners. This modified speech is often referred to as "foreigner talk."

Unfortunately, it appears that some of the same theoretical assumptions that are used within the transmission model have been used for a large portion of the research and instructional recommendations that have emanated from these studies. The very label "input" suggests a one-way, teacher gives/student receives conceptualization of language teaching and learning. Thus, many reports and professional resources center on what to do either to give input or to get output rather than on the overall exchange or negotiation of meaning-making occurring *between* speakers. (In real-life conversation, all input is also output and vice versa!)

Fortunately, as our conceptualization of the overall process of language acquisition has continued to broaden, so too have the studies of the place of input and foreigner talk within this overall process. In keeping with the current conceptualization of oral language acquisition as a strongly interactive process that is influenced by a large number of variables, a growing number of researchers are now attempting to take into account its interactional properties (its properties as *intake* as well as *input*). Thus, studies today have begun to focus not only on the linguistic properties of second language input, but also on its other properties: paraverbal (the characteristics of speech not pertaining to its content or linguistic structure); nonverbal (the nonverbal actions that accompany the oral language); discourse (the ways in which different utterances or speech acts are organized and related to one another); contextual (the settings in which it is created) and interactional properties (its characteristics as part of the social organization and negotiation of the overall flow of discourse).

Questions remain as to the best way to define the process of oral second language development and the nature and role of input within that process. Still, the literature concerning these issues offers several insights and teaching ideas that can be highly useful in integrated classrooms. Much of this literature indicates that teachers can indeed tailor their own instructional language to fit the language-learning needs of their various students (e.g., Burt and Dulay 1981; Krashen 1981, 1982; Saville-Troike 1982; Ventriglia 1982; Krashen and Terrell 1983; Genesee 1986; Hudelson 1984, in press; Wong-Fillmore 1985; Lindfors 1987). In general, three modifications are suggested:

1. Make classroom oral language *understandable* (i.e., concentrate on communicating, not on providing linguistic forms), and use your knowledge of students' previous experience (criterion no. 4) with the second language to provide whatever extra resources are needed for students to be able to understand it. This modification is often referred to as providing "comprehensible" input (Krashen 1981).

2. Make it *relevant* (i.e., make sure that students are paying attention to it and that it is appropriately geared to their experience and interests [criterion no. 3]).

3. Make it *useful* (i.e., choose what to talk about and how you talk about it so that it can be immediately used by students for their own meaning-making purposes [criterion no. 2]).

Following Urzúa (1985), from now on we will refer to classroom language that has undergone these modifications as "real input."

It is important to note that you can use these three input directives to think language and to create real input whether or not the primary function of your speech at a given moment is specifically to teach language. In other words, it's just as possible to make your speech understandable, relevant, and useful during dismissal time as during story time or current events time. If there's "English everywhere," then there's also the opportunity for real input everywhere! This also means that you can turn your ongoing speech into real input whether you are talking to your second language students in a grade-level classroom, a bilingual education classroom, or an ESL classroom. However, as Wong-Fillmore (1982) and others have suggested, the degree to which you can be successful in this endeavor will depend on the size and the language abilities of the group of students to whom you are speaking. Wong-Fillmore explains:

> Teachers find it considerably more difficult to tailor instructional language to the needs of language learners in classrooms where there are both language learners and fluent speakers of the target language . . . It is hard to make the adjustments the language learners need for figuring out what is being said in the presence of others who find such efforts unnecessary and boring. The tendency for most teachers in a mixed language situation is to talk to the students who understand best rather than in ways that can be understood by everyone. Often, the easiest solution is to aim at a point somewhere in the middle of the various abilities, and hope for the best. Indeed, this is what we have frequently observed during group instruction in mixed classes. (1982:293)

Both the difficulty itself and the solution of "teaching to the middle" which Wong-Fillmore describes here can be seen whenever any teachers are faced with teaching a large number of students with a wide variety of learning abilities and needs in the full group setting. So what is the solution if you happen to be a teacher whose students' language experiences and needs vary widely? We do not believe that the solution is to aim your classroom speech to only full second language and native English speakers or to permit beginning and mid-second-language students to "skip" or to "opt out" of your full group instruction. At the same time, we do not believe in segregating beginning and mid-second-language students by removing them from mixed language situations, either by placing them in other classes by themselves or by placing them in within-class groups by themselves. Having beginning second language students color pictures or do workbook pages while the rest of the class views and discusses a film is no better a solution to the oral input dilemma than just pretending that those students don't exist while you do the film activity. Both options deny these students access to the knowledge, language, and ways of interacting that are bound up in the film activity and which they will eventually need in and out of school in order to succeed. They also deny both first language and second language students the opportunity to learn about and learn from one another.

The solution that we propose is a three-step one. First, use variety (criterion no. 6) in your speech within your mixed, full group activities to make that speech as understandable, relevant, and useful as possible for the diversity of students who are experiencing it. Second, organize full group activities in which you are not the major discourse provider (e.g., group discussions, games) and also arrange for many times when students are learning in small groups and alone instead of in the full group, teacher-led activities. Third, and most important, use these small group and individualized activities to construct real dialogues with your students about the authentic tasks in which they are engaged. Thinking language in terms of real dialogues places students back where they belong, at the center of the language teaching picture, as junior partners in their own language learning.

Step 2 of our solution to the input dilemma is addressed in Chapters 2 and 3, where we made some suggestions for organizing your grouping and learning activities to include variety. In the rest of this chapter, we shall offer some suggestions for accomplishing steps 1 and 3.

5.4 REAL INPUT FOR THE LARGE GROUP: TEACHER TALK AND INTERACTIONAL TALK

The challenge in thinking language to transform your speech into real input during mixed, large group activities is that you must simultaneously address the learning needs of students at many different points in both their English language development and their conceptual development. As the preceding excerpt from Wong-Fillmore suggests, language that is perfectly suited to one subgroup of students may be of little or no use to another group; full second language and native English speakers may *drop out* of the learning activity if the only speech you use is completely understandable, relevant, and useful to beginning second language speakers, and the latter may never be able to *get into* the learning activity if the only language you use is useful and relevant to the former.

Two broad methods or techniques can be used for applying the variety criterion within your input to address the diversity of language needs that occur in a mixed, full group setting: adapting your overall "teacher talk" and adapting your "interactional talk." These two techniques make use of a different subset

The teacher is using the contextual, the discourse, and the interactional dimensions of this trip to a farm to turn everyday speech into real second language input.

of the major dimensions of input mentioned earlier. The first technique —adapting your teacher talk—consists of using all of the linguistic, paraverbal, nonverbal, and discourse dimensions of input to add variety to your own speech in order to make it both more understandable for your beginning and mid-second-language speakers and more relevant and interesting for your full-second language and native English-speakers. The second technique —adapting your interactional talk—consists of using the limited interactional and discourse dimensions of your full group discourse to add variety to that discourse in order to keep all students tuned in and to constantly give different types of students turns at taking in and giving out language that is appropriate for them. Here are some specific strategies to use, along with illustrations of the strategies in practice from our colleague Molly's actual teaching.

Adapting Teacher Talk

It is not just what you say but how you say it that makes the difference in turning your regular speech into real input. Using real input within your full group activities consists of consistently tapping what are usually untapped classroom natural resources for meaning-making: namely, your body (the nonverbal dimension); your voice (the paraverbal dimension); the types and the sequence of utterances you use (the discourse dimension); and your materials and physical environment (the contextual dimension). Figure 5.1 presents some of the ways in which you can adapt your teacher talk using each of these resources.

Nonverbal Strategies. As Figure 5.1 indicates, you can use three nonverbal strategies to adapt your teacher talk for a variety of first and second language students. You can use gestures along with your speech, both to illustrate its meaning and to heighten its appeal. Gestures can be as simple as pointing to objects and locations (e.g., pointing to the door while saying "Go over to the door") or as complex as a careful set of gestural jokes and contrasting definitions. To illustrate the latter, when Molly was joking on one occasion with her full class about a student's mother cutting his hair with a hammer, she made hammering motions above the child's head. Then, when the class uproariously corrected her by providing the appropriate word ("scissors"), she corrected her speech and gestures and shifted to making snipping and cutting motions around the head of the same student. Molly used a brief piece of discourse and gesturing to teach new vocabulary to her beginning and mid-second-language students while using a joke to keep her more advanced students attending to her discourse and to check on their comprehension.

Adding bodily motions to your speech is a second strategy for using the nonverbal input dimension. Bodily motions are best thought of as extensions of gestures. In transforming her speech into real input, Molly spent very little time

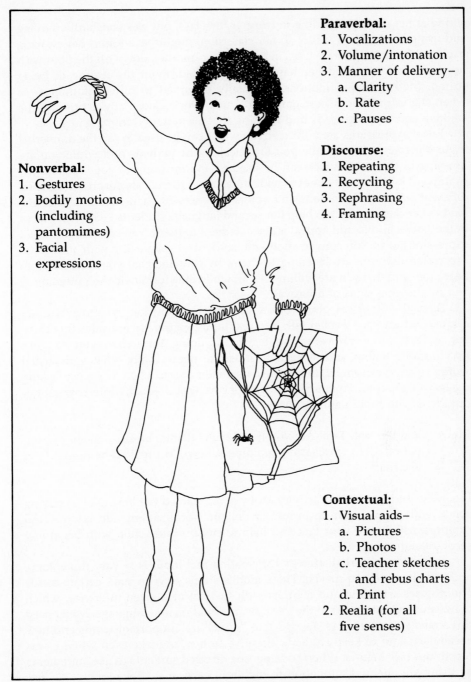

Paraverbal:
1. Vocalizations
2. Volume/intonation
3. Manner of delivery–
   a. Clarity
   b. Rate
   c. Pauses

Discourse:
1. Repeating
2. Recycling
3. Rephrasing
4. Framing

Nonverbal:
1. Gestures
2. Bodily motions
   (including
   pantomimes)
3. Facial
   expressions

Contextual:
1. Visual aids–
   a. Pictures
   b. Photos
   c. Teacher sketches
      and rebus charts
   d. Print
2. Realia (for all
   five senses)

Figure 5.1: Strategies for Adapting Teacher Talk

sitting at her desk or standing in front of the class, but was constantly moving and using her body. A visitor to her classroom might have found her swaying back and forth to illustrate trees in the wind or huddled down on the floor with her face hidden behind her hands as she talked about the feeling of being scared. Molly's bodily motions eventually extended to full pantomimes, as when she introduced a new game of "Duck, Duck Goose" by acting out the walking and tapping heads and running that are required in the game.

Facial expressions are a third strategy that can be used to tap the nonverbal input dimension, both while you are speaking to students and while you are listening to them. Your face can be used to add meaning to your speech. For example, Molly opened her eyes wide and smiled to indicate surprise. She used different facial configurations and voices to represent characters in stories she read to her class in order to help her second language students keep their places in the stories and to add appeal and excitement to them. You can also use facial expressions to sustain conversation with students, by signaling with your facial expression that you are listening to them, by showing that you would like to hear more and that you are willing to wait while they formulate their utterances, and by showing signs of approval.

Paraverbal Strategies. Your voice is another natural input resource that you can use to turn your teacher talk into real input. Figure 5.1 indicates that there are at least three paraverbal strategies for doing this. First, you can use vocalizations within your speech to illustrate paraverbally what your actual words mean. For example, during field day, after a race, when Molly was asking a beginning second language boy whether he was tired, she interspersed her questions with rapid panting noises:

Molly: You ran fast, Tam! Are you tired? Huh? (Pants, breathes deeply in and out rapidly.) *Tired!* (Pants rapidly.) Whew! *I'm* tired! I'd be tired if I ran like that!

Similarly, during a baking activity Molly accompanied her licking of a cooking spoon with a long "Um-m-m-m!" of delight. Vocalizations add interest and comprehensibility to your talk and help to sustain interaction with beginning second language speakers.

A second paraverbal strategy for creating real input is to vary the volume and intonation of your speech. These modifications serve to make certain words and phrases stand out and contrast with the rest of a given utterance, which draws students' attention to the key new information and language. Molly used this strategy constantly as she spoke to "punch up" important words and new vocabulary, and to keep students attentive to her language even when it was repetitious (see below). When cooking, she directed students to use ingredients by using volume and intonation to highlight each one: "Take an *egg.* An *egg.* Now take your *milk.* Take your *milk.*" She also drew students' attention to critical meanings in a story to assist them in responding to her inferential questions: "But what will happen when that dog sits down? Remember, it said that the *dog* was *big* and the *chair* was itsy-bitsy *little!*" Notice that what Molly did *not* do was to indiscriminately increase her volume across all of her speech whenever she was directly addressing second language students—they are not hard of hearing, just learning a new language!

The manner of delivery of your speech is a third paraverbal strategy. Adjust the clarity of your speech, the rate at which you deliver it, and the pauses that you use within it to enable all your students to process and use what you are saying to learn language. In general, clearly articulating your words and minimizing "Sandhi variations" (running words together so that, for example, "Did you eat yet?" sounds more like "Jeet-jet?") will increase the likelihood that the words will be understood and used by second language learners. Slowing down your delivery and adding pauses throughout your speech will also give second language students a better opportunity to attend to it and to process and use it. You can then use your students' nonverbal and verbal feedback to decide whether you should alter your speech even further, for example, by slowing down or pausing even more. However, this strategy should not be used to such an extreme degree that your speech sounds unnatural, dramatically different from normal conversation, or condescending. Second language students are also not stupid!

Discourse Strategies. Even when you are doing all the talking in your learning activity—which wouldn't happen very often in the integrated classroom—you can use specific discourse strategies within the flow of that discourse to turn it into real input. Figure 5.1 presents four possibilities. First, you can use repeating within your discourse to give second language students many opportunities and contexts for hearing and using the same language. Here's an example from Molly's teaching (she is directing six students in making individual cup recipes of pancake batter):

Molly: All right, look here. OK—
Alberto: Break an egg.
Molly: —now. Did you hear Alberto say "Break an egg"? *"Break the egg!"* Look here, everybody needs to put *one egg* in their cup. All right Jaime, take an egg and then you pass it to Lin and say "Lin, take an egg."
Jaime: (to Lin) Take the egg.
Lin: (to Mary) Take an egg.
Molly: I heard Lin. I heard you say it. I didn't even need to tell you! (An egg falls off the table.) What happened?
Jaime: It fall.
Molly: *One egg* on the floor. This egg's no good. (Enright 1986:131)

It's important to note that each time Molly repeated the word *egg* in the preceding excerpt, she used a slightly different utterance, meaning, and context. This is a key attribute of the repetition strategy. Your repetitions should be meaning-based, not just repetition for its own sake. (This same principle holds for asking students to repeat as well.)

Recycling language, the second discourse strategy, builds on the repetition strategy. It is also closely related to the "incorporation" phase of the language teaching cycle discussed in Chapter 1. There, we suggested that the language and context that you use in your integrated units should be incorporated into succeeding units and activities. In the same vein, the language you use in speaking to students should be reintroduced and practiced in new settings and for new purposes. The recycling strategy is often applied spontaneously as well. For example, when Molly and her class were reading a story that had a river in it, she exclaimed to the class: "A river. Remember, we have talked about the *river.* 'Jump the river!' Remember? We talked about rivers when we learned to play that game!"

Just as you can repeat your words and utterances or reintroduce them at other times, you can also rephrase them to enrich their meaning and to provide different forms of real input to different students. Like repeating, rephrasing recasts the same meaning onto new vocabulary and utterances. Thus, when Molly was talking about balloons, she said, "We'll have balloons! Big colored balls of air!" and when she introduced the word pancake to some beginning second language students, she said, "We're going to make pancakes! Flat round circles to eat. Sort of like bread."

The fourth discourse strategy is framing. This consists of marking off the topical and meaning boundaries within your discourse by using a combination of words or phrases (such as "OK," "Fine," "All right," "Now") along with intonation and pauses. Framing helps second language students to keep their place within the discourse and lets them know when a new idea or concept is being introduced. An example from Molly's teaching follows. (She had demonstrated the action that students were to use during a finger-play and was now ready to have them do it with her):

Molly: (Raises her hand and opens and closes her thumb and fingers.) Here is an alligator . . . (bends her arm into "log" position) and here is a log. *OK. Now. Watch.* Here is an alligator sitting on a log. (She rests her hand on her arm.) See? Let's try that together. *Ready?*

By using the "OK. Now. Watch." set of utterances to set off, or frame, each segment of her input, Molly was able to build meanings one upon another within her discourse. The "Ready?" utterance is also an example of framing, used here by Molly not only to cue her students as to a meaning boundary but also to signal that a new participant structure or phase of the activity is to occur—in this case a shift from [teacher demonstrate] to [students practice with teacher]. The framing strategy can also be used to set clear boundaries between learning activities within the overall flow of classroom discourse (Wong-Fillmore 1985).

Contextual Strategies. Much has been written in this book about the authentic, functional uses of speech and print and about developing a physical and social environment to support those uses. You can also use these contextual resources to help you turn your oral language into real input. Anchoring your teacher talk within the rules, activities, and participant structures of your social environment was discussed in Chapter 2. Figure 5.1 presents the strategies you can apply using the materials you have gathered together in your physical environment.

Tapping all five of your students' senses by using different kinds of materials while you talk will provide contextual information and increase the comprehensibility, relevance, and usefulness of your talk. Visual aids such as photos, pictures, and even sketches and rebus charts made by you (such as the ones suggested in Chapter 4 for classroom rules, schedule and jobs, as well as the recipe chart in the "Rain Makes Applesauce" unit in Part II of this book) can bring comprehensibility and a much needed focus to newly introduced language and concepts. The rebus charts also exemplify how you can link concrete objects and oral language with print. Eventually, print can become a visual aid by itself, as in using a chart showing the words of a song to teach the song.

"Real world" objects, or realia, can add a visual component to your oral language and can be used to incorporate students' other senses into your instruction as well. For example, Molly used many cooking activities in her classroom to give her students opportunities to take in and give out measuring language, nutrition and food language, cooking terms, descriptive and comparative language, and sensory language. Molly's students also saw and counted (and then ate!) M & M's during a color graphing activity; they smelled and tasted beets and blueberries during a natural dyeing activity; and they saw, smelled, and touched a real fish when they made fish prints. Molly also used recordings of natural sounds to add an auditory dimension to her input, and, like Ms. Kay, she had her students tape-record themselves and listen to the results to improve their own output.

Adapting Interactional Talk

In addition to adapting your own teacher talk within your large group, teacher-led activities so that it becomes real input, you can work to maximize the amount of *interaction* that takes place within that setting and to adapt the ways in which you use the interactional dimension of your own speech in calling on and responding to students within these activities. As Figure 5.2 shows, the strategies that you can use for this purpose include ones for getting student output (i.e. to get students to participate and respond using their oral second language skills) and strategies for responding to that output (and to provide additional, follow-up input). The word *survey* in Figure 5.2 is a reminder that all of the full group interaction strategies presented there depend for their successful implementation upon your constant surveying and monitoring of your students as you speak and interact with them. This enables you to make moment-to-moment decisions about how you will use those interaction strategies.

To Get Student Output:
1. Vary participant structures.
2. Vary elicitations.
3. Vary output requests according to student ability and social style (across time: "raise the ante").

To Respond to Student Output (according to the student speaker's ability and social style):
1. Use confirmation checks and clarification requests.
2. Use student rephrasings and expansions.
3. Give extra chances—
   a. Pauses
   b. Prompts
   c. Self-rephrasings
   d. Requests for more information (probes)
4. Correct by focusing on the message (its meaning and intelligibility)—
   a. Explicit corrections
   b. Models of appropriate forms

Figure 5.2:   Strategies For Adapting Group Interaction

Requesting Student Output. Three general strategies can be used for adapting oral requests for output from your second language students so that the oral discourse within your full group activities will be turned into real input for them. First, it is important to apply the variety criterion within your learning activities—particularly those in which a large number of students at different levels are involved. Each of your students brings a distinctive set of abilities, previous experiences with speech and print, and ways of interacting to the full group setting. The exclusive use of one or two participant structures within your activities might help those few students whose abilities, social styles, and previous experiences happen to already match those structures, but it will also systematically prevent the rest of the class from tying back the new language and interaction of the activity to their experiences and resources. The only way to avoid this is to have "something for everyone" at some point in the schedule by employing a variety of forms of participation across the set of full group activities that you use.

As we've suggested, one way of adding variety to your full group participation is to have some activities in which you are not the major director and speaker. But you can also use different kinds of rules and participant structures when you are the main speaker. One of these is the "lesson" format that was described in Chapter 3 (the typical full group, teacher-led activity used most of the time in transmission classrooms). Lessons consist of teacher lectures followed by cycles of [teacher asks question/student replies/teacher evaluates reply]. This format is useful and should be included in your planning, especially since it is the one that your students will be exposed to most often in other classroom settings. However, it should be only one of many kinds of participation that you use.

In addition to the lesson format, there are many other ways to organize your full group, teacher-led activities. For example, one teacher we know has a weekly "Mr. Wizard" time in class during which he demonstrates a piece of science "magic" to the full group. Following this, there is a period during which students try to figure out the real explanation for what happened by asking the teacher questions and following up on those questions. Other teachers we know have "class meetings" (Glasser 1969) in which students initiate topics and the teacher acts as the moderator of the discussion and the synthesizer of students' ideas (class meetings will be explained further in Chapter 7). Sharing, or "show and tell," is another common activity in which students practice public speaking and giving extended oral narratives by taking turns talking about a familiar object or event. Other routine events—such as calling roll at the beginning of the day and discussing the weather conditions and the date—can also be used to provide alternative forms of participating and using language.

Another strategy for adding variety to your requests for student output is to vary your use of elicitations—the ways in which you call on students for contributions. Again, the transmission lesson format provides us with one useful type of elicitation—the nomination—in which students are called on to contribute one at a time and by name. For example: "Now conjugate the present tense of the verb 'to be'—Amanda") However, this is not equally effective with every student. Using nominations to call on students who are from cultures in which individualized public speaking is considered rude or to call on beginning second language students who are still heavily involved in trying to take in the new language and in trying to form some preliminary hypotheses about how it works is more likely to lead to embarrassment and unwillingness to participate than to language learning. Therefore, other types of elicitations besides nominations should be used in the full group to include these students.

At least four other types of elicitations can be used in your full group, teacher-led activities. Volunteer nominations are elicitations that allow students to indicate (by raising their hands or by looking at you or giving some other signal) that they wish to be called upon, while still leaving in your hands the selection of who will "have the floor." Open-ended elicitations give control of the floor to the students to the degree that anyone who wants to is allowed to speak up and share in response to that particular elicitation. (For example: "An eclipse is very hard to explain. Anyone want to give it a try?") In choral elicitations, the entire group responds to a question, recites a poem, or uses oral language in some other manner ("We practiced the names of all the planets in our solar system yesterday. Let's go through them together again today as I point to the chart. Everyone.") Patterned elicitations set up a specific form of turn-taking and speaking which is usually explicitly set in advance (e.g., the full group is sitting in a circle and the teacher says, "I'd like to go around the circle and have each of you tell what your favorite food is and why"). None of these methods will be equally appealing and useful to all the students in the group, so it is important that you use a variety of them within your full group instruction. We don't believe that within your full group interactions you can reach *all* of your students *all* the time. We do believe that it's possible to reach all of your students at *some* time or another if you use a variety of elicitations and participant structures.

The third strategy has to do with varying the kinds of output that you ask for when you call on students. As Wong-Fillmore (1985) points out, the best way to organize output requests within the mixed, full group setting is not to ask questions of your best English speakers only or to ask only low-level questions of everyone or to skip asking questions altogether! The best way is to match your output requests to the current oral language proficiency and individual social styles of your students—an enterprise that requires a large variety of requests and responses and that requires thinking language within the full group setting at its highest level of sophistication! In order to do this, you will have to make use of all of the types of elicitations that we have mentioned, along with a wide range of discourse acts. The output that you request from a student can (and should) include simple nonverbal signs of comprehension (a nod of the head, a smile); nonverbal "explanations" (a gesture, pointing to an object, a nonverbal demonstration or pantomime); one-word responses; phrases; single complete utterances; and extended narratives. Similarly, the content of your utterances can (and should) make full use of Bloom's taxonomy of educational objectives (1956), requiring students, for example, to make inferences and predictions in addition to recalling facts.

Let's look at how this third strategy might work in practice. Let's say you are reading a children's novel to your group each day (we'll use *Charlotte's Web*) and you want to start off a particular day's reading with an update of what has happened so far. Using your knowledge of your students' abilities and their social styles, you might start off by asking the entire group to remind you (chorally) of the identity of the heroine ("What was the name of that old spider again?"). Then you might hand the book to Rafael—an outgoing and confident beginning second language student—and ask him to find a picture of Charlotte and show it to the class. ("Rafael, help me find Charlotte in here! Can you show a picture of her to the class?") This requires that Rafael comprehend your request and demonstrate his comprehension through a public act, but it does not require that he say anything at all! As Rafael holds the book up for the class to see, you might have Moon Hee, a beginning-second language student who is not yet ready for public displays, confirm whether the animal Rafael has found is indeed Charlotte by nodding her head yes or no. ("Is Rafael right, Moon Hee? Is that Charlotte?") Then you might do a quick review of the other items that Rafael has found in the picture—asking some students for one-word answers ("Raise your hand if you know what that thing hanging above Charlotte is called"), asking other students to simply point ("Wilbur? Is Wilbur the pig in this picture? Bui, come show me where Wilbur is"), and asking still other students to provide full utterances about the picture ("Lacretia, where are all those cows and sheep going?"). After you finally let poor Rafael sit down, you might have the students review what happened the day before ("What was Wilbur's boast? What did the rat tie on Wilbur? Where did he tie it? Where did Wilbur get that idea that he could spin a web?") and speculate on what might happen today ("Do you think Wilbur can spin a web? Why not? What's going to happen? How will Wilbur feel? How many people think that Wilbur will spin a web? What's the name of the rat again?"). Of course, it's very likely that some students in the group will want to initiate and tie in or tie back the story's characters, plot, and language to their own experiences ("You have a stuffed pig, Maria Elena? What's his name?" or "You read a book about pigs, Earl? What was it called? What did it say about pigs?"). Or you might find an opportunity to do this yourself ("Remember the movie we saw about spiders?"). Now, after only four or five minutes of conversation, the whole class can be warmed up and "ready to roll," and you can begin today's reading happy in the knowledge that you have provided real input for your second language students!

Teacher talk and student participation are equally important instructional components of large group activities like "story time."

Besides illustrating the complexity and difficulty of using the third "output getting" strategy in the full group setting, this brief imaginary scenario illustrates three other key points. First, it demonstrates the need for multidimensional and multicontextual materials within the classroom and within the full group setting. If *Charlotte's Web* had no pictures, it would be much harder to involve the beginning-second-language students in the group within the activity. On the other hand, if the book were not a complete story, with a plot and characters, it would be much harder to involve the full-second-language and native English speakers in the activity, and it would have been impossible to give everyone the opportunity to tie in and tie back the book's content and language to their own experiences.

Gibbons (1985) describes the "silent period" that has been posited for early second language learning—that initial period when new second language students are still trying to make sense of all the input they are receiving and do not as yet have the information, hypotheses, and confidence they need to begin to speak. Gibbons further points out that the silent period can be seriously prolonged by not giving beginning-second language students enough opportunities to produce language and communication at the appropriate level and in the appropriate circumstances. We agree with this position. More specifically, it may be that our second language students remain "silent" not because they are still unable to produce output but for two other reasons. One, we aren't asking them for the simpler, more "reduced output" (Gibbons 1985) that they are ready and able to use, and two, we aren't asking for it within the kinds of familiar and supportive circumstances in which they would be willing to try to give us that output (or as Molly put it, "to dare to risk speaking English"). The key to providing such opportunities is to constantly *invite* every member of the group to participate in the activity and in the discourse that is being construct-ed, and to show through your actions and input that you both expect that students will accept this invitation and care whether or not they accept it. Inviting Moon Hee to nod, or even simply calling her name as you talk, with no expectation of a reply ("That *is* a web. Charlotte lives in that web, huh, Moon Hee. See it, everyone?") will reassure her that you know she is there and that she is an important member of the group whom you expect to participate and contribute just like everyone else, even if it is only by being attentive. If you continually invite all the students in your class to participate, eventually they will all accept that invitation.

Finally, the scenario with *Charlotte's Web* illustrates the dynamic potential of full group interaction and of your output requests. Your output requests can supply students with real input according to the initiations that the students themselves make and how they respond to you. But this dynamic potential will be realized only if you *share* control of the floor and the conversation with your students. Student efforts to initiate and communicate might be labeled as "off-task" or "interruptions" in some classrooms. In integrated classrooms, they are valued and celebrated; moreover, they are integrated into the ongoing discourse and the teacher's instructional goals.

The dynamic potential of your interactional talk can also be expressed over time. As your students' language abilities and social styles develop during the school-year, so will your output requests. For example, during story time in September you may ask Moon Hee only to pay attention to your discourse, but by December you may be asking her to locate and show a picture to the class; by March you may be asking her to answer your questions orally. Like parents teaching their children the first language, it is important in providing oral discourse to your second language students to raise the ante communicatively. As they continue to develop their second language abilities, you should make output requests that "push" them to use these abilities to the utmost (Swain 1985), while at the same time providing the linguistic and emotional support that they need. As we have said, this is accomplished much more easily and effectively when you are talking with only one or two second language speakers, which is why we suggest that you include lots of times for such interactions within your schedule.

Responding to Student Output. Once you have managed to use your output requests successfully, you can try four major strategies for responding to that student output. These four strategies are also presented in Figure 5.2. Like the output request strategies, all four of these strategies should be selectively applied to your responses to students' output.

The first response strategy involves the use of confirmation checks and clarification requests. Confirmation checks are designed to obtain confirmation from the speaker that you have understood the output. (Student: "A big house." Teacher: "A house?" Student: "Yes.") Clarification requests are designed to get the student to clarify or restate the output so that it can be understood. ("I missed that." "Try it again." "Sorry?" "Would you please repeat that?"). Both these techniques induce students to perform to the fullest extent of their abilities as they speak. They also often act as "probes," getting students to add information to their output, and as "sustainers," getting students to continue to speak. Caution must be applied in using this strategy, since confirmation checks and clarification requests can make students feel that they have made some kind of mistake or that they are on the spot in front of the class. The strategy is used most effectively when it is an authentic part of the ongoing discourse and when you and the students are focusing on communicating through oral language rather than on performing with oral language.

Another useful response strategy is to rephrase or expand on what the speaker has said. This strategy functions much like the teacher talk rephrasing strategy in that it gives the speaker highly relevant and useful feedback regarding what he or she is saying and also adds to its comprehensibility and usefulness for the entire group. Here's an example of this strategy from Molly's teaching (The students are passing a bag with a plastic alligator in it around the group, during the first part of the alligator finger-play activity):

Molly: What does an alligator have in his mouth? If it's an alligator?
Chau: Teeth.
Molly: Chau says if it's an alligator that he can feel *sharp teeth!*
  Lee: It'll bite me!
  Sam: Uh-uh! (Negative)
  Lee: I can feel 'em!
Molly: Be careful when you feel his long, sharp teeth! He might bite you!

Here's another example, from Molly's introduction of an art activity involving paper-towel folding and dipping into food coloring:

  Molly: See, then you fold it over and then over again.
Alberto: Two times?
  Molly: Yes, two times. Twice. You fold it once, twice.

Through her application of the rephrasing and expanding strategy, Molly provides tailored input to individual students in her group, thereby using the student's present language to introduce new language to that student.

The third general strategy for responding to student output is used to sustain interaction with a student speaker and to give that speaker an extra chance to contribute. This includes giving extra chances both to students who have been called on and who haven't contributed yet and to students who have just spoken and who want to speak some more! One simple way to give an extra chance to students who have not responded to your invitation is simply to lengthen your pause before "giving up" and going on to the next student. Teachers often provide extremely short pauses between elicitations (Rowe 1969; Swift and Gooding 1983; Tobin 1986; Fagan, Hassler, and Szabo 1981). Native speakers often find it difficult to get their thoughts and their language together to speak before the time interval allotted to them for that purpose elapses. Therefore, you can imagine what this is like for second language learners! Pausing in requesting student output is as important as pausing within your teacher talk. You can also give nonresponders extra chances to speak by prompting them (e.g., repeating your elicitation). This gives them an extra chance to process your input, in addition to "holding the floor" for them in a way that will maintain a comfortable group atmosphere. Rephrasing your elicitation—which operates just like rephrasing your teacher talk—is another way of giving nonresponders an extra chance to respond. It *lowers* the ante within your speech, which is helpful if the reason for the lack of a response is noncomprehension. Here's another example from the bag-passing portion of Molly's alligator finger-play activity. In this exchange, Molly is talking with a beginning second language student:

Molly: Sarig, did you feel?
Sarig: (No response.)
Molly: Could you feel it? (Pats hands together as if feeling an object.) *Feel* it, Sarig. (Imperative.)
Sarig: (Feels around in the bag).
Molly: Did you find it? Can you feel it?
Sarig: (Nods.)
Molly: What can you feel?
Sarig: Alligator.
Molly: Good! Sarig felt the alligator too!

Often, your goal in giving students an extra chance to respond is to raise the ante, soliciting further output from them at the highest level of their oral language capacities. Therefore, requests for more information (or probes) are also very useful. In the preceding excerpt, Molly used this strategy with Sarig when she followed up Sarig's nod with a request for more information ("What can you feel?"). Here's another example of Molly raising the ante, this time with a student during a story-reading activity:

Molly: What did the blue and yellow do, Chau?
Chau: They go together.
Molly: Yes, they went together, and then what happened?
Chau: Me?
Molly: Um-hmm. (Affirmative.)
Chau: They make green.
Molly: Yeah, they made *green*, didn't they?
Chau: They make green, uh—and they made a long string of green!
Molly: Yeah, and what kind of green, what *shade* of green was it?
Chau: (No response.)
Molly: Was it light green or dark green or sort of regular? Remember we talked about different shades of green? (Points to glasses with various colored liquids.)
Chau: Oh! . . . It's dark. Dark?

Here, Molly raised the ante with a mid-second-language speaker while continuing to provide the real input support that he needed in order to meet her higher discourse requests.

Providing appropriate corrections is the last important strategy to use in responding to student output. This is done in following up on students' output as part of the key language that they need. Correcting students is a topic that continues to engender lots of discussion among language teachers, and indeed there are many ways to correct. In keeping with the instructional criteria of support and purpose and with the definition of real input that we have outlined, the best rule of thumb in correcting students in all settings is to focus on the message (the communication) that the student is attempting to convey and on the ongoing negotiation of conversation rather than on the form or the pronunciation of the students' utterances in isolation. This implies that problems of syntax would be addressed when they affected the intended *meaning* of the student's message (i.e., when the message is in danger of being misunderstood) and that problems of pronunciation would be addressed when they affected the *intelligibility* of the student's message (i.e., when the message is in danger of not being understood at all). Here's an example from Molly's pancake-making activity:

Hong: Two spoon.
Molly: You have two spoons. Spoons. Z-z. Hear the difference?
Hong: Spoon-z-z.
Molly: Aw-*right!*

This excerpt illustrates Molly's use of explicit correction. She draws Hong's attention to the problem, but she does so as it occurs in an authentic, message-oriented context. She also does it clearly and in a matter-of-fact way, as a natural part of the ongoing activity, so that Hong does not feel embarrassed or put on the spot. Another way to follow up on students' oral errors is to model the appropriate form of the student's utterance. This is illustrated twice in the previous excerpt, where Molly and Chau were discussing "dark green"; first when Molly followed up Chau's utterance, "They go together," by modeling the correct form and requesting further language ("Yes, they went together, and then what happened?"), and later when Molly followed up on "They make green" with "Yeah, they made green, didn't they?". As with all of the real input strategies for responding to students' output, you should make your corrections while keeping in mind the speaker's abilities and social style. Moreover, in deciding whether to correct a student explicitly or just model the appropriate utterance, you should use the instructional criterion of support. This will enable you to determine whether any given correction would embarrass the student or discourage his or her genuine attempts to communicate with you. Remember that you can always file away the student's error and wait for a more appropriate, private moment to deal with it.

When used together, all of these real input strategies can assist you to use your large group, teacher-led activities as vehicles for fulfilling language instruction goals as well as procedural and content-teaching goals. It's important to recall here, however, that these strategies can fulfill their functions only if they are used within activities and discourse that follow the criteria of the ILT model. Adding rephrasings and confirmation checks to language lessons in which meaningless facts and fragments of speech are repeated and drilled might improve these lessons a little, but not nearly enough!

It's also important to note here that we have deliberately chosen the large group, teacher-led setting as the context for our discussion. We know that many teachers feel most at ease in this setting and that they are using it for much of the school day. We are also aware that matters of practicality dictate that this setting be used. Still, we do not believe it to be the most effective setting in which to teach and learn language, for at least two reasons.

First, there is the matter of quantity. No matter how skillful you are in tailoring your teacher talk and your interactional talk to take into account the diverse needs of your class, you will only occasionally be able to provide specific real input to a particular student. Most of your activity's discourse will have to be suited to the majority of your students. As we stated earlier, the best you can do in the full group setting is to provide real input to each student in the full group, some of the time. In contrast, during dyadic (one-on-one) and small group activity settings, you can focus on the student or few students in that activity for its entire duration.

Second, there is the matter of quality. The strategies we have provided so far will provide somewhat helpful oral language to your second language learners in the full group setting. However, the organization of that setting implicitly precludes providing maximally helpful oral language. The collaboration that we believe is crucial to successful second language development is by definition limited in the full group setting.

Once you move from providing oral discourse in the full group setting to providing it in small group and dyadic settings, you can add a number of collaborative strategies to your real input repertoire. Input collaboration leads to the construction of sustained, responsive, and individually tailored real dialogues with students. In contrast to the input/output patterns of the full group setting, real dialogues involve students more fully in the construction of the ongoing discourse and in their own second language development. In your full group settings you can only think language in talking *to* students, but in your small group and individualized settings you can think language in talking *with* students. Let's see how this might be done.

5.5 REAL INPUT WITH FEWER STUDENTS: REAL DIALOGUES

Figure 5.3 presents the major strategies that you can use to engage in real dialogues with your students. The word *real* in "real dialogue" signifies that these dialogues must involve language that is comprehensible, relevant, and useful to the student(s) engaging in the dialogues with you. In addition, like the jar of spiders in the picture, the word signifies that these language-teaching conversations must center on an authentic or real task and on materials with which the student is engaged. This harks back to our original conceptualization of integrated curriculum (Chapter 2) as the union of teacher, students, and the real world. Once you have completed the difficult task of planning and getting students involved in your integrated learning activities, you can then use these activities to engender and engage in real dialogues. The following transcribed excerpt illustrates the various strategies that you can use to do this. In the excerpt, a teacher has come into a classroom to borrow some materials. While he waits for the other teacher to get the materials, he watches the students. He is standing across from a group of six students (seven to nine years old) who are seated at a table chopping vegetables for a class snack. Bakir, a nine-year-old Lebanese beginning-second language student who has been in the United States for less than a month, initiates the real dialogue by smiling and waving hello.)

Bakir: (Smiles and waves.)
   T: Hey, Bakir, how are you doing? You look busy!
Bakir: Fine! (He gestures amusedly to the vegetables.)
   T: What are you doing? What are you guys making?

Figure 5.3:   Real Dialogue Strategies

Bakir: Kah-kah-kah-rotes. (Carrots.) We . . . kah-rotes.
    T: You sure do! You do have carrots. Wow! What are you doing with those carrots?
Bakir: We, uh-h . . . we . . . (he makes chopping motions with the knife) . . . kah-rotes.
    T: Oh yeah, I see. You're *chopping* those carrots. I should have known. You've got some *big* carrots! And you're chopping them.
Bakir: Yes! (He pauses to think. His grin slowly widens.) Big kah-rotes . . . (he makes chopping motions) . . . little kah-rotes! Fine!
    T: (Laughing.) You got *that* right! You're chopping those big carrots into little carrots. You're quite a chopper! You're quite a chopper, all right! You're quite a cook!
Bakir: (Puzzled.) Cook?
    T: Yes, you know, uh, someone who makes the food. Like Mrs. Sprague at lunch. *She* chops! She chops too! She's the *cook!*
Bakir: Oh! Oh yes. Oh yes, lunch. (Slyly.) But I no . . . (shakes head, negatively).
    T: You're not what?
Bakir: I no kah-rote!
    T: (Scoffingly.) No, you're not a carrot. You're a *cook!* Like Mrs. Sprague!
Bakir: (Grins widely, stands up very straight, and makes body rigid with arms held to his sides.) I a kah-rote!
    T: (Dubiously.) What?
Bakir: (With emphasis.) I a *kah-rote!*
    T: (Amazed.) You *are* a carrot? OK, then I'll chop you! (He makes pretend chopping motions, tickling Bakir as he does so.) Chop! Chop! Chop that carrot! Chop, chop, chop.
Bakir: (Collapses, giggling.) No! No chop! No kah-rote! I no kah-rote! No chop! I cook! I a cook! I a cook!

Getting Started

You can use two primary strategies to begin a real dialogue. One strategy permits the students themselves to initiate a dialogue and to respond appropriately to their initiations. This is illustrated in the above "chopping" episode. Bakir initiates the conversation by smiling and waving to engage the teacher in an exchange. He then goes on to set the initial topic of the conversation by gesturing to his carrots. The visiting teacher responds to both initiations with language and signs of interest. This strategy of giving control over the beginnings of the dialogue and the topics within that dialogue to students represents a key difference between real dialogues and the exchanges that typically occur in full group settings.

The other strategy that you can use to begin a real dialogue is to invite a student or students to talk with you about what they are doing or about something that is of importance to them. For example, you might begin a real dialogue with two girls reading a storybook during "book time" by sitting with them at their table and (at the right moment) joining their conversation (e.g., "That silly purple monster is in trouble again!" or "I think that monster is silly too.") Of course, invitations, can be formal, too. For example, you could call a student or two over to read with you the book that they have chosen. However, *inviting* students to talk with you is different from *commanding* them to listen to you and speak to you. It means that you signal through your opening comments and actions that you are willing to let the student(s) choose a different topic or focus and that you are willing to give them some control over the negotiation of the conversation. Inviting students to talk with you also means that you will allow them to decline the invitation completely and that you will subsequently look for other situations and topics that might result in your invitation being accepted. (With respect to this strategy, there is no such thing as a forced dialogue.)

Getting Grounded

After you and your student(s) have "connected" and are ready to converse, it is your important duty to establish and maintain the interpersonal and contextual "ground" upon which the dialogue will occur. In order to ground topics within a real dialogue, you must orient the student(s) to the key features of each topic being discussed and provide the linguistic and nonlinguistic context that the student(s) need in order to take their turns in discussing the topic within the dialogue. You must also check to make sure that the various participants in the dialogue are paying attention to one another and that they have a mutual focus with respect to the topic being discussed. In the chopping excerpt, once Bakir has successfully initiated the conversation and has (nonverbally) selected the initial topic—the carrots and the chopping—the teacher provides the linguistic and nonlinguistic context for the dialogue and continuously monitors his dialogue partner, repeating and adjusting his own speech as necessary to preserve intersubjectivity and to propel the dialogue forward (e.g., "What are you doing? What are you guys making?" and "You sure do! You do have carrots. Wow! What are you doing with those carrots?"). This continuous grounding is accomplished through the use of the real input strategies described earlier in the chapter.

In everyday life, the responsibility for grounding a conversation is generally shared by the various participants in that conversation. The speaker who introduces a new topic will usually take primary responsibility for doing the groundwork that enables everyone engaging in the conversation to use the topic. In contrast, in the real dialogues that take place in your classroom, *you* take on the continuing responsibility for grounding the conversation each time a new topic is introduced, whether it is introduced by you or by the students. Although real dialogues are shared constructions, the construction process is an asymmetric one, with you as the senior partner taking responsibility not only for fulfilling your own conversational duties but also for fulfilling many of those that would usually be fulfilled by the other speaker(s). Without the advantage of this asymmetric relationship, second language students would not even be able to get started on the developmental process that results in oral fluency, nor would they be able to concentrate on the specific new oral discourse that is being offered to them within your real dialogues.

Building the Dialogue and the Students' Oral Language: Scaffolding

Once the foundation for a real dialogue has been put in place, you can begin to use the mutual construction of the conversation, along with your real input strategies, to provide oral language instruction to your second language student(s), while simultaneously sharing feelings, experiences, and new ideas with them. You can build this new language, meaning, and shared experience by providing an interactional "scaffolding" (Wood, Bruner, and Ross, 1976; Greenfield 1984) for your junior partners' construction of their part of the dialogue. The scaffolding typically used by construction crews in erecting buildings is a useful metaphor for the set of strategies that you use at this point in the real dialogue. In Greenfield's words:

> The scaffold, as it is known in building construction, has five characteristics: it provides a support; it functions as a tool; it extends the range of the worker; it allows the worker to accomplish a task not otherwise possible; and it is used selectively to aid the worker where needed. To illustrate this last point, a scaffold would not be used, for example, when a carpenter is working five feet from the ground. (1984:118)

It is at this point in the real dialogue process that we can clearly distinguish between the kinds of instructional collaboration and support that you can provide in small group and dyadic situations as compared to the full group setting. The dynamic and highly sophisticated attributes of the scaffold as described here by Greenfield would be very difficult to provide for even one student (much less the entire class) in the full group setting.

To provide a scaffold for your second language students within the real dialogue, you must perform four key operations within your discourse and interaction: supporting, adapting, providing, and withdrawing. As Figure 5.3 illustrates, all the operations except withdrawing are performed at the same time; they are interdependent and overlapping; and they culminate in the fourth operation, that of withdrawing the discourse scaffolding when the student(s) no longer need it. Figure 5.3 also shows that the student(s) who are collaborating with you to produce the dialogue are busy performing their own operations—attending, using (or practicing) and extending—in synchrony with your actions in order to take advantage of the scaffolding that you are providing and in order eventually to incorporate the new meanings and capacities they are learning into their overall discourse repertoires.

Just as construction scaffolds support carpenters as they erect new parts of buildings, so do the scaffolds that you create in your real dialogues support your second language learners as they construct new meanings and extend their meaning-making capacities. Dialogue scaffolds support students in a number of ways. First, by removing much of the discourse responsibility that would usually be assumed by students, they free students to concentrate on the language and conversational dimensions within the dialogue that they need to learn. This is done while maintaining the full, normal contours of everyday conversation, as illustrated in the "chopping" dialogue. Even though Bakir had only sixty to eighty words in his English vocabulary at the time this conversation took place, the visiting teacher was able to create (with Bakir's collaboration) a "natural," meaningful conversation. This method of supporting students' language constructions highly resembles parents' use of "proto-dialogues" with first language infants to establish the conversational conventions of turn-taking and to supply meaningful oral input. Greenfield also distinguishes between this support dimension of scaffolding and the behaviorist method of "shaping":

> Shaping involves a series of successive approximations to the ultimate task goal. While the learner is successful at every point in the process, he or she starts with a simplified version of the ultimate task. Scaffolding, in contrast, does not involve simplifying the task during the period of learning. Instead, it holds the task constant, while simplifying the learner's role through the graduated intervention of the teacher. (1984:119)

Greenfield also suggests that elements of shaping do appear in scaffolding tasks but that modifications of learner role rather than task simplification predominate.

Another way that scaffolds support students' language constructions is in supplying emotional support for language building activities. Whether you are repeating, correcting, or introducing new language, it's important for your dialogues to take place in a clearly positive social atmosphere in which you express genuine interest in what your students are trying to communicate, as well as genuine responses to their contributions; in which you demonstrate your confidence and faith in students' abilities to extend their language capacities; and in which you ensure the smoothness of the conversation by "repairing" any potentially embarrassing breakdowns that occur. For example, throughout the chopping dialogue the visiting teacher not only accepted Bakir's verbal and nonverbal efforts to communicate, but delighted in them and incorporated them directly into his responses. ("You sure do! You do have carrots. Wow!" and "You got *that* right! You're chopping those big carrots into little carrots." and "You *are* a carrot? OK, then I'll chop you!") This teacher also helped Bakir maintain his dignity after the student was asked an obvious (but linguistically and interactionally helpful) question, by acting as if it was his own dimwittedness that prompted the question. ("Oh yeah, I see. You're *chopping* those carrots. I should have known.") The support strategy of accepting and using students' language to provide them with new language is apparent throughout the excerpts of Molly's teaching as well.

Scaffolds can also support students' language constructions linguistically when you adapt your language to fit their current language capacities and needs. As Greenfield's description suggests, without the support that scaffolding provides, there would be no way for a carpenter (the student) even to begin to extend the building (the student's language capacities) upward. However, just as we do not expect carpenters to create the eighth floor of a building before they have built the seven floors beneath it, so too should we not ask our second language students to practice or to produce linguistic forms and discourse that are far beyond their current capacities. In other words, students can't "skip floors." This is true for all second language students, including older students whom we often ask to skip floors so that they can close up the space between where they are and where their native English-speaking age-mates are in their English language and literacy development.

On the other hand, we must not underestimate our students' language levels or only make demands of them that are considerably below their current capacities. If we do so, we will deprive them of the opportunities they need to perform their third operation within the scaffolding process, that of extending their language capacities. In adapting your language to create a scaffold for your second language students, aim for what Vygotsky (1978) calls the "zone of proximal development," or "the distance between the actual developmental level as determined by independent problem solving and the level of potential development as determined through problem solving under adult guidance or in collaboration with more capable peers" (1978:86). When you adapt your language to create a scaffold at this level of your students' development, not only will they be able to extend their language use in new directions, but they will eventually be able to incorporate it into their own language capacities. When this happens, they will no longer need the scaffold that you have provided.

In the chopping excerpt, the visiting teacher makes constant efforts to "drop" his discourse to Bakir's level by repeating, rephrasing, providing extra meaning (e.g., gesturing, using the carrots and the knife and Bakir himself as he pretends), and using a number of other real input strategies. Specifically, the visiting teacher adapts his speech to Bakir's level when he adapts his original output request ("What are you guys making?") to encompass Bakir's response ("We . . . kah-rotes") within his subsequent output request ("What are you doing with those carrots?"). Later, the teacher also adapts his speech to Bakir's level by embedding vocabulary that is new to Bakir ("cook") in language and meanings that he and Bakir share (T: "You're quite a cook!" Bakir: "Cook?" T: "Yes, you know, uh, someone who makes the food. Like Mrs. Sprague at lunch. *She* chops! She chops too! She's the cook!") The intimate and collaborative nature of this informal small group setting allows the visiting teacher to use all the full group input strategies to maximum effect and to tailor their use specifically to Bakir's language needs. Throughout the dialogue and Bakir's contributions within it, Bakir also aptly demonstrates the student's role in collaborating with the teacher to take advantage of these adaptations as he carefully focuses on what is being said and how it is being said. Throughout the excerpt, Bakir works as hard to process the teacher's input and to fulfill his share of the conversational responsibilities and keep it going as the visiting teacher does to provide the real input and the scaffold that Bakir needs! Bakir's successful use of pantomime and speech to make a nonverbal joke ("I a kah-rote!") to take his turn in the dialogue and to sustain the interaction is an excellent example of this continual focusing and refocusing activity.

As you use your scaffold to support your second language students' language construction at their present levels, you also then provide them with new discourse (including vocabulary, syntax, pronunciation, and functions) which they can use to build their own language capacities. As Greenfeld points out, it is here that the analogy between learning and the scaffold "breaks down" (1984:125). Scaffolds do not provide carpenters with the actual bricks and mortar that eventually make up the product of their labors, and do not supply them with the tools they use to put these materials in place. As the teacher, on the other hand, you not only supply the scaffold upon which the student works, but also the raw materials and tools which they use to build their new language capacities. In the cooking excerpt, the teacher provides materials and tools to Bakir, supplying this beginning second language student with new vocabulary when it is needed (Bakir: "We, uh-h . . . [he makes chopping motions with the knife] . . . Kah-rotes." T: Oh yeah, I see. You're *chopping* those carrots"); providing new syntax and discourse elaborations (Bakir: "Big kah-rotes . . . [he makes chopping motions] . . . little kah-rotes. Fine!" T: "You got *that* right! You're chopping those big carrots into little carrots"), and providing numerous models of the correct pronunciation of the dialogue's major topic ("carrots").

The numerous examples of the visiting teacher's provision of real input to Bakir also illustrate four key characteristics of provisions as part of the scaffolding of real dialogues: (1) they are connected to the students' own language and language capacities; (2) they are provided to the student at those times during the dialogue when they have the potential for being maximally attended to, understood, and used; (3) they are all meaningful; and (4) they are all useful to the students on the scaffold. With regard to the meaningfulness of your discourse, however, it should also be noted that your utterances do not all have to make a direct contribution to the communication being negotiated within the dialogue, but can instead serve primarily teaching functions. For example, many of the visiting teacher's repetitions ("You're quite a chopper! You're quite a chopper, all right!") were probably not needed to engender successful communication or even to sustain the dialogue, but rather were uttered in order to promote Bakir's second language learning. The key is that they successfully performed this teaching function *because* they exhibited all of the scaffolding characteristics we've mentioned.

While it is your duty to work with your dialogue partner(s) to provide them with the materials and tools they need in order to build their language capacities, it is their job to practice and use these materials and tools in order to get on with the building. Bakir lives up to his using/practicing duties through-out the dialogue, struggling to comprehend the materials and tools, or input, that he is receiving (T: "You've got some *big* carrots. And you're chopping them." Bakir: "Yes. [He pauses to think. His grin slowly widens.] Big kah-rotes . . . [he makes chopping motions] . . . little kah-rotes! Fine!"), and making original and creative use of those materials and tools (e.g., moving from "I no kah-rote" to "I a kah-rote" to "I a cook"). Different students participate differently within the real dialogue setting, and these differences should be taken into account when you create the scaffolding for their language use and development. However, if the students do not become engaged in the dialogue, that is, if they do not genuinely attempt to use the language that is being offered and to take their turns within the dialogue, there is very little likelihood that language learning will occur. Thus, the importance of applying the instructional criteria of purpose and student interest within the integrated classroom is once again made apparent.

Finally, if your scaffolding has performed its function successfully, your students will incorporate the new language into their present language capaci-ties and will no longer require the scaffolding you have provided in order to use these extensions. At this point, it is your job to withdraw the scaffolding so that students can use their new capacities independently and creatively, and then to seek out new opportunities for raising scaffolds to the new language capacities and needs that your students display! Unlike buildings, which have a finite number of floors and windows, the language-learning potential in your second language students is infinite. The challenge is to enable your students to continue to reach new heights!

As you can see, the strategies we have been discussing are not rigid formulas with strict requirements for application. They are fluid and dynamic methods for "tuning in" to students and collaborating with them to develop their oral language abilities. While all real dialogues exhibit the overall operations and strategies described here, each one is also unique! This is

This teacher engages in real dialogues with her students during a cooking activity.

because of the uniqueness of the human beings who fill our classrooms and the unlimited meaning-making capacities that they bring to those classrooms.

Dialogues supply you with the tools and settings not only for effective language instruction, but also for effective instruction in general—for collaborating with students to develop their full creative and reasoning capacities (thought discourse), their memory capacities (fact discourse), and their communication capacities (share discourse). As Parker (1983) eloquently attests:

> If pupils have regular opportunities to engage in the kinds of dialogue, the "give and take of reciprocal discussions" (Barnes, 1976, 1977) which encourage and support higher order uses of consciousness, then the operations involved in these interactions may be reconstructed internally as permanent processes. When the opportunities for dialogue are sharply limited by the structure and content of classroom uses of language, then it would seem the growth of mind is sharply curtailed. (1983:153)

Creating real input and real dialogues for second language students will not only facilitate the development of their English, it will facilitate the development of their minds! The use of all the strategies discussed in this chapter will enable you not only to address the educational goal of literacy for these students, but also to address the educational goal of empowering them—of giving them control over their own meaning-making powers and their own destinies.

The following lists summarize the strategies you can use to provide oral discourse across all of your integrated learning activities:

HOW TO TURN YOUR ORAL DISCOURSE INTO REAL INPUT

1. *Make it understandable.*
2. *Make it relevant.*
3. *Make it useful.*

HOW TO PROVIDE REAL INPUT TO STUDENTS

1. *Adapt your teacher talk:*
   a. *Nonverbal adaptations (gestures, bodily motions, facial expressions).*
   b. *Paraverbal adaptations (vocalizations, volume/intonation, manner of delivery).*
   c. *Discourse adaptations (repeating, rephrasing, recycling, framing).*
   d. *Contextual adaptations (visual aids, realia).*
2. *Adapt your interactional talk:*
   a. *To get student output (vary participant structures, vary elicitations, vary output requests).*
   b. *To respond to students' output (use confirmation checks and clarification requests, use student rephrasings and expansions, give extra chances, correct by focusing on the message).*

HOW TO ENGAGE IN REAL DIALOGUES

Use all of your real input strategies to:
1. *Invite students to converse (or respond to their initiations).*
2. *Supply the grounding for the dialogue (context, orientation, intersubjectivity, mutual focus).*
3. *Furnish the scaffolding for your students' construction of new language:*
   a. *Support their language use (interactionally, emotionally, linguistically).*
   b. *Adapt your language to their abilities and needs.*
   c. *Provide the new language that the students need and can use at the appropriate time.*

5.6 CONCLUSION

In this chapter, we have described several strategies for providing oral discourse within the integrated classroom and curriculum. Next, let's look at some ways in which you can think language and apply the criteria of the ILT model to provide meaningful written discourse to your second language students and make connections between oral and written discourse in your classroom.

ACTIVITIES AND DISCUSSION

1. Review two recent lessons you conducted or observed, one primarily concerned with teaching language and one primarily concerned with some other topic or content. Describe the management, content, and oral language dimensions of each lesson. Assess how fully you or the instructor took advantage of the oral discourse teaching potential of the activity and come up with a few ways that the activity could have been altered to maximize this potential.

2. Review your planning book or lesson plans for a few days. For each major activity, plan at least one strategy for increasing the oral discourse teaching potential of the activity. Then, monitor your performance during one or two of these activities to see if the strategies worked.

3. If you can, videotape yourself or a colleague during one or two lessons. If possible, again try to observe and record one language-centered activity and one activity centering on another topic. (It would be interesting to tape one large group and one small group activity or activities with very different participant structures). Review the videotapes a few times for instances of the teacher talk and interactional talk adaptations described in this chapter (see Figures 5.1 and 5.2). Assess whether or not these adaptations are contributing to the comprehensibility, relevance and usefulness of the teacher's oral language.

4. Using the tapes you recorded for no. 3 above, observe the kinds of elicitations used by the instructor and the number of each kind of elicitation (see Figure 5.2). Were the elicitations successful? What kinds of oral discourse did they engender? Also review the tapes and tally the number of times that each student participating in the activity spoke. Are there any patterns? If so, can you explain what the instructor did or did not do to create these patterns?

5. Audiotape or videotape yourself or a colleague during one or more real dialogues. (It would be interesting to tape at least one real dialogue with a beginning or mid-second language student and one with a full-second-language or native English-speaking student.) Review the

tape(s) several times to find instances of the various strategies employed during real dialogues (see Figure 5.3). Remember that you will need to observe for *two* sets of strategies since both partners in real dialogues have responsibilities and strategies for meeting them within the dialogues.

6. Monitor your class or a chosen class for a few days to determine the topics and materials students use the most frequently for initiating real dialogues with the teacher. Use one of these topics to plan and then conduct a real dialogue with a second language student and one with a native English-speaking student. Make sure that the linguistic and cognitive scaffolds you have in mind for the dialogues are at the appropriate levels for the students who will be participating in them. Also keep in mind that you may have to plan (and try to conduct) more than one dialogue for each student since you cannot *force* them to accept your dialogue invitation.

FURTHER READING

Cherry-Wilkinson, L. (Ed.) 1982. *Communicating in the classroom.* New York: Academic Press. This collection of papers provides an excellent overview of the many ways of viewing and analyzing classroom communication. The essays by Dickson ("Creating Communication-Rich Classrooms") and Wong-Fillmore ("Instructional Language as Linguistic Input") are particularly useful in thinking about providing real oral discourse.

Enright, D. S. 1986. "Use everything you have to teach English": Providing useful input to young language learners. In P. Rigg and D. S. Enright (Eds.) *Children and ESL: Integrating perspectives* (pp. 115-62). Washington, D. C.: Teachers of English to Speakers of Other Languages. This article describes Molly's transitions from teaching in an all native English-speaking grade level classroom to teaching in a mixed (native English speakers and beginning, mid, and full second language speakers) summer school classroom, including her input adaptations.

Gass, S. M. and Madden, C. G. (Eds.) 1985. *Input in second language acquisition.* Rowley, MA: Newbury House Publishers. The papers in this volume discuss many of the major issues in second language input research.

Genishi, C., and Dyson, A. H. 1984. *Language assessment in the early years.* Norwood, NJ: Ablex Publishing Corporation. A careful look at young children's oral language development and ways of supporting and assessing it. The book is filled with wonderful examples of children's talk and writing.

Greenfield, P. M. 1984. A theory of the teacher in the learning activities of everyday life. In B. Rogoff and J. Lave (Eds.) *Everyday cognition: Its development in social context* (pp. 117-38). Cambridge, MA: Harvard University Press. A clear description of the scaffolding process derived from observing Los Angeles parents teaching language to their children and Zinacanteco (Mexico) mothers teaching weaving to their children.

Heath, S. B. 1985. Literacy or literate skills? Considerations for ESL/EFL Learners. In P. Larson, E. L. Judd and D. S. Messerschmitt (Eds.) *On TESOL '84: A brave new world for TESOL* (pp. 15-28). Washington, D. C.: Teachers of English to Speakers of Other Languages. Writing as both a researcher and a teacher, Heath details various students' tying in and tying back of their new literacy experiences in school.

Jaggar, A., and Smith-Burke, M. T. (Eds.) 1985. *Observing the language learner.* Newark, DE: International Reading Association. Appealing and sensible recommendations for observing children's oral and written language development which can be put to work immediately in first and second language classroom settings.

Krashen, S. D. 1982. *Principles and practices in second language acquisition.* Oxford: Pergamon Press. Krashen's five hypotheses about second language acquisition and their implications for practice in the second language classroom.

Tough, J. 1985. *Talk two: Children using English as a second language in primary schools.* London: Onyx Press. (U. S. Distributor: Heinemann Educational Books, Portsmouth, NH). This noted first language development educator applies many of her theories to working with children developing language number two. Many practical teaching suggestions and actual samples of conversation are in the book. It also has an appendix of pictures and instructions for surveying children's oral English use.

Wells, G. 1986. *The meaning makers: Children learning language and using language to learn.* Portsmouth, NH: Heinemann Educational Books. A comprehensive description of children's language and literacy development from infancy through elementary school, based on the author's fifteen year longitudinal study. While in many ways the book is a research report, in other ways it is a blueprint for thinking about and supporting students' language and literacy development at home and at school.

Chapter 6

Providing Real Written Discourse

Too Many Names

Mondays are meshed with Tuesdays
and the week with the whole year.
Time cannot be cut
with your exhausted scissors,
and all the names of the day
are washed out by the waters of night.

No one can claim the name of Pedro,
nobody is Rosa or Maria,
all of us are dust or sand,
all of us are rain under rain.
They have spoken to me of Venezuelas,
of Chiles and Paraguays;
I have no idea what they are saying.
I know only the skin of the earth
and I know it has no name.

When I lived amongst the roots
they pleased me more than flowers did,
and when I spoke to a stone
it rang like a bell.

It is so long, the spring
which goes on all winter.
Time lost its shoes.
A year lasts four centuries.

When I sleep every night,
What am I called or not called?
And when I wake, who am I
if I was not I while I slept?

This means to say that scarcely
have we landed into life
than we come as if new-born;
let us not fill our mouths
with so many faltering names,
with so many sad formalities,
with so many pompous letters,
with so much of yours and mine,
with so much signing of papers.

I have a mind to confuse things,
unite them, make them new-born,
mix them up, undress them,
until all light in the world
has the oneness of the ocean,
a generous, vast wholeness,
a crackling, living fragrance.

–Pablo Neruda (Alastair Reid, Translator)

6.1 INTRODUCTION

One of the most potent methods that you can use to meet the educational goal of empowering second language students is to provide opportunities in class for them to use the written word to accomplish their purposes and to construct and share their personal meanings. You can address this goal in your own classroom by using the assumptions and criteria of the ILT model to provide your students with real written discourse. In this chapter we will suggest several strategies for doing this. Of course, in integrated classrooms, the two resources of real oral discourse and real written discourse are always provided together and are used to support one another. Written discourse in integrated classrooms is introduced as another way for students to accomplish their meaning-making goals, and therefore speech and print are constantly used (and taught) together.

6.2 "ACADEMIC" VERSUS "SURVIVAL" ENGLISH?

In recent years, considerable attention has been focused within the second language education field on the overall gains that the students in our programs have made and have failed to make. A prevalent view is that most of our students today are managing to become fairly proficient in "survival English," or the oral communication skills that they need in order to negotiate the demands of daily life in their new culture. While this gain is surely to be celebrated (so goes this view), the problem is that our students are not managing to become proficient in "academic English," or the language and skills needed to negotiate the demands of the classroom and the highly formal, "abstract," and "decontextualized" knowledge that is found there. The solution that has been most often proposed to solve this problem, of course, has been to directly teach (i.e., transmit in the form of isolated facts and skills) these "higher" forms of language skills to our students in order to bolster their achievement.

There are two implicit notions within this view which we are quite willing to accept. The first of these is that many of our students today are still not "making it" in school—their achievement levels are not rising and their dropout rates are not falling in the way that we would all like them to. The second tacit notion is that our second language students are also still not being granted full access to the cognitive and linguistic (and for that matter, economic and political) resources that many of us and many of their peers have secured. However, beyond these notions, we find much that is troublesome in this view and in the instructional applications that have emanated from it.

We doubt that the reason many of our students are succeeding in acquiring survival English is that we are successfully teaching it or transmitting it to them in the classroom. Rather, we suspect that the students are for the most part *teaching themselves* the language that they need to get along in the real world. They are doing this, we think, by taking advantage of the "English everywhere" present in their new culture, using the strategies detailed by the recent second language acquisition research. Peers, neighbors, bus drivers, and the language of the streets play a greater role in the successful learning of everyday, conversational English than the transmission-oriented bilingual and ESL and other language-oriented instructional programs that have been typically provided for these students. The real (if limited) language gain that many of our second language students are making is occurring, we maintain, more in spite of our instructional efforts than because of them.

Unfortunately for our intrepid second language students, while the street may be a great classroom for "picking up" or "acquiring" (Krashen 1981) survival English, it is not nearly as good a place for picking up certain formal uses of oral discourse within the new culture, such as making speeches or moderating discussions. It also isn't such a good place for picking up certain formal uses of written discourse which are much more prevalent at school and in specific segments of the workplace, such as locating, extracting and synthesizing themes from a number of differently organized print sources or writing compositions for a specific audience according to a complex set of conventions. Thus we suspect that the full explanation for why our second language students are not performing well with respect to these activities is that they are not getting the appropriate opportunities to use and learn them either in the classroom or anywhere else in the real world of their daily experience (Heath 1985; Heath and Branscombe 1985).

If these explanations are indeed accurate, what is the path to reform? Adding these formal, "academic" uses of discourse to the subject-matter skills and habits that we plan to transmit in our classrooms is *not* the answer. Neither, we believe, is the answer to step up efforts that are already under way to transmit this knowledge by providing even more lessons, drill, practice, and "remediation" in our second language programs. Adjusting or adding to meaningless skills, facts, and competencies won't solve the problem. The answer is to change the entire process of instruction. We must turn it upside down to organize language and literacy activities that are by, of, and for meaning-making, and we must turn it inside out to organize activities that are of, by, and for our students. Only in this way will we address the considerable deficiencies that we and our programs (not our students and their families) face. Then, only by additionally ensuring that this new student- and meaning-centered program encompasses the full range of meaningful uses of oral and written discourse will we be able to effectively include "academic English" within our programmatic offerings. As Greene (1986) explains in her essay entitled "Expanding the Range of Literacy," our educational goals of literacy and empowerment can be realized if we construct real dialogues between students, texts, and ourselves and if "the young have opportunities to rewrite what they read, to create their own knowledge, to pose their own questions, to reach towards what is not yet" (1986:241). We long to offer our students the chance to write poetry in addition to writing business letters; to become the next generation of Shel Silversteins and Judith Viorsts and Pablo Nerudas, in addition to becoming the next generation of the labor force. We believe we are more likely to realize this longing by giving students chances to read Silverstein and Viorst and Neruda and to write their own poetry rather than by lecturing and drilling and then testing them on subject matter such as famous poems and their rhythmic conventions.

This group of students is involved in a real writing activity: conducting a "pollution hunt" around the school grounds to collect and record trash samples and then to write up and report their findings.

6.3 PROVIDING REAL WRITTEN DISCOURSE

With the above conception of second language literacy and literacy development in mind, let's look in more depth now at how written discourse is likely to be provided. In transmission classrooms, written discourse and the processes of reading and writing are presented and taught in much the same manner as the rest of the subject-matter curriculum (including oral English): they are organized into discrete and isolated skills and competencies and are taught as content all by themselves. Written discourse—like oral discourse—is studied *about* rather than genuinely *used* to accomplish the purposes it was designed for. Students in transmission classrooms are generally required to read for the sake of practicing reading and to write for the sake of practicing writing. Is it any wonder that, stripped of the opportunity to use print for real purposes, many students in these classrooms complain that they "don't know what to write" and that reading is "boring" to them? Reading and writing are not *inherently* meaningless and useless activities, they are extremely useful ones—except in many classrooms, where they are made explicitly meaningless and useless and where often their authentic use is explicitly prohibited! In many of the classrooms we visit, the only authentic, real uses of written discourse we witness are students stealing peeks at comic books and novels they have hidden inside their desk tops and furtively "passing notes" underneath their desks to friends around the class! In transmission classrooms where real reading and writing is illegal, these processes are made into instructional ends to be reached through repeated drill and practice. The fact that this often turns them into dead ends for students seems to matter little.

In contrast, in integrated classrooms, written discourse and the processes of reading and writing are presented and taught as useful, important, and exciting new means for reaching a diversity of student meaning-making ends—for exploring, sharing, enjoying, and thinking about the world. Students in integrated classrooms read and write to have pleasure (fun discourse); to communicate with other people (share discourse); to get and give information (fact discourse); and to imagine and reflect (thought discourse). All of these real uses of print are also often embedded within thematic, integrated curriculum units and real learning activities that make use of all four language processes.

6.4 THE SPEECH-PRINT CONNECTION

One of the key theoretical assumptions of the ILT model is that all students use their previous experiences with oral and written language to construct new meanings and to develop their oral and written language capacities. This principle holds for both native English-speaking students developing literacy in English (e.g. Doake 1979; Teale and Sulzby 1986) and second language students developing literacy in English as a second or additional language (e.g., Au and Jordan 1981; Cummins 1981, 1984; Hudelson 1984, 1986; Edelsky 1986; Rigg 1986; Jones and Tetroe 1987). For second language learners, the strategy of using previous experiences manifests itself in two ways. The first way, the "tie back" strategy, is when learners use their previous experiences with their native language to develop their English language and literacy capacities. The second way, the "tie in" strategy, is when learners use their experiences in one of the four language processes of listening, speaking, reading and writing in English to help them develop their experiences and capacities with the others.

Teachers in integrated language classrooms reject the myth (which many of us language teachers were taught) that in order to become proficient or competent in a "foreign" language, one must master listening before speaking, speaking before reading, and reading before writing. As with all myths, there are some grains of truth in this one. For example, it is indeed impossible to speak a new language before you've even heard a word of it or to write it before you've seen it in print, and when teachers ask their newly arrived, beginning second language students to read a basal selection or to complete a phonics ditto before they've had a chance to hear and to speak some English, they are making meaningless and more or less impossible requests. However, teachers in integrated classrooms realize that their second language students' use of *"all of their available resources"* to develop their English language and literacy capacities (theoretical assumption no. 5) includes using all of the various discourse resources that are available to them—oral and written alike—as long as these resources help the students to make and share meanings (i.e., as long as they are *real* resources). To illustrate, if a beginning second language high school student has just arrived in an English class in which all the concepts being discussed are written as a list on the blackboard and are frequently referred to by the teacher, what will she do? Will she turn her head away from the blackboard or disregard the references to it just because it involves reading and she is not ready to read? No. She will use the print that is available for meaning-making along with whatever other resources that are available to her to try to figure out what is being discussed and to participate in that discussion. Included in these resources will be her previous experience with settings such as this one, her knowledge of the subject, her first language literacy capacities, and the actions of the students around her. Teachers using the integrated model operate under the assumption that their students, like this one, will use anything they can to make and share personal meanings that are important to them.

As the previous discussion of survival English and academic English indicated, many second language students bring with them oral language experiences and abilities in both English and in their first language which—like the oral experiences and abilities of their native English-speaking peers—can be productively used as the vehicle for integrating written discourse uses into their meaning-making repertoires. Cook-Gumperz and Gumperz (1981) summarize this in reviewing first language speakers' "transitions to literacy":

> Children need experiences in school that favor the learning of written culture through the *medium of the oral culture,* thus building on the interpretative skills and linguistic understandings that children bring to the school experience, as a basis for further learning. . . . In fact, children need a saturation experience of orally transformed "written prose" in as many culturally "neutral" ways as possible (such as through the teaching of science) in order to transform, for themselves, the *rhythms* of spoken language into the written modes. (1981:107-108)

The linkage between the oral language and cultural knowledge resources that students bring to the classroom, on the one hand, and the new "written culture" that is made available to them in the classroom, on the other hand, is what we are calling the speech-print connection. Providing the kinds of speech-print connections that Cook-Gumperz and Gumperz call for within meaningful and interesting learning activities will permit your second language students to tie in their new experiences with written discourse to their existing oral language processes and tie back their new second language experiences to their previous experiences with speech and print.

Several strategies have been developed to facilitate students' construction of meaningful speech-print connections, both for first language and second language students. Among the strategies that can be productively utilized within the integrated curriculum are key vocabulary and word banks; the use of environmental and functional print; the language experience approach; story-telling and the use of home and personal oral narratives; and reading aloud and the use of "Shared book" experiences. Each of these strategies is briefly described in the sections that follow. Some additional resources for each of these strategies are listed at the end of this chapter, should you desire to explore them further.

Key Vocabulary and Word Banks

The "key vocabulary" strategy was first proposed by Ashton-Warner (1963) in her book describing her literacy instruction of Maori children in New Zealand. Key vocabularies are sets of words requested by students themselves which are then written on cards (or on some other material that can be saved by the student) and collected by each student. These collections of key vocabulary words are often referred to as word banks.

The key vocabulary strategy facilitates students' transition to literacy through their own personal experiences and language and through the start of what Ashton-Warner (1963) sees as an "unbroken" speech-print connection:

> Back to these first words. To these first books. They must be made out of the stuff of the child itself. I reach a hand into the mind of the child, bring out a handful of the stuff I find there, and use that as our first working material. Whether it is good or bad stuff, violent or placid stuff, coloured or dun. To effect an unbroken beginning. And in this dynamic material, within the familiarity and security of it, the Maori finds that words have intense meaning to him, from which cannot help but arise a love of reading. For it's here, right in this first word, that the love of reading is born, and the longer his reading is organic the stronger it becomes, until by the time he arrives at the books of the new culture, he receives them as another joy rather than as a labour. I know all this because I've done it. (1963:64)

Since Ashton-Warner's report of how she used the strategy appeared in print, it has been developed further for use in a variety of teaching programs. Following are four basic steps for using the key vocabulary strategy which are based on those proposed by Veatch, Sawicki, Elliott, Barnette, and Blakey (1973).

   1. *Elicit the key word.* Key words should come out of students' experiences and should be words that they themselves want to read and preserve.

At first, the words can be deliberately elicited by setting aside specific times during the day to ask students to choose words or by following up on especially exciting classroom activities with a "key word time," but after a while their use becomes an ongoing part of the literacy activities in the classroom, and students often spontaneously ask for key words as they talk with peers or as they write.

2. *Write the word.* Write the word for the student and let the student watch you write it.

3. *Have students use the word.* This can include having students trace the word; copy it; draw an illustration of it; put it into a story; share and learn peers' words; classify words (by initial letter, sound, function, etc.); act out words; and make up new stories with the words.

4. *Store the word.* Students can collect their words and use them over and over again as they build their personal second language print vocabulary. We have seen word banks made out of key rings and flash cards or tagboard cards with punched holes. We have also seen older students take file boxes or small spiral notebooks, divide them into alphabetical sections, and use them as "personal dictionary" word banks. You can create large group, class word banks by displaying a "path" of favorite or most requested key words winding around the room, on mobiles, or in a class word-bank book stored near Webster's "word bank book"! You can also develop a key vocabulary or word bank for each new integrated unit that you introduce in class to support students' retention of the new concepts and language in the unit and to support their reading and writing within the unit. After students collect a sufficient number of key words, the words can occasionally be reviewed and used to replace required school spelling lists and to inspire new reading and writing activities.

Environmental and Functional Print

This strategy involves deliberately taking advantage of your classroom environment and the "English everywhere" in the school and in the surrounding community. *Environmental print* includes all of the print that naturally exists in the "real world" surrounding the classroom. Examples of environmental print in the school might include signs on doors (e.g., Office, Teachers' Lounge, Custodian); posted bulletins, announcements, advertisements, schedules, and menus for the week; labels on equipment and materials; and even words on clothing (e.g., "Have a Nice Day" T-shirts and "Kiss Me, I'm Irish" buttons). Examples of environmental print in the community might include street signs and traffic signs; vehicle print (e.g., license plates, model and company names such as Mustang, Cadillac, Suzuki; company titles and advertisements such as

"Redi-Freddy's Rapid Delivery Service" or "Backgammon's Pizza—We Deliver!"); signs on buildings and fences; print on federal mailboxes (e.g., delivery times); trash (e.g., discarded fast-food cups and bags, newspapers, cans, plastic wrappers, and containers); and even print on trees and lampposts (e.g., "Vote for Leland Culpepper," "Garage Sale Saturday at 2438 Saltshaker Drive").

Functional print is the real world print that has been produced for a specific, concrete purpose and that generally accompanies a specific material or specific context—for example, labels and directions on packages, boxes, and containers; ads; posters; phonograph album covers; TV, cable, and radio guides; bus schedules; job applications; contest and order forms; and programs for sports and entertainment events. Students have many examples of these and other forms of functional print in their own homes (quite often in both their first language *and* in English!), and they may or may not be aware of or using this print. Functional print also includes the print (and the suggestions for using it) that you yourself embed within your classroom spaces, materials, routines, and learning activities in order to add a written discourse dimension to students' *real* learning experiences, such as the job chart and schedule chart figures in Chapter 4.

The strategy for using environmental and functional print calls for you to do three things: (a) to be aware of the naturally occurring real print that is already available in the environment; (b) to use this print to add a functional and environmental print dimension to your learning activities (whether or not they are literacy development activities); and (c) to focus students' attention on this print and facilitate their real use of it within your activities to develop their written discourse capacities.

One way of applying this strategy in your classroom is to organize activities in which real environmental and functional print are themselves the main focus—the "English search" described in Chapter 5 is an example of this. Another example would be taking the class on a tour of the school at the beginning of the year to read all of the print there and later repeating the tour in order to incorporate new students into the classroom community (see Chapter 7). Still another example would be having the class take turns reading the class job chart and schedule chart at the beginning of each day or week.

The most important way to apply this strategy, though, is to arrange opportunities for second language students to use environmental and functional print within your integrated units and learning activities as well as to take advantage of any naturally occurring opportunities to use this print that arise. For example, during a cooking activity, when students read and follow the directions on a cake mix package to make a cake, they are using functional print along with real oral discourse to make real speech-print connections. Other applications of this strategy include using copies of menus from students' favorite restaurants to plan a banquet menu; using newspaper ads and television commercials to plan a budget for furnishing a "dream apartment";

using toys, empty cans and containers, and other items that students bring in from home to create a classroom grocery store; and using real road maps, travel guides, and brochures to plan a fictional "Walk Across America." Making deliberate use of real print in these ways will alert students to the power of print and the potential usefulness of literacy in their lives and will increase the likelihood of their "taking in" written discourse of this kind outside the classroom.

You can also take advantage of spontaneous occurrences of environmental and functional print in order to make speech-print connections. Suppose a group of fire fighters with a fire truck were to visit your school and some of the students noticed the print on their helmets and uniforms and on the truck. You could draw everyone's attention to this "surprise" print and ask the students (and the fire fighters) to tell you what it said and what it meant. This print could then be used in follow-up activities, after the visit had ended. To further illustrate, let's suppose you were trying out Activity A-3 of the Superheroes unit in Part II (Tallying Cartoon Heroes' Speech and Characteristics). Suppose the students were watching cartoons with captions or with lots of print (e.g., a Las Vegas street scene!). You could read this print with the students and have them use it throughout the unit. Similarly, a student's matchbook collection brought to school for "sharing time" could inspire sorting and classifying exercises, matchbook hunts in businesses and shops around the area; original matchbook designs; and discussion and analysis of matchbook slogans and advertising designs. An action as simple as labeling the different people, places, and objects in a class mural for subsequent reference while it is being displayed on the wall provides speech-print connections for second language students! Several other examples of using environmental and functional print to inspire real speech-print connections and real reading and writing can be found in Chapter 4 (e.g., the suggestion box, the *Ranger Rick* display) and throughout Part II of this book.

The Language Experience Approach

This approach is perhaps most familiar to early childhood and primary school teachers, since it has long been used with first language speakers to make meaningful speech-print connections and to introduce these students to written discourse and its conventions (e.g., K. Goodman 1971). The approach has been successfully adapted for use with second language students (e.g., Rigg 1981; Feeley 1979) and with students of all ages (e.g., Hall 1970; Dixon and Nessel, 1983).

The essence of the language experience approach lies in directly transcribing students' own speech onto the page and subsequently using it for reading activities and (eventually) to inspire writing. This strategy can be used in both the full group and in the small group or dyadic situation. *Real dialogues* about any topic would be an excellent source of language experience stories and narratives; for example, the Bakir/carrot excerpt could be turned into a wonderful carrot-chopping report using this strategy! The following paragraphs describe four basic steps for implementing the strategy with second language learners.

1. *Share and discuss an experience.* This is the warm-up phase of the activity, in which the students share and discuss an experience with you. The experience can be anything of interest to the students (criterion no. 3), such as something they did with their family or friends, a movie they saw, or a book they have been reading or that you have been reading with them. Rigg (1977) describes how wordless picture books can be used to create a rich, complex, and enjoyable shared experience as students discuss it and "read" it with you. Cartoon strips with the dialogue removed and "silent" or "wordless" films are also good candidates for this step—the antics of Charlie Chaplin or the Road Runner can be used with high school students to elicit the same rich dictation that a wordless picture book like *Pancakes for Breakfast* (DePaola 1978) elicits from younger students!

2. *Ask students to dictate a story or report based on the previous shared experience and discussion.* Write down what is said for everyone to see as it is dictated, in a clearly visible way such as on an overhead transparency, on the blackboard, or chart paper. Write down students' exact words without rephrasing or correcting them, and periodically read back what you have transcribed to make sure that you're "getting it right" and to help the students begin to associate their speech with the text that you are creating (the speech-print connection!). In taking dictation in the full group setting, use your real input strategies (see Chapter 5) to get contributions from as many members of the group as possible.

3. *Read and reread the finished story with students.* Once the dictation of the experience story or report has been completed, read the entire piece with students again a few times. Encourage the students to edit the piece further and to make any improvements that they would like to make. Also encourage them to read the piece out loud with you. Students may read the story (or parts of it) individually or chorally. Once a final version has been agreed upon, it should be copied to be used in subsequent reading events.

4. *Use and reuse students' dictated writings.* The product of steps 1 through 3 is a continually expanding set of real reading materials that can be used with or in place of basal reading materials to provide students with integrated second language activities; to familiarize them with print conventions and the uses of print; and to give them needed practice in reading aloud and reading for comprehension (see Van Allen 1976; Van Allen and Allen 1976; Hall 1970; Dixon and Nessel 1983). Individual

students can collect and read their own language experience stories or can read and share one another's stories. Language experience stories can be dictated to accompany the display of artwork or a valuable possession (e.g., a rock). Conversely, illustrations can be added to a language experience story to be published as a book or displayed on the wall. Full group language experience stories can also be illustrated and displayed. Class language experience reports can be turned into letters to go home and into class archives (see Chapter 7).

When students have begun to recognize and copy English words and have begun to try to write words of their own, language experience stories can also be used to make this speech-print connection. One teacher we know files away most of her "letter forming" and "cursive writing" drill sheets and instead has beginning writers copy their own transcribed stories onto a page for letter formation practice. Another teacher we know has her students dictate a short three-to-five sentence report or story to her. She then (within her transcription) draws blanks in the text where words appear which she knows the students know how to write or which they can find in the classroom environment or in their word banks and has them write in those words. Whether they are dictated reports about Spidey's visit to the class or dictated fantasies about what happened to Charlotte the spider's children after the end of *Charlotte's Web*, language experience stories are a productive way of providing real written discourse to second language students as single activities and within integrated units.

Even computer language and concepts can be introduced through making real speech-print connections, as illustrated by this "robot" being programmed to exercise by his classmates.

Storytelling and the Use of Oral Narratives

Another strategy that can be used to permit students to tie in and tie back new written discourse is the use of storytelling and oral narratives in the classroom. Researchers such as Bauman (1977, 1982) have documented the complex and culturally diverse folklore and folkways of children from around the world, along with the riddles, jokes, taunts, word games, jumprope rhymes, and other oral activities that they use within their juvenile subcultures. There is also strong evidence that children as young as four years old have begun to develop a sense of story (Applebee 1978; Sutton-Smith 1981) and that they use this device to entertain themselves and their peers and to organize and make sense of the world. Many of our second language students are familiar with and have often enjoyed the folktales and storytelling traditions of their own native countries and cultures.

Van Dongen (1987) explains the full potential of students' own home narratives and narrative thought when they are used in the classroom:

> In classrooms where there are many opportunities to engage in the narrative mode of thought, literacy and literature become an entity. For children encounter and use narratives in a variety of ways: (1) they tell and retell personal experiences, (2) they create stories in play and social experiences, (3) they read and listen to stories through literature, reading, and writing, and (4) they use and encounter narrative in texts where the narrative is used to explain an event, an idea, or some phenomena. (1987:80)

If Van Dongen is correct, then using home narratives at school would be a very useful way to make real speech-print connections and to facilitate second language students' literacy development. As with the language experience strategy, the products of storytelling and oral narratives will also provide a rich, and culturally relevant and appropriate set of real reading materials to be used over and over again in class (Baynham 1986).

Storytelling and oral narratives can be used in many different ways to promote language and social development for both first and second language students. We recommend the following steps for using them specifically to make speech-print connections.

1. *Collect stories and narratives.* When you first introduce storytelling and the use of oral narratives in class, you yourself should have some stories ready to tell. (Several resources for this are provided at the end of this chapter.) However, once students understand how this activity works, they can begin to bring in stories and personal oral narratives to tell in class themselves. Thus, you will be sharing this task with your students.

2. *Tell stories and narratives.* Besides actually telling stories to your students, you should be modeling storytelling so that students can begin to take over this role in the full group and with one another. As

students take in your stories and begin to give out their own narratives, they will learn new vocabulary and new grammatical structures. They also will further develop the literate, school-oriented "ways of telling" that Van Dongen describes and that will subsequently appear in their texts. They will do this using familiar and interesting materials from their own background. And they will have fun doing it!

Again, ideally this task will be shared by you and your students. Both you and they should choose stories that you enjoy telling and remember or know well. Barton (1986) maintains that the three essential components, or "building blocks," for "making a story your own" in order to tell it well are learning the plot (story structure), creating characters (character awareness), and adding details (style and patterns of language). You can use these building blocks in your own preparation for telling a story, and you can use them to help students organize, practice and tell their stories for maximum effect. Often there are professional or practiced storytellers nearby who can be invited to class to launch your use of this speech-print strategy. Community members and students' families are good sources of both stories and storytellers. (Remember the Grandparent's Day storytelling celebration?) If a student or family member is more comfortable telling the story in another language, you can either use a story translator during the story event or use that particular story and teller with a group of students from that language background. These students can then translate (orally or in written form, or both) and retell the story to the entire class.

3. *Add real input components.* You should make the language of your stories as comprehensible, relevant, and useful as possible for your class by using your voice, body, and discourse effectively and by adding a visual component to the story. In many cultures, storytelling includes a visual accompaniment. Two examples are making marks in the sand (e.g., the Walbiri of Australia, as reported by Munn, 1973, in Pellowski, 1984) and using "story knives" to carve in the snow (e.g., Eskimos, as reported by Tafoya 1983). Using the playground gravel or sand area for storytelling would be a great way to include markings like these in your storytelling. You can also use string stories, finger-play stories, and figurine stories to provide a visual component. Pellowski (1984) has collected stories that use all of these visual devices and has included directions for using them. Our favorite is a story that uses Russian nesting dolls—a set of successively smaller dolls, each doll "nested" within the next biggest one. You can also adapt your own stories to include these visual devices.

At an even more basic level, you can create sketch or picture stories to tell. During key points in the story, you add an element to the drawing (again, see Pellowski [1984] for examples). You can also use the felt board and simple felt pieces and figures to add a similar cumulative visual dimension and focus to your story. Many of the stories your students bring to class will also have a visual component. For example, we have had Japanese students tell folktales as they fold paper origami figures related to them. However, even if students don't use a visual focus for their stories initially, they soon will be able to include one if they can repeatedly watch you doing it.

4. *Review, discuss, retell.* Once a story has been related by you or by a student, review the event and the highlights of the story with students. Use the story to familiarize students with the building blocks mentioned above. Discuss the characters; ask students to predict what will happen next; let students retell their favorite parts of the story and relate stories and personal anecdotes similar to the ones just recounted. Students' favorite stories can be retold on the same occasion or at another time. Once students have become accustomed to this event, they will even dare to retell one another's stories for the group!

5. *On occasion, use the language experience approach to transcribe and preserve stories (and to collect stories in written form).* Stories that you tell and that students tell can also be transcribed and even illustrated and published. The language experience approach can be utilized for this, or students can "retell" their stories in print. One teacher we know has a "story of the month," with each gigantic, teacher-transcribed page of the story illustrated in mural-like fashion by the students. Another teacher develops a class folk-story collection each year (which she displays next to her *Grimm's Fairy Tales* and *Mother Goose*). The collection is comprised of students' own transcribed and illustrated oral narratives and folktales, compiled in a large spiral notebook. The teacher also uses this method to collect proverbs and riddles from her students' homes and native cultures.

6. *Bridge to formal print.* Use the written products from your storytelling activities as real reading materials for your students. These new "readers" can be reused each year, inspiring adaptations and new products. You can also use the storytelling event and these products to introduce commercially published legends, folktales, and fairy tales with equally familiar themes from around the world (see additional references at the end of the chapter). It's fun to collect all of the variations on a single folktale theme, too—the various versions of *Cinderella*, for example, or *Little Red Riding Hood*. These materials can be used to inspire students' own reading explorations and to read individually with them.

In like manner, students can begin to transcribe their own folktales and oral narratives, and can write down stories and narratives from their own neighborhoods and cultures and from around the school. A good illustration of just how successful and exciting this approach can be is the *Foxfire* project and magazine published by the students of the Rabun Gap-Nacoochee school in northern Georgia (Wigginton 1985). The teacher and students in this unique high school collect oral histories, poems, descriptions of customs, reports, anecdotes, folktales, and many other kinds of oral narratives from the people of northern Georgia using notes, tape recorders, and their own minds and memories. The printed articles and stories that result form a permanent record of a fragile and changing culture which might otherwise have been lost to future generations.

The six steps just outlined are not just for storytelling. They can be used to incorporate many of your students' home oral and written discourse resources directly into your classroom and curriculum. We've already mentioned a few of these—oral histories, proverbs, riddles, songs, insults (older students love collecting these!), jumprope rhymes, and poems. There are many others as well. Using home language and literacy materials in class to promote second language students' learning will be further discussed in the next two chapters.

Reading Aloud and the Use of Shared Book Experiences

A natural adjunct to storytelling in integrated classrooms is story reading, which continues the bridging between familiar oral discourse and new written discourse. The importance of "book talk" and of understanding the conventions of story reading and the story-reading event as a precursor to literacy has been made more apparent than ever before in recent years. Frequently reading aloud to students from books that have been selected with their backgrounds and needs in mind can provide students with new "ways of taking" from books (Heath 1982)—which in turn emanate from their own "ways of telling" oral narratives (Wolf 1985) that have been developed at home and through such school experiences as the storytelling event. Reading aloud often to second language students introduces them to the conventions, ritual, and language (e.g., "book talk") of school literacy events (Heath 1982; Hudelson 1984); provides them with lots of real oral language input; and offers them further real experiences with the structure, conventions, and components of different written genres. Just as important, reading aloud often is likely to result in children mirroring your enthusiasm for the second language and for reading and developing a permanently positive and warm attitude toward reading (Trelease 1982).

Here are a few things to consider in preparing and conducting your read-aloud sessions:

1. *Make the environment of these sessions an intimate, comfortable, and pleasant one.* Reading aloud in class should parallel storytelling and reading aloud at home. It should allow students to experience the story comfortably and to participate fully in the event. A carpeted area is a good place for a read-aloud session; so is the grass outside the classroom during a quiet part of the day.

2. *Choose books carefully.* Choosing books to read to students is just as complicated a proposition as organizing any other part of your curriculum! What the "right" book is for a read-aloud session will depend on you and your interests; the size of the group; the backgrounds and language capacities of the students within the group; and the other activities that are taking place in class. In general, we recommend choosing books that you like and that you are comfortable reading, since you will be the main interpreter of them for your students. Trelease (1982) maintains that a "good" read-aloud book should (1) "be fast-paced in its plot, allowing children's interest to be hooked as soon as possible"; (2) "contain clear, rounded characters"; (3) "include crisp, easy-to-read dialogue"; and (4) "keep long descriptive passages to a minimum, at least at the start" (1982: 73-75). These four characteristics nicely parallel the building blocks suggested in the previous section. If you plan to read to the full group, you will have to choose a book that appeals to a wide range of interests and that presents opportunities for involving students who are at a number of points in their language development. The best books for full group read-aloud sessions are those with large, clean pictures, those which provide the opportunity for sharing experiences similar to those recounted in the story, and those which provide opportunities for asking a variety of questions. We also strongly recommend that you use reading aloud and storytelling often with small groups so that you can maximize the opportunity to choose books that are suited to your diverse student population.

3. *Focus students' attention before reading through warm-up activities.* It is important to make sure that your students are "with you" and are ready to participate in the reading *before* you launch a read-aloud session. First, make sure that everyone is paying attention to you. Then make sure that students' interest is aroused so that they will continue to pay attention throughout the reading. The *Charlotte's Web* scenario in Chapter 5 and the "Rain Makes Applesauce" read-aloud activity in Part II illustrate how this can be done. Finally, it is very helpful to students—particularly second language students—to provide a back-

ground framework, or schema, for what they are about to see and hear. You can do this by deliberately tying back the content of a story chapter to their own lives and previous experiences (Johnson 1982; Carrell 1984; Rigg 1986).

4. *Add real input components as you read.* Books with a large number of clear and interesting illustrations that are closely tied to the language and actions in the text are very helpful to beginning and mid-second-language learners, as are predictable books (books that have a pattern, refrain, or predictable sequence). Because these kinds of books are also helpful to students learning English as a first language, there are many good ones available. Predictable books allow students to predict and learn the discourse of the text quickly, and second language learners can use the consistency of plot and language patterns within the text to hear and practice vocabulary and larger chunks of discourse in a way that is highly useful and interesting to them (Hough, Nurss, and Enright, 1985). Once you have chosen the appropriate book for the small group or full group you are going to read to, you can then use all of the real input strategies presented in Chapter 5 as you read to facilitate students' speech-print connections and language learning (see the *Charlotte's Web* example in Chapter 5 for a detailed illustration of this). If you are hesitant about starting up read-aloud activities in your classroom, or if you just want to make sure that you are squeezing as much out of these activities as you can, you can obtain good read-aloud collections and programs which provide suggestions for warm-up, questioning, and follow-up activities to go along with various reading selections (see the resources at the end of the chapter).

5. *Branch out!* The stories you read aloud in class can provide the impetus for all sorts of follow-up activities involving both speech and print. In fact, entire integrated thematic units can be built around good read-aloud storybooks, novels, and literature! (For examples, see Moss, 1984). The read-aloud activities detailed in Part II of this book are embedded in integrated units and contribute to and flow out of these units. The number of ways in which you can follow up on read-aloud sessions with related oral and written activities is limited only by the limitations of your time, resources, and imagination!

A popular and useful variation on the read-aloud strategy is the "shared book experience" or "big book" read-aloud activity, which adds even more real input, more exposure to literacy conventions, and more direct student involvement. Big book activities make use of predictable and well-illustrated books; moreover, the books used in these activities are poster-sized, and enlarged print is used so that the students and the teacher can jointly participate in, or "share" in, the book-reading experience. This reading experience is like that of young children reading in the lap of a loved one, which has been shown to have strong associations with success in learning to read (e.g., Holdaway 1979). Shared book experiences take advantage of the attributes of the read-aloud strategy and the attributes of the environmental and functional print strategy to make critical speech-print connections. As Holdaway (in Park 1982), one of the most prominent advocates and developers of the shared book experience, explains:

> Signs, advertisements, and print on TV have these qualities of visual impact for very sound economic and psychological reasons—they *work* in controlling attention. But it is the learning possibilities of using these dominant print forms which embody the real purposes of so-called "shared book experience" techniques. The natural setting of young children gathered around a big book or chart in a shared experience of literary pleasure with the teacher offers the possibility of powerful learning within a context of satisfying meanings.

Sharing the enjoyment of literature can help children develop a love of books and an understanding of conventions of sharing.

> . . . Gathered around a book as a natural, sharing community children learn more from actual participation than from direct instruction: they learn from the teacher's model, from their own sensible involvement, and from each other, without any sense of competition or pressure. They also learn from judicious instruction which is more intelligible because of its real and obvious purposes. (1982:815,819)

Shared book experiences follow the same basic pattern as that used in conducting a read-aloud activity, except that the reading aloud includes the students themselves! Through the use of real input strategies (such as pointing to the words as they are read, using intonation and pointing to indicate punctuation, etc.), you can read a big book aloud to your students and then they can "read" it (some by actually decoding, some by memorizing and reciting) with you again and again. Big books allow you to share the print and the actual act of reading with students in the full-group setting. This allows you to translate to the full-group setting and the read-aloud event many of the real dialogue strategies from Chapter 5, which you can create in small group and dyadic settings using regular books. Several commercial publishers (e.g., Scholastic Books) currently produce big books for use in shared book experiences. You can also make them yourself or have students make them or help in making them. We have seen wonderful teacher-made big books of favorite multicultural stories and poems from favorite class books like *Where the Sidewalk Ends* (Silverstein 1974). We have also seen wonderful teacher-made materials for older students which use the shared-book-experience strategy to produce big books with predictable text but age-appropriate themes, such as big book versions of rock songs.

The strategies we have outlined here are just a sampling of the many innovative and exciting ways that teachers, researchers, and other educators have found for integrating students' own backgrounds and experiences —including their oral language experiences—with new written discourse experiences. Each of these strategies ensures that *students have ownership* of their new experiences with print and that these experiences indeed expand the range of students' capacities to communicate (share discourse), gain information (fact discourse), reflect (thought discourse), and have fun (fun discourse) using their second language.

6.5 EXTENDING READING AND WRITING

The meaningfulness and usefulness that reading, writing, listening, and speaking have for students should not decline as students' sophistication in using them increases. Making speeches, reading reference books, and writing research reports can and should be as exciting and authentic as the simple activities that preceded them. Composing and delivering a speech can be just as meaningful and functional as talking about chopping carrots (see the "I Have a Dream" activity [no. 8] in the Superheroes unit in Part II.) Each of the four main types of discourse that we identified in Chapter 1 can continue to be developed in functional, real ways—even as students come to rely less and less on their oral language and on the surrounding context for using these four kinds of discourse in their written form.

In reporting on their longitudinal examination of students' writing development, Applebee and Langer (Applebee and Langer 1983; Langer and Applebee 1984) point out that when students use print as a tool for learning and when their reading and writing emanate from their own interests and purposes, then it is possible to mediate and to facilitate their reading and writing development with the same processes of instructional scaffolding and other real dialogue strategies that are used to promote students' oral language development. The topic in the Bakir transcript in Chapter 5 happened to be carrot chopping, but it could just as well have been a picture book or a reference book that Bakir was consulting or a poem or report that he was writing. Applebee and Langer (1983, 1984) provide a case illustration of an adult providing scaffolding for a student's writing during a conference held to organize a report that the student was planning to write. This student's senior partner used the strategies described in Chapter 5 to provide a scaffold for this student's composition planning. Of course, using *real dialogues* to support and extend students' written discourse development in this way will entail the extensive use of small groups and dyadic groupings, just as it does in creating oral dialogues and scaffolding! It will also entail giving invitations to students to share what they are reading, and providing responses to their initiations and requests for assistance in their reading and writing activities. Finally, it will entail the provision of a variety of opportunities for students to engage in different reading and writing activities as part of their classroom pursuits. Integration comes into play here, too, since in the process of providing scaffolding for your second language students' written discourse development, you will also be providing them with real oral input and support for their oral language development!

Further Extensions of Writing

The continuing development and the meaningful extensions of your second language students' writing capacities hinge on your establishing a *real* writing environment in your classroom, namely, an environment that is filled with real print; that encourages collaboration and mutual support among writers; and that provides numerous opportunities for students to create and use the four kinds of meaningful discourse in writing. A real writing environment also continuously encompasses the "writing process" as developed and described by Graves (1983) and Calkins (1983, 1986). A brief description of these steps follows.

The six general steps in the writing process are as follows:

Step 1—Prewriting. Prewriting involves oral language experiences that are designed to help students to develop the need and desire to write; to acquire information or content for writing; and to acquire the necessary vocabulary, syntax, and language structures. Activities that help students get ready to write include talk and listening time; a shared experience such as a trip, an interview, or a cooking activity; the reading of literature (including predictable books or wordless books, and literature that is appropriate to the students' interests, age, and English proficiency); fantasy activities such as role playing, puppetry, and storytelling; brainstorming of words and ideas through "word shaking" (i.e., eliciting from students lists of many words about a given topic); "webbing" (i.e., creating interrelated word lists with lines to show relationships, as in our curriculum "webs"); encouraging children to explore, through writing, what they know (e.g., their own personal experiences of subjects they have learned a lot about); and teachers writing and sharing their own writing with children.

Step 2—Drafting. This step involves writing quickly to get ideas down. It involves working for fluency and not worrying much about mechanics. Students are encouraged to think of writing as mutable, not as "done" once it is put to paper. Young children are encouraged to "invent" spellings on the basis of letters, words, or sounds that they know. Activities include teachers writing in the way that students write in order to model being a writer and to produce pieces to share with students; encouraging students to "spell as best they can," using their knowledge of the alphabet, phonics, familiar words, and information around the classroom (such as the alphabet and language experience stories); and writing daily in journals.

Step 3—Sharing and responding to writing. This step involves writing in small groups, large groups, or individually with the teacher. Teachers and students give one another encouragement and feedback on the writing in preparation for revision. Activities might include sharing and discussing an anonymous piece of writing displayed on an overhead projector; peer conference groups (see following chapter); training students to use PQP—*positive* feedback, *questions* to clarify meaning, and suggestions to *polish* writing (Lyons 1981) having regular individual or small group conferences with students about their writing; and responding to children's writing in an interactive journal.

Step 4—Revision. In this step, students revise selected pieces of writing for quality of content and clarity of expression. Not all pieces are revised, only those in which the student has a particular interest and for which the student has a particular audience in mind. This step might include the teacher's demonstrating revision techniques, such as cutting and pasting (using scissors and tape to physically manipulate the copy on a transparency or chart); students using the word processor to make revisions on a piece; mini-lessons, such as discussions of what makes good writing (e.g., clarity, voice, sense of audience, appropriate sequencing, word choice, use of a lead, ending, transitions, etc.) in preparation for revision (Calkins 1986); and students applying revision techniques to their own work.

Step 5—Editing. In this step, with the help of peers and teachers, students fix up mechanics of usage and spelling. Standards vary, depending on students' ages and on their stage of writing. This step is used only when there is a purpose and an authentic audience for the writing—as when a piece is going to be published. Activities can include making a chart of editing skills as they are taught for students to use as a checklist when they edit; creating an editing center; having editing conferences; providing individual, student-made spelling, translation, or picture dictionaries for students to use in checking spelling or usage; and organizing peer editing conferences (see Chapter 7).

Step 6—Publishing. Through publication, students' writing is presented to an audience and is celebrated. Young children's writing is often published in draft form; the writing of students who are older or more proficient, or both, will be revised and edited before publication. Ways of publishing often emanate directly from the writing activity itself, such as performing a play once it has been written or putting a story into the class library once it has been finished. Other ways of sharing or publishing students' writing include putting writing on bulletin boards, walls, and halls; reading writing to the class (or to another class, to a parent group, over the intercom to the school, etc.); making a video of a reading of pieces; making class books (including big books) or books for the school library or other classes; and making a class newspaper or literary magazine.

The six steps in the writing process can be used in full group and small group settings to guide students through the completion and presentation or publication of a piece of writing. After students have become accustomed to using these steps and to producing original works, they will be able to use the steps independently (with your supervision and support) for whatever writing project they are engaged in. We have found it helpful to present these steps to students and provide practice using them. For example, you can have a writing conference in front of the class in the full group setting and have students suggest questions and responses for you to use before having students go through writing conferences in pairs. After such demonstration and practice, strive to incorporate conferences into your classroom as an ongoing part of the language and literacy environment (e.g., students who have written up a science discovery trying out their report on some colleagues to get feedback and then revising it without your direction). In using the six steps of the writing process to help you establish a real writing environment in your classroom, keep in mind that not all the steps are used with all types of writing, nor are they all needed with every piece of writing that a student creates. Certain stages may be altered or omitted, depending on the student's age and proficiency at writing. For example, young children and inexperienced writers are not expected to use revision extensively; they often publish "first drafts." Experienced writers, on the other hand, often do not need elaborately structured prewriting experiences, but can write privately and independently. In general, however, if you can embed these six steps into your daily classroom life, your second language students will continue to grow in their use of written discourse across all of your integrated curriculum activities.

Students grow as writers by being given many opportunities to engage in the six steps of the writing process. This kindergarten student is already beginning to write in two languages!

As students continue to become familiar with and comfortable using English print and as they practice using the six steps in the writing process, you can continue to raise your expectations for their use of the writing process. Here are a few additional suggestions for continuing to build a real writing environment and for extending your second language students' writing:

Sensory writing and memory writing. Moffett (1968a) describes many developmental writing activities which can be productively used with second language learners, including sensory writing and memory writing. *Sensory writing* involves students carefully observing a place or a scene using all five of their senses, making observational notes of the scene and writing down thoughts and sensations, and then taking these notes back to class and using them to create different kinds of writing (e.g., a descriptive paragraph, a poem, a story). Students can visit different spots around the school for sensory writing, and it can also be turned into a home FUN activity (see Chapter 8.) Students can also observe, experience, and write about the same scene on more than one occasion and then compare their notes and subsequent themes.

Memory writing can be used to get second language students started writing or to get them more comfortable and confident with writing. There are many ways to begin a memory writing experience. Students can just look around the room until they see something that reminds them of something in their past. Or they can close their eyes and picture a specific scene or locale (e.g., a room where they live; a back yard; a classroom or another place in their native country; a place where they play; their "favorite place"; their "secret" place) and then use the picture they have created to write a composition. Memory writing encourages students to use their imaginations; to get at core experiences and to map them into print; to sequence; and to tie emotion, experience, event, and plot to setting. What better way to tie back students' emergent writings to their previous experiences?

Autobiographies. Writing autobiographies is a natural follow-up to writing memories. Students often spend a good deal of time in the prewriting stages of this activity, thinking about their past lives and organizing their ideas before writing. Memory writings; personal time lines (the interesting, key events in the student's life arranged chronologically on a yearly time line); family photos; and interviews with parents and other family members can all help students obtain the raw material they need in order to write autobiographies. Also, peer conferences and full group discussions can enhance the richness of this activity. Autobiographies have a natural homeFUN component (see Chapter 8) and directly tie back second language students' composing efforts to their previous cultural experiences. However, because many of our students have had several painful events in their lives—the death or loss of loved ones; the loss of home and country; physical and mental abuse; and poverty and hunger, to name just a few examples—you should prepare yourself to deal with these experiences and the pain and need for counseling or consoling that goes along with them using both your own resources and the professional resources you have available in your particular school setting.

Following a model. Another fun way to support second language students as they extend their writing development is to use patterned stories and poems as models for students to follow in venturing forth with their own poems and stories. Cramer and Cramer (1975) suggest using predictable storybooks with patterned language (e.g., *The Little Red Hen; The Three Billy Goats Gruff; Brown Bear, Brown Bear*) and then assisting students to use their own themes and to write, following the model. Thus the " 'Not I!' said the dog. 'Not I!' said the cat" pattern of *The Little Red Hen* might become " 'I will,' said the mamá. 'I will,' said the papá" of a second language student's composition! Cramer and Cramer provide a list of predictable storybooks to use in this way. Many big books could be nicely adapted for model writing as well. Dr. Seuss—who often uses simple discourse patterns but complex and fantastic language in his stories—also works for inspiring older students' model writing. We have seen wonderful new songs written through use of the model-writing strategy, such as an ESL group's theme song entitled "This School Is Your School, This School Is My School"—patterned after (and sung to the tune of) "This Land Is Your Land."

"Parody poetry" is also great fun to do in this context. Students can bring in their own favorite poems to use as models to imitate; particularly vivid, and rhythmic, and playful poems such as those by Charlotte Zolotow, Shel Silverstein, and Ogden Nash also work well. (For some lighthearted parody poetry examples, see Stegall [1977] for a set of Ogden Nash parodies which her class did.)

Skits and plays. Writing pieces to be read aloud or performed is another good way to extend second language students' writing development in English and to give them speech-print connections. It also gives them lots of practice in using the six steps of the writing process while preserving access to nonverbal communication and the social and physical context. Inspiring students to prepare puppet shows or reader's theater or full play productions promotes cooperative learning and gives beginning second language students an opportunity to collaborate with and learn from their native English-speaking and full-second-language-speaking peers. Writing dialogues to "act out" a favorite scene or a new chapter in a storybook is a good way to extend read-aloud and storytelling sessions. Finally, for older students, simulations can be used to help make historical events and characters "come alive" and to give your students exciting opportunities to work out historical dilemmas and to rewrite history as they would have it be. We have seen stock-market crashes, Declaration of Independence signings, and customs searches of new arrivals at Ellis Island during the 1800s! Also don't forget that works of theatrical discourse have a quadruple payoff in your classroom—the students writing them get practice in writing; the students performing them get practice in using oral language; the students (and any others) who serve as the audience get practice in listening to oral language; and the scripts and other products of the show can be edited and published for real reading practice by students on future occasions! And everyone gets to have fun!

Further Extensions of Reading

We have seen that meaningful extensions of your students' writing abilities depend on establishing a *real* writing environment in your classroom. In the same way, extending your students' reading abilities depends on establishing a *real reading* environment! In a real reading environment, reading does not only occur at one specific time during the day or in one setting or with one kind of text (e.g., a basal reader). Rather, it occurs throughout each day as students use a variety of print forms—functional print, reference books, literary works, picture books, and self-created print, to name a few—to create the four types of purposeful discourse. Every activity that we have suggested in this chapter for encouraging and extending writing also encourages and extends reading! Moreover, all the oral discourse activities that we have described in this book have the potential to become extended to print and therefore to reading and writing. That's what thinking language and integrating the four language processes is all about!

Here are three other key strategies for encouraging and extending your second language students' reading development: making basal reading groups into *real* reading groups; having reading conferences; and celebrating reading.

Making basal reading groups into real reading groups. Most teachers are familiar with the traditional, round-robin reading group activity used in almost all U.S. classrooms, the kind of event and participant structure which is supported and maintained by the large number of basal reading programs published in the United States. Unfortunately, most basal reading programs are designed to carry out the transmission model's one-way drilling and practice of disconnected and pre-determined skills and facts. This orientation presents some daunting problems for using basals effectively to provide students with real written discourse and to extend their reading in English.

The first problem is that since most basals have been designed with the intention of teaching predetermined and isolated skills, the occasions when they tap students' interests to get them excited about and involved in using print to communicate, have fun, and think for themselves are all too rare. The organization of the language selections as well as the exercises and activities in most current basals have been governed by formal, highly sophisticated notions about controlling students' access to language in order to "reinforce syntactic habits" or "orchestrate the incremental addition of comprehension processes." Not used are mundane notions about sharing the experiences and the power of literacy with living, breathing people who appreciate and respond to high-quality language and literature, and who, if given an appropriate stake in the language and literacy development process, will respond with gusto. Diane Ravitch sums this up the best when she asks, "What child won't plead to stay up 'just a little longer' if he or she is in the middle of an exciting story? . . . Did anyone ever take a flashlight to bed to read a basal reader under the covers?"

The second problem that basals pose for their effective use in the integrated classroom is that too often they have been designed for drill and practice, so it is also very rare when the exercises that they provide to accomplish these tasks involve any kind of purposeful student language use. Children in basal programs often practice reading by reciting meaningless lists of "base" words or by making diphthong sounds or by filling in worksheets that concentrate on particular reading skills. That is, they study *about* reading rather than directly *engaging in* reading. This is particularly damaging to beginning and mid-second language students who have had little exposure to or experience with English of any kind. In *Becoming a Nation of Readers*, the National Commission on Reading of the National Academy of Education (1985) makes clear its views of these exercises:

> In summary, while it cannot be doubted that well-designed workbooks and skill sheets can provide worthwhile practice in aspects of reading, many of these exercise activities are poorly designed. The most notable shortcomings are the dubious value of a large share of the activities to growth in reading proficiency and the lack of integration of the activities with the rest of the reading lesson. For these problems, the publishing industry is responsible. Moreover, in the all too typical classroom, too much of the precious time available for reading instruction is given over to workbook and skill sheet tasks and students invest only the most perfunctory level of attention in the tasks. For these problems, teachers and school administrators are responsible. The conclusion is that workbook and skill sheet tasks should be pared to the minimum that will actually contribute to growth in reading. (1985:76)

What the experience of researchers and teachers such as these authors of *Becoming a Nation of Readers* seems to be saying is that it is important to provide children with specific skills, but that their introduction and instruction must be *embedded* in students' ongoing, authentic use of language to communicate, have fun, and think for themselves. In other words, the best way for children to learn how to read is to read, to learn how to listen is to listen, and learn how to speak is to speak, and to learn how to write is to write! Besides, of course, to learn how to read through writing and to learn how to write through reading and so on. Yet most basal series—in obedience to the dictates of the atomistic, transmission teaching model—organize language and literacy instruction so that children spend very little time actually *doing* any of these things.

The final problem that basals pose for their use in the integrated classroom has to do with their being designed often to support the drill and practice of artificially isolated facts and skills which are sequentially and hierarchically organized (i.e., "scope and sequence"). The reading selections that they employ to provide that required drill and practice are often artificial and contrived. Most basal series either create artificial new reading selections or alter already published selections to provide maximal exposure to a particular skill or fact of form (e.g., a phonics rule like "e at the end makes the vowel long"). They also use discourse-altering formulas to control the "difficulty" in the kinds of vocabulary, order and kinds of language forms, and length and complexity of sentences used in the selections.

The problem with these transformations is that they change much more than the vocabulary or sentential length that they set out to change. They also change the style and the internal organization and structure of the selections (K. Goodman and Y. Goodman 1977; Morgan 1983; Gourley 1984; K. Goodman 1986) and can even dilute or change their meaning (Armbruster, Osborn, and Davison, 1985). This makes it much more difficult for children to apply what they already know to reading and trying to understand the basal selections that they are exposed to.

If all of this makes basal selections of questionable value to first language students, it makes them even more harmful to second language students. Researchers examining the reading performance and reading development of both young readers (e.g., Hodes 1981; Rigg 1986) and college and adult readers (e.g., Johnson 1982; Carrell 1984, 1985) have found that second language students' background and knowledge and experiences (or "cultural schemata") as well as their knowledge and previous experience with the way that stories and other written genres are organized (or "story schemata") affect how much they are able to give to and take from their reading experiences. The typical reading and language basals of today do not give second language students access to their previous experience, nor do they give them access to the everyday "real world" discourse and the school-centered "text" discourse that they must learn in order to be successful students.

Given these problems with using basal reading materials with second language students, what can you do to turn your basal reading groups into *real* reading groups? First, you can modify some of the ways that you use the basal reader in your reading groups. If you want to (or are forced to) really go through the basal reader, lesson by lesson, and exercise by exercise, try to highlight those activities in which students use language in meaningful ways. They often are found at the end of a unit and are labeled as "supplementary" or "extension" or "enrichment" activities to be completed only after the memorization and drill that precede them. Quite often these activities are clever and creative and nicely fulfill the seven instructional criteria of the integrated model. For example, in one basal that we've used, the teacher's guide directs the teacher to have the students read the basal version of the story and then drill them on "long vowel sounds" and factual recall questions. Then the guide suggests that the students act out the story for another group or the rest of the class. Using this basal unit in the integrated classroom, you could skip several of the drill exercises, substitute some predicting, inferring, generalizing, and imagining questions for some of the factual recall questions; point out and practice vowel patterns in context, and spend the majority of your basal group time doing the "extra" activity of writing and acting out a student version of the story!

We have two other suggestions for using basal materials in real reading groups. First, you can introduce reading materials other than basal readers into them. How exciting it would be for your group if you were to make multiple copies of a student's own composition or "published" book and use *it* to organize your activity for the day! What a message it would send to students about the power of reading if you were to allow them to take turns choosing a favorite story to be duplicated (or collected as multiple copies) and read by the group one time each week! How helpful it would be to second language students if you were to use some of the folktales and other reading selections that you'd collected from students' own native cultures and communities to serve as the reading selections in the reading group (Hudelson and Barrera 1982; Rigg, 1986)! *Real* print—reading matter that is comprehensible, interesting, and useful to students—is key to making reading groups real, whether it results in a group of fifth-grade boys reading *Sports Illustrated* or in a group of first-graders finding and reading words in *My Weekly Reader*.

Finally, you can turn your basal reading groups into real reading groups by changing the *internal organization* of the reading group to maximize meaning-making and to maximize students' tying back and tying in of the reading materials being used (including basal reading materials). Begin by adding *pre*-reading and *post*-reading activities to your reading group sessions. The addition of a warm-up, pre-reading segment in your session will give your second language students an adequate opportunity to become familiar with, think about, talk about, and connect to themselves the discourse and ideas that are to come in the reading. If you are using a basal reader in your reading groups, you can utilize the real activities that appear at the ends of the units and lessons both before and after students' reading to do pre- and post-reading. You can also use what is called the ETR approach (Betts 1950) to organize the three phases of the reading lesson. Using ETR, you dedicate your pre-reading time to eliciting personal *experiences* (the "E") from the students which are related to the events and characters that will appear in the text for the day. During and after reading the *text* with the students (the "T"), you can help them to develop explicit *relationships* (the "R") between what they know and what they read. The ETR approach, while originally developed for first language students, is an example of the tie back learning strategy used by second language students which has appeared throughout the second language education literature and throughout this book, and has been successfully implemented with second language students in the reading group setting (Au 1979).

Another reading strategy that you can use to facilitate second language students' reading in your reading group event is usually referred to as the "Directed Reading-Thinking Activity (DRTA)" approach, developed by Stauffer (1975). You begin a "DRTA" reading lesson by getting students to predict what they think the reading selection for the day is going to be about or what they think will happen in the selection. You use the title, the pictures, or the first few lines of the selection to do this, or a combination of these. Then, you continue to ask students to build meanings by stopping them every so often and asking them to summarize what they've read, to make new predictions and speculations about the themes, characters, and events of the story, and to pick up on new questions and mysteries that have developed within the text. What ETR and DRTA have in common is that they emphasize involving students actively and fully in all stages of the reading event (before, during, and after), in creating and using meanings and in relating these meanings to themselves and their own experiences and ideas. These principles should not only be central to your reading group sessions, but they should be central to all of the reading activities that go on in class.

Reading conferences. Engaging in real dialogues with your students and providing scaffolding for their reading as well as their writing, listening, and speaking demonstrates to them the importance that you place on their independent reading efforts. The material that you share with students during their reading conferences with you can include material that you've chosen because of a particular conferee's reading need as well as the stories, personal essays, and so on which the student chooses to bring to the conference. Continued reading from a longer novel or story of the student's choice works well in conferencing as well. You can also work out specific support activities to accompany students' individualized reading efforts, such as having students record questions they have about their story or about new words (which can become part of their word banks!); creating related research investigations; or writing and completing projects related to the book (e.g., making a Big Book of a regular book read in a conference or putting on a skit of one of the scenes in a story read during a conference). In other words, you can adapt all of the full group and small group print activities that we have described and use them in your reading conferences to extend students' reading!

Celebrate reading! Finally, continuously celebrating reading in your classroom life will make it into a real reading environment above anything else. You celebrate reading when you reveal to children the joy and power that reading has for you and that it can have for them, and when you give it a special place within the ongoing life of your classroom in addition to incorporating it into all of your integrated units and other instructional activities. Having regular times when everyone reads a book silently (including you) is a way to celebrate reading. So is having a comfortable, special place to go to read (a library corner or a "book nook" or a reading chair) or having regular read-aloud and storytelling times. You also celebrate reading when you share your own reading experiences and when you embed your knowledge of books and reading anecdotes in your daily conversations with students—and encourage them to do the same. Through your example and through their own positive experiences, your second language students will not only come to read, but they will come to understand the power and potential of reading and will come to celebrate and love reading!

The following list summarizes some ways to provide real written discourse in the integrated classroom.

TO PROVIDE REAL WRITTEN DISCOURSE

1. *Make meaningful speech-print connections such as:*
   a. *Key vocabulary and word banks: Write and give to students words they want to use and save.*
   b. *Environmental and functional print: Be aware of and use the print in the environment within your learning activities.*
   c. *Language experience approach: Have students share and discuss an experience, have them dictate a story to you based on the experience. Transcribe what they say. Then read the students' narrative to them and use and re-use these writings.*
   d. *Storytelling and oral narratives: Collect students' stories (and your own), tell them in class, and use them to develop related reading and writing activities.*
   e. *Reading aloud and shared book experiences: Choose and read story books and full-length books regularly in class. Have books available for student use, develop integrated units based on favorite books. If appropriate, use "Big Books" to give students the maximum opportunity to participate in the reading occasion.*
2. *Continue to extend writing.*
   a. *Set up a real writing environment: Give students lots of opportunities within your learning activities to plan, draft, talk about, revise, edit and publish their writing.*
   b. *Provide additional creative extensions of writing: such as sensory writing, memory writing, autobiographies, following models and skits and plays.*
3. *Continue to extend reading:*
   a. *Set up a real reading environment: Integrate many varieties of print and reading into all parts of the curriculum.*

b. *Make basal reading groups into real reading groups: High-light meaningful uses of language, supplement the basal reader with real reading materials and give second language learners opportunities to tie in and tie back the reading content to their own experiences.*
c. *Have individualized reading conferences.*
d. *Celebrate reading!*

6.6 CONCLUSION

In this chapter we have completed the task begun in Chapter 5 of depicting your critical role as senior discourse partner to your second language students in providing both real oral discourse and real written discourse to them in your classroom. In the chapters that remain, we shall describe the last critical role that you must assume in implementing the ILT model, that of being a community leader inside and outside the boundaries of your classroom and your school.

ACTIVITIES AND DISCUSSION

1. Make a written language inventory of a classroom (your own or another). What kinds of print are displayed there? What kinds of written discourse are available to be used by students? How much of the written discourse that you have found is *real* (i.e., there for a meaningful, interesting purpose)? Also make a written language inventory of the lesson plans and learning activities for one week in that class. How much of the reading and writing that students are to do is real? How much of it is there to practice the process of reading and writing alone?

2. Make a written language inventory of your school or a school you visit. Make a list of all of the places in and around the school which are shared by everyone (e.g., the office, the cafeteria, the front of the school, the playground). For each place, record the kinds of print you see and how and by whom it is used. (This can be done in conjunction with the oral language inventory suggested at the end of Chapter 3.) Think of some ways that you could bring students' attention to this print surrounding them in the school.

3. Make a written language inventory of the neighborhood around the school. Develop some activities which tap the real written discourse which you find there.

4. Keep a personal written language "log" for a 24–48 hour period. Write down each kind of written language that you read during that time and each instance of writing that you yourself did. Review your log. What kinds of written language were the most common? How did the two written language categories (print you read and your own writing) compare? How could you use the varieties of written discourse from your log in your instruction?

5. Have a group of students make written language inventories in their homes or keep their own personal written language logs. How do their inventories/logs compare with the ones you did for the school-related settings and in your own life?

6. Choose one of the strategies for making speech-print connections discussed in this chapter (i.e., key vocabulary, environmental and functional print, language experience, storytelling, or reading aloud) and try it out with a group of students. After the activity is complete, review what happened. What kind of oral discourse was used? What kinds of written discourse? How does the writing that emerged from the activity compare with the other writing the students have been producing? What are some ways that you can follow up on this activity and the writing it produced in future activities? How can the written discourse which you produced be integrated into your other learning activities or the rest of the curriculum? Repeat this activity using one or more of the other strategies or come up with your *own* speech-print connections and try *them* out!

7. Review your current learning activities and lesson plans to find places in them where you can add speech-print connections and then add some of them into your plans. (Examples are provided in this chapter!)

8. Review a content area textbook. (If you are presently using a content area textbook, review it.) Add speech-print connections to some of the textbook activities.

9. The next time that you create a complete piece of writing (e.g., a school brochure, a term-paper, a letter to the Editor), consciously monitor the various kinds of activities that you go through to produce your final draft and keep track of the sequence in which you went through them. Compare your activities and steps to the six steps in the writing process described in this chapter. How is your process the same? How is it different?

10. Observe a group of students during a single writing session or across many sessions as they prepare a final draft of a piece of writing. Do their activities and steps fit the six steps of the writing process? How so? How not so? Are there specific suggestions that you can make to

assist them in developing their pieces without taking away their ownership of their own writing?

11. Choose one of the strategies for extending writing discussed in this chapter (i.e., sensory writing, memory writing, autobiographies, following a model, or writing skits and plays) and try it out with a group of students. Use the questions provided in no. 6 above to review the activity and the writing that resulted. Also use the students' work to identify individual writing strengths and needs. Repeat this activity using one or more of the other strategies or come up with some of your *own* writing extensions and try *them* out!

12. Review a basal reading text. (If you are presently using a basal reader, review it.) Choose one unit or section from the text and adapt its activities and exercises for a *real* reading group. That is, adapt the specific activities that are provided for each lesson so that they follow the seven criteria of the integrated model, and adapt the overall organization of the reading lessons using either "ETR" or "DRTA" to integrate the students' previous experience into them.

13. Plan a reading group activity or set of activities centering on real reading materials (e.g., students' own compositions, library books, newspaper articles, functional print). Use the seven criteria of the ILT model to do this, and also make sure that you have located all the learning objectives/potentials present in the materials you plan to use. Then try out and review the activity(ies) using the questions outlined in no. 4 above.

14. Use one of your students' favorite children's literature selections to develop a thematic, integrated curriculum unit following the steps provided in Chapter 2.

FOR FURTHER READING

Applebee, A. 1984. *Contexts for learning to write: Studies of secondary school instruction.* Norwood, NJ: Ablex Publishing Corporation. A fascinating collection of reports from the National Study of Writing in the Secondary School examining the settings, processes, and development of high school students' writing. In the last chapter, Applebee applies the concept of instructional scaffolding to composition and also presents some provocative recommendations for improving secondary composition instruction.

Calkins, L. M. 1986. *The art of teaching writing.* Portsmouth, NH: Heinemann Educational Books. In this beautiful book, Calkins expands and develops many of the central themes of her seminal work, *Lessons from a Child* (1983), including the developmental changes that children undergo as writers, the teacher's role in students' writing development, the use of writing conferences, reading-writing connections and writing across the curriculum. A particular strength of the book is its consistent relating of writing research and theory to the realities of the classroom.

Cantoni-Harvey, G. 1987. *Content-area language instruction: Approaches and strategies.* Reading, MA: Addison-Wesley Publishing Company. A broad, practical survey of techniques and materials for developing language, cognition and content knowledge together. The book is written for grade-level as well as bilingual and ESL teachers.

Commission on Reading, National Academy of Education. 1986. *Becoming a nation of readers.* Champaign, IL: Center for the Study of Reading, University of Illinois. A clear, readable synthesis of current language arts and reading research and theory along with convincing recommendations for teaching.

Cummins, J. 1984. *Bilingualism and special education: Issues in assessment and pedagogy.* Clevedon, England: Multilingual Matters. This book includes a clear statement of Cummins' influential conceptualization of the construct of bilingual language proficiency and its cognitive and linguistic components. Cummins also focuses on the issues of assessment of bilingual students, the construct of learning "disability" as applied to bilingual students, and "immersion" and other instructional programs that have been designed for "at-risk" and learning disabled language minority children.

Graves, D. 1983. *Writing: Teachers and children at work.* Exeter, NH: Heinemann Educational Books. Graves' eloquent, whimsical and well-grounded reflections about how children's writing develops and how teachers may encourage and support that development.

Harste, J., Woodward, V., and Burke, C. 1984. *Language stories and literacy lessons.* Postmouth, NH: Heinemann Educational Books. The authors present a delightfully readable and incredibly rich portrayal of young children's language stories (their own comments on their developing powers of reading and writing as well as many samples of their work) and the literacy lessons that adults can draw from these stories. The dedication in this book reads, "To literacy learning."

Macnamara, J. 1973. "Nurseries, streets and classrooms: Some comparisons and deductions." *Modern Language Journal* 57(5-6):250-54. In this article, Macnamara makes comparisons among the language settings of his title. In spite of over a decade of subsequent research and curriculum development, "foreign" and second language classrooms today are strikingly similar to the ones he describes.

Mohan, B. A. 1986. *Language and content.* Reading, MA.: Addison-Wesley Publishing Company. This book deals with important issues of conceptualizing and carrying out a program of coordinated language and subject-matter instruction.

Parker, R. P., and Davis, F. A. 1983. *Developing literacy: Young children's use of language.* Newark, DE.: International Reading Association. Excellent collection of essays exploring the many aspects of young children's literacy development, including the beginnings of literacy, parental and school literacy instruction, and children's uses of language and literacy.

Rigg, P. 1986. "Reading in ESL: Learning from kids." In Rigg, P. and Enright, D. S. (Eds.) *Children and ESL: Integrating perspectives.* Washington, D. C.: Teachers of English to Speakers of Other Languages. Rigg's careful analysis of the oral reading performance of four second language learners as well as the texts they read from provides a number of key insights regarding how second language learners approach the English reading task and what teachers can do to support them in mastering it.

Smith, F. 1985. *Reading without nonsense (Second edition.)* New York: Teachers College Press. One of the definitive statements of the psycholinguistic, student- and meaning-centered approach to reading instruction. The "nonsense" in Smith's title refers to the meaningless "exercises, material and drills" which he finds in most skills-oriented programs of reading instruction.

ADDITIONAL RESOURCES

Speech-Print Connections

Key Words.
Ashton-Warner, S. 1963. *Teacher.* New York: Bantam Books.
Veatch, J., Sawicki, F., Elliott, G., Barnette, E., and Blakey, J. 1983. *Key words to reading: The language experience approach begins.* Columbus, OH: Charles E. Merrill Publishing Company.
Functional/Environmental Print
Prizzi, E., and Hoffman, J. 1985. *Reading around the world: Functional reading fun.* Belmont, CA: David S. Lake Publishers (19 Davis Drive 94002).
Prizzi, E. and Hoffman, J. 1985. *Reading everyday stuff: Functional reading fun.* Belmont, CA.: David S. Lake Publishers.
Short, T. R., and Dickerson, B. 1980. *The newspaper: An alternative textbook.* Belmont, CA.: David S. Lake Publishers.
Language Experience Approach
Hall, M. A. 1970. *Teaching reading as a language experience.* Columbus, OH: Charles E. Merrill Publishing Company.
Rigg, P. 1981. Beginning to read in English the LEA way. In C. W. Twyford, W. Diehl and K. Feathers (Eds.) *Reading English as a second language: Moving from theory* (pp. 81-90). Bloomington, IN.: Indiana University, School of Education, Monographs in Teaching and Learning, 4.
Van Allen, R., & Allen, C. 1976. *Language experience activities.* Boston: Houghton-Mifflin Company.
Storytelling and Home Narratives
Barton, B. 1986. *Tell me another: Storytelling and reading aloud at home, at school and in the community.* Markham: Ontario, Canada: Pembroke Publishers Limited.
Foxfire Magazine. Subscriptions available for $9.00/year (4 issues). Write to: The Foxfire Fund, Rabun Gap, GA, 30568. Available from the same group and address: *Hands On Newsletter,* geared for teachers using community-based cultural and literacy educational projects.
Pellowski, A. 1984. *The story vine: A source book of unusual and easy-to-tell stories from around the world.* New York: Collier Books.
Van Dongen, R. 1987. Children's narrative thought, at home and at school. *Language Arts,* 64(1): 79-87.
Reading Aloud and Shared Book Experiences
"Big Book" publishers: Addison-Wesley Publishing Company, Inc. (Route 128, Reading, MA 01867) Rigby Education (454 S. Virginia Street, Crystal Lake, IL., 60014), Scholastic, Incorporated. (P. O. Box 7501, 2931 E. McCarty Street, Jefferson City, M. O., 65102), and The Wright Group (10949 Technology Place, San Diego, CA., 92127).

The Wright group also has a newsletter centering on integrated techniques called "The Whole Idea."

Holdaway, D. 1979. *The Foundations of literacy.* Sydney, Australia: Ashton-Scholastic. (Available through Heinemann Educational Books, Portsmouth, NH).

Trelease, J. 1982. *The read-aloud handbook.* New York: Penguin Books.

Whitehead, R. J. 1975. *The early school years read aloud program.* (Four Volumes, Fall, Winter, Spring, Summer). Homewood, IL: ETC Publications.

Extending Writing

Cramer, R. L., and Cramer, B. B. 1975. Writing by imitating language models. *Language Arts,* 52(7):1011-18.

Fox, M. 1986. *Teaching drama to young children.* Portsmouth, NH: Heinemann Educational Books.

Geller, L. G. 1985. *Wordplay and language learning for children.* Urbana, IL.: National Council of Teachers of English.

Jones, K. 1982. *Simulations in language teaching.* Cambridge, England: Cambridge University Press.

Kirby, D., and Liner, T. 1981. *Inside out: Developmental strategies for teaching writing.* Montclair, NJ: Boynton/Cook.

Maley, A., and Duff, A. 1978. *Drama techniques in language learning: A resource book of communication activities for language teachers.* Cambridge, England: Cambridge University Press.

Moffett, J. 1968. *A student-centered language arts curriculum, grades K-13: A handbook for teachers.* Boston: Houghton-Mifflin.

Scardamalia, M., Bereiter, C., and Fillion, B. 1981. *Writing for results: A sourcebook of consequential composing activities.* LaSalle, IL: Open Court Publishing Company.

Smith, S. M. 1984. *The theater arts and the teaching of second languages.* Reading, MA: Addison-Wesley Publishing Company.

Extending Reading

Au, K. H. 1979. Using the experience-text-relationship method with minority children. *The Reading Teacher* 32(6): 677-79.

Moss, J. F. 1984. *Focus units in literature: A handbook for elementary school teachers.* Urbana, IL.: National Council of Teachers of English.

Simmons, J. S. and Palmer, B. C. 1985. *Reading by doing: An introduction to effective reading.* Lincolnwood, IL.: National Textbook Company.

Stauffer, R. G. 1975. *Directing the reading-thinking process.* New York: Harper and Row Publishing Company.

Chapter 7

Building the Classroom Community

All the colors of the race

All the colors of the race
are
      in my face, and just behind my face:
                 behind my eyes:
      inside my head.

And inside my head, I give my self a place
    at the end of a long
          line   forming
              it self into a
                  circle.

And I am holding out my hands.

—Arnold Adoff

7.1 INTRODUCTION

We have discussed the role of the teacher as planner and designer of the integrated curriculum; ways for the teacher to make the classroom social environment meet the criteria for the integrated language model by evaluating and adjusting rules, activities, and participant structures; criteria and suggestions for adjusting the classroom physical environment to meet the seven criteria; and the teacher's multiple roles as students' senior discourse partner. In this and the following chapter, we will shift our focus to the use of some of the most important resources for strengthening our second language learners' language and literacy development.

What are these valuable classroom natural resources? People! An important type of integration predicated by the ILT model is the uniting of all of those who are involved in our students' language and literacy development. The first step toward accomplishing this key human integration is to work in your classrooms to unite your personal resources with those of your students, and to unite each student's personal resources with those of every other student. That is, you must work to create a genuine integrated classroom literacy community—a place where the experiences, capacities, interests and goals of every classroom member are simultaneously utilized for his or her own learning benefit and for the benefit of the rest of the class. By including "literacy" in the title of this community, we signify our belief that full communicative competence in English is one of the most important benefits that we expect this new community to provide. In the pages that follow, we will first identify those components of the integrated classroom community which also comprise the human resources available for use in assisting second language students' learning. Then we will discuss the major characteristics of the integrated classroom community: multiculturalism and cooperation. Finally, we will describe teacher roles and teaching strategies for building and maintaining a multicultural, cooperative, integrated classroom literacy community.

7.2 COMPONENTS OF THE INTEGRATED CLASSROOM COMMUNITY

Figure 7.1 presents the components of the integrated classroom community. The figure includes both the personal resources and experiences that second language learners bring to the classroom and those which the classroom offers them.

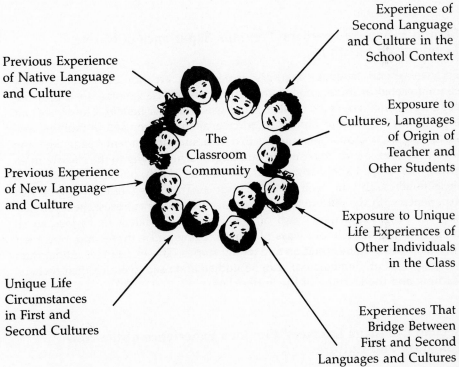

Components of the Classroom Community

What Second Language
Learners Bring to the
Classroom Community

What the Classroom
Community Offers to
Second Language Learners

Experience of
Second Language
and Culture in the
School Context

Previous Experience
of Native Language
and Culture

The
Classroom
Community

Exposure to
Cultures, Languages
of Origin of
Teacher and
Other Students

Previous Experience
of New Language
and Culture

Exposure to Unique
Life Experiences of
Other Individuals
in the Class

Unique Life
Circumstances
in First and
Second Cultures

Experiences That
Bridge Between
First and Second
Languages and Cultures

Figure 7.1: Components of the Integrated Classroom Literacy Community

7.3 WHAT SECOND LANGUAGE LEARNERS BRING TO THE CLASSROOM

In many of today's transmission-model classrooms and within the one-way transmission curriculum, students are passive receptors of the knowledge that is being instilled in them. This remains true in spite of the considerable evidence which indicates that learning is highly interactive and that students bring a rich and diverse array of valuable resources to the learning process. In the transmission environment, neither native speakers' nor second language learners' previous linguistic, cultural, or cognitive experiences are likely to be used to their fullest extent in the students' learning.

Second Language Learners' Previous Experience of Native Language and Culture

Because second language learners' experiences are not instantly or easily communicated or understood in these transmission classrooms, their previous experiences are even more unlikely to be used for their benefit. These previous experiences are a major human resource available to be used in building and sustaining a classroom community that will support students' language and literacy development. Your second language learners bring to the classroom an already-developed knowledge about the people, places, objects, and events in their families and in their native cultures. They also often bring a rich experience with the discourse traditions of their native cultures: their peoples' ways of conversing, their ways of behaving appropriately in various social settings (including school); ways of using reading and writing; and even their ways of presenting information and telling stories. These resources, rather than being ignored or "remediated," can be studied and used to enrich their owners' learning and the learning of the entire class.

Second Language Learners' Previous Experience of the New Language and Culture

Second language learners bring more to your classroom than their previous native language and cultural backgrounds. They also bring previous experience (from a few days to a few years) with English and North American culture, and some human experiences which might be described as belonging to all cultures—we will refer to these as pan-cultural experiences.

Many times not only are second language learners' native language backgrounds ignored; but their backgrounds in the new language and culture are ignored as well. Many second language learners have been in an English-speaking country for some time and have English discourse capacities which, if identified, can be utilized to help them learn more English. Other second language learners come from cultures where English as a second language was a part of their schooling. Some of these students have developed academic English literacy abilities that outstrip their oral English abilities. If these former are identified, they can be used to develop the latter. Similarly, many second language learners are familiar with a variety of North American cultural resources which can also be used to bring the members of the class into concert and to provide language and literacy instruction. Haven't you had second language learners in your classroom who could sing several verses of popular songs in English even if they didn't quite understand all the words?

Pan-cultural experiences, which are also present in sometimes quite painful abundance in classrooms with second language learners, should be used to unite our students. The experience of war belongs to no single culture, nor does the experience of hunger, fear or losing a loved one. On the other hand, the experiences of safety, of accomplishing something, of joy, of loving and being loved also do not belong to a single culture. These experiences are an intense and living part of our classrooms. If they are recognized, they can be tapped to facilitate instruction and to strengthen the classroom community.

Second Language Learners' Unique Life Experiences in First and Second Cultures

While second language learners' current lives certainly include their previous experiences and their lives at school, the home lives and circumstances that these students return to after school each day resemble neither their previous existences in their native countries nor the comfortable, middle-class world that tends to be portrayed in most schools. Many of the parents of second language learners have exchanged professional employment (and concomitant living circumstances) in their native countries for employment as waiters, orderlies, sales clerks, or janitors in their new country. Many of your second language learners have lost or have been separated from one or both of their parents and are living with family friends, sponsors, or relatives not much older than themselves. Many may be experiencing culture shock or may be undergoing anxiety over their families' welfare. It is important to take all of these circumstances into account in working with your second language students. They have been included in Figure 7.1, as resources that should be considered and used in building an integrated classroom literacy community.

7.4 WHAT THE CLASSROOM COMMUNITY OFFERS TO SECOND LANGUAGE LEARNERS

The English language and North American culture are obviously a major part of every U.S. or Canadian classroom in which second language learners are placed. They are present in the school culture and in the cultural experiences that the teacher and students bring with them to the classroom. But in many classrooms, including those adopting the transmission view of instruction, English and North American culture are largely present as quantitative future ends—as the objectives that are to be reinforced or the content that is to be "covered" in lessons, exercises, and tests. In this way, language and culture are treated as something "out there" which must first be somehow converted into a finite and controlled form as curricula and textbooks before being brought into the classroom to be divulged and transmitted to students by the teacher (Barth 1972). In this view, the acquisition of language and culture stops at the end of the textbook and at the classroom door.

In contrast, language and culture in the integrated classroom community are present as both exciting dreams and as useful tools—as unlimited resources for meaning-making which comprise both the means and the ends of educational experience. They are not studied about in the present so that they can be used later. Rather, they are used in the present for the purposes of the present and to aim for the future. In this way, the new language and culture are treated as something "in here" as well as "out there," and the traditional boundaries between the classroom and the real world of English language and North American culture are relaxed to allow for a full range of real, meaningful, integrated language and learning experiences. In this view, the acquisition of English and of North American culture can take place whenever and wherever they are available to be experienced, not just in the classroom. Moreover, the teacher serves as the instructional director and mediator of these experiences, not as their transmitter.

The Experience of Second Language and Culture in the School Context

To the student who is newly arrived from another country, the school itself is a new culture within the new English-speaking culture. The school represents a microcosm of the greater cultural experience, and is often the first place where second language learners come into contact with the new culture. The texts and the curricula formally present the history and language of the new culture. But the ways in which school life is carried on—its bells, announcements, cafeteria lines and foods, assemblies and student council elections—present the ways in which things are done in the new culture. This experience of culture is one that new students cannot avoid, but you can do more with the experience of the school culture than merely permit them to experience it. You can directly and consciously teach students about the school culture; structure student interactions with important people in the culture; and help students learn about how this institution, which is typical of the new culture, is governed and operated.

Exposure to Cultures and Languages of Origin of Teacher and Other Students

In the integrated language classroom community, textbooks, formal curricula, and school procedures are certainly not the only places where English and North American culture can be found as potential learning resources for second language learners. They can also be found in the personal resources of the teacher—in your own language and experience of your culture and in your knowledge of teaching and your work with and for students. They can be found within the personal resources of the students themselves—within your native English-speaking students, if you have any, and within whatever previous experience your second language students have had with English and North American culture. As an integrated language teacher, you can develop a classroom community that takes advantage of all these cultural resources and the opportunity they afford for exchanging, sharing, and eventually integrating cultures in the classroom.

Exposure to Unique Life Experiences of Other Individuals in the Class

The many unique experiences of the individuals in the classroom are also available as resources in the integrated language classroom. The North American culture is pluralistic, not unitary. Not only is there more than one language spoken in the classroom, there is undoubtedly more than one "English" spoken. Even native English-speaking students use different dialects of English from different regions or ethnic groups of origin, and they use different forms of English when speaking to peers than when speaking to teachers. Second language learners can acquire the concept that there is more than one appropriate way to speak in different situations, more than one right tradition, more than one right way to believe and to act, just from learning about the unique life experiences of other individuals in the class. In the transmission classroom, there is little opportunity for such interchange. In the integrated classroom, learning about one another is a legitimate and important focus. A favorite unit we observed as it was used in a classroom, entitled "Developing a Classroom Community," exemplifies how a classroom focus on students' unique characteristics and preferences and on cultural and family backgrounds can be used to develop a sense of unity and community in the class. In the unit, students wrote and told about their special talents, their favorite things, and their personal preferences. They studied one another's physical characteristics, countries of origin, and family characteristics. In becoming familiar with one another's similarities and differences, students begin to develop the tolerance, appreciation and understanding that are necessary to any genuine community.

Experiences That Bridge Between First and Second Languages and Cultures

English and the larger North American culture can also be incorporated into the classroom community as they are found in the world of people outside the classroom—either by taking the students directly out to the real world (e.g., school tours, field trips) or by bringing the real world directly into the classroom (e.g., invited guests and speakers, use of radio or television, use of realia, or corresponding with persons outside the classroom). This will be discussed further in Chapter 8 which describes the crucial role of the teacher as a provider of experiences that form a bridge between the classroom community and the other communities of the students, including those of school, family, neighborhood, and work.

We note here that in recommending that you not limit the exposure to English and North American culture in your classroom to textbooks, we do not mean to imply that any old materials or experiences or "exposure" will do. Obviously they will not. The philosopher Martin Buber (1965) describes one of the educator's critical duties as the selection of the resources, materials and experiences from the real world that will be used to enter into a teaching relation with students. If the goals of literacy, access, joy, community and power for your students are to be met, then you must first carefully become aware of and select from all of the available language and cultural resources that can help you meet these goals, and then use these resources fully within your instruction. The integrated classroom community is not an island. Rather, it is firmly situated within the larger language and culture. The teacher selects parts of that larger language and culture to use in the classroom to forge the multicultural community ties that will further support language and literacy development.

Teachers can support students as they meet the challenges learning a new culture presents, as with this student learning to conquer fingerpainting!

More, Not Either/Or

By now it should be obvious that the abundance of human experiences and human resources that are available for use in your work with second language learners is nothing short of astounding! But has this abundance typically been utilized to enrich the learning and experience of either first or second language learners? We think not. All too often in the recent past, the discussions surrounding second language learners' education and the educational programs that have come out of these discussions have been based on politics, not pedagogy; on adults' fears and prejudices, not on young people's interests and needs. All too often the education these programs have offered second language students has been a matter of "either/or": either mother-tongue maintenance or English learning, either native-culture preservation (and separation) *or* assimilation into the new culture. All too often the "bi-" in "bilingual education" and the "second" in "English as a second language education" have been neglected or forgotten, and these terms themselves have been used to fragment the extremely limited monies available to assist second language learners, and to alienate from one another the people dedicated to working with second language learners. We believe that as teachers, you can serve your students best by refusing to participate in the contest of either/or and by instead aiming for "more"! We believe that the whole of students and teachers working together for themselves and one another is greater than the sum of the individual learning and teaching efforts that might otherwise take place. The "more" that we speak of in the ILT model is the sharing and using of all the diverse human resources of the classroom by all of the participants in the classroom life for the benefit of all. In the rest of this chapter, we will describe some ways of using the human resources we have identified to build and maintain the integrated classroom literacy community.

7.5 CHARACTERISTICS OF THE INTEGRATED CLASSROOM COMMUNITY

All of the seven key instructional criteria of the integrated model lead toward the development of a genuine classroom literacy community. This community's rich resources give it the potential to provide support from teachers and peers; many opportunities for collaboration; group goals and purpose; opportunities for students to explore and develop their own interests and share interests with the group; chances to share and build on previous experiences in their native countries and in the new one; the necessity of seeing the world from a variety of points of view; and the need to integrate students from broad backgrounds into a new community of shared goals.

The integrated classroom literacy community has two primary characteristics. First, it is multicultural. Students' native cultures and various subcultures in the new English-speaking country are fully respected as all students learn about and form a new classroom culture. In this way, learning the cultural and linguistic ways of the new country is an additive process, not a subtractive or substituting one. Second language learners need not give up their past and present cultural ways in order to learn other ways. In the integrated classroom literacy community, developing "awareness of and competence in multiple cultures is indeed the normal human experience" (Grow-Maienza 1984). This community must be a place where cultures of origin and various cultures of the new country are treated with respect, while the students' cultural repertoires are expanded to provide them with the power of choice over their own futures.

Second, and equally important, the integrated classroom is cooperative. The primary goals in the class are shared goals which students help one another to attain. The students are not competing for a limited good that only some can acquire (e.g., a certain percentage of A's). They are cooperating toward a shared end—acquiring knowledge and strategies for furthering their knowledge.

Although in many ways classrooms can be described as having their own cultures (e.g., Trueba, Guthrie, and Au 1981; Erickson 1984; Spindler & Spindler 1987), teachers are rarely aware of their roles in creating those cultures. Because we are asking you to take on the new roles of classroom community creator and community leader, we will take great pains to clarify those roles in the sections that follow. In many ways, each of the two characteristics of the classroom literacy community—multiculturalism and cooperation—requires the other for its fulfillment, but for the sake of simplicity, we will discuss them one at a time.

7.6 THE MULTICULTURAL
CLASSROOM COMMUNITY

The first major characteristic of the integrated classroom community is that it is multicultural. In their review of the literature on multicultural education, Grant, Sleeter, and Anderson (1986) note that the term *multicultural* is used in many ways, and they recommend that its users carefully clarify the meaning they intend. The approach we advocate is most closely related to what they call "multicultural education":

Multicultural Education

Purpose: Reduce social stratification and assimilation by promoting knowledge and appreciation of America's cultural diversity.
Assumptions: Assimilation is undesirable; standard school curricula and practices are biased; all aspects of schooling should reflect diversity, which will eventually lead to reduction in prejudice and social structural change.
Practices: Re-write curricula to reflect ethnic, gender, social class, and handicap diversity; promote diverse learning styles; promote use of more than one language; provide nontraditional staffing patterns. (1986:48).

Our viewpoint also incorporates several aspects of what Grant, Sleeter, and Anderson call "education that is multicultural and social reconstructionist." Practices of this include "in addition to those of multicultural education, organiz[ing] curriculum around current social issues, actively engag[ing] students in problem-generating and problem-solving, teach[ing] members of oppressed groups political action skills." (1986:49)

Why is multicultural education so essential for our second language students? Besides the social purposes cited above, it fulfills important language learning purposes. In order to take advantage of the many learning resources available to a classroom community that includes second language learners, the classroom must be organized to use these resources for students' language learning. In order to do this, the classroom community must be open to the various cultures represented. Multicultural education takes place in a classroom community in which developing competence in multiple cultures is seen as the normal human experience. The goals for a truly multicultural classroom community are twofold, as follows.

The first goal is students' development of pride in their varied cultures of origin. This pride is not developed on a surface level, for example by simply comparing and contrasting easily observed differences in food, costume and holidays (Saville-Troike 1980; Ehlers and Crawford 1983; Grant and Sleeter 1985). It is also not developed just by looking to the past, in discovering one's roots and drawing family trees. These activities may be helpful for getting students started in understanding one another's different cultural points of view, but they are not enough. Cultural pride is not developed merely through studying fables and literature of one's native culture out of context or through a separately taught thematic unit on a culture. We cannot "take time out for Black history," for example, one month a year. In the multicultural classroom we must integrate the study of other cultures into our daily classroom life and everyday curriculum (Piper 1986). Pride must be developed for the culture of origin, which is part of the students' *present* lives (as is shown in Figure 7.1) and for the new cultures, or complex ways of living, that students are learning to understand.

The second goal for a multicultural classroom is the development of hope for and pride in the shared culturally diverse life in this country, which is new for some. Implicit in this goal is the assumption that there is no one desirable mainstream, "target" culture, that instead there are many cultural ways of doing things, some of which are necessary for students to attain power and access to their personal goals. Learning necessary ways of communicating in different situations to attain goals is part of the shared culture children learn in a multicultural classroom. As Figure 7.1 illustrates, the cultures of students who make up a classroom community cannot be sorted into separate, neat little boxes. Students bring different but interacting and intersecting cultural viewpoints into the classroom community. Learning to be part of that community can help students develop a "transcendent identity," which combines attachment and detachment, freedom and self-actualization, commitment and objectivity (Ehlers and Crawford 1983), and which looks toward the future of larger national and world communities.

These goals affect the ways in which teachers go about planning the curriculum, and organizing the physical and social environments. They affect

teachers' relationships with students by making them partners in the educational enterprise, not just providers of information. They reveal the essential role of
the teacher as being community builder and community leader. They also point
to the importance of the teacher as provider of experiences that bridge between
students' previous culture and language and the new ones. This bridging is the
topic of Chapter 8, in which we will discuss ways in which you can help your
students reach out to the communities of school, home and beyond. Of course,
the two goals we have just described will be difficult to reach, if not unattaina-
ble, unless they are the goals of the whole school, not just of your classroom.
Creating a multicultural classroom is not only the topic of this chapter, but is a
theme that runs throughout this book. In this chapter we will confine ourselves
to discussing your roles within a truly multicultural classroom, along with
strategies for working with students to bring about a cooperative, multicultural,
integrated classroom literacy community.

The Teacher as Student of Culture

In order to create a multicultural classroom, you first must become a researcher,
a student of culture. You must be open to and interested in actively seeking new
knowledge about the cultures of your students. You can do this in three ways.
The first is to study about other cultures. Seek out information about the native
cultures of the children with whom you work, and read it. Ask the students,
their parents, and colleagues in the school who are more informed than you are
about the given culture to talk with you and to share resources with you. If you
have students from just one or two cultures of origin, you have the luxury of
studying these cultures and perhaps their languages in some depth. Butterfield
(1983) gives a specific example of learning about and integrating Native
American cultural ways into classrooms for students from that culture. Of
course, if you have students from many cultures, you may not become an expert
on each culture, but you can locate materials about them and refer to these
materials when the need or occasion arises. In this way, you can gradually learn
a great deal about many cultures as you continue to teach from year to year.

The second means for learning about your students is to make a study of
how to learn about culture. Effective multicultural teachers are "culture
watchers" who share the methods of an anthropologist, learning how to stand
back a little and look, listen, and ask the right questions about cultures that are
different from their own. Saville-Troike (1978) has collected an excellent set of
questions to use in learning about the cultures of students in your classroom.
Learn to ask such questions and to use them when meeting parents, visiting
students' homes, and dealing with students. Heath (1983) describes how
teachers in the southeastern United States learned about the oral and print
traditions of the different English-speaking sub-groups in their classes by both

studying these traditions directly and having the students act as community ethnographers to collect cultural information to share and use at school.

The third means to learn about your students' cultures is similar to the second, but it works on a more personal, individual level. It is to be interested, open, sensitive, and observant. Can you notice the effects that your behaviors and classroom events have on students from other cultures, and ask yourself if these effects could have a cultural origin? Can you pause before reacting (within your own cultural expectations) to your students' behavior in class to make sure that you are interpreting their behavior correctly and fairly? Perhaps a student who will not contribute in class or look you in the eye is behaving in a way that shows respect in his culture, although it seems to indicate apathy and insolence in yours. Perhaps the student next to him interrupts classroom discussions frequently to share her ideas and seems fond of yelling out, "Teacher! Teacher!" throughout the class day because this participation style and form of address are appropriate in her culture, although they seem to be excessive and uncontrolled in yours. The cultural backgrounds students bring into the classroom have an effect on the success of methods of grouping students (Jordan 1985; Bassano 1986; Heath 1983), on language schemata (Heath 1982; Butterfield 1983) and on how one's nonverbal behavior is interpreted (Hall 1976). If you can keep yourself open to explanations outside your own cultural experience and continually broaden that cultural experience and utilize it in making instructional decisions, you will be much more successful in a building multicultural classroom community.

The Teacher as Promoter of a Multicultural Point of View

In addition to learning about culture, the teacher in the integrated classroom is the model and the leader who establishes the expectation that the class as a whole will take a multicultural point of view. Cultural awareness and tolerance are integrated into daily classroom life. In your organization of classroom activities, be aware that students' cultural ways may influence what kind of learning environment helps them most. Students from Asian and Middle Eastern cultures where schools often operate in accordance with a very strict transmission model (large classes and teachers controlling all interaction) will need to adjust and gradually adapt to your integrated classroom environment. Students from traditionally cooperative, peer-oriented cultures might have difficulty with several aspects of transmission-model teaching, such as being expected not to help one another and being singled out for responses (Au and Jordan 1981; Erickson and Mohatt, 1982). Besides respecting and learning about the cultures of your students, you must develop your repertoire of teaching styles so that you can make adaptations in your classroom rules, procedures, and groupings to accommodate these students' needs.

Things will not always run smoothly in your integrated classroom. You should expect cultural conflicts to arise, and you should develop effective processes to deal with them, processes that resolve the conflict at the same time that they help students become more tolerant and respectful of one another and of one another's respective cultures. The multicultural classroom community faces potential or real cultural conflicts openly and directly. Students are able to use introspection to explore their own cultural stereotypes and to learn that one another's cultures, dialects, and languages have equal worth as a source of linguistic and conceptual growth. Later in this chapter, we will describe two processes that will help you to prevent such clashes and to deal with them should they arise.

The Teacher as Culture Educator

The integrated curriculum takes advantage of the many cultural resources available in the classroom by making culture part of its content. Not only teachers, but also students become researchers and students of culture. Help your students to use one another's cultures as the focus of study. You and your students can use the anthropological research techniques of introspection, interviewing, collecting records and artifacts, observation, and participant observation to study similarities and differences in cultural and language ways of students in the class, of families of class members, and of other members of the community (Heath 1983; Wigginton 1985). The homeFUN activities in your integrated units and curriculum can also be consistently employed to integrate students' home lives and cultural experiences with their school lives in the multicultural classroom community. Not only should you make the direct study of culture part of your curriculum, you should also try to incorporate an international point of view in whatever you are studying. For example, rather than teach a separate unit on the contributions of immigrants, your everyday study of history (or science or literature) can consistently make students aware that among the important figures in North American history, many were immigrants or came from minority ethnic groups. Only by *integrating* a multicultural perspective into the daily life of the classroom can you make it into a true community.

The following list summarizes two primary goals of multicultural education and three essential roles of the teacher in making the classroom community a multicultural one.

THE PRIMARY GOALS OF MULTICULTURAL EDUCATION

1. *That students develop pride in their varied cultures of origin.*
2. *That students develop hope for and pride in the shared culturally diverse life in their new country.*

THREE ROLES OF THE TEACHER IN THE MULTICULTURAL CLASSROOM COMMUNITY

1. *Become a student of culture who is sensitive to cultural nuances and who actively seeks knowledge about other cultures.*
2. *Actively promote a multicultural point of view, infusing cultural awareness and tolerance, and appreciation of differences into all aspects of classroom life.*
3. *Help students become students of culture, teaching them processes for studying culture and providing resources and information about culture as part of the curriculum.*

7.7 THE COOPERATIVE CLASSROOM COMMUNITY

In transmission classrooms, most events fall into one of two categories. The first category consists of competitive events, in which students vie for limited rewards. The underlying premise of these activities is, "If you succeed, I fail; if I succeed, you fail." Competitive events include trying to win in classroom contests, working for a limited number of high grades, and trying to get the right answer first in a question-and-answer session or in a reading group. The second category includes individualistic events, in which students work alone toward a goal and are evaluated on the basis of their performance. The underlying premise of these individualistic events is, "My success or failure is unrelated to your success or failure." These events include the lessons, seat work, workbooks and homework that fill most of the typical school day. Cooperative events, whose premise is, "We succeed or fail together," are rare in typical classrooms (Moorman et al 1984; Goodlad 1984; Combs 1979). Yet this third category of classroom events has great potential for enhancing learning, in particular in the multicultural classes of second language learners.

Effectiveness of Cooperative Teaching

In Chapter 3, we suggested that activities such as the competitive or individual-istic ones just described can be altered to become more collaborative and cooperative. There are compelling reasons why this change is desirable. Indeed, a considerable body of evidence contributed by researchers from a wide range of backgrounds indicates that cooperative teaching and learning offer advantag-es over other styles, particularly within heterogeneous and multicultural classes. Adding cooperative learning to the classroom has been found to have advantages for students' academic development; in the quality and quantity of language input provided; in student motivation; in increased opportunities for higher level learning; and in students' acquisition of social and interactive skills. We shall briefly summarize recent research in each of these areas.

Contributions of Cooperative Learning to Academic Achievement

When it comes to creating opportunities for teaching and learning, many heads (the students') are better than one (the teacher's). Peer and cross-age tutoring and cooperative/small group learning are two major approaches used by teachers to enhance learning. These approaches enable teachers to tailor instruction to meet individual student needs and allow teachers to work with smaller groups or individual students. Considerable evidence documents the generally positive academic achievement effects of both dyadic, tutoring interactions (Allen 1976; Cohen and Kulik 1981; Kulik & Kulik 1982; Levin, Glass & Meister 1984) and small, cooperative learning task interactions (Sharan 1980; Slavin 1983a, 1983b, Kagan 1986). However, this literature also indicates that these achievement effects differ considerably, depending upon the manner in which the peer interactions are organized and conducted.

Effects of Cooperative Learning on Quantity and Quality of Language Input and Output

As stated in Chapter 1 and elaborated upon in Chapter 5, the current theoretical consensus within the field of second language education is that second language development is a highly interactive and collaborative process in which second language learners actively engage in constructing and testing out hypotheses about how language works as they participate and communicate with others in meaningful activities. Cooperative classrooms provide the rich context required for language learning and provide opportunities both for the input and the output needed for language development. Using paired and small group activities increases the amount of meaningful and interesting language provided to second language learners and can also greatly multiply the number of opportunities available to them to practice and use the target language (Long,

Adams, McLean and Castanos 1976; Cathcart, Strong and Wong-Fillmore 1980; Johnson 1980, 1983; Enright 1982; Enright and Gomez 1985; Long and Porter 1985; Gomez 1987). Cooperative classrooms provide the rich social environment needed for the language play without requiring a presiding "judge" to develop the student confidence that permits language acquisition. Cooperative classrooms, in summary, provide the "share discourse" and "thought discourse" situations that demand that students use language in many ways, for many purposes.

Cooperation and Motivation

Cooperative learning is also fun! Peer interaction is intrinsically motivating to students. It provides "fun discourse" which increases students' willingness to communicate. Sutton-Smith (1982), in discussing his theory of children's play, observed that when children are left to themselves, they ordinarily choose to spend much of their time interacting with others. Educators have the opportunity to engage children much more fully in their own learning and in school tasks by bringing playtime energy, excitement, and communication into classrooms. When peer interaction is carefully incorporated into instruction, curriculum objectives and materials become an integral part of children's experience instead of serving as external impositions.

With specific regard to the second language learner in school, meaningfulness is an essential element of successful language input (Krashen 1982; Ventriglia 1982; Littlejohn 1983; Urzúa 1985; Enright and McCloskey 1985). Interaction with peer language models has been shown to be one of the key potential sources of such motivated learning intake (Wong-Fillmore 1976; Peck 1978; Cathcart, Strong and Wong-Fillmore 1980; Johnson 1980, 1983, Ventriglia 1982; Gomez 1987). Cooperative learning, which demands significant peer interaction, provides highly motivating learning opportunities to second language learners.

Cooperation and Higher Order Thinking Skills

Peer interaction learning activities have the potential to involve students frequently and fully in using their powers of critical thinking and problem-solving. Further, they can involve students in the "higher-order" cognitive operations identified by Bloom and his colleagues (1956), such as making inferences and generalizations and summarizing and evaluating information. Studies of cooperative small group activities in both native English-speaking classrooms (Johnson, Skon and Johnson 1980; Sharan, Hertz-Lazarowitz and Reiner 1980; Sharan 1984) and bilingual classrooms (Cohen 1986) have demonstrated the positive contribution that peer interaction can make to the development of students' critical thinking processes. Among these new ways of using language which can and should be developed in our second language students is that of *thinking* in English—that is, second language learners should be provided with multiple opportunities to develop both their intra-personal as well as their inter-personal English language skills. Cooperative learning activities can help us to reach this goal.

Cooperation and the Development of Social Skills and Interactive Competence

Cooperative learning activities can give second language learners the opportunity to develop *interactional* competence in the new culture at the same time that they are developing *analytic* competence in their new language. The opportunity to develop interactional competence is one that may not be readily available to these students in settings outside the classroom. Native English-speaking students from the majority culture arrive at school with interactive repertoires and experiences with print that largely match those which are required for academic success. Second language learners, on the other hand, often arrive at school with interactive repertoires and literacy experiences that are discontinuous (Ogbu 1982) from school repertoires. Cooperative peer interaction activities offer teachers the opportunity to create "mixed forms" of interaction (Erickson and Mohatt 1982) which tap the students' previously developed interactive and cognitive repertoires in order to add new ways of interacting and using oral and written language for creating meaning (Au and Jordan 1981). In addition to the development of interactive skills, cooperative interactive learning has been shown to improve relations among different racial and ethnic groups, to develop mutual concern among students, and to develop student self-esteem (Slavin 1980, 1981; Parker 1985).

Cooperative interactive learning is the means by which you can take full advantage of the rich resources in your classroom and provide your students with a social learning environment that gives them more, not either/or.

7.8 CREATING A COOPERATIVE CLASSROOM COMMUNITY

In your role as leader of a classroom community that aspires to be cooperative and multicultural, you will become more than an evaluator and one who imparts information. You will become a facilitator, a fellow participant, a group process trainer, an interactionist, and a consultant who helps students who are working together to solve their own problems. While no longer being at the center of all communication and collaboration, you will still play a central role

Cooperative, collaborative learning is the means by which students can take full advantage of the rich human resources in the multicultural classroom.

in setting forth the rules and expectations for how interaction is to occur. As with any educational goal for students, a classroom won't become a cooperative, multicultural community just because you wish it to be. You will have to carefully build it with and for your students. This building process should begin as the year begins. It can be summarized in three steps: (a) developing classroom community identity; (b) formulating cooperative goals and activities which help students to learn about and through one another's cultures; and (c) training students in group process skills. Each of these steps is described below. Following each step is a set of specific teaching strategies that will help you with its implementation.

Developing a Classroom Identity

A class becomes a cohesive and cooperative community as it identifies itself as a unit. Developing this unit, of course, will be much easier for classroom teachers who have students for all or most of a day. It is also certainly possible for a teacher who has students for short periods periodically, and even for itinerant (no-classroom) teachers. One way to begin this task is to create a specific class identify. Select with the students some class symbols that can be used often in class and that will quickly identify students with the class. These symbols will become immediately recognizable and meaningful even to beginning second language students. Some examples follow.

A class name. A positive, affectionate, catchy name for the room, class or class members helps students feel they "own" the group. It certainly is better than referring to a group by its teacher's name (Ms. Peacock's class) or the room number (205z). Encourage student nominations, add a few of your own, and then take a vote. The name that is selected can be used as a label outside the classroom door, and when talking to and about the students as a group. One international school uses the word for "friend" in many different languages to identify classes (*amigo, tomodachi, ami, rafiki,* and so on). Some students like to include the teacher's name in some alliterative way in the class name (e.g., Hart's Heroes, Galbo's Gators). Others have an affectionate name for the room with reference to its activities (e.g., The Mad Tea Party, The Carnival, The Circus) or make use of favorite places in literature to create a warm classroom identity (i.e., Sherwood Forest, Wonderland, Narnia, Marvel Universe). Still others use an admired animal (e.g., Eagle, Owl, Leopard) or plant (e.g., redwood, foxfire, columbine).

A class mascot. Bring a "friend" to school for the class to adopt as the class mascot. Relate the mascot to your class name or to a common interest held by students of the age you teach. We've seen a teddy bear, a lion puppet, a burro piñata, and a stuffed eagle used affectionately to create a sense of community. Your class mascot may not even need to be visible: you could use a six-foot invisible pookah named Harvey! One class had an imaginary class member named David Rostimodo who moved along with the students in the class from year to year. David was never seen, but his name appeared in every issue of the class paper, on every play program, and even on the list of graduates when students moved to the next school! David Rostimodo was a delightful shared secret among class members and gave them something to remember for a lifetime. Make sure that your mascot is active in the class on a daily basis, not just sitting in a corner. A creative teacher used her class mascot, an Ernie doll (from Sesame Street), as the correspondent in interactive journals. Another playful teacher we know helped the Pink Panther to leave pink footprints all over the room at night when the students were gone. In the morning, students would follow the trail to see what mischief the panther had been up to or what surprise he had left. With help from you and the students, your mascot can read stories, take attendance, lead songs, or give homeFUN assignments (see Chapter 8). Puppets and stuffed friends are helpful icebreakers for students who are reluctant to speak. Young students in particular lose their self-consciousness and fear of making mistakes when talking to an inanimate friend.

A class logo. A lively integrated art and writing activity for the beginning of the year which will also support the development of classroom identity is the design of a class logo. Discuss with students what you want this symbol to communicate, and have students make up a logo that incorporates the class name, a mascot, and, perhaps, a motto. As your classroom community develops throughout the year, symbols of its identity may grow. Perhaps students will add door decorations featuring the logo or costumes for the mascot (featuring the logo) for various holidays or special events.

And more. . . . A class song; a poem; an adopted zoo animal; a tree planted, named, and marked by the class; class plays; class projects; a newspaper; a newsletter; a literary magazine; or a scrapbook all can contribute to developing and maintaining a sense of class identity. Projects that students cooperate to produce and that are a product of their learning together are the best unity builders. A written and pictorial record of class events will help to celebrate what the class has accomplished and to promote the class in the school and in the greater community.

The following list summarizes the steps involved in creating a classroom community identity:

HOW TO DEVELOP A CLASSROOM COMMUNITY IDENTITY

1. *Help the students choose a positive, catchy name for the class.*
2. *Choose a class mascot to lead and participate in class activities.*
3. *Design a class logo and use it on class products, etc.*
4. *Create a class scrapbook.*

Formulating a Class's Cooperative Goals, Rules, and Activities

Edelsky, Draper, and Smith (1983) wrote an insightful article about the beginning of the year in the classroom of an exemplary second language teacher whom they called "KS." The study illustrates the powerful effect that changing rules, activities, and participant structures to meet the criteria of the integrated model can have on the creation of a cooperative classroom community. KS began the first activity of the first day of school with a clear expectation that students would cooperate. The expectation was made clear to students by the nature of the task and by the teacher's directions. KS's directions were often not completely explicit for her sixth-grade students. She gave a direction that established a cooperative procedure, such as, "If there are more than five waiting, do something else." She did not specify what "something else" was, but communicated high expectations for students to make decisions that would benefit the smooth running of the class. Students in this class worked independently and cooperatively, and the class ran smoothly even on the first day!

Starting the Year

Formulating cooperative goals and activities should also begin as the year begins. Research on first language classrooms also suggests the importance that effective activities at the beginning of the school year have for establishing a classroom climate that will be successful all year (Emmer, Evertson, and Anderson 1980; Brooks 1985). Teachers who are effective managers tend to exhibit behaviors and select activities that meet students' needs; to model and teach a clear set of rules; to show interest in individual students; and to use nonverbal means to enhance clarity and understanding.

Comfort and safety are the first order of business in developing cooperation and community. To provide for safety needs, anticipate and answer as well as you can the questions students are asking as they enter a new room. These will include questions about safety and belonging ("How do I belong and succeed here?"); questions for information ("Where do I sit?" "What do I do?" "What will this teacher be like?" "What will the other students be like?"); questions about students' individuality ("Will people here respect me as an individual?" "Will they respect my cultural differences?"); and questions about rules ("What are the rules here?" "Does this teacher mean what (s)he says?"). Anticipate these questions and provide answers in a comfortable fashion. A great way to launch a new classroom community is to greet students as they enter, showing interest in them and helping them to find a seat. Check carefully the proper pronunciation of students' names. Tell students a little about yourself. You might feature yourself on a Citizen of the Week bulletin board, placing items on the board that tell something about you even to beginning second language learners (show pictures of your family and pets and bring in realia symbolic of your favorite hobbies).

The next order of business in developing cooperation as part of your classroom community is to create room for students to initiate and to make decisions within the expectations you have established for them. Rules will vary depending on your students' ages, your teaching situation, and your style (see Chapter 3). Your rules should communicate your basic expectation that the classroom is for learning, that there is enough learning to go around so that everyone can succeed and that it is everyone's job to help everyone else succeed. The classroom rules and your behavior should explicitly communicate that in your classroom, intolerance or ridicule of someone else's differences is unacceptable. As students are able, encourage them to help you refine the rules and turn them into a "classroom constitution." Stevick's (1982) image of the jungle gym conveys the value of establishing rules and procedures for your integrated classroom:

> Children build their muscles by climbing around on a jungle gym in any way they like but they can do so only because the apparatus itself is both rigid and open. (1982:65)

The integrated classroom supports students' linguistic, cognitive, and social "muscle building" because it is both rigid—with clear goals, rules, and procedures—and open—with room for and direction toward student initiative (see Chapter 3). The "jungle gym" provided by the integrated classroom teacher is always there to support the students as they climb, offering alternate routes to the top.

Changing Tasks to Make Them Cooperative

As the school year starts, make sure to lay the groundwork for the cooperative, communicative activities that will characterize your classroom throughout the year. Depending on your students' age and proficiency, you can begin with a very simple cooperative task (e.g., students asking the person next to them a few simple get-acquainted questions) or a more complex task (e.g., students in small groups completing and putting up bulletin boards you have planned).

The integrated teaching model proposed in this book mandates both the integration of learning, that is, subject matter and language; and learners, that is, the classroom participants in a classroom community. Thus, tasks must be designed to be genuinely cooperative—involving students working together toward a goal that is both shared and authentic.

Cohen (1986) provides clear and useful lists of some of the characteristics of tasks that either do or do not support productive classroom peer interaction and group work. According to Cohen, the characteristics of a task that supports group work are as follows:

- Has more than one answer or more than one way to solve the problem
- Is intrinsically interesting and rewarding
- Allows different students to make different contributions
- Uses multimedia
- Involves sight, sound, and touch
- Requires a variety of skills and behaviors
- Also requires reading and writing
- Is challenging
  (1986:57–58)

Here are the characteristics of a task that does *not* support group work:

- Has a single right answer
- Can be done more quickly and efficiently by one person than by a group
- Is too low-level
- Involves simple memorization or routine learning (1986:58)

As Cohen's lists suggest, part of what is involved in planning tasks to be used in peer interaction activities is the selection of the materials and discourse that go with the task. The selection of these two components of the activity should be aimed at giving focus and structure to the task. In this way, students' collaboration will be maximally purposeful and related to the instructional goals of the activity, and you will be free to exercise your role as the students' discourse partner.

To be most effective, materials and discourse should be chosen so that activities are both cooperative and real. If students are sitting together helping one another with individual work sheets, the task is not a truly cooperative one, but rather a cooperative version of an independent task. If teams of four compete to see which team can finish a set of math problems first, the task again is not truly cooperative, but a cooperative version of a competitive task. Students collaborating to complete a work sheet may work in a manner that is cooperative; however, unless the students see a genuine purpose for the work sheet, the task is not "authentic," or "owned" by the students (Edelsky and Smith 1984). In this case, the task is not of the highest possible interest and usefulness to students.

All of these variations of traditional classroom tasks add a "must cooperate" component and lots of share discourse to the learning activities. As such, they represent great improvements over the exclusive use of the lecture, question-and-answer, and seat work teaching that presently characterize a large proportion of classroom time. We ask you to take your planning one step further by designing tasks for your classroom which meet Cohen's criteria and are thus both cooperative and authentic, with the outcome being one that students "own." The idea of ownership doesn't necessarily imply that the task has been selected by the students. Rather, it suggests that they understand its purpose and accept it as their own (Edelsky and Smith 1984; Wigginton 1985). An authentic, real task is one whose purpose makes sense to students. The task becomes its own reward. An example of such a task is students working together to decide on a community hero they would like to interview; making an appointment for that interview; doing background reading; and writing a set of questions to prepare for that interview (see "Heroes and Superheroes" in Part II). Other such tasks might include making a Big Book adaptation of *Rain Makes Applesauce* (Scheer and Bilek 1964), to be shared with family and friends (see "Rain Makes Applesauce" in Part II) or working with a fellow student to make pizzas that are tailored to both students' personal preferences.

7.9 COOPERATIVE ACTIVITIES

We offer the following set of learning tasks which provide students with both cooperative and authentic experiences working with peers.

Cooperative Projects

One broad type of peer interaction activity is the small group project or investigation, in which groups of students must work together to complete an assignment—a question that needs to be answered, a puzzling situation, or a task with several different steps. Projects usually involve research, paper-and-pencil tasks, and concrete, "hands-on" things to do. Generally, projects are completed over a relatively long period of time. They may be incorporated into all subject-matter areas of the curriculum. They can also be used to integrate different content areas and language processes. One project activity might be groups of students learning about city wildlife. Students could conduct "wildlife surveys" of the numbers and kinds of wildlife spotted on the school grounds and in the neighborhood. They could then write up their findings for the school paper (science). For another project, groups of students could locate and examine myths from different countries along with the types of heroes and heroines who appear in them. Students could then compare their results with those of other groups (language arts). Or groups of students who lived near one another could investigate changes in housing in their home neighborhoods over the past fifty years by looking at historical records and interviewing neighbors who had lived there that long (social studies). Or student groups could plan a duck pond for the school yard by researching the environmental needs of ducks; making scale drawings; computing the cost of the necessary materials; raising the necessary funds; buying the materials; and then doing the actual construction (mathematics).

Jigsaw

Students use division of labor to simplify a difficult task in this more sophisticated cooperative learning activity (Aaronson 1978; Cohen 1986). The class is divided into teams. Each team works on the same set of learning tasks, and each group member within a team has a different task. Members of different teams with the same learning task come together and collaborate to become "experts" in that area of the learning unit. The experts in each area then return to their original teams and teach what they have learned to the rest of their group. For example, a class studying a unit on their home state could be divided into six groups, each with five members. In each group, one person would become an expert on a different topic relating to the home state: its history, its people, its products, its climate, and its tourist attractions. Students studying each area would meet together to learn all that they could about their respective topics. When students returned to their original groups, each one would be an expert holding one piece of the puzzle. Students could put the jigsaw puzzle together as they taught one another about the state and put together a product—such as a book—to show what they had learned.

Writing Conferences

The process approach to writing, discussed in Chapter 6, is highly appropriate in the integrated language classroom. This approach can add a sense of shared purpose, a spirit of cooperation, and significant oral and written discourse experiences to your curriculum and classroom.

Proponents of a "process" or "workshop" or "developmental" approach to writing (e.g., Graves 1983; Kirby and Liner 1981; Calkins 1986) place great importance on the presence of an authentic audience for student writing that is undertaken, and peers are an obvious first choice. In Chapter 13 of her recent book, *The Art of Teaching Writing,* Calkins describes how a teacher named JoAnn goes about teaching students to be effective "writing teachers" by helping them learn to respond in genuine and useful ways to one another's writing. JoAnn begins the day's writing workshop by saying to her students:

> Yesterday I talked with you about being writers. Today I want to talk with you about being writing teachers. There is not just one writing teacher in this room—there are thirty of you. Every one of you needs to become a writing teacher. (1987:129)

JoAnn then lists on the board a simple framework for peer conferences:

a. The writer reads out loud.

b. Listeners respond or, if the piece is confusing, the listeners ask questions, then respond.

c. Listeners focus on the content, perhaps asking questions about it. The writer teaches them about the subject.

d. The focus shifts to the text. What will the writer do next and how will he or she do it? (1987:129-30)

JoAnn then takes students through the steps of the framework with one writer: modeling, questioning, and guiding students in the use of the steps. She helps them through this and future conferences to become genuine and encouraging listeners to one another, to know when a conference has been successful, and to work toward asking open-ended questions that will help the writer develop his or her thought. As JoAnn develops these skills with the whole group, she encourages students to practice them with peers in pairs and in small groups.

JoAnn follows a learning cycle similar to the one presented in Chapter 2 of this book. She sets a purpose for what students are doing; introduces behaviors; models the behaviors; gives students a chance to practice them under her supervision, then independently; and finally encourages students to incorporate these newly learned behaviors into their writing repertoires.

Peer conferences like the ones used in the process writing curriculum can be used in other ways in the integrated classroom. Brainstorming sessions can be scheduled in which student authors, playwrights, inventors, and scientists together can come up with many ideas for their writing, inventions, and experiments, and then cull them for the more useful ones. Once conferences have been well established in the classroom, students will use this peer interaction activity spontaneously throughout their daily activities.

Cooperative Games

Cooperative learning can be extended to the playground through the use of cooperative games (see the resource list at the end of this chapter). These games have been designed so that students can have a good time while using lots of oral fun discourse and share discourse to learn positive things about themselves and others and about how they should behave in the world. They are games in which everyone wins. As the factory model has come to dominate our schools, so production, machine orientation, and overspecialization have become central to our games. Our games have become rigid, judgmental, highly organized, and excessively goal-oriented. In contrast, cooperative games stress cooperation, acceptance, involvement, and fun.

Traditional games can easily be changed to cooperative games through the adjustment of rules. For example, you can have students focus on how many times they can hit the volleyball continuously, rather than on trying to make their opponents miss. You and your class can play nonelimination Simon Says (a great activity for practicing receptive language) by having two games occurring simultaneously. When students miss, they simply move to the other game, instead of having to sit out!

Cooperative games can also be created or adapted to become a part of an integrated thematic unit. (For examples of this, see "Where's Spidey?" in "Heroes and Superheroes," Part II.) For a large assortment of games which you can use or adapt for your own purposes, see the resources listed at the end of this chapter.

Learning Centers

Learning centers are an excellent resource for providing students with opportunities to practice and extend skills and concepts learned in more direct instruction. In a learning center, students can work without direct teacher supervision. They can use centers either individually or cooperatively with peers. A lot of planning time is required to create and run a "learning-centered" classroom that will entice and involve your students as well as meet their instructional needs. However, this kind of teaching has tremendous benefits. Learning centers permit some students to work independently and productively while the teacher is free to work individually or in small groups with other students. Center activities can be organized so that students of various language backgrounds and abilities must pool their linguistic, cognitive, and cultural resources to complete the learning center task. (Typical learning center activities incorporate two or more of the four types of discourse.) Perhaps the most important aspect of learning centers is that they make learning more fun both for the students using them and for the teachers who are free to participate in "real" discourse with individuals and small groups while spending less time disciplining uninterested students.

In planning a learning center, consider the following questions (based on Wayant and Wilson 1974):

Where will the center be? Provide enough space to accommodate at least one or two students, the materials they will be using, and activities they will be doing without interfering with others in the class. Separate noisy activities from quiet ones: a drama center where students are rehearsing a comic skit should not be placed near the quiet reading corner.

How will the center be managed? Ground rules must be set for who can use the center and how and when it will be used. On some occasions you may want to assign students to the centers, but try to make centers so inviting that students will choose to work there. Set limits on how many students may work at the center at one time. You can have students sign up for centers, hang student name tags on hooks, have young students wear color-coded center assignment cards around their necks, or think of another clever way to designate that a center is full. You should clarify to students what work should be completed by them before they may go to the center, and design activities so that students know when they have completed a turn and should allow other students to come to the center.

How will the center be constructed? Materials for the center should be sturdy enough to be reused. They may take some time to make, but that time can be regained many times over if they do not have to be remade each year and if they are interesting enough that students want to spend lots of productive time with them. Materials can be made which serve several purposes: a pegboard can be used to hold a variety of center activities; a spinner and a universal game board could be used in many games related to many themes throughout the year.

How will the center be introduced? Do not expect students to know how to use centers the first time they appear in the room. Teach the activities carefully. Start slowly, with one activity. Work with the whole class or with small groups and help students try out the center under your guidance. During the introduction time, you can remove any "bugs" in center procedures. Gradually, you can add more centers and introduce new procedures for learning how to use them, such as peer instruction.

Also, consider the following guidelines for making centers especially conducive to cooperation and second language and literacy learning (also based on Wayant and Wilson 1974):

1. *Directions should be appropriate for independent use.* When introducing each new center to the class, review all center activities. Give instructions to the full group by demonstration and explanation, but also provide directions for activities at the center itself in a manner that is appropriate for students of all language proficiencies. You can record the oral instructions on an audiocassette recorder, display them pictorially, write them, or use some combination of these means (see Chapter 4). If directions are written, include in each center group at least one student who reads well enough to comprehend the directions.

2. *Centers should include a number of activities at several language and learning levels.* A range of center activities will provide choices for the students and will increase their interest in the center. The time that you spend creating the center will be paid back by the time students spend engaged in learning and using language! Providing activities that vary according to difficulty—from basic drill (matching words to pictures) to creative synthesis (composing a song)—will give full second language and native English-speakers a chance to utilize the range of their language and literacy abilities while also allowing them to help beginners use the simpler activities at the learning center. Beginning and mid-second-language students, on the other hand, will be able to experience success with at least one or two center activities while also receiving challenging input.

3. *Centers should have hands-on activities as well as pencil-and-paper tasks.* Hands-on activities will increase interest in centers and will accommodate the different learning styles and second language capacities of students. In addition, a variety of materials often inspires increased student interest (and language use). For example, having an erector set in a science learning center about simple machines will produce much more language than having students fill in blanks on a worksheet, or even draw machines. Student inventions and descriptions can be inspired by real machines (e.g., old clocks, pencil sharpeners, and hand tools) displayed in the center.

4. *Centers should provide a way for students to evaluate themselves either while they participate in the activities or afterward.* Methods for students' self-evaluation include placing answer sheets at the learning center with which students can check their responses when finished; using

activities that require that charts be filled in or scores be kept; and having students cross their names off a class list when they have completed an activity. See that some record of the students' participation is left at the center so you can monitor what students are doing there and evaluate the effectiveness of the center. Use students' records from centers and your observations to determine what adjustments need to be made to centers. Many examples of student self-assessment are included in the portions on learning centers in Part II.

5. *A versatile design for the physical environment will facilitate the effective use of learning centers.* Your classroom design should permit both full and small group instruction with the teacher and independent activities of individuals, pairs, and small groups of students at centers. The sample room design in Figure 7.2 shows such a versatile classroom. The centers should be designed to make their purpose and intended use clear to students, since they are to use centers without direct teacher supervision. Label centers clearly with numbers and/or rebus symbols (see figure), and make the location of materials within the center clear by using picture labels so students can easily find things and put them away (see Chapter 4).

The Computer as Learning Center

The potential of the computer for second language teachers and learners is just beginning to be discovered. Teachers are often hesitant to use these machines because they are uncomfortable with computers, and because no traditions exist for their use in the classroom. These teachers might be helped by envisioning the computer as an exciting and powerful learning center. All of the suggestions for making learning centers effective in the second language classroom are appropriate for computer use. The advantage of using a computer in the classroom is that once good software has been selected, much of the preparation for the center is complete. The challenge of using a computer as a learning center in the classroom is the selection of that good software.

Unfortunately, much of the educational software that has been designed for use with classroom computers has utilized a transmission view of curriculum. Frank Smith (1984) describes this one-way, "drilling software" in this manner:

> It is as drill machines that computers are widely seen today as most relevant in education and where I think they are potentially most dangerous. . . . *Drill and Kill* can fatally damage both literacy and teaching. To anyone who holds that the development of language ability is a matter of learning basic skills through systematic instruction—and there seem to be many well-meaning but misguided people who have that belief—computers can not only do the job of teachers, but they can do it better. They can lead us faster all the way down the path to totally controlled programmatic language instruction (1984:13-14).

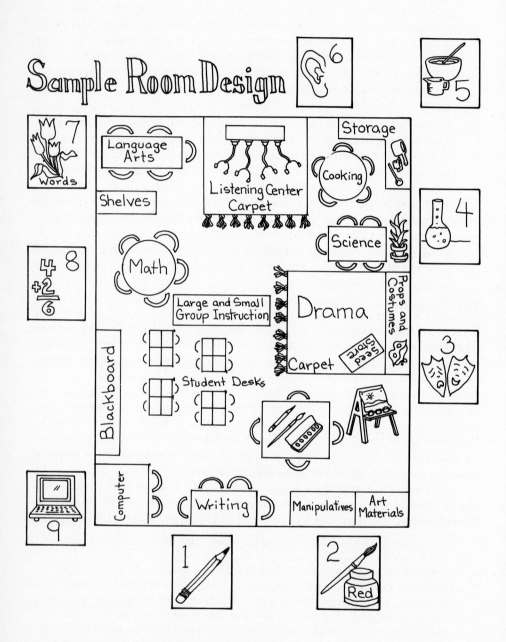

Figure 7.2: Learning Center Room Design

Like Smith, we do not see the role of the teacher as a comprehensive drill provider, nor do we see the potential of computers in language education as lying in their drilling capability. Fortunately, computers can play other roles besides the one of "drill instructor" that Smith describes. Computers can provide the reinforcement and extension of skills and concepts taught in the classroom—one of the purposes of a learning center. They can also be powerful tools for students to accomplish their own goals. As Canale and Barker (1986) point out, in addition to its tutorial role, the classroom computer can also be used as a tool—for communicating, thinking, and having fun—and as a tutee—to be controlled by students (i.e. to respond to commands and to be programmed). Our suggestion here is to choose software, including word processing software, data base management software, and graphics software that utilizes the microcomputer as a powerful tool for your students, and to help students learn to program computers using a programming language such as LOGO (Papert, 1980). LOGO was developed by Papert and his colleagues at the Artificial Intelligence Laboratory at the Massachusetts Institute of Technology to help children learn how to master the technology of the computer and, in the process, to come into contact with deep ideas from science, mathematics and model making.

You can also look for ways to create and/or incorporate the computer learning center into your integrated units. For example, a computer game about finding buried treasure can be incorporated into a unit on pirates, or children's word processing and graphics software can be used for publishing "superheroes" comic books (see Activity No. 4 in the "Heroes and Superheroes" unit). With ingenuity and commitment, computer use in the language classroom can be incorporated in a way that fits the ILT model.

Classroom Correspondence

At the beginning of this chapter, we specified that the integrated classroom community is a literacy community. In this community, writing can be used to help to create community and, in turn, the community aspects of the classroom can be used to organize opportunities for students to use real oral and written discourse. Classroom correspondence is an excellent vehicle for helping you do both.

Dialogue writing, in which two participants "converse" in writing, incorporates the interactive aspects of conversation and the solitary nature of essayist writing. Thus, it can bridge the gap between these two forms of communication (K. Goodman and Y. Goodman 1983; Kreeft 1984). Classroom correspondence can provide a natural means by which students can move from oral communication in English to a new skill: writing for an unseen audience. To encourage written exchanges in the classroom, provide a print-rich environment in which there are interesting and important things to read all over the room, change a few rules or routines (e.g., teach students that they may not interrupt your small group lesson, but may pass you a note), and set up particular activities for written exchanges. Three examples of classroom correspondence activities are:

Message board/mailboxes. Set up a bulletin board where folded notes can be tacked with the name of the intended recipient on the outside, or individual mailboxes in which messages can be placed. Begin writing short notes to students in which you ask questions, comment on their successes in school, relate interesting events, or perhaps just draw and label a small picture. Encourage students to respond to your notes and to begin exchanging notes with one another. Remember that the success of the message board depends on your enthusiasm. Encourage students to explore their own topics on the message board and suggest topics of your own, for example, a joke or riddle exchange.

Interactive journals. Encourage students to write frequently in a bound journal about topics they choose. Carry on a conversation with your students in the journals. They can be a vehicle for you and your students to exchange questions; report personal experiences; make promises; evaluate classroom activities; offer contributions to the class; offer an apology; give directions; and complain or state opinions (Staton 1981). In your responses to student writing, remember these basics:

- Use a direct conversational style. Match the length of and reasoning level of your response to the student's language proficiency and cognitive abilities.

- In your responses, provide new and interesting information that models more complex language and makes the response interesting to read.

- Ask real questions that seek student opinions and information that you don't already know.

- Rather than correcting mechanical errors and focusing on form, correct by focusing on what students are trying to say. In Chapter 5, we discussed "correcting for meaning" in oral discourse. This same method can be used in print in interactional journals. When students make mistakes, use the same language features in your response, but use them correctly.

Letter Writing. Letter writing is a more formal method of carrying on written dialogue in the classroom. It can be utilized by students who have attained some proficiency with written language. Instead of having students write letters as an exercise, use any occasion that comes your way to have them write letters with real purposes. They can write letters home to parents to give important messages about events at school; letters to pen pals in other schools or classes; invitations to special events; thank-you notes to visitors; letters requesting information; fan letters to sports or movie stars or opinion letters to school officials or politicians (Arnow and Byrd 1986). Use the writing process when appropriate to produce polished letters for mailing.

Resources, Roles, and Student Characteristics

Three other factors must be considered in planning cooperative activities: the use of resources; types of participation in the activities; and types of members assigned to groups.

Resources. Selective use of resources can contribute to the "must cooperate" nature of a task. In Chapter 4, we described the functional storage of materials near where they are to be used. Limited resources, for example, an inadequate number of scissors or crayons, can actually be considered an advantage rather than a problem. Such circumstances compel students to set up a division of labor that utilizes both human and physical resources efficiently. For example, in the "Supervehicles" learning center activity in Part II (the "Heroes and Superheroes" unit), Ms. Kay provided plenty of junk materials for making the vehicles at the center. She assigned four students to work together at the center, but she provided only two pairs of scissors, one pair of pliers, and one bottle of glue. The conversations that can be resulted from the "tool scarcity" were more important to Ms. Kay than keeping every student busy every moment.

Roles. Students can participate in groups through a variety of roles. Three of the most commonly used ones are equal roles, differentiated roles, and self-selected roles. *Equal* roles might be played in a group organized to brainstorm ideas for celebrating the fiftieth anniversary of the founding of its school. In a brainstorming activity, the task is to get many ideas for the solution to a problem. Students "bounce" ideas off one another as quickly as they can, with one student taking notes. All ideas are accepted without criticism, even the most ridiculous ones (although it is permissible to laugh!). Using equal roles, all the students (except the note taker) have the same responsibility: to come up with as many ideas as possible.

Differentiated roles involve refinements in the roles students assume when performing a task. This type of role can also add a "must cooperate" component to group activities. Students can specialize—each one can having a piece of the information needed to complete the task. This can be done by having each student do a different part of the research and present it to the rest of the group; by students being assigned different roles in the group (leader, observer, praiser, etc.); or by assigning students to the group to balance their skills and abilities. A differentiated group might be assigned to select from a brainstormed list three workable ideas, which the group could further develop and then present to the class for a vote. This group might have different students appointed to act as chair, recorder, illustrator, and presenter.

A third way to organize participation in peer cooperative groups is to allow the students themselves to determine their roles and responsibilities within these activities. In order for students to assume *self-selected* roles, they must have had considerable experience working together in pairs and groups and in learning how to identify and carry out the various roles and duties involved in classroom learning activities. This manner of organizing cooperative group roles might be feasible only after you had firmly established your overall classroom constitution and a sense of cooperation and community that would support student autonomy. If, in the differentiated group just described, students experienced with group work could appoint members of the group to serve as chair, recorder, illustrator, and presenter, this would be an example of self-selected roles. An even more sophisticated group of students might not be given a list of roles, but would determine for itself what roles were needed and then make the assignments.

Student characteristics. In addition to considering ways in which students may participate in groups, teachers must also consider whom they put together in cooperative groups. Students can be grouped or dispersed in accordance with expertise, interest, social style, and language proficiency.

Students' natural expertise can be deliberately used within peer activities, or expertise can be developed in advance of an activity in class (i.e., the teacher can teach the student a skill, a process, or content information and then the student can become an instructor to peers).

Individual interest in activities will vary and, group assignment can take this factor into account, either by having students choose the task that most interests them or by placing highly interested students in each group, with the hope that their excitement about the topic will be contagious. For example, in designing comic book adventures ("Heroes and Superheroes," Part II), Ms. Kay included both student writers and student artists in each group.

Social style and interactional skills will also vary among students and should be observed closely by the integrated classroom teacher before decisions are made about group placement. Some students are good listeners; some are talkers; some are good at drawing out others; some tend to dominate the conversation; some get along with others easily; some do not. Second language learners approach the classroom interactive environment and the language learning task in a variety of ways (Ventriglia 1982; Gomez 1987). All these factors should be considered. In addition, teachers should vary group composition in order to offer students many different interactional experiences.

Of course, in classrooms with second language learners, the native language of students and their English proficiency and interactional competence should also be considered when teachers create peer learning groups. Placing students in small groups in which no other student speaks the same native language is often desirable, because it produces a "must speak English" component. For some tasks, such as planning an interview of an oldtimer in the neighborhood, a balance of language abilities might be important. Students with similar language abilities might be assigned for other tasks, such as making a diorama showing city wildlife in the area. Opportunities for English language practice in the multilingual classroom can be considerably multiplied if native English-speaking or full second language students are placed with second language learners to collaborate on learning tasks and are provided with oral and written discourse and materials that will support their collaboration (Enright and Gomez 1985).

Many scholars and researchers have focused their attention on the needs, abilities, and learning styles of second language learners, and we have attempted to reflect this work in the assumptions and criteria of the integrated model and in the instructional recommendations that we have made up to this point. However, in the multilingual classroom and wherever there are bilingual or English-speaking peers, or both, working together with second language students, it is also important to consider the proficiency and interactional competence of these student "models" in assigning students to small groups. In her year-long ethnographic investigation of the second language development of three Cambodian kindergartners, Gomez (1987) suggests some of the characteristics of "good" peer language teaching models that can help in doing this. Figure 7.3 lists these characteristics.

Characteristics Resulting in Input to Second Language Learners	Characteristics Encouraging Output from Second Language Learners
Social	*Social*
Friendly, outgoing (a comrade to learner)	Responsive to learner
Facility with language (able and willing to talk)	Facility with language (verbalizes during interactions)
Conversational manner (talks with learner)	Conversational manner (lets learner have turn) Solicits output from learner
Linguistic	*Linguistic*
Adjusts input to learner's proficiency	Provides feedback for learner
Uses verbal cues to supplement environmental cues	Uses variety of linguistic structures (asks questions)
	Uses word play, "follow-the-phrase" routines. (1987:231)

Figure 7.3: Characteristics of Good Peer Language Teaching Models (from Gomez 1987)

While it is doubtful that any student can provide a second language student peer with real input and real dialogue in as sophisticated and careful a way as you can, the results of Gomez's study remind us that some bilingual and native English-speaking models are more helpful than others. You can use these attributes both in making small group assignments and in talking with and preparing English peer models for collaborating with second language colleagues.

The following list summarizes the key steps involved in developing cooperative goals and activities:

HOW TO DEVELOP COOPERATIVE GOALS AND ACTIVITIES

1. Set up rules and procedures that promote cooperation, collaboration, and multicultural understanding. At the beginning of the year:
   a. Establish a supportive environment that provides for students' safety and information needs.
   b. Involve students in writing a classroom constitution that promotes class goals.
   c. Involve students immediately in collaborative, cooperative activities that help them learn about one another and about the cultures represented in the classroom.

2. Build cooperation into the learning tasks students perform by creating "must cooperate" tasks. Include such activities as:
   a. Cooperative projects: Have peer groups conduct investigations and create products to show what they have learned; use "jigsaw" to create situations in which everyone is an expert on some part of a task.
   b. Peer conferences: Help students learn to use brainstorming and feedback conferences with peers.
   c. Cooperative games: Use games that are cooperative, and adapt competitive games to the cooperative model.
   d. Learning centers: Provide students with opportunities for many kinds of discourse in a situation in which they work independently, without direct teacher supervision.
   e. Classroom correspondence: Provide students with opportunities for real written discourse with one another, with the teacher, and with others outside the class.

3. Consider three other factors:
   a. Resources: Use materials and supplies in ways that foster collaboration and cooperation.
   b. Student roles: Use various roles for students which are matched to their needs, including equal roles, differentiated roles, and self-selected roles.

c. *Student characteristics: Group or disperse students in accordance with expertise, interest, social style, and language
proficiency to promote collaboration and language learning.*

7.10 TEACHING GROUP PROCESS SKILLS

"I tried small groups, but they didn't work. The students just couldn't handle them." This statement typifies the feelings many teachers have expressed about their experiences with small classroom groups. What would happen if you tried reading and the students just couldn't handle it? You would try again! It seems that the most important life skills we teach in school are those which often are only implicitly communicated, such as skills for getting along with people and getting things done with groups of people. In Chapter 3, we discussed how rules can be changed to facilitate language learning in the integrated classroom. We also discussed how time could be used differently—for example, with several activities going on at once, including small group activities without the teacher. We cannot expect students to work well in cooperative groups if we just put them there and say, "Work together!" any more than we would expect them to learn to read if we handed them *War and Peace* and said, "Read!" Putting students in groups is not enough. Putting them in groups and giving them appropriate tasks is not enough. Students cannot be expected to begin to read *War and Peace* without first having developed the background experiences and the reading ability appropriate to the content and writing level of such a book. Likewise, students will not work well in cooperative groups without being given the prerequisite skills, practice, and experience in using those skills. Thus the final order of business in making your classroom a cooperative community is to teach group process skills to your new community "citizens." You must design appropriate tasks for practicing and mastering cooperative learning; communicate appropriate expectations for students; and provide support as students work to acquire these skills.

If you want your fledgling students to soar in their cooperative learning, you must first begin with some flight preparation on the ground. The basics include such interactive skills as listening, turn taking, and learning how to "get the floor," and such task-orientation skills as learning to take responsibility and staying with an assignment without constant supervision.

After students have been given training and preparation on the ground, they are ready to move on to short, trial flights. At this level, students must learn to manage group activities; to develop effective working relationships among members; to monitor progress and express support; to bring a stray member back into line with the group goals, and to sustain group energy.

Finally, you must prepare your students for long-distance flying and fancy maneuvers in their group activities. At this level, they develop and use high-level reasoning. They learn the skill of summarizing; they seek accuracy; and they cultivate the ability to elaborate on their work. In this way, they move toward deep understanding of the material at hand and toward mastery of the assigned materials. The goal is that these students will eventually be in charge of their own flight plans. As independent learners, they will seek to reconceptualize the material being studied; resolve cognitive conflict; search for more information; and communicate the rationales behind their conclusions.

We suggest that you make these essential group process skills explicit in your teaching. Write them directly into your plans, giving them the prominence they deserve. In this section we offer you a starter set of strategies to help you begin teaching your students to work together effectively and cooperatively. For further study, we refer you to the suggested resources at the end of this chapter that describe the teaching of cooperative social skills and that suggest cooperative teaching exercises.

Strategies to Teach Cooperative Group Process Skills

Taking Responsibility: Classroom Jobs

We saw earlier in this chapter and in Chapter 3 that in the integrated classroom, many leadership functions that are typically performed by the teacher become student responsibilities (e.g., the maintenance and distribution of materials; the operation of audiovisual equipment; attendance taking; lunch count; greeting and providing tours to visitors; maintaining the classroom library; preparing bulletin boards and learning centers; dismissing the class for activities; chairing discussion groups, and so on). Helping students learn to take on classroom responsibility is an effective way to develop the independence and commitment to a task that are necessary for group work.

Before giving students classroom jobs, see that they are trained, by you or by another student, to perform the task well. Then see that a "coach" is available to give them encouragement and feedback on their performance, with occasional suggestions for improvement. Give students the opportunity to try out different roles. Students can be matched to roles in a variety of ways. Some teachers use a chart to rotate responsibilities. Other teachers require students to make oral or written "applications" for new jobs periodically. On these "applications" and in a follow-up "job interview," students are given opportunities to make it clear that they understand the requirements of the new task. You also might choose to issue "licenses" for classroom privileges. In this procedure, after students have been trained and have demonstrated competence and responsibility, they may receive a license for some activity, such as operating the record player or tape recorder; using the restroom with a wooden pass; correcting their own papers, using an answer key; or taking home materials from the classroom library. Although these responsibilities and procedures may take more time to organize and establish at first, in the end they will produce a classroom that operates smoothly and efficiently, with minimal teacher direction.

Working in a Group: Class Meetings

Glasser (1969) describes his use of classroom meetings, "in which the teacher leads a whole class in a non-judgmental discussion about what is important and relevant to them" (p. 122). Such meetings, held periodically in your class to discuss issues and solve problems, can provide diagnostic information and numerous opportunities for share discourse, fact discourse, and thought discourse. They also provide an excellent opportunity for you to model effective group leadership and participation.

As you lead a class meeting, you can demonstrate the skills you want students to use in later small group work. Be explicit. Label the actions that you are performing (e.g., "I'm trying to make sure that everyone has a chance to talk"). Explain that students should use these same actions when they have their own small group meetings. See that everyone talks in turn and listens

During class meetings students can be introduced to and practice the cooperative skills that they will need for small group work.

while others talk and that all students understand the issues being discussed as much as possible. If necessary, restate the issues until beginning second language learners understand. Make sure that everyone has an opportunity to participate (call on students who are hesitant to volunteer). Show that you are aware of others' feelings by restating their ideas to check your understanding of their point of view. Providing encouragement to others and accepting their contributions as valuable even when others disagree with them should be a central premise of the group.

Seeing Other's Needs and Helping: Welcoming a New Student

The ranks of second language learners include families of immigrants, migrants, refugees, and international employees whose life situations often don't permit them to arrange to enter new schools neatly at the start of a new school year. A new student arriving in the middle of the school year can provide an opportunity to teach and reinforce group process skills. Review classroom rules by having students role-play them for the new student. Assign a helpful "coach" or "buddy" to make sure that the new student understands classroom procedures, activities, and assignments, and to help him or her learn beginning language. Finally, incorporate the new student into the classroom by giving him or her visible classroom responsibilities. If necessary, select a student who is experienced in that responsibility and use her or him as a coach to demonstrate and explain how to perform the job.

To help the new student become oriented to the school, assign peers to accompany him or her on errands to various locations in the school building, for example, the office, the library, or the music room. To help the new student practice language learned on the errand, ask the students to reverse roles on the way back—the new student will be the guide leading the old student on the return route to the classroom.

If peer or adult native language interpreters are available, they can provide a valuable bridge to the new classroom culture for an entering beginning second language learner. It is also your job, however, to determine when the native language bridge is turning into a crutch and to restructure peer pairings to help students develop English skills.

Group Self-Evaluation: Observation of Group Process Skills

In the same way that students learn to make their own language and culture the content of their learning in the integrated language classroom, they can make group process a part of what they study in the classroom community. Students can be taught to evaluate their own groups after they have finished an activity, not only for the quality of the product, but also for the quality of the group process they used. You can suggest that they ask themselves questions like the following: Did everyone participate? Did everyone listen to one another? Was everyone given some responsibility in the task?

Students can be taught observational techniques to measure the group participation. One way to do this is to appoint a student to tally, on a class list, how many times each student was called on and how many times each student volunteered during the entire class discussion or class meeting. Although it may not be perfectly accurate, this information will be invaluable to you in your efforts to distribute your attention equitably. Once the observational technique has been learned, students can repeat the process in their small groups. As students' observational skills improve, they can be encouraged to look at the quality of questions asked (Did we ask open-ended questions sometimes?) and at the types of responses they gave to group members (Were we encouraging? Were we polite in disagreeing? Did we make sure we understood what the other person had to say before we stated our point of view?).

Helping students develop their awareness of their performance as leaders, participants, and observers of groups will help them improve group process skills.

Cooperative Conflict Resolution: Active Mediation

Both language skills and group process skills can be modeled by the way in which a teacher handles conflict situations. We propose a technique that we call "active mediation." You can use this technique to resolve a serious conflict between disputing class members. There are five steps in the procedure.

a. Separate and isolate students (e.g. at their own desks or in separate corners of the classroom) and give them time to calm down.

b. Bring the students together to talk with you, away from the rest of the class, and give each student in turn an opportunity to tell what happened, without interruption. Encourage students to use mime, props, a peer translator, or whatever is needed or available in order to make themselves understood.

c. Ask for clarification. Your highly developed cultural sensitivity is brought into play to help make students aware of misunderstandings related to cultural differences. Ask questions about major discrepancies. A witness may be called in briefly for questioning if a major discrepancy occurs. Usually this is unnecessary. Minor discrepancies should be ignored.

d. Ask students for suggestions about a resolution of the issue and the prevention of another occurrence in the future.

e. Resolve the dispute, incorporating student suggestions if possible. The resolution reflects natural consequences (e.g., repair of any damage done, reparation for disruption, etc.). In almost all conflict situations, some responsibility for the conflict lies with each party. If at all possible, the resolution should involve some sort of compromise that "saves face" and promotes social learning for both parties.

The following list summarizes strategies for teaching cooperative group process skills.

HOW TO TEACH COOPERATIVE GROUP PROCESS SKILLS

1. *Help students feel ownership of the class and learn to take responsibility by providing them with classroom jobs.*
2. *Help students acquire and practice group process skills in class meetings.*
3. *Use the arrival of a new student as an opportunity to teach and reinforce group process skills. Peers can orient the new student, teach classroom rules and procedures, and provide friendship and support in the new situation.*
4. *Teach students to evaluate their group process skills through observation and discussion.*
5. *Use active mediation to solve student conflicts and cultural clashes in ways that build community.*

7.11 CONCLUSION

In this chapter, we have discussed the components of the integrated classroom literacy community—those things which second language learners bring to the classroom and those which the classroom community offers them. We have discussed the two major characteristics of the classroom literacy community: its multiculturalism and its cooperative nature. We have provided a set of activities to help you to create that community, including ways to create classroom identity, formulate cooperative goals and activities, and teach group process skills. Combining the principles and suggestions from this chapter with your integrated curriculum and classroom and with the oral and written discourse that you are providing to your second language students will go a long way toward creating the maximal conditions for supporting your second language students' language and literacy development. In the following chapter, we will explain how to help your students expand their knowledge of their new community by stepping outside the classroom to reach out to and to interact with the larger cultures of the school, the home, and the greater community.

ACTIVITIES AND DISCUSSION

1. Interview a student who is acquiring English and make an individual model of the components of the integrated classroom community (Figure 7.1), showing the background and knowledge this student brings to the class and what the classroom community offers him/her. Try to discover several things that this student knows that you don't—things that this student could teach you. Also try to find out what the student would most like to know about his or her new culture here.

2. List activities of a school day that might be unfamiliar to a student from another culture. Ask acculturated students from other cultures which aspects of school were particularly difficult for them when they first entered North American schools.

3. Observe your own (or a chosen) classroom and note unwritten cultural expectations—ways of behaving that are not written anywhere, but are nevertheless expected of students. How did you discover these expectations? How would you expect a student who was new to the culture to discover them?

4. In your own classroom or one you visit, break a cultural norm, e.g., wear unmatched shoes to class, sit in an unusual place in the classroom, change time limits to assignments to make them unusually short. After observing student responses to your behavior, tell them that you have purposely broken the norm and ask them to describe their feelings and explain reactions. Ask the students how they would treat a peer who broke such norms.

5. Recall a time in your own life when you were in a different cultural setting (in another country or in another area of your home country). How did you feel? How did you cope? What were some of the dimensions of the setting you found to be strange and different? What did you do to become more comfortable and to learn how to act in the setting? What did the "natives" in the new setting do to help you act appropriately within it? How could you use some of the strategies that you and they used with second language students?

6. Create a resource list about a culture of origin of students you teach/may teach/have taught. Include books, magazine articles, names of individuals who are familiar with the culture, and physical resources, e.g., stores where foods from the culture are sold; museums with art or artifacts from the culture; etc. Be "resourceful"! Use materials suggested in this chapter, the library, the yellow pages and talk to lots of people, asking each of them to suggest other resources.

7. Choose a typically competitive classroom activity, e.g., a spelling bee

or flash card drill. Redesign the activity as a cooperative one. If you can, conduct the original activity one day and the cooperative one another. Observe and note changes in student interactions. Ask students to compare and contrast the activities and state their preferences and reasons.

8. Re-design a classroom activity, e.g., book reports, as a jigsaw activity. Compare the opportunities for oral and written discourse in the original activity and your new version.

9. Analyze and list the skills needed for a student to lead a small, cooperative group. Write plans for "coaching" and providing students with practice at some of these skills.

10. Write lesson plans for a first day of school that establish a smoothly run classroom with a supportive and collaborative atmosphere. How will you determine and teach the classroom rules?

11. Observe a classroom where learning centers are used successfully. Note how centers are managed by children and teachers. Interview the teachers about how this management system was established. Interview students about how they like the centers and how much they feel they are learning.

12. Visit a school microcomputer lab or a classroom where computers are used. Survey the software available to students. Categorize software using these categories (or develop your own):

GAMES	DRILL/PRACTICE	TUTORIAL	SIMULATION	TOOL
for fun	including games for drill/ practice	to learn a new skill, e.g., typing	including some form of problem solving	e.g., word processor, data base, spreadsheet, draw

FOR FURTHER READING

De Costa, S. B. 1984. Not all children are Anglo and middle-class: A practical beginning for the elementary teacher. *Theory into Practice*, 23:2, 155-162. Along with a number of suggestions for multicultural approaches and activities for elementary students, this article includes a list of addresses of agencies which provide high quality resources and materials concerning various ethnic groups for classroom use.

Newman, J. M. *Whole language: Theory in use.* Portsmouth, NH: Heinemann, 91-98. A chapter on the message board provides an anecdotal record of lively interactions of fifth graders and teacher through the message board, along with general suggestions for use of this strategy.

Schmidt, V. E., and McNeill, E. 1978. *Cultural awareness: A resource bibliography.* Washington, DC: National Association for the Education of Young Children. Provides a comprehensive cultural awareness bibliography.

Tiedt, P. L., and Tiedt, I. M. 1979. *Multicultural teaching: A handbook of activities, information, and resources.* Boston: Allyn and Bacon, Inc. Comprehensive source including overview of the multicultural approach, and ways to build self concepts, language skills, intergroup relations. The book incorporates a myriad of classroom activities.

Waynant, L., and Wilson, R. 1974. *Learning centers: A guide for effective use.* Paoli, PA: The Instructo Corporation. Clear guide for organizing, developing and using learning centers in the classroom.

Wigginton, E. 1985. *Sometimes a shining moment: The foxfire experience.* Garden City, NY: Anchor Press/Doubleday. A high school English teacher's reflections about his career which includes the story of a publishing project to relate local culture and heritage that has never stopped developing and expanding.

ADDITIONAL RESOURCES

Resources for learning about culture:

Condon, J. C., and Yousef, F. 1975. *An introduction to intercultural communication.* Indianapolis, IN: Bobs-Merrill.

Hall, E. T. 1976. *Beyond culture.* Garden City, NY: Anchor Press/Doubleday.

Gilmore, P., and Glatthorn, A. A. (Eds.). 1982. *Children in and out of school: Ethnography and education.* Washington, DC: Center for Applied Linguistics.

Grant, C. A., Sleeter, C. E., and Anderson, J. E. 1986. The literature on multicultural education: Review and analysis. *Educational Studies,* 12:1, 47-71.

Saville-Troike, M. 1980. Cross-cultural communication in the classroom. In J. E. Alatis (Ed). *Current issues in bilingual education.* pp. 348-355. Washington, DC: Georgetown University Press.

Resources for multicultural activities:

Appleton, N. 1983. *Cultural pluralism in education: Theoretical foundations.* New York: Longman.

Baker, G. C. 1983. *Planning and organizing for multicultural instruction.* Reading, MA: Addison-Wesley Publishing Company.

Kendall, F. E. 1983. *Diversity in the classroom: A multicultural approach to the education of young children.* New York: Teachers College Press.

Lynch, J. 1986. *Multicultural education: Principles and practice.* London: Routledge and Kegan Paul.

Pasternak, M. G. 1979. *Helping kids learn multi-cultural concepts.* Champaign, IL: Research Press.

Trueba, H. T., and Barnett-Mizrahi, C. (Eds.). 1979. *Bilingual multicultural education and the professional: From theory to practice.* Rowley, MA: Newbury House Publishers, Inc.

Williams, L. R., and De Gaetano, Y. 1985. *A multicultural, bilingual approach to teaching young children.* Reading, MA: Addison-Wesley Publishing Company.

Resources for cooperative games:

Gregson, B. 1982. *The incredible indoor games book.* Belmont, CA: Pitman Learning.

Grunfield, F. V. 1982. *Games of the world.* Zurich: Wsiss Committee for UNICEF.

Michaelis, B., and Michaelis, D. 1977. *Learning through noncompetitive activities and play.* Palo Alto, CA: Learning Handbooks, Pitman Learning.

Milberg, A. 1976. *Street games.* New York: McGraw-Hill Book Co.

Orlick, T. 1978. *The cooperative sports & games book: Challenge without competition.* New York: Pantheon.

Orlick, T. 1982. *The second cooperative sports & games book.* New York: Pantheon.

Page, L. G., and Smith, H. (Eds.). 1985. *The Foxfire book of toys and games: Reminiscences and instructions from Appalachia.* New York: E. P. Dutton.

Sobel, J. 1983. *Everybody wins: 393 non-competitive games for young children.* New York: Walker.

Resources for learning centers:

Enright, D. S. Ed. 1983. *From pancakes to puppets to poison ivy: The Garden Hills international summer school curriculum guide, Vol. I.* Atlanta, GA: Georgia State University.

Enright, D. S., and McCloskey, M. L. (Eds.). 1984. *From balloons to bubbles to banana bread: The Garden Hills international summer school curriculum guide, Vol. II.* Atlanta, GA: Georgia State University.

McCloskey, M. L., and Enright, D. S. 1985. *From rainbows to rhythms to runaway cookies: The Garden Hills international summer school curriculum guide, Vol. III.* Atlanta, GA: Georgia State University.

McCloskey, M. L., Ed. 1987. *Turn on units.* Atlanta: State of Georgia Board of Education.

McCloskey, M. L. and Nations M. J. 1987. *English everywhere: An integrated English as a second language curriculum guide.* Atlanta: Educo Press.

Morelan, J. E. 1974. *Classroom learning centers: Planning, organization, materials, and activities.* Belmont, CA: David S. Lake Publishers.

Wendelin, K. H., and Greenlaw, M. J. 1984. *Storybook classrooms: Using children's literature in the learning center.* Atlanta, GA: Humanics Limited.

Resources on group process and teaching social skills:

Carteledge, G., and Milburn, J. F. Eds. 1980. *Teaching social skills to children: Innovative approaches.* New York: Pergamon Press.

Cohen, E. G. 1986. *Designing groupwork: Strategies for the heterogeneous classroom.* New York: Teachers College Press.

Dishon, D. and O'Leary, P. W. 1984. *A guidebook for cooperative learning: A technique for creating more effective schools.* Holmes Beach, FL: Learning Publications, Inc.

Johnson, D. M. 1983. Natural language learning by design: A classroom experiment in social interaction and second language acquisition. *TESOL Quarterly, 17:1,* 55-68.

Johnson, D. W., Johnson, R. T., Holubec, E. J., and Roy, P. 1984. *Circles of learning: Cooperation in the classroom.* Alexandria, VA: Association for Supervision and Curriculum Development.

Kagan, S. 1986. Cooperative learning and sociocultural factors in schooling. In *Beyond language: Social and cultural factors in schooling language minority students*, (pp. 231-298). Los Angeles, CA: Evaluation, Dissemination and Assessment Center, California State University, Los Angeles.

Schmuck, R., and Schmuck, P. 1979. *Group processes in the classroom. (2nd ed.)*. Dubuque, IA: William C. Brown.

Slavin, R. E., Sharan, S., Kagan, R., Hertz-Lazarowitz, C. Webb, N. and Schmuck, R., Eds. 1985. *Learning to cooperate, cooperating to learn*. New York: Plenum.

Smith, C. A., and Foat, C. 1983. *Once upon a mind: Using children's literature for self-discovery*. Manhattan, KS: Kansas State University Extension.

Stocking, S. H., Arezzo, D., and Leavitt, S. 1980. *Helping kids make friends*. Allen, TX: Argus Communications.

Chapter 8

Developing Ties with the School, Home and Community

Honey, I Love

I love
I love a lot of things, a whole lot of things
Like
My cousin comes to visit and you know he's from the South
'Cause every word he says just kind of slides out of his mouth
I like the way he whistles and I like the way he walks
But honey, let me tell you that I LOVE the way he talks
　　　I love the way my cousin talks
　　　　　　　and
The day is hot and icky and the sun sticks to my skin
Mr. Davis turns the hose on, everybody jumps right in
The water stings my stomach and I feel so nice and cool
Honey, let me tell you that I LOVE a flying pool
　　　I love to feel a flying pool
　　　　　　　and
Renee comes out to play and brings her doll without a dress
I make a dress with paper and that doll sure looks a mess
We laugh so loud and long and hard the doll falls to the ground
Honey, let me tell you that I LOVE the laughing sound
　　　I love to make the laughing sound
　　　　　　　and

My uncle's car is crowded and there's lots of food to eat
We're going down the country where the church folks like to meet
I'm looking out the window at the cows and trees outside
Honey, let me tell you that I LOVE to take a ride
    I love to take a family ride
          and
My mama's on the sofa sewing buttons on my coat
I go and sit beside her, I'm through playing with my boat
I hold her arm and kiss it 'cause it feels so soft and warm
Honey, let me tell you that I LOVE my mama's arm
    I love to kiss my mama's arm
          and
It's not so late at night, but still I'm lying in my bed
I guess I need my rest, at least that's what my mama said
She told me not to cry 'cause she don't want to hear a peep
Honey, let me tell you I DON'T love to go to sleep
    I do not love to go to sleep
But I love
I love a lot of things, a whole lot of things
And honey,
I love you, too.

—Eloise Greenfield

8.1 INTRODUCTION

James Coleman (1985) describes two schools where what he calls "intergenerational closure" exists among faculty, students, and parents. In these schools, children's friends and associates are sons and daughters of friends and associates of the children's parents. Many teachers live in the school communities and have considerable out-of-school contact with parents and students. Coleman describes the areas in which these schools exist as "functional communities"—built around work and residence and sometimes also kinship and church. The advantage of these communities for the schools are many. Information flows freely from school to community and, parents provide support or feedback to the school. Instead of having to depend on the child alone for information about what is happening in and out of school, the parent has many channels of communication, including the child's acquaintances, *their* parents, and school staff. The school, the child, and the parent are all more closely accountable to one another.

The functional schools that Coleman describes are rare today. They are throwbacks to the small-town past of North American schools, when community involvement was a natural part of community life. They are not typical of the urban, pluralistic, anonymous communities that many of our schools serve. The situation is quite different for most schools that serve second language students. These students usually come from uprooted and perhaps separated families and are often located in "anonymous" communities where there is little intergenerational closure. They can have the advantages of a functional community only if the school and the teacher create it. More traditional schooling will not effectively educate students who are from a new kind of community (Sanders and Schwab 1981). A new approach is required. Schools need to take on the task of closing the intergenerational gap.

A functional community fosters a partnership among those who participate in students' education. It uses parents' potency as teachers to its fullest potential. Your classroom is not an island. You cannot assume total responsibility for your students' academic and linguistic growth. Nor can you assign to parents the entire responsibility for your students' success or failure. Education results from the efforts of several participants, not only one. The student, the teacher, the school, the community, and the family all have roles to play, (Smith and London 1981; London, Molotsi and Palmer 1984).

Research evidence has led to a wide consensus concerning the value of parental participation in students' school achievement and social development (Clark 1985; Comer 1986; Leichter 1974; Lightfoot; 1978; Majoribanks 1979; Bronfenbrenner 1975; Heath 1983) and specifically reading and language development (Silvern 1985; Temple, Nathan and Burris 1982; Tizard, Schofield and Hewison 1982). To paraphrase Beane (1980), clearly the time has come for teachers to start working *with* parents instead of avoiding them. The time has also come for teachers to encourage the flow of communication between students and others in the school community and in the greater community.

This chapter is designed to provide many ideas and activities that you can use to develop such communication. It also will provide both a rationale and procedures for building and sustaining a functional community that includes your class and the families and neighborhoods to which your students belong.

8.2 REACHING OUT TO THE SCHOOL COMMUNITY

In Chapter 6, we described the school as a microcosm of the greater community, where second language students could begin to learn about their new culture. In school effectiveness research, the school culture has been called the "key to more effective instruction" (Firestone and Wilson 1984). School culture is a key that can open many doors for second language learners. Students can learn about culture through activity in the school. They can learn to claim power in that culture by learning about how decisions are made and how to affect these decisions in schools. We have spoken frequently of the need for students to feel ownership of their classrooms. This same feeling of ownership is important at the school level.

Reaching out to the school community offers clear language benefits as well. In establishing strong classroom-community ties, you let the students experience an expanding menu of language models of different ages, backgrounds and roles in the school. Students have a chance to be givers and helpers to other students and to the school community in general, instead of just being recipients of help, and they learn the new "ways with words" (Heath 1983) that those roles entail.

Activities for Involving the Class in the School Community

What we are talking about goes far beyond a school spirit campaign. The following strategies and activities are designed to help you and your class begin to move out into the school community.

Interviews. Interviews involve having students initiate conversations with other individuals to collect and report information that their interviewees can provide. Interviews with important individuals in the school community have a number of benefits. They are an effective way to expose students to a wide range of people who held various positions. They can help students begin a continuing relationship with various adults in the school. Once initiated, further communication between students and school personnel is likely to follow. Students and their interviewees will have learned one another's names. Students will feel more responsible to persons with whom they have had one-to-one interactions.

Interviews are far more meaningful for students if they involve preparation, execution and follow-up. The first step is to make sure that students have a clear reason in mind for the interview. They may wish to conduct a poll or a survey to answer a particular question, such as "What flavor ice cream is the most popular in this school?" or "Who do you want to win the presidential election?" or "Have you ever personally experienced prejudice because of your race, ethnic origin, gender or age?" They may wish to investigate a particular issue, such as why the library doesn't have more books about the cultural groups that are represented at the school. Or they may be preparing to write articles about the interviewees for a class newsletter. Help students prepare for the interviews by obtaining background information and writing out and role-playing questions. After the interview, help students transcribe or summarize the information, or both, producing a product which has meaning to them. "Heroes and Superheroes" in Part II provides lesson plans for interviews of "school heroes."

Although we describe interviews here as a strategy for involving students in the school community, interviews can also be conducted within the classroom community; at home (see "Heroes and Superheroes" in Part II); and in the greater community (see the field trip in "Rain Makes Applesauce").

Inter-age grouping and cross-class tutoring. One of our favorite teaching memories goes back to watching a kickball game in which two classes were cooperating. Both classes had a large proportion of second language learners. One was a high school class and one was a primary class. Each position was covered by two students. The primary student did the actual playing, and the high school student was the coach. These students' teachers used the game to create an information gap—the older students knew the rules of the game, but the younger students, who had never played before, were the players. Imagine, if you can, the confusion, and fun, the talking, and the helping of one another that went on during that game! It was agreed by teachers of both classes that both age groups learned a lot of new English, and that the high schoolers got the most out of the activity. Cooperative activities with interage groups are not difficult to implement; they just require a little cooperation among teachers. You could have your students plan a party that would include decorations, refreshments and games for a neighboring special education class. Or your middle school students could take a joint field trip with a primary class, taking responsibility for guiding and supervising their charges. After publishing stories using the writing process (see Chapter 6), students might enjoy reading their books to students in another class. Older students enjoy writing and illustrating story books with a younger audience specifically in mind. Experiences with older classes can provide students with language models and role models and can supplement supervision for small group or individual activities. Experiences with younger classes provide older students with valuable opportunities to give from their strengths. These activities may also lead to recruiting older tutors to work with younger students (Allen 1976, Farmelo 1987).

Study school culture. Your students can learn language and literacy and gain content area knowledge while they learn about the school culture. Think of important sets of questions to ask, such as, "Who decides what foods are served in the cafeteria? What are the governmental requirements for food served? How are changes effected in the menu?" Or, "Is our school multicultural? Does it reflect the racial, ethnic, and language backgrounds of the student body in the library collection, in the staff representation, in the artwork on the walls?" Or "Is there prejudice at our school? Why do people act that way?" Studying culture that directly affects them provides students with meaningful opportunities for use of oral and written language. It also helps them see how a culture operates, how the culture is designed to serve them, and what roles they can play in that culture. Studying school culture provides students with greater understanding and access to that culture and to its members.

Try to effect a change. Once you and your class have investigated an issue in the school community, help them learn how change takes place in an institutional structure by trying to make a change in their school. You could have students figure out the steps to take in getting the cafeteria to provide a salad bar or to offer food that is more representative of the ethnic groups in the school. Perhaps your students would like to undertake a schoolwide campaign to make persons in the school community aware of the damage caused by prejudice. Community-wide campaigns can also be used to stimulate classroom and school campaigns. For example, during the city's "Eco-week" a class could seek out pollution on the school grounds and clean it up.

The following list summarizes our suggestions for developing ties with the school community.

HOW TO INVOLVE THE CLASS IN THE SCHOOL COMMUNITY

1. *Help students to conduct and report on interviews of important individuals in the school community.*
2. *Involve your class in activities with classes of students of different ages and different backgrounds. Tutoring, celebrations, performances, and field trips are all possibilities for inter-age activities.*
3. *Help your students to study the school culture.*
4. *Work with students to effect a change in the school culture.*

8.3 INVOLVING THE FAMILY IN THE SCHOOL AND THE SCHOOL IN THE FAMILY

Parents' attitudes about education can have a powerful effect on student success in school (Clark 1985), and the teacher can help to influence these attitudes. Just influencing a parent to read aloud to students daily (in any language) has a powerful effect on children's literacy learning. In *Becoming a Nation of Readers* (1985), The National Academy of Education stated that "the single most important activity for building the knowledge required for eventual success in reading is reading aloud to children" (1985:23). Although parents are powerful teachers, we do not limit our view of parent involvement to a one-directional "let's straighten those parents out" approach. This is a form of blaming the victim. Schlossman warns against such blame-assignment in these words: "It is fruitless to try to isolate the impact of individual educational institutions —whether the family, the school or the television—and assign them full responsibility for educational outcomes. The incredible variety of institutions that socialize children and the complex manner in which they touch, overlap and interact, demands that we exercise considerable caution in parceling out blame for educational failures." (1978:807-808) You can undertake educating the parent about activities that can promote student learning. However, you must also be educated by the parent in order to better educate the child. Au and Jordan (1981), Jordan (1983), and Hansen (1986) have discussed the problem of the "interaction rule mismatch" and "cultural incompatibility." Students' home interaction rules are often quite different from school interaction rules. A mismatch between the two can lead to learning and social problems in the classroom. Closer communication and frequent interactions between you and your students' parents centering on mutually purposeful activities (i.e., the education of the children), along with considerable openness and sensitivity on your part, can lead to better understanding of cultural differences, including those in communication patterns. This communication will also assist you in fulfilling your role as a student of your students' cultures (see Chapter 7).

You can serve as a bridge between home learning and school learning in several ways. Regarding home-school interactions with the families of second language learners, who are often hesitant to initiate contacts with the school because of cultural differences, difficult work situations, difficulties with the language, or a combination of these, you should be willing to take the initiative. Previously, we have discussed ways to study home culture and ways to carry out interviews to get information from family members. Two other ways in which you can initiate contact between families, students, and school are bringing families into the classroom and "homeFUN."

Bringing the Family to School

Parent participation in your classrooms and schools presents its challenges: parents often lack time or confidence or both; each party fears being examined too closely by the other; and management and scheduling are difficult. But the rewards are increased richness and variety in the learning environment; greater classroom enthusiasm; parents understanding the learning process better and thus being more capable of helping their students with academics; and greater support for the school from parents (Johnston and Slotnik 1985). Rich (1985) of the Home and School Institute offers a rule that is most relevant to teachers who seek to bring parents into the classroom: "Link parents' involvement directly to the learning of their own children" (1985:80).

When developing activities to bring parents into your classroom, remember that rule. The experience in your integrated classroom should be as meaningful and real for the families of your students as it is for the students themselves. The activities we have selected respect and take advantage of the rich resources parents have to offer and provide the flexibility that parents with busy schedules need. You may want your first parent involvement to be with a parent volunteer from your class or with someone from the school parent-teacher organization. Such a person might be willing to call other parents to help you to solicit assistance from parents with the events described in the sections that follow.

Bring parents in for special celebrations. The easiest way for parents to find their way into your classroom is to help you celebrate something. Plays and programs always provide a good draw; parents enjoy seeing their own children perform. When you plan performances for parents, you can maximize student participation and minimize preparation by using a chorus or by having a number of small parts or several small skits rather than one long play. In the latter case, each student has a role, and the language demands of the role are not overwhelming for language learners. Instead of giving students long parts to memorize, have a narrator read parts while other students pantomime and say a few short lines that can easily be remembered (or ad-libbed). Other celebrations that would lure parents into your classroom include a publication party for a book (see Supercelebration'' in the ''Heroes and Superheroes'') or an opening of a show of student artists' work. Special relationships can also be featured. As we saw earlier, one class celebrated Grandparents' Day, to which students invited their grandparents and grandparent-figures. The students prepared refreshments, recited original poems, and sang for their guests. One family was represented by four generations!

This child is wearing her grandmother's baby bonnet as she helps to provide entertainment for ''Grandparents' Day.''

Bring parents in as resources, to share special knowledge and skills. Now that your parents know the way to your classroom, find ways to involve them in your curriculum as participants, not just spectators. Invite parents in to give talks and answer questions about their native countries, their occupations, their hobbies, and their favorite stories. A resourceful teacher we know had a year-long integrated thematic unit about careers. He invited the parents of every student in the class to come in at some time during the year to share what they did for a living, and to bring in some representative tools of their trade or hobby. One father played the guitar and helped the students compose original songs; a sheep-shearer sheared a sheep; a mother brought in her word processor and helped the students write stories; another parent came in with a collection of toys and clothing from South America; still another came in to show the students how to make spring rolls.

Parents who are able and willing can participate by helping you to read aloud to small groups in school. If you have several students from the same language group, find a parent who will read or tell stories to them in their native language. We know that native language development can contribute to English language development. A great deal of background information, paralinguistic learning, and story knowledge can be transferred from one language to another (Cummins 1981; Walters and Gunderson 1985).

Bring parents in to help with small groups and individuals. Parents can provide a valuable extra pair of hands in many activities that are used in the integrated classroom. For example, in Activity 11 of "Heroes and Superheroes" parent volunteers are used to help small groups bake a Superman cake. Carefully plan your activity ahead of time, and spend a few minutes explaining the ground rules of the activity to the parent. Your time and thought will be rewarded by a successful experience for both students and parents. Parents can help to supervise small teams of students on a field trip (see the farmer's market trip in "Rain Makes Applesauce") or assist students at the learning center. Parents may be willing to return often to your classroom to assist you. Some of the most successful parent volunteer programs that we have seen operate in multilingual schools where second language learners' parents (who often are also still learning the new language and culture) help out in the classrooms, cafeteria, library, and playground and by doing so help both their children and themselves.

HomeFUN: Family and School Working Together

Homework is another area in which parent involvement has been shown to be effective (Paschal, Weinstein, and Walberg 1985). Homework has mixed potential, however. Ways in which it is organized by teachers and dealt with by families can make it have positive or negative effects (McDermott, Goldman, and Varenne 1984). Families of second language learners are particularly prone to problems surrounding homework because often parents don't speak, read, or write the language of the assignment. We propose an alternative to homework. This alternative enables parents and students to work together on meaningful academic tasks and turns language and cultural differences into resources. We call our proposal homeFUN.

HomeFUN is a teaching strategy that helps you to promote family involvement in students' language and literacy learning. Here are some suggestions for its effective use.

Choose activities that are engaging and fun. HomeFUN is not a time for language drill and practice, but a time for meaningful language play and discovery. Devise activities that children and family members enjoy and look forward to. For example, to help students practice and improve spelling skills, don't give them an assignment to copy and memorize spelling words. Children can improve these skills as they increase their awareness of functional print in their environment and learn how advertisers and others change spellings to get attention. Encourage students and parents to hunt for words which appear in the print environment intentionally misspelled, such as those in Figure 8.1.

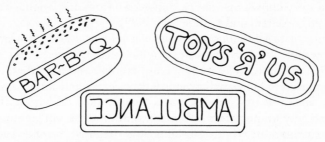

Figure 8.1:   Misspelled Environmental Print

Choose activities that integrate language. Instead of choosing activities from one compartment of language, such as reading, spelling, grammar or handwriting, choose activities that include more than one medium and that encourage children and family members to use higher-level skills, such as summarizing, organizing, and synthesizing information. For example, you might ask family members and students to do a set of "kitchen chemistry" experiments to find out what happens when certain cooking ingredients are combined and heated. Students could describe the reaction that occurs when baking soda and vinegar are combined (wild bubbling!) or their own reactions when eating the product of a "sugar inversion" experiment (fudge). Depending on their level of proficiency, students can describe these experiments by drawing pictures of results; dictating to family members about results in English or their native language; filling out a chart summarizing results; or telling about results in class.

Make sure that the activities necessitate both parent (or other older person) and child participation. To make sure that parents become involved, assign activities that a student cannot do alone. You might ask students to interview parents or other older family members about what school was like when they were children. Students could then draw comparisons between the schools of yesterday and their own school. It is important to adapt the activities to students' home situations. If no one in a student's home can read English, ask another parent, an older sibling, or a paraprofessional to translate the assignment. If translation is not possible, explain and demonstrate the activities thoroughly to the students so that they can explain them to their parents. If, after a number of tries, you are sure that no one in a family is willing or able to help a student in your class with homeFUN activities, find an older student or adult volunteer to work with that student.

Respect and utilize home language. As we have stated, "school talk" and "home talk" are not the same for students from various ethnic and native language backgrounds. In the classroom, you have many opportunities to teach standard English forms, but the sharing of homeFUN projects is not an appropriate time for correcting grammar. HomeFUN activities, if they are to help to bridge a home-school language gap, should not "put down" language and dialect differences but should celebrate and incorporate them. If children are not helped to feel proud of the communication that takes place in their homes, they will not want to share it with teachers and peers at school. Assign activities that develop this pride. For example, in "Heroes and Superheroes," Ms. Kay could ask students to tape interviews with family members about their memories of persons they had known whom they consider heroes. These tapes could be shared with the class, and students could discuss the language use of the individuals interviewed as well as the content of the interviews. Heath (1983) and Moll (1987) describe a number of similar activities. These kinds of homeFUN activities have a double value: they celebrate students' home language and they help you to learn more about that language so that you can use this knowledge throughout your curriculum.

Give families adequate time for completion of the HomeFUN activity. Rather than giving an assignment one day and expecting it to be completed by the next, allow families several days or a week to fit these activities into their busy schedules. Assigning the activities regularly will help family members and students learn to expect them and to plan ahead for them. Plan to educate parents about the homeFUN activities at Open House at the beginning of the school year and through class newsletters (translated when necessary) and conferences.

Present the activities with both preparation and follow-up. Motivate students through your enthusiasm and give them prerequisite skills. For example, introduce the elements of a fairy tale, including the characters (protagonist, evil person, magical person), setting (far away and long ago place), and plot (problem, complication, resolution involving magic) before asking students to collect such stories from their parents or other older family members. Plan time to share and respond to the homeFUN activities. For example, help students write down, illustrate, and bind together their fairy tales in a book.

Provide variations based on students' language levels. The homeFUN activities that you provide for your students should challenge them without frustrating them. Offer parents ways to adjust the activities to their children's proficiency levels. This will help them learn about their children's capabilities. For example, some family members and children might search kitchen shelves or road signs for symbols or letters that the students could recognize, while others might search for words or phrases that the students could read by sight. Parents of younger students could take dictation for the children, while parents of older students could expect students to copy the words themselves.

Work with other teachers to develop and exchange activities. Bouncing ideas off your peers can spark your creativity and decrease your work load.

HomeFUN activities should be a part of the ongoing curriculum. Every integrated unit that you plan for your students can and should have a homeFUN activity or two to extend your students' language and content learning to their homes. Following is a small selection of sample homeFUN activities to get you started. (See Part II.) We encourage you to go on to create your own.

Assign students, with family members, to:

- Make a personal time line of the student's life.
- Make a map of family or ancestral migrations.
- Collect insults, jokes, or riddles.
- Make a family tree.
- Study how family members use reading or writing: list the many ways in which a family member uses print in one day.
- Sketch bedrooms, houses, blocks.
- Make maps of routes commonly traveled, for example, to school.
- Get a library card and learn how to use it.
- Write down an unwritten family recipe as a family member prepares the dish.
- Collect family stories in a certain category—humor, superstitions, ghost stories.
- Collect funny stories about the student's childhood.
- Study a particular aspect of parents' childhood: work, housing, television, radio, segregation.
- Make lists and sketches of wildlife near the home in a certain category, for example, insects, mammals, birds.
- Collaborate on a cooking activity.

Involving parents in your classroom and incorporating home involvement into your curriculum can help your teachers to know the parents better and to value their involvement (Epstein 1985), and it can help students academically (Combs 1979; Becker and Epstein 1982; Walters and Gunderson 1985). Involving parents in your classroom will also have a self-perpetuating effect—once the process has begun, both parents and teachers are likely to want more of the same (Becker and Epstein 1982). The following list summarizes our suggestions for helping school and family work together.

HOW TO INVOLVE THE FAMILY IN SCHOOL AND THE SCHOOL IN FAMILY

1. *Bring family members into school for special celebrations.*
2. *Invite family members in to serve as resources and to share special knowledge and skills.*
3. *Ask parents to help with small groups and individuals, and on field trips.*
4. *Provide homeFUN activities for parents and students to do together. Make sure that these activities*
   a. *are engaging and fun*
   b. *integrate language*
   c. *necessitate both parent and child involvement, and*
   d. *respect and utilize the home language.*
   e. *allow adequate time for families to complete.*
   f. *are introduced carefully and are used in class when they are completed.*
   —provide variations based on students' language levels.
   —work with other teachers to develop and exchange activities

8.4 REACHING OUT TO THE GREATER COMMUNITY

Become a Language Advocate

The first step in reaching out to the greater community is for the teacher to learn about that community and take an active role in its affairs. The community is rich with resources for language teachers and learners and for families of the language learners. Teachers who are knowledgeable about school and community resources become valuable language advocates for language learners. (Cazden 1986.) Second language teachers have an important role to play in working with school administration and other teachers of the learners to see that these students receive appropriate placement and instruction. They also can play an important role in connecting parents to school and community resources. Learning about all the resources that are available in the community should not be the task of each individual teacher, however. Through a network of school staff and parents, resources can be solicited, organized, and filed so that they are accessible to anyone in the school.

Help Students Study the Community

Morin (1986) describes a series of projects in which she worked with three teachers in three different communities to develop curriculum that was relevant to each community around the theme of "House Sense." A class of fifth- and sixth-grade students in a lower-income urban neighborhood studied housing problems in the neighborhood, role-played housing disputes, and visited Housing Court to observe cases and to interview the judge. A special education class of four- and five-year-olds discussed shapes and features of houses and their functions; drew houses; and discussed the drawings. A fourth-grade class in a girls' boarding school in a well-to-do neighborhood took a field walk to a golf course and planned hypothetical developments for the site, taking into account ecological issues.

All of the classes described by Morin were involved in a theme that helped them learn about housing features in their communities, but each class made specific adaptations to the composition of the class and to the community in which their school was located. In developing your integrated curriculum for second language learners, these same adjustments must be made. Look around at what your school community has to offer and develop your curriculum to take advantage of these offerings: Develop authentic activities around your community's resources.

Activities whose purpose is learning about communities can result in valuable contributions to the local community. A class of students whose school was located on a street that had been through many changes over the years (it had gone from being an elite community to a poverty community to a community in transition) undertook a project to write a history of the street. Students studied the street from many angles: they interviewed long-time residents; surveyed restaurants and gas stations, graphing how many had restrooms and soda machines; and wrote about these and other features of local color. The class revised their writing and published a book about their study. Each student also made a square of a quilt that showed something about the locality he or she had studied. The squares were sewn together and quilted by the class, and the beautiful quilt was later raffled off, with the benefits going to the school.

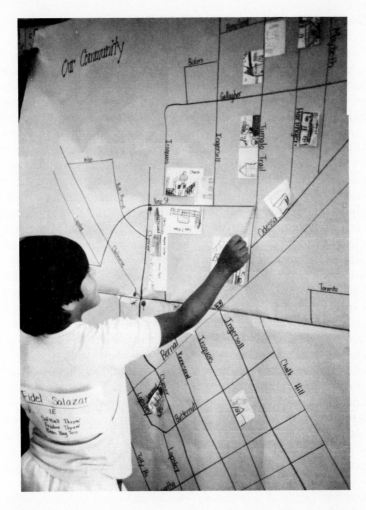

Having students trace their daily routes to school on a map of the neighborhood is an example of the authentic classroom use of community resources.

To illustrate further, students can develop a slide show featuring important or interesting locations near the school and accompanied by a student-made tape describing the slides. They might write a restaurant directory of the local community, including student reviews (Lauterbach 1986). You and your class can also move your focus beyond the local community and study problems of the world community. Donnan (1985) reports on a school campaign to fight world hunger which united the school around an important issue and which also provided the funds to save many lives, thereby encouraging the growth of a sense of community in the school as a whole.

Going Out into the Community: Field Trips

Field trips have been mentioned many times before in this book because of their value in so many aspects of language learning. They are an integral part of the curriculum. They lead to development of social aspects of language. They foster development of oral discourse skills. They provide purpose for bridging from oral to written discourse. They help students to learn about the new culture. Of course, they develop ties between school and community. Indeed, field trips are the perfect synthesizing activity for the integrated curriculum. They make the acquisition and practice of language immediate and concrete, and they require generalization of classroom-acquired language skills to deal with new and exciting situations. Motivation is an intrinsic part of the field trip experience. Students meet people and discover places and things. These experiences invite them to use and improve various of types of discourse. Language use on a field trip has natural and positive consequences: the hot dog ordered is delivered; the child's curiosity about how a photograph is developed is satisfied; the letter mailed at the post office appears in someone's mailbox a few days later.

Field trips encourage students to venture out and to overcome fears of interacting in the new culture. Once students have learned how to use public transportation to get to the public library, the museum, or the baseball stadium, they will repeat the outings on their own or with their families.

Out-of-school experiences can be confidence-building for second language learners. Talents and areas of expertise that are outside school-related reading, writing, and mathematics can be explored and the students can take a turn in the spotlight. We witnessed a dramatic change in one second language student's willingness to take risks and make contributions after he showed a younger class how to make a bamboo fishing pole and then demonstrated its use on a trip to a pond (they caught a few small fish and one large turtle). This student, who was not particularly successful at classroom tasks, had helped to support himself and his family in Southeast Asia by fishing. Field trips offer many opportunities for similar student contributions.

Planning a field trip. To derive the greatest benefit from field trips, careful planning is required. Each trip involves three plans: one for before, one for during and one for after the trip. When converging these three plans in a delicious "field trip sandwich," there are a few important things to remember, as follows.

Before the trip: (a) To be successful, a field trip should be an integral part of the classroom curriculum and language learning process. Both the language and the content that will be involved in the field trip should be introduced in before-field-trip activities that explicitly relate them to the rest of the curriculum. (b) Use pictures, visitors, and conversation to prepare students for what they will experience. Help them plan questions to ask guides and others whom they will meet on the trip. Help them make record sheets or notebooks to write or sketch what they observe, and set up specific purposes for these observations. (c) Make sure students have a task and a goal for the trip. Each student should have at least one question to ask the museum guide, one item to price at the grocery store or one animal to spot, sketch, and describe at the zoo.

During the trip: (a) Set clear expectations for behavior and responsibilities. Make sure that students know where they should be at all times, what it is they are trying to learn on this trip, and what to do if a problem occurs, for example, if someone is lost or hurt. (b) Consider seating and grouping arrangements. Pairing children of different native languages, or native speakers with non-native speakers, will encourage the natural use and modeling of English. (c) Include parents. They can provide extra supervision and assistance, and their inclusion will strengthen home-school ties. Consider the language proficiency of parents when giving them responsibilities. A parent who speaks little English might be comfortable helping with snacks, but uncomfortable with helping students interview a state senator. (d) Make use of travel time. The ride to and from the destination can be a source of valuable learning time *and* fun. Plan to sing songs and play games such as Twenty Questions en route. Have students record and graph the number of animals in different categories that they see en route, or have a contest to see who can be the first one to find all the letters of the alphabet on signs. (e) Expect and incorporate the unexpected. A successful trip is the result of planning carefully and making good use of the unavoidable (and most desirable) unplanned events. If you have a flat tire, share stories about other mishaps that you and the students have experienced. If someone scrapes a knee, teach students what to do if they are hurt and tell them the names of first aid items. If you meet some interesting character, tape an interview. If someone gives you lemons, make lemonade!

After the trip: (a) Make connections. Tie together what students learned before the trip, what they expected from the trip, and what they actually saw. How was the cookie factory different from what the children thought it would be? Have students write about the trip in their journals. Find activities that give students another chance to use and thus retain vocabulary, language structures, and concepts learned before and during the field trip. (b) Complete projects (See chapter 7). Use what students have learned and collected on the trip. Complete the graphs of the numbers of different types of animals seen; chart the prices of vegetables at the farmer's market; classify the leaves that students collected. (c) Celebrate and share what you have learned. Use the language experience approach or the writing process (See chapter 6) to prepare and publish writings about the trip on walls and in halls. Make a videotape of students reading or talking about the trip or showing items they have made, and present the video to parents and to other classes in the school.

Even the ride to and from a field trip destination can be valuable learning time and *fun!*

The following list summarizes our suggestions for reaching out to the greater community.

HOW TO HELP YOUR CLASS REACH OUT TO THE GREATER COMMUNITY

1. *Become a language advocate for students and their families. Be knowledgeable about the community and its resources and help your students and their families to connect with them.*

2. *Help students study the community. By making the community a part of the content of your curriculum, you serve students' language-learning and culture-learning needs together.*

3. *Go out into the community on field trips. When planning field trips, remember that the plan has three parts: activities and preparations for before, during, and after the trip.*

8.5 CONCLUSION

We will use the seven criteria of the ILT model to summarize this chapter.

Collaboration. Through interactions with the school, home, and greater community, students collaborate with many individuals besides their teachers and one another. They expand their vistas through cooperation and collaboration with their own family members, with other students' family members, with school officials, and with many different individuals in the greater community.

Purpose. When students are involved in activities that help them learn about and possibly improve community life, they are making a difference in their own lives and in the lives of others. This provides them with many clear purposes.

Interest. Students are interested in their own lives and in their own surroundings. Activities that help them investigate the wider community enable them to expand their interests and make them aware of their responsibility and their power in the community.

Previous experience. Students who study the contexts in which they and their families live, work, and learn are beginning with the known and moving out to the unknown. They are using home experiences, home language, and home culture to move on to the next step. These experiences with various communities can help them tie back the new to the old.

Support. These activities help teachers to reach out to the communities of school, home and community to expand the support students receive. As they receive this support, students prepare themselves to become support providers themselves, to contribute to the overlapping communities in which they live and learn.

Variety. It's a pluralistic world out there. Exposure to a wide variety of languages and dialects, ways of interacting and new situations which will foster students' learning of language and the new culture is a natural product of expanding the classroom community out to the school, home, greater community and eventually the world.

Integration. Discovering ever expanding communities means the integration of education and life. Students move out of the "ivory tower" and into the "thick." They integrate forms of language,—reading, writing, listening, and speaking—in the process of preparing for, carrying out, and writing up an interview. They also integrate the learning of language and culture. Through studying issues and perhaps even taking action on them, they integrate learning about culture in various settings and contexts.

If you choose to use the resources offered by the school, home, and greater communities as fully as possible, the responsibilities with respect to creative thinking, planning and following through are many, but the rewards will make your hard work pay off many times over: students who find joy in life and learning; who feel that they are valuable contributors to their new communities; who have access to the resources these communities provide; who are fully literate in their new language; and who have the skills and the power to control their own lives and improve their society.

ACTIVITIES AND DISCUSSION

1. List the advantages to the language learner of increased communication among students, teachers, school community, the family and the greater community. What are the advantages of such interactions to the teacher? Are there disadvantages as well? What are these?

2. Design an activity for students that, like the kickball game described in the chapter, involves combining students of different ages. What are the advantages of this grouping to language learning? Are there any disadvantages?

3. With peers, or alone, brainstorm a list of questions about the school culture for students to investigate, and a list of community or school issues of problems for them to address. Which ideas from this list might interest/benefit language learners most? Why?

4. Recall the involvement of your own parents in your education. Did they visit your school? Did they talk to your teachers frequently? Did your parents' participation enhance your school experience, your learning? How? Were your parents involved with your homework? How was this beneficial? Compare/contrast your experience with your parents with that of your students who are acquiring English. Generate some explanations for how the experiences are the same or different and how you can respond.

5. Using the questions outlined in #4, compare/contrast the parent involvement of different students in your class, for example, native speakers and second language learners.

6. List the resources of the parents in your class or in a class with which you are familiar (e.g., jobs, languages, skills, etc.). How could you find out about more parents' resources? How could you put these resources to work for your students?

7. Ask a group of second language students to do a home print inventory, listing all the kinds of print (both English and native language print) they have and use at home. Brainstorm ways to use these kinds of print in instruction.

8. With a group of students, parents, or peers, brainstorm field trip opportunities for your school. Include promising field trips in the greater community, walking field trips in or around the school, and a list of individuals from the community who might be willing to come to the class to work with the students, thus bringing the field trip to school.

FOR FURTHER READING

Ashworth, M. 1985. *Beyond methodology: Second language teaching and the community.* New York: Cambridge University Press. This book provides a great deal of information for teachers and schools that are interested in researching community resources and developing community involvement.

Berger, E. H. 1981. *Parents as partners in education: The school and home working together.* Toronto: The C. V. Mosby Company. Comprehensive overview of the field of parent involvement and home-school programs today. The chapters "Effective home-school-community relationships" and "Resources for home and school programs" are particularly valuable for second language educators.

Bronfenbrenner, U., Ed. 1975. *Influences on human development.* Hinsdale, IL: Dryden Press. Includes conclusions from early childhood education research regarding the importance of parent involvement in children's learning.

Combs, A. W. 1979. *Myths in education: Beliefs that hinder progress and their alternatives.* Boston: Allyn and Bacon, Inc. False myths which create educational problems, and ways of revealing and overcoming them.

Comer, J. P. 1986. Parental participation in the schools. *Phi Delta Kappan, 67*(6), 442-446. Proposes a new model for parental participation that meets the needs of today's students, given the complexity of the modern world.

Cummins, J. 1981. The role of primary language development in promoting educational success for language minority students. *Schooling and language minority students: A Theoretical Framework.* Los Angeles: Evaluation, Dissemination, and Assessment Center, California State University. The author's ground-breaking explanation of the processes underlying first and second language acquisition and how the former are used in the service of the latter.

Davies, D., Ed. 1981. *Communities and their Schools.* New York: McGraw-Hill Book Company. Essays dealing with critical issues concerning relations between schools and the communities they serve.

Epstein, J. L. 1985. Home and school connections in school of the future: Implications of research on parent involvement. *Peabody Journal of Education, 62*(2), 18-41. Research on teacher practices of parent involvement has implications for the use of home computers to boost school skills, including use of technology at home, use of technology to communicate from school to home, and school and family cooperation using the computer at school.

Heath, S. B. 1983. *Ways with words: Language, life and work in communities and classrooms.* Cambridge, England: Cambridge University Press. An ethnographic investigation of the cultural context of literacy development in three communities in the Piedmont Carolinas and descriptions of teaching practices, including having teachers and students become ethnographers, designed to promote literacy for children from these communities.

Jordan, C. 1983. Cultural differences in communication patterns: Classroom adaptations and translation strategies. In Clarke, M.A. and Handscombe, J. (eds.), *On TESOL '82: Pacific Perspectives on language learning and teaching* (pp. 285–294). Washington, DC: Teachers of English to Speakers of Other Languages. Classroom practices were adapted to adjust to children's cultural communication patterns, with considerable success.

Lombana, J. H. 1983. *Home-school partnerships: Guidelines and strategies for educators.* New York: Grune and Stratton, Inc. Directly written for teachers to use in developing better communication and partnerships with their students' families, this book is filled with useful insights, resources and classroom-based techniques.

ADDITIONAL RESOURCES

Becker, H. J. and Epstein, J. L. 1982. Parent involvement: A Survey of Teacher Practices. *The Elementary School Journal. 83*:2, 85-102.

Coleman, J. S. 1985. Schools and the communities they serve. *Phi Delta Kappan, 66*(8), 527-532.

Commission on Reading, National Academy of Education. 1985. *Becoming a nation of readers: The report of the commission on reading.* Champaign, IL: Center for the Study of Reading, University of Illinois.

Donnan, C. S. 1985. Tackling world hunger in an elementary school. *Educational Leadership, 43*(4), 49-52.

Firestone, W. A., & Wilson, B. L. 1984. Culture of school is a key to more effective instruction. *NASSP Bulletin, 68*(476), 7-11.

Greany, V. 1986. Parental influences on reading. *Reading Teacher. 39*:8.

Hansen, D. A. 1986. Family-school articulations: The effects of interaction rule mismatch. *American Educational Research Journal, 23*:4, 643-659.

Epilogue

Listen to the Mustn'ts

Listen to the MUSTN'TS, child,
Listen to the DON'TS
Listen to the SHOULDN'TS
The IMPOSSIBLES, the WON'TS
Listen to the NEVER HAVES
Then listen close to me—
Anything can happen, child,
Anything can be.

—Shel Silverstein

Part II

Integrated Thematic Units

Unit A

Rain Makes Applesauce: An Integrated Unit For Second Through Fifth Grade Students

INTRODUCTION

The apple is a fine theme for a unit for second language learners because it is familiar to students in many cultures and liked by all. The inclusion of activities for cooking and eating food, the universal motivator, assures the direct involvement of everyone.

This unit was inspired by a wonderful picture book called *Rain Makes Applesauce,* by Julian Scheer and Marvin Bileck (1964). In the book, the authors blend lots of silly talk ("Monkeys mumble in a jelly bean jungle") with marvelous picture science lessons showing how rain really does make applesauce. This unit, like the book, mixes fun with language and learning about many subject areas, through many mediums, as can be seen on the planning web, Figure A-1. Through science, math, literature, art, field trips, and cooking experiences centered on the theme of apples, students will learn and use language and concepts of the plant cycle, states of matter, arithmetic processes, measurement, and folk history of the United States.

Fall would perhaps be the most appropriate time for teaching this unit, because of the possibility of seeing apples as they are harvested or visiting a cider press. However, because of the year-round availability of apples, any time will do. In order to give you the opportunity to select appropriate activities, we have deliberately overplanned the unit, providing more activities than could possibly be used in one two-week period. We encourage you to select those activities most relevant to the interests and needs of your students. We invite you to have a wonderful time!

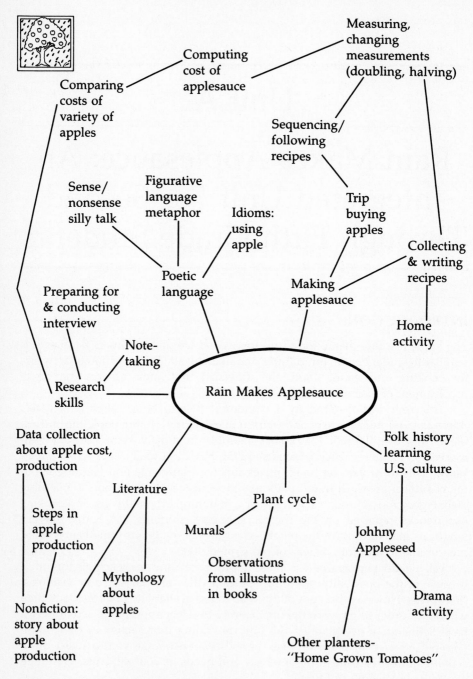

Figure A-1:   Unit Development Web

UNIT OBJECTIVES

The objectives for this unit selected from objectives set forth in the *Basic Curriculum Content for Georgia's Schools* for grades two through five. Language objectives are featured, but content area objectives in science, social studies, mathematics, and art are incorporated as well. Objectives for each unit activity are shown in Figure A-2. A suggested two-week schedule for the unit is included in Figure A-3.

Activities:	1. Literature: Applesauce	2. Language Experience	3. Before the Trip	4. During the Trip	5. After the Trip	6. Plant Cycles	7. Johnny Appleseed	8. HomeFUN	9. Applemath	10. Appletalk	11. Applelit
Language:											
1. Follows oral directions	•	•	•	•	•	•	•	•	•	•	•
2. Interprets nonliteral meanings of words	•										•
3. Interprets instructions		•		•	•	•	•	•	•		•
4. Selects and uses reference sources	•		•		•	•					
5. Makes predictions and comparisons	•		•	•	•				•		
6. Demonstrates an interest in literature by choosing appropriate books	•										•
7. Uses creative arts to interpret literature	•	•				•	•				•
8. Participates in the writing process	•	•	•	•	•	•		•			•
9. Shares and discusses ideas gained from independent reading			•				•				•
10. Distinguishes between fact and opinion	•	•	•	•							
11. Acquires and uses vocabulary related to the theme	•	•	•	•	•	•	•	•	•	•	•
Science:											
12. Demonstrates heat as change agent	•				•			•			
13. Describes chemical and physical change	•				•			•			
14. Describes models of interdependence of living things						•	•				
15. Describes mixtures and solutions	•					•		•			
16. Describes states of matter by special characteristics	•					•		•			
17. Reads information in tables, charts, and graphs				•		•		•	•	•	
18. Describes changes in living things and in systems	•	•	•	•		•					
Social Studies:											
19. Describes cultural expression of values							•	•			
20. Identifies selected cultural regions to study in regard to geographic patterns, climate, topography, natural resources								•			

Activities:	1. Literature: Applesauce	2. Language Experience	3. Before the Trip	4. During the Trip	5. After the Trip	6. Plant Cycles	7. Johnny Appleseed	8. HomeFUN	9. Applemath	10. Appletalk	11. Applelit
21. Identifies ethnic groups and linguistic patterns							•	•			
Mathematics:											
22. Identifies different names for numbers: whole numbers, fractions					•			•	•		
23. Determines pairs of numbers when given relations									•		
24. Selects and applies units of measurement					•			•	•		
25. Determines amounts of money: collections up to \$5, amount spent and change up to \$1			•	•							
26. Estimates results of measurement or computation			•	•	•			•	•		
27. Identifies geometric shapes						•					
28. Identifies geometric relations						•					
Art:											
29. Draws the outlines and details of forms and objects	•				•	•					
30. Creates artworks that demonstrate an awareness of details observed in the environment	•				•	•					

Figure A-2:   Rain Makes Applesauce Unit Objectives

Week 1

Monday	Tuesday	Wednesday	Thursday	Friday
LG GP UNIT INTRO Intro Center A SM GPS 1. "SILLY TALK" 2. LISTEN- ING CENTER GROUPS SWITCH LG GP ASSIGN HOME FUN APPLE RECIPES	LG GP Intro Center B SM GPS 1. PEER CONF., REVISIONS ILLUS. 2. CENTER GROUPS SWITCH LG GP SHARE WRITINGS	BEFORE THE TRIP LG GP DISCUSSION SM GPS RESEARCH LG GP APPLE ESTIMATION TRIP QUESTIONS	THE TRIP TO THE FARMER'S MARKET LG GP TRIP DISCUSSION	AFTER THE TRIP LG GP INTRO ACTIVITIES SM GPS 1. APPLESAUCE (Parent) 2. CENTER (Indep.) 3. THANK-YOU LETTERS (Teacher) LG GP REMIND ABOUT HOME FUN

Week 2

Monday	Tuesday	Wednesday	Thursday	Friday
LG GP DISCUSS HOME FUN SM GPS REVISE BIND INTO BOOK FOR CLASS/ CENTER LG GP READ JOHHNNY APPLESEED IND INTRO CENTER C	LG GP INTRO SKITS SM GPS PLAIN SKITS REHEARSE IND INTRO CENTER D	LG GP PERFORM SKITS LG GP PLANT CYCLE INTRO IND INTRO CENTER E	LG GP/IND PLANT CYCLE POSTERS SM GPS INTRO APPLEMATH/ CENTERS IND INTRO CENTER F	SM GPS APPLEMATH IND INTRO CENTER G (Continue centers for 1-2 weeks)

Figure A-3: Sample Schedule for Pull-Out Class or 45 Min/Day of Grade-Level Class

RAIN MAKES APPLESAUCE:
OUTLINE OF UNIT ACTIVITIES

Part A: Introduction to the Unit
     Activities:
       1. Literature: *Rain Makes Applesauce*
       2. Writing/Language Experience: "Silly Talk"
Part B: A Field Trip to the Farmer's Market
     Activities:
       3. Before the Trip
          a. Trip Discussion
          b. Apple Research Groups
          c. Applesauce Estimation Contest
          d. Preparation of Trip Questions
          e. Assessment/Evaluation
       4. During the Trip
       5. After the Trip: Making Applesauce
          a. Applesauce Activity
          b. Assessment/Evaluation
Part C: More Apples!
     Activities:
       6. Plant Cycles
          a. Learning about Cycles
          b. Making Cycle Posters
          c. Assessment/Evaluation
       7. Johnny Appleseed
          a. Sharing the Literature
          b. Acting out the Story
          c. Assessment/Evaluation
       8. HomeFUN—Apple Recipes
          a. Collecting Recipes
          b. Publishing an Apple Cookbook—Options:
             1. Publish "As Is"
             2. Use the Writing Process
             3. Use an Adult Volunteer
       9. Applemath
          a. Apple Cost Comparisons
          b. Computing the Unit Price of Homemade Applesauce
          c. Cooking for One or a Million
          d. Assessment/Evaluation
      10. Appletalk: Idioms and Figurative Language
          a. Learning about Idioms and Figurative Language
          b. Assessment/Evaluation

11. Applelit Learning Center: Reading, Listening, Talking, and Writing about Apples
    a. The Little Red House
       1. Independent Reading
       2. Listening
       3. Peer Storytelling
    b. Steps in Growing and Selling Apples
    c. Apples of Love and Discord
    d. Apple Recipe Cards
    e. *Apples:* A Wordless Book
    f. Assessment/Evaluation

UNIT ACTIVITIES

Part A: Introduction To The Unit

Groupings:
    Small or large group, teacher-led
    Individual work with teacher assistance
Materials:
    Apple
    Knife
    Rain Makes Applesauce, by Julian Scheer and Marvin Bilek
    Opaque projector or slides (if book will be shared with large group)
    Drawing, coloring, and writing materials
Procedures:

Activity 1: Literature—*Rain Makes Applesauce*

Show everyone the apple. Talk about what it is, ask if everyone has tasted one and if apples are grown in everyone's native country. Ask where apples come from. As this discussion takes place, cut the apple into little pieces and give everyone a taste. Practice basic vocabulary (*apple, taste, cut, mouth, good, skin, seed, core*), and simple phrases ("tastes good," "comes from," "eat apples") for beginning students.

Show the students *Rain Makes Applesauce*. The book is a predictable poem that uses nonsense phrases such as the following:

Stars are made of lemon juice

                    and rain makes applesauce.

I wear my shoes inside out

                    and rain makes applesauce.

My house goes walking every day

                    and rain makes applesauce.

Do not try to share the illustrations with the large group. They are full of tiny details that children need to be close to the book to see. Either show the pages on a screen using the opaque projector; make slides of the illustrations; or share the book with small groups. Before reading, name the author and illustrator, and ask children to predict what the book will be about. Ask them if they think that rain makes applesauce. Also ask the students to look for patterns in the language of the book, and, if they are able, to look at the pictures to see if they all tell the same story as the words.

Read the book. Encourage students to join in on the repeated phrase "and rain makes applesauce." You may occasionally need to stop in order to develop vocabulary skills for students who need them, for example, to demonstrate what *mumble* means.

After reading, discuss the pattern of the book: a silly phrase, followed by "and rain makes applesauce." Ask such questions as, "Why are these things so silly?" "Is it silly to say that rain makes applesauce?" "Why?" "Why not?" Elicit descriptions of the sequence of events pictured in the book that shows the relationship between rain and applesauce.

Motivate the students further by giving them a unit overview and by introducing the unit projects, all of which will be centered around the theme of apples: learning about the plant cycle and making posters to show others; going on a trip to the farmer's market to learn more about growing apples; making applesauce; reading and acting out *Johnny Appleseed*, a homeFUN activity that will lead to making an apple cookbook; figuring out how to make recipes for more people or fewer people; studying Appletalk (idioms and figurative language about apples) and Applelit (literature including the apple theme). Mention how interesting the activities will be and how much students will learn from them.

Activity 2: Writing/Language Experience—"Silly Talk"

Return to talking about *Rain Makes Applesauce*. Ask students to write or dictate (depending on student level) examples of silly talk followed by the phrase "and rain makes applesauce." Write these (or have students write them) on strips of lined chart paper. Glue the strips to large drawing paper and have students illustrate the sentences. The finished products can be stapled or bound into a Big Book, the students' own version of *Rain Makes Applesauce*, and added to the classroom or school library. Students will enjoy having their book read out loud, reading it themselves during free time, and checking it out to take home and show off to the family.

Here are some examples of student writings that this activity has elicited:

I eat mice for breakfast

and rain makes applesauce.

All we do at school is play, play, play

and rain makes applesauce.

I can jump a mile high

and rain makes applesauce.

A rhinoceros sleeps in my bed

and rain makes applesauce.

Part B: A Field Trip To The Farmer's Market

For the apple unit, we have chosen to provide a plan for a visit to a farmer's market. You may need to adjust the plan for a destination that is appropriate for your purposes and convenient to your school. The plan can be easily adapted for many other trips, including trips to a cannery, a truck stand, a grocery store, an apple farm, a cider mill or the home of a community resident who has a garden and cans many food items.

Thoughtful advance planning is a must for any field trip. If at all possible, visit the destination ahead of time. At least phone and interview individuals who will guide the group or talk to the students. Prepare these persons for speaking to beginning and mid-second language learners. Explain that they may need to adjust their speech somewhat by speaking a little more slowly and clearly so that students can understand. Encourage them to check whether they're being understood by asking the students many questions.

Activity 3: Before the Trip
Grouping:
  Large group, teacher-led
  Small, independent groups, with teacher available
Materials:
  Paper, pencils, wallpaper samples
  Reference books on apples, e.g., encyclopedias, suggested references at the
end of the unit
Procedures:

(a) *Trip discussion.* Tell students about the planned trip to the farmer's market. Ask if any of them have ever been to a farmer's market, and from those who have, elicit a description of the place and its purpose. Talk about the purposes for the trip, and, with students dictating, list the purposes on the blackboard or on a chart. The purposes are to (a) learn about where apples come from; (b) learn about how they are bought and sold; (c) collect data about different varieties of apples and their relative costs for use in a later project; (d) study other plants that are used for food (where they come from, what part of the plant is used for food, how they are grown, etc.); and (e) purchase apples for making applesauce.

(b) Apple research groups. Assign groups for different areas of data collection, and help each group design forms for data collection. Two sample forms are included.

Comparing Apple Quantities and Varieties

Variety	Quantity	Price	Price per Pound

Figure A-4:   Comparing Apple Quantities and Varieties

Other Plants Used for Food

Plant	Part of Plant Eaten	Price	Quantity	Price per Pound

Figure A-5: Plants for Food

Next, have the children conduct research on varieties of apples that are good for making applesauce. Books such as *Apples, A Bushel of Fun and Facts,* and encyclopedias contain such information. Students may also choose to interview experienced cooks (parents, for example) for their expert opinions. If time allows, students can send letters to apple growers asking for information about cooking with apples.

Help the children to select several varieties that would be acceptable, and plan to price these and choose the least expensive, best-quality apples. Also help them estimate how many pounds of apples the class will need to make applesauce. Estimate how many apples will make one pound. Plan to bring a calculator to help with computing unit prices.

(c) Applesauce estimation contest. Introduce a contest to estimate the cost of the materials needed to produce one quart (32 oz.) of homemade applesauce. Assign students to record apple and applesauce prices on their next trip to the grocery store. Once this information has been collected, ask each student to record a guess as to the cost of one quart of homemade applesauce. Offer a prize (free time, a trip to the library, apples, etc.) for the closest guess. Later in the unit, when students make applesauce and compute the unit price, they can check the accuracy of their guesses.

(d) Preparation of trip questions. Plan questions for apple growers/marketers. See that each student has a question to ask. Some students will be more comfortable if the question is written on a slip of paper to which they can refer on the trip. Sample questions might be:

> Where were these apples grown?
> Who grew the apples?
> When were they picked? Who picked them?
> What did they cost you?
> Why is the price lower if we buy more?
> How old does an apple tree have to be to produce apples?
> What do you think are the best kind of apples for cooking?
> How can apples be for sale all year when they're
>   on the trees only in the fall?

Help students staple several small sheets of paper together with a wallpaper cover to make a notebook for questions, answers, prices, sketches, and so on, of information collected on the trip.

(e) Assessment/evaluation. Students will receive feedback on the accuracy of their estimates during Applemath Activities 9a and 9b.

Activity 4: During the Trip
Grouping:
Small groups, with an adult assigned to each one
Materials:
Notebooks, pencils, money to purchase apples
Procedures:
On the day of the trip, review rules and expectations. Assign an adult to stay with each small group to assist with its task. You may choose to use color-coded name tags for students and adults to help keep groups together. Review the objectives for the trip.

Explain to the adults who are helping the small groups that their role is to encourage the students to talk, to ask the questions they have prepared, and to

record the information needed in later activities. Encourage all of the adults to
incorporate language into the exploration of any unexpected discoveries at the
market which might appeal to the children, such as home-baked or canned
goods or live animals.

At the farmer's market, have students complete data collection forms;
compute unit pricing on apple varieties in which they are interested; interview
vendors; make notes on other products for sale; and purchase apples.

Use travel time on the bus to teach and review unit concepts and
vocabulary. Teach the children to sing "Apple Blossom Time" or "Found an
Apple" (a takeoff on "Found a Peanut"). Provide a card game, such as Ròtten
Apple (played like Old Maid with pairs of apple vocabulary cards and one
rotten apple card). Talk about the trip en route, anticipating what students will
see, and on the way home review what was seen.

Activity 5: After the Trip—Making Applesauce
Groupings:
    Small groups of 4 to 8 students with an adult nearby
    Small groups with a student leader
Materials:
    Recipe on chart (rebus or written, depending on student level)
    One apple for each student (Tart apples work best.)
    ¼ cup sugar for each 3 cups of cut-up apples
    ½ teaspoon cinnamon for each 3 cups of cut-up apples
    ½ cup water for each 3 cups of cut-up apples
    Hot plate
    Large pot
    Large spoon
    Knife and potato peeler for each student in small group (Students can bring
these from home.)

Procedures:

(a) *Applesauce activity.* Help students "read" the rebus recipe. Discuss the
meanings of terms for ingredients, utensils, and cooking procedures which
might be new, for example, *peel, core, simmer.* Have one student follow the recipe
through step 4 (see the rebus recipe, Figure A-6) as others watch and check to
see that instructions are followed and that the student knows how to use
utensils safely. If you are working with several small groups, ask one member
from a previous group to be the leader of the current group, giving her or him a
chance to apply the information learned. Then have each student follow
instructions through step 4 independently, with supervision from you or the
student leader, or both.

Figure A-6: Rebus Recipe for Applesauce

Have the students keep a record of the quantities of ingredients used and the quantity of applesauce produced for use in Applemath Activity 9b.

When all the apples have been prepared, guide the students through steps 5 through 8. As the apples simmer, discuss how heat changes liquids to gas and how sugar dissolves in the liquid and "disappears." Introduce the terms *solid, liquid, gas, suspension,* and *solution* orally and by writing them on the board. Discuss how solid apples are changed into liquid applesauce, and why a gas, water vapor, is produced in the process. Discuss how the sugar suspension or mixture is changed to a sugar solution. Use these terms to compare cooking applesauce with cooking other foods (such as cake, fudge, soup). If the students are ready for even more information, discuss how cell walls are broken down during cooking, and how this process changes flavor and texture.

As students observe the cooking process, help them describe the changes in the apples. Ask for suggestions for ways to describe what the texture is like when the apples are done ("mushy," "thick," "like oatmeal," etc.). Compare how full the pot was at the beginning of the cooking and how full it is at the end, and discuss reasons for the change, for instance, elimination of air space between apple pieces, evaporation of water.

While the students eat the applesauce, discuss how apples are prepared and eaten in different students' homes. Use descriptive words for the taste and texture.

Review the cause-effect relationship between rain and applesauce, and elicit more silly talk which claims an impossible relationship.

(b) Assessment/evaluation. Ask each student to read the recipe independently.

Check selected students' comprehension by asking them to give instructions to other students.

Encourage students to discuss the success of the recipe or how it might be improved.

Part C: More Apples!

Activity 6: Plant Cycles
Groupings:
    Large group with teacher
    Small, independent groups
Materials:
    Large mural paper
    Construction paper in assorted colors
    Paint, brushes, markers, pencils
    Rain Makes Applesauce, by Julian Scheer and Milton Bileck
    Opaque projector, slides and slide projector, or pictures from *Rain Makes Applesauce* showing the steps in the transformation from apple seed to applesauce
    What's Inside of Plants, by Herbert S. Zim
    Bits That Grow Big, by Irma E. Webber
    Encyclopedias and other plant reference books
    Films or filmstrips on the plant cycle
    Language master and cards
    Pictures of steps in plant cycle and labels (see Applelit Learning Center, Activity 11).
Procedures:

(a) Learning about cycles. Introduce the concept of cycle by drawing a bicycle on the board. Ask students to name other "cycles" and what they have in common (tricycle, unicycle, motorcycle—wheels that go around). Ask what a plant cycle might be. Talk about how plants grow in a cycle, like a wheel.

Draw a large circle on the board and review the pictures from *Rain Makes Applesauce.* Elicit the steps in the cycle from the children, and write them on the circle as they are suggested. Review the cycle and have students help to rearrange the order if necessary. Use simple line drawings so that children whose English vocabulary is limited can acquire the concept of the plant cycle. Your result should look something like this:

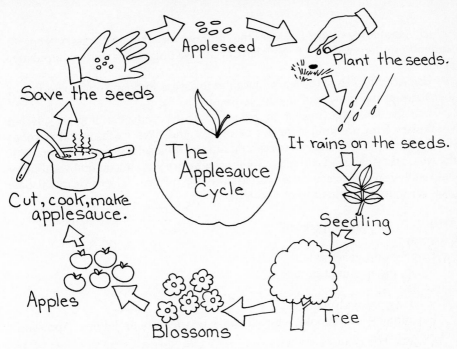

Figure A-7: The Applesauce Cycle

(b) Making cycle posters. Divide students into small groups and tell them that each group will choose a plant, learn about it, and make a plant cycle chart. In the library, help students use reference books to find and sketch the stages of growth of their chosen plants. Help them to make a small sketch of the mural, and then assign each student in the group one or more stages (e.g., for apples: seed, seedling, tree, blossoms, green fruit, ripe fruit, seed; for gill fungi [a group of mushrooms]: spores, mycelium, buttons, young plant, and mature plant). (*Note:* This would be an appropriate time for an art lesson on drawing plants and trees from nature.)

When the groups are ready to begin applying their individual drawings and cutouts to the mural paper, show them how to make a large circle using a pin, a pencil, and a string. Introduce or review the geometric terms *center, radius, diameter,* and *circumference* during this process.

Provide strips of lined paper and help the groups make labels for each stage. Then help them apply the labels to the murals. Refer the students to the dictionary and the plant books from the library to find the correct names and spelling for their labels. Display the finished murals in the classroom or hall. Have the groups hold a "mural tour" in which each group explains its mural to the class. Invite the principal or another VIP to the mural tour, to enhance the importance of the event for the students.

(c) Assessment/evaluation. Use the murals for diagnostic assessment of students' understanding of the plant cycle, writing skills, and manipulative skills.

Use Activity 11b of the learning center to assess students' understanding of the stages in the growth of the apple tree.

Use the language master to assess students' understanding of selected vocabulary from the unit. One set of cards could have words, another could have pictures. Students who are reading can test themselves to see how many of the words they can read correctly. Students who are working on oral vocabulary can test themselves to see if they can identify the pictures. The cards can also be used for independent study of vocabulary.

Activity 7: Johnny Appleseed
Groupings:
    Large group, teacher-led
    Small, independent groups
Materials:
    Cooking pot with handle
    Biographies, storybooks, encyclopedia articles about Johnny Appleseed (see references)
    Sacks, pots, and other props brought from home by students
Procedures:

(a) *Sharing the literature.* Introduce the character Johnny Appleseed by placing a pot on your head. See if anyone knows who you might be playing. Tell the students that Johnny Appleseed was an American folk hero who planted apple trees all over the United States as it was being settled by families moving west. Discuss how stories of the lives of folk heroes are often part fact and part fiction. Ask students to listen to the story of Johnny Appleseed and decide what parts they think are probably facts and what parts are probably fiction.

Read from a book, tell from your own knowledge of the story, or show a film or filmstrip on the life of Johnny Appleseed (a.k.a. John Chapman). Have students retell parts of the story in their own words and discuss favorite events from his life. Talk about which events are true and which are not, and how one could know for sure. Talk about what character traits Johnny had that made everyone admire him.

(b) *Acting out the story.* Divide students into pairs or small groups and have each group select an incident from Johnny Appleseed's life to act out for the class. Examples might be Johnny's promise to a small child to plant apples; Johnny gathering seed from mash at a cider mill; Johnny's relationships with animals; Johnny's pet wolf; Granny's coat; healing the Indian; individuals who reported seeing Johnny after his death. (All these incidents are written about in Le Sueur's *Little Brother of the Wilderness: The Story of Johnny Appleseed.*)

Give students time both in and out of class to prepare the skits so that they can bring in simple props or costumes from home. While they are rehearsing, set expectations for the skit. It should be one to two minutes long. Lines may be improvised, read, or memorized. Groups may use pantomime with a narrator or dialogue. They may act out the parts themselves or use puppets. All students in the group must play an active, though not necessarily speaking, role.

Have students perform the skits before the class. Encourage students to give one another feedback on the skits, including both praise and suggestions for improvement or elaboration. Have the students revise and rehearse skits and then put on a second performance for another class.

(c) *Assessment/evaluation.* A picture assessment could be devised to determine whether students remember the events in Johnny Appleseed's life and the order in which they occurred. Select several pictures that depict events in the life of Johnny Appleseed and several that do not. Have students choose which pictures belong, and arrange them in the order in which they happened in Johnny's life.

A checklist of skills demonstrated in the performance could be devised for diagnostic purposes. Skills assessed could include willingness to get up before the group; participation of all group members; appropriate voice volume; expression; speech length and complexity; use of language conventions; and success of the skit in holding the attention of other class members.

Activity 8: HomeFUN—Apple Recipes

Grouping:

    Large group, teacher-led

    Children working with family members at home

    Small, independent groups with teacher support

Materials:

    Paper, pencils

    Art supplies for illustrating and binding books

Procedures:

(a) *Collecting recipes.* Review the discussion of different ways of preparing apples and how apples are eaten in different individuals' homes. Review the recipe used to make applesauce. Explain to students that their homeFUN assignment is to make a rebus recipe for something that is made with apples in their homes.

Explain that parents may not actually measure all ingredients and that the students may have to watch the preparation of the dish in order to estimate the measurement of each item. Provide options for students who say that apples are never cooked in their homes (e.g., write another recipe or give instructions for how to eat a raw apple).

Elicit a list of food preparation and cooking equipment terms from the students (e.g., *peel, chop, core, simmer, boil, bake, knife, pot, strainer, peeler*), and duplicate the list or have students copy the words into their own notebooks or personal dictionaries for their use in making the recipe. Encourage them to choose a dish that is not too complicated. Encourage students to share ideas about the recipe they will write in order to assure a wide variety of dishes. Distribute printed recipe cards or provide a form for the recipe (see Figure A-8). Ask students to include some information about the country from which the recipe originated, such as location, climate, topography, natural resources, and important local foods.

Encourage students who are not ready to write recipes in English to bring in recipes in their native languages (preferably with pictures). These recipes can either be included in the cookbook in the native language, or you can find someone to translate them before inclusion.

Give the students and their families several days to a week to complete the assignments. This will take into account the busy schedules of working parents.

HomeFUN Apple Recipes

Name of Recipe _____

English Name _____

From the Kitchen of _____

Serves _____

Ingredients: _____

_____

_____

_____

_____

Procedures: _____

_____

_____

_____

_____

_____

Serving Suggestions: _____

_____

_____

_____

Figure A-8:   HomeFUN Recipe Form

(b) Publishing an apple cookbook. HomeFUN assignments that are brought to class by students can be handled in a number of ways, depending on the amount of available time and the inclinations of both student and teacher. Here are three options:

1. **Publish "As Is."** Assign volunteer students to make a cover and table of contents, and bind and publish the recipes without revision or editing for the classroom or school library.

2. **Use the writing process.** Follow the steps in the writing process (see Chapter 6) to revise and publish the apple cookbook. Have the students give one another feedback on the recipes in small groups, on the basis of such criteria as completeness and understandability. Provide feedback to students in individual conferences. Have students revise and illustrate recipes, and then bind them into a cookbook, as in option 1.

3. **Use an adult volunteer.** After the revision process (see option 2), find a volunteer to type the recipes; have the students illustrate them; and duplicate the booklets for students to give as a special gift for Mother's Day or Father's Day, some other holiday, or just as a nice surprise.

Activity 9: Applemath
Groupings:
    Large group, teacher-led
    Small groups with and without teachers available
    Independent, individual work
Materials:
    Information collected during shopping and applesauce making
    Paper and pencils
    Blackboard and chalk, or chart paper and markers
    Calculators
Procedures:

(a) Apple cost comparisons. Reproduce the field-trip chart that shows costs of different varieties and quantities of apples. Help students determine the steps involved in answering the following questions:

> What was the price of each variety of apple per half peck, per peck, and per bushel?
>
> What was the price per pound for each variety and quantity?
>
> What variety was the cheapest?
>
> Was the same variety cheapest in all quantities?

How much did the price per pound vary for each variety between buying a peck and buying a bushel?

Compare costs of several kinds of apples in several quantities.

Have individuals complete the necessary computations; enter them on the chart, and perform comparisons. Discuss the advantages and disadvantages of buying in quantity.

(b) *Computing the unit price of homemade applesauce.* As a large group activity, compute the price of applesauce. Determine and then collect the information needed (this collection is best done on the field trip and during the cooking activity).

Price of apples per pound (a)

Number of pounds used (x)

*Price of sugar per cup (s)

Number of cups used (y)

*Price of cinnamon per teaspoon (c)

Number of teaspoons used (z)

Number of quarts of applesauce made (q)

Explain the formula for computing the cost per quart.

Cost of one quart of applesauce = $(ax + sy + cz) \div q$

Review and practice the meanings of the units of measurement used: pound, cup, quart, teaspoon. Although all students may not completely understand the mathematical process for determining the formula, they can understand the general idea and perform individual computations, and they can develop vocabulary and concepts for measurement.

Have various students perform the calculations by hand and by calculator to check accuracy. Use the results of the computation to decide on the winner of the contest set up in Activity 3c, the Applesauce Estimation Contest. Discuss variables that might change the answer (quantity of applesauce made; variety of apples; change in price; amount of sugar needed depending on sweetness of apples; etc.). Compare the cost of homemade applesauce with the cost of applesauce at the grocery store. Questions for discussion might include "Is it economical to make one's own applesauce?" and "Are there other reasons besides economy to make homemade applesauce?"

*Use information on bag or container to estimate these.

(c) Cooking for one or a million. Select, with students, a favorite recipe from the class apple cookbook. Explain that recipes are often made for six or eight servings, whereas many times people either are cooking for fewer than six or are cooking for a crowd and need to find a way to adapt the recipe to their needs. Ask students how this might be done.

Write the ingredients and quantities of the chosen recipe on the board, along with the number that the recipe is expected to serve. Determine a formula for dividing the recipe in half and another formula for doubling the recipe. Assign pairs or small groups to perform computations for each ingredient. List the new quantities on the board.

After solving these problems as a class, ask each student to select a recipe and perform the computations individually. Provide a calculator for checking computations. (*Note:* This activity provides an excellent opportunity to introduce or review the process of changing fractions to decimals.)

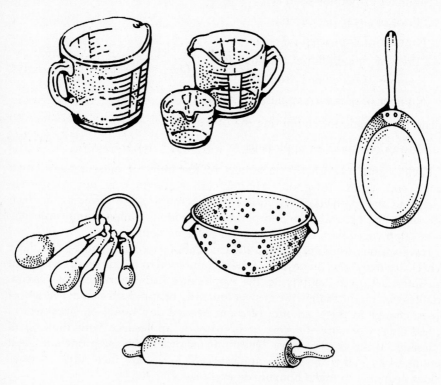

(d) Assessment/evaluation. Have students check their own computations by using a calculator.

Request students to choose a recipe from home and either double quantities or divide them in half. Evaluate students' assignments for correct applications of the procedures used in class.

Assess understanding of measurement terms by having pictures of the various quantities on language master cards. Have pairs of students quiz one another on whether they can name the term for the pictured quantity.

Activity 10: Appletalk—Idioms and Figurative Language
Groupings:
  Large group led by teacher
  Individual, independent work with teacher support
Materials:
  Chart paper, drawing paper, paint, markers, etc.
Procedures:

(a) Learning about idioms and figurative language. In preparation for this activity, ask students to listen for and bring in any idioms, metaphorical terms, or sayings using the word apple throughout the earlier activities in this unit. Make sure that the students know what idioms and metaphors are by providing some examples, such as "apple of my eye," Big Apple, Windy Apple, sour apple, apple cheeks, candy apple red, apple blossom time, "An apple a day keeps the doctor away," "An apple for the teacher." To increase the number of examples brought in, you may wish to include other fruits: "The car was a lemon," "You're a peach," "sour grapes."

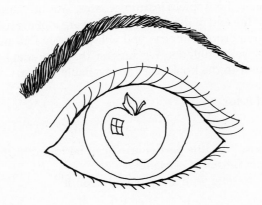

As students bring in the terms or sayings, discuss their meanings and add them to a list on a wall chart. When quite a few have been collected, review their meanings and ask each student to use his or her imagination to illustrate one of the terms or phrases. Some may wish to illustrate a figurative meaning (e.g., a child with rosy cheeks for "apple cheeks"); a humorous literal illustration (e.g., a person with an apple in her eye for "apple of my eye"); or a combination of the two (e.g., a skyline of New York City inside a large apple for "Big Apple").

When the students have completed their illustrations, ask them to display their work individually in front of the class. Have the class guess which term or phrase the student has illustrated. Ask them to discuss whether the interpretation was figurative, literal, or a combination of the two. Make labels for the illustrations and display them.

(b) *Assessment/evaluation.* Cover the labels on the illustrations. Ask each student to name the phrase depicted and to tell whether the illustration is figurative, literal, or both.

Activity 11: Applelit Learning Center—Reading, Listening, Talking, and Writing about Apples
Groupings:
   Individuals
   Pairs for some activities
   Small groups for many of the learning center activities, with or without the teacher
Materials:
   We suggest some delightful and interesting literature around the theme of apples for inclusion in the Applelit learning center. This literature is listed in the reference section at the end of the unit. While you are looking for these books in your school or neighborhood library, you will probably find many others that are appropriate for your students. We suggest that you adapt the procedures suggested in this unit to the books that are available to you.

(a) *The little red house.*

Materials:
   The riddle/poem "A Little Red House" can be found in the book *Yakima, Washington: An Apple Growing Community*
   Tape recorder, cassette with story recorded on it
   Apples
   Knife

Procedures:

In an old folk tale a boy searches for the answer to a riddle:

A little red house
Just three inches wide
As round as can be
With a star inside.

The child goes from person to person repeating the riddle rhyme, but no one knows the answer. Finally, as the boy recites the rhyme to his grandmother, an apple falls out of a tree beside them. His grandmother cuts the apple in half crosswise and shows him the five-pointed-star pattern made by the arrangement of the seeds.

Activities based on this story can be offered on several levels:

1. *Independent reading.* Students who read English can read the story and then tell it to someone at home.

2. *Listening.* Students who do not yet read at the appropriate level can listen to the story on tape while looking at the illustrations. Then they can cut open an apple to see if there is a star. Finally, of course, they can eat the apple.

3. *Peer storytelling.* Older students can listen to the rhyme and learn it, then visit a younger class to tell the story of the riddle to a child or a small group. They can end the storytelling by cutting open an apple and sharing it with the younger children.

(c) Apples of love and discord.

Materials:

Book of Greek Myths (1962), by Ingri and Edgar Parin D'Aulaire

The Labors of Hercules (1965), by Paul Hollander

Cassette recorder and blank tape

Procedures:

The D'Aulaires' *Book of Greek Myths* includes two Greek myths about apples in the chapter entitled "The Apples of Love and the Apple of Discord." *The Labors of Hercules,* by Paul Hollander, describes Hercules' quest for golden apples and how he outsmarted Atlas to succeed. Depending on their reading skills, students could either read the myths for themselves or listen to them at the learning center.

After students have heard the stories, have them retell one of the stories into a tape recorder, then play the tape back to a small group. Outstanding tapes could be played for the whole class.

Have students discuss the apple stories in their small groups. Ask the students to explain how apples led to good things in one story and bad things in another. Ask them to tell one another any other stories they know about apples.

(d) Apple recipe cards.

Materials:

The students' own cookbook (see Activity 8b, Publishing a Cookbook)
Assorted illustrated cookbooks for adults and children
Apples: A Bushel of Fun, and Facts (1976), by Bernice Kohr (The last chapter includes a number of apple recipes for children to try.)
Recipe cards
Pens and pencils

Procedures:

Provide the students with several cookbooks as resources. Mark the pages with apple recipes that they might like. Encourage students to browse through the pictures and recipes and find one they'd like to try. Have them copy the recipe on a 3-by-5-inch card and take it home. Encourage students to bring in samples of dishes they've prepared and to report on the cooking.

(e) Apples: A wordless book

Materials:

Apples (1972), by Nonny Hogrogian
Cassette recorder and taped instructions

Procedures:

This activity is provided for beginning second language learners. Pair a beginning student with a verbal and compatible partner. Provide taped instructions for the partner to use in leading the lesson. On the tape, instruct the partner to have the beginning student tell the story of *Apples* while looking at the pictures. Tell the partner to ask questions and give encouragement, but *not* to tell the story. Explain that the job of the partner is to elicit the story from the beginning student. After the story has been told once, the students may reverse roles, with the beginning student asking the questions and the partner telling the story. On the tape, provide discussion questions for the pairs to use after the storytelling. Students should be instructed on the tape to listen to a question, then stop the tape and discuss the question, then turn on the tape for the next question. Questions might include the following: How did the stories you told differ from one another? What were the steps in the plant cycle in this story? How much time passed from the beginning to the end of the book? Was there anything impossible about the story the book told? Why was the book funny?

(f) Assessment/evaluation. For record keeping at the learning center, you may find a chart helpful. With the chart, you can assign centers to students according to their needs, assign partners that are appropriate, and monitor students' completion of the activities. We have included a sample chart in Figure A-9.

NAMES	A	B	C	D	E	Partner's Name	
Tomie							Assigned (date)
							Checked (date)
Charlotte							Assigned (date)
							Checked (date)
Maurice							Assigned (date)
							Checked (date)
Paulo							Assigned (date)
							Checked (date)
Crescent							Assigned (date)
							Checked (date)
Margaret							Assigned (date)
							Checked (date)
Anno							Assigned (date)
							Checked (date)

ACTIVITIES

Figure A-9: Applelit Center Chart

REFERENCES

D'Aulaire, Ingri and Edgar Parin. 1962. *Book of Greek myths.* Garden City, NY: Doubleday & Company.

Educational Research Council of America. 1970. *Yakima, Washington: An apple growing community.* Boston: Allyn and Bacon.

Hogrogian, Nonny. 1972. *Apples.* New York: Macmillan.

Hollander, Paul. 1965. *The labors of Hercules.* New York: G. P. Putnam's Sons.

Kohr, Bernice. 1976. *Apples: A bushel of fun, and facts.* New York: Parents' Magazine Press.

Le Sueur, Meridel. 1947. *Little brother of the wilderness: The story of Johnny Appleseed.* New York: Alfred A. Knopf.

Scheer, Julian, and Bileck, Marvin. (1964). *Rain makes applesauce.* New York: Holiday.

Webber, Irma E. 1949. *Bits that grow big.* New York: William R. Scott.

Zim, Herbert S. 1952. *What's inside of plants.* New York: William Morrow & Co.

Unit B

Heroes and Superheroes: An Integrated Unit for Third through Sixth Grade Students

INTRODUCTION

The idea for "Heroes and Superheroes"* came directly from a group of middle elementary students who were bringing superhero figures to school and animatedly discussing superhero cartoon programs. Interest in superheroes seems to have some durability, as stories about remarkable humans and mythical figures have been told in just about every culture as far back as we have records of stories.

As the Heroes and Superheroes Unit Planning Web in Figure B-1 shows, student interest in contemporary superheroes is used as a jumping off place to study language through a variety of content areas. The famous television and comic book hero Spidey pays a visit to the class to set the unit into motion. Students learn about mythical superheroes from various cultures and compare them to contemporary superheroes. They review science concepts about simple machines, electricity, light, and magnetism by inventing superheroes whose powers are based on these concepts. They review their understanding of story structure while they create adventures for their original superhero characters.

In the second part of the unit, students turn their attention to real-life heroes.

---

* For purposes of clarity and simplicity, we use the terms *hero* and *superhero* to refer to both males and females throughout this unit.

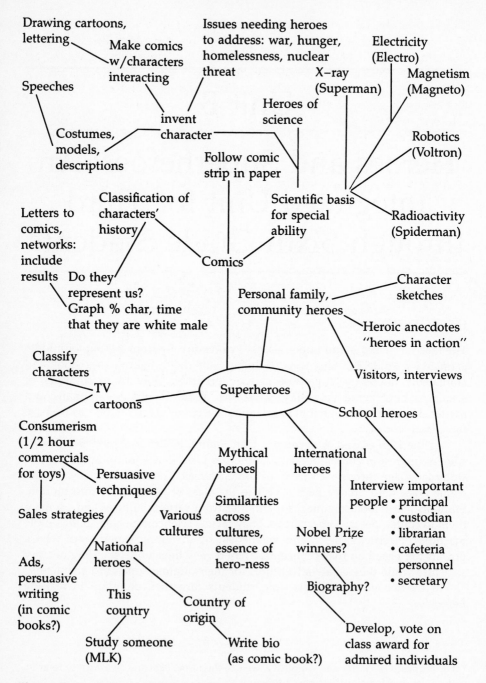

Drawing cartoons, lettering

Make comics w/characters interacting

Speeches

Costumes, models, descriptions

invent character

Issues needing heroes to address: war, hunger, homelessness, nuclear threat

Heroes of science

Follow comic strip in paper

Electricity (Electro)

Magnetism (Magneto)

X-ray (Superman)

Robotics (Voltron)

Scientific basis for special ability

Radioactivity (Spiderman)

Letters to comics, networks: include results

Classification of characters' history

Do they represent us? Graph % char, time that they are white male

Comics

Personal family, community heroes

Character sketches

Heroic anecdotes "heroes in action"

Classify characters

TV cartoons

Visitors, interviews

School heroes

Superheroes

Consumerism (1/2 hour commercials for toys)

Persuasive techniques

Sales strategies

Ads, persuasive writing (in comic books?)

National heroes

This country

Study someone (MLK)

Various cultures

Mythical heroes

Similarities across cultures, essence of hero-ness

Country of origin

International heroes

Nobel Prize winners?

Biography?

Write bio (as comic book?)

Interview important people • principal • custodian • librarian • cafeteria personnel • secretary

Develop, vote on class award for admired individuals

Figure B-1:   Planning Web for Heroes and Superheroes

They learn about civil rights hero Martin Luther King, Jr., and then expand their study to other real-life heroes, including school and community heroes, whom they interview, and heroes from family stories. Students study speeches of famous heroes, then write and present speeches for their own superheroes.

A learning center where students practice and expand on concepts learned in the other unit activities plays an important role in the unit.

Objectives for the unit come from the *Basic Curriculum Content for Georgia's Public Schools* and cover a wide range of third- through sixth-grade objectives in many subject areas, addressing many aspects of language learning. These objectives for the unit are shown in Figure B-2.

The unit concludes with a Supercelebration, during which family, school, and community visitors are treated to the sights, sounds, and tastes of the products of students' labors.

Heroes and Superheroes: Outline of Unit Activities*

Introduction
Part A. Superheroes
    Activities:
      1. A Visit from Spidey
        a. Before the Visit
        b. During the Visit
        c. After the Visit
      2. Legendary Superheroes
        a. Collecting Legends and Myths
        b. Assessment/Evaluation
        c. Extensions
      3. Tallying Cartoon Heroes' Speech and Characteristics
        a. From Tally to Graph
        b. Assessment/Evaluation
        c. Extensions
      4. Individual Superheroes and Group Adventures
        a. Developing Individual Superheroes
        b. Group Adventures
        c. Assessment/Evaluation
        d. Extensions
Part B. Heroes
    Activities:
      5. HomeFUN: Family/Community heroes
        a. Sunshine Outline
        b. Assessment/Evaluation
        c. Extensions
      6. In-School Field Trips: School Heroes
        a. Before the Trip
        b. During the Trip
        c. After the trip
        d. Assessment/Evaluation
        e. Extensions
      7. A Civil Rights Hero: Martin Luther King, Jr.
        a. A Real-Life hero
        b. Assessment/Evaluation
        c. Extensions
      8. I Have a Dream: A Hero's Speech
        a. Listening to Speeches
        b. Writing and Delivering Speeches
        c. Assessment/Evaluation
        d. Extensions

UNIT ACTIVITIES

Part A: Superheroes

Activity 1: A Visit from Spidey

Groupings:
 Small groups
 Full group, teacher led
Materials:
 Paper and writing materials
 Chalk, blackboard, bulletin board
 Spiderwoman (man) costume or mask (draw a red and blue spider face on
an old sheet or pillowcase with magic markers)
Procedures:

(a) *Before the visit.* A week or two before the unit is to begin, start leaving
hints around the classroom that Spidey is coming to visit. Leave spiderwebs on
blackboard; tack a note saying "Spidey is coming" on the bulletin board, on the
classroom door, in the restrooms; leave *Spiderman* comics around the room.

A day before the planned visit and unit introduction, ask students to make a
list of questions they would like to ask Spiderman or Spiderwoman, should he
or she decide to visit the classroom. Remind students that Spidey has no mouth,
and thus can only nod or shake his/her head in response to questions:
therefore, the questions should be answerable by yes or no. Encourage students
to learn more about Spidey by reading the comics, and do so yourself. You may
choose to read the comics aloud to the class.

Have students meet in small groups to brainstorm additional questions and
write them down. Make sure that each student is armed with a question before
Spidey's visit. Students might ask questions to find out how Spidey got
web-spinning powers, why he/she is visiting the classroom, who Spidey's
principal enemies are, what kinds of problems Spidey solves with his/her
superpowers, why he/she wears that funny costume, and so on.

(b) *During the visit.* Ask a colleague do a little research on Spidey, then to don
the costume and make a surprise visit to your class. Warn your confederate not
to speak but just to nod or shake his/her head. Encourage students to ask all of
the questions they have prepared and to record the information they obtain for
later use.

(c) *After the visit* Talk about what students have learned. Write down what students say and have them help you group the information. Get students to define what a superhero really is—what characteristics a superhero has that no other persons or characters have. Make a list of characteristics that constitute a superhero profile, as in Figure B-2.

Superhero Profile Chart

Name	Superman
Alternate identity	Clark Kent
Costume	Red and blue with cape
Logo	Large yellow "S"
Superpower	Strength, X-ray vision, etc.
Source of power	From another planet
Goals	Help people in trouble
Enemies	Lex Luthor, etc.
Weakness	Kryptonite
Where born/originated	The Planet Krypton
Where based	Metropolis

Figure B-2: Characteristics of a Superhero

(d) *Assessment/evaluation.* Observe the quality of students' questions. Which students can ask questions that require yes or no answers? Which students are able to record the answers fully in English?

(e) *Extensions.* Encourage students to write in their journals about Spidey's visit.

If you are computer-inclined, help students keep track of the information you and the students collect about heroes and superheroes, then have students help you put a superhero data base on the computer as you do the unit activities. You can also keep information on a data base bulletin board and do manual searches for information. This bulletin board will come in handy as the unit progresses and can be used at the end for additional writing and game activities.

Use the game Twenty Questions to help students practice thinking up questions that require a yes or no answer. Students can choose a favorite comic book or real-life hero and the rest of the class can try to guess the hero's identity.

Activity 2: Legendary Superheroes

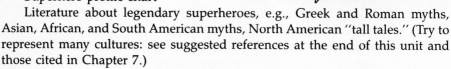

Groupings:
    Full group, teacher-directed
    Individuals working independently
    Dyads
Materials:
    Superhero profile chart
    Literature about legendary superheroes, e.g., Greek and Roman myths,
Asian, African, and South American myths, North American "tall tales." (Try to
represent many cultures: see suggested references at the end of this unit and
those cited in Chapter 7.)
Procedures:
    (a) *Collecting legends and myths.* Visit the school and local public libraries to
collect superhero myths from many cultures. Share these stories with the
students by reading them aloud, by storytelling, by playing cassette tapes, or by
showing films or video. Ask parents and students to bring/send in stories/
myths about superheroes from their native cultures.
    Make the stories available to students for sustained silent reading and for
listening at the learning center. (If you like, have students vote on favorite
stories they would like you to tape.)
    Have pairs of students select a mythological hero, read or listen to stories
about him/her, and then fill in the profile sheet with information about that
hero.
    Bring the students together to discuss these mythological superheroes and
compare them to the contemporary superheroes of comic books and cartoons.
Generate additional or alternative mythical hero characteristics to add to your
original profile list.
    Have the pairs meet to use information from the profile sheet and
discussion in order to write a short narrative about their chosen mythological
superhero.
    Use the writing process (see Chapters 6 and 7) to edit and revise narratives,
and bind them into a class book to be shared with parents and other classes.
(For the book's title, you could use something like "Mythological Superheroes
from Many Cultures.")

    (b) *Assessment/evaluation.* Evaluate students' profiles and narratives to assess
writing needs. Are students able to plan and write short, coherent, sequenced
narratives with help? Without help? Observe discussions of pairs. Use "follow
the phrase" (Ventriglia 1982) to extend language used by students.

(c) Extensions. Repeat the same process, choosing comic book or cartoon superheroes, or permit students to select a mythological, comic book or cartoon superhero for developing the profile.

Discuss why we humans have always invented superheroes. Help students reflect on the human needs that are fulfilled by inventing myths and heroes.

If you are developing a database, explain that the computer understands only "yes" and "no" questions and numbers and that students will have to code the information so that the computer can understand. For example, the data entry for Superman might look like this:

Name:	Superman
ID:	001
Origin:	0 (not on earth)
Present location:	3 (North America)
Sex:	1 (male)
Age:	3 (20–30)
Race:	3 (Caucasian)

Activity 3: Tallying Cartoon Heroes' Speech and Characteristics

Groupings:

Full group, teacher-directed

Small groups

Materials:

Video cassette recorder

Videotape of segment (10 to 15 minutes, one story) of Saturday morning superhero cartoon (the school librarian or a student may volunteer to help you with this). The tape should be about 10 to 15 minutes long, of one story, with at least three or four characters and with some conflict and resolution.

Stopwatches or watches with second hands (Ask students to bring in or borrow from PE teacher.)

Writing materials

Almanac with current national population statistics

Graph paper

Procedures:

(a) From tally to graph. As you and students in the full group watch the tape the first time, list the superhero characters as they appear.

Have the students select a character to observe more closely as they watch the tape a second time. Assign a third of the students to keep track of the character's time on the screen, another third to keep track of how many times that character speaks, and the last third to record other information about the character: approximate age, race, gender, "good" or "bad" affiliation.

Record (have students write or dictate) and discuss findings. Compare conflicting evidence and develop ways for students to be more accurate.

Before watching the tape a third time, assign three students to observe each character, each taking one of the tasks from the second viewing of the tape.

Record the information obtained on a chart like that in Figure B-3.

	Time on screen	Times spoke	Gender	Age	Race	Good/bad
Character 1 Name:						
Character 2 Name:						
Character 3 Name:						
Character 4 Name:						

Figure B-3: Superhero Cartoon Graphs

Have students help you use the information on the chart to make graphs and compute answers to questions like the following:

How many times did women speak during the segment?

How many time did men speak?

What is the average age of the characters?

What percentage of the characters belong to each gender?

What percentage of the characters belong to each race?

What percentage of characters of each gender are "good?"

What percentage of characters of each race are "good?"

Using information you have recorded and graphed, compare percentages of persons of different races and genders in cartoons to those in the general population (using information from the almanac). Discuss implications of the answers.

(b) Assessment/evaluation. Observe students' use of various categories in the chart. Do the students classify correctly? Do they understand the terms? Observe students' knowledge of terms for numbers and mathematical operations, and use symbols to help them learn correspondences.

Ask each student to come up with a question that can be answered by the information on the chart. Evaluate students' questions and offer other students a chance to find the answers.

(c) Extensions. Assign students a homeFUN exercise in which they watch a particular TV cartoon and record information. Compile this new information to see if the results are the same as in the pilot study.

Have students, in pairs, make graphs that show the answers to the questions.

Students may wish to write to television stations or companies that produce comics or cartoons, telling them the results of their research.

Activity 4: Individual Superheroes and Group Adventures

Groupings:
  Full group, teacher-directed
  Individual, with teacher available
  Small groups, dyads
Materials:
  Superhero profile chart or transparency
  Blank superhero profile sheets
  Writing and drawing materials
  Science texts, science magazines, and illustrated science books for reference on scientific principles upon which to base superpowers
Procedures:

(a) Developing individual superheroes. In she full group, review categories of characteristics of superheroes, referring to a large superhero profile chart. Ask students for examples of each category. Discuss the science fiction aspects of contemporary superheroes. Many of the superpowers refer to actual scientific principles; for example, Spiderman—radioactivity; Superman—X-ray.

Brainstorm with the class, and list possible scientific connections between imaginary superheroes and their powers, for example:

Rocky   gravity
Flame Woman   fire
Geiger Girl   radioactivity
Laser Lad   lasers
Robert Robo   robotics

Ask each student to think up a personal imaginary superhero and to research the scientific basis of the hero's superpower. Ask each student to come up with a unique character. Give the students time to think, to browse through science materials, and to talk to friends and family members about the assignment.

When the students have completed the assignment, have them work in pairs, in turn presenting the character to the partner and giving feedback suggestitons for elaboration or improvement. Students can then revise their characters.

(b) *Group adventures.* Once characters have been revised, have groups of two or three pairs of students meet to plan an adventure for their characters to have together. Before the groups meet, go over the basic elements of a story (e.g., setting, characters, problem, complication, resolution) and basic comic-book techniques (narration, balloons for speech or thought, drawing simple stick figures). Have students draft and discuss a "story board" before writing the final version of their adventures.

Have students share adventures orally, and mount the strips on a "Superheroes Adventure" bulletin board.

(c) *Assessment/evaluation.* Plan an individual conference with each student to discuss the character that has been created. Provide students with encouragement and specific, constructive feedback.

(d) *Extensions.* You may choose to publish a classroom *Marvelous Universe* along with the comic adventures. Have each student contribute a one-page comic biography of a character to the book.

Part B: Heroes

Activity 5: HomeFUN—Family/Community Heroes

Groupings:
  Student/older family member dyads
Materials:
  Writing materials
  Copy of newspaper or magazine record of "heroic" act by community member (e.g., "Scouts in Action" section in *Boys' Life)*
  Sunshine outline chart
  Individual, duplicated copies of the sunshine outline
Procedures:

(a) *Sunshine outlines.* Share stories of heroism from newspapers or magazines. Discuss what makes an act heroic (e.g., courage when facing personal danger, quick thinking, crucial special knowledge).

Have students ask family members to tell the story of a heroic act they experienced or heard about, either in this country or in their native country. Students may choose to write the story and read it to the class; to tape the story and play it to the class (and translate it if necessary and possible); or to present the story orally, using an outline. Show students how to use a "sunshine outline" for note taking to make sure they get all the essential information in their interviews of family members.

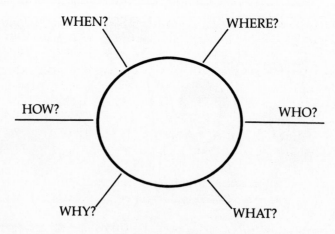

SUNSHINE OUTLINE

Figure B-4:   Sunshine Outline

Have the students present the stories they have collected. Post a sunshine outline chart in the room. At the end of the presentation, ask participants to refer to the sunshine outline chart to note which questions the presenter has not yet answered. Then have participants ask these questions.

(b) Assessment/evaluation. Observe students' presentation. Look over the sunshine outlines to make sure that students understand the question words and that they have answered them appropriately. Observe the quality of questions that students ask one another during presentations.

(c) Extensions. Revise and compile heroic stories in a book. After students have all taken turns sharing the book with their families, donate the book to the school library for other students to read.

Activity 6: In-School Field Trips: School Heroes

Groupings:
    Full group, teacher-led
    Small groups
    Small groups with school community "hero"
Materials:
    Writing materials
Procedures:

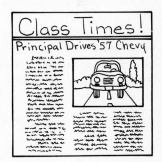

(a) Before the trip. Discuss how our leaders and community helpers are in a sense heroes to us. Use the profile characteristics generated earlier to focus the discussion on characteristics of real-life heroes. Ask students to name persons that they think are the heroes of the school community (e.g., the principal, librarian, custodian, cafeteria worker, nurse, secretary, counselor, etc.).

Explain to the students that they are going to interview these school community heroes. With the students, develop a model list of questions they might ask. Explain that effective interviewers usually leave their "script" and ask unplanned questions to follow-up on interesting things the interviewees say.

Divide students into groups of about four. Have each group meet and come up with a list of questions to ask their interviewee. Make sure that each student has two or more questions to ask.

Have students role-play the parts of interviewer and interviewee until they are comfortable asking the questions. Again, explain that they will probably find themselves asking questions they had not thought of before the interview, and that this is desirable.

(b) During the trip. Have students take audiocassette recorders with them to tape the interviews. They may also take a camera to photograph the interviewee.

(c) After the trip. After the interviews, students may follow up in a number of ways, depending upon how much time is available and upon their language levels. They may transcribe the interview or parts of the interview and revise and publish them; summarize the information gained on a school heroes profile sheet; orally present a summary of the interview to the class; make a school heroes bulletin board in the hall with pictures of and stories about the persons interviewed; and write articles for the class newsletter or school newspaper telling about the school heroes.

(d) Assessment/evaluation. Ask students to write short summaries of the interview. Take dictation from students who are not yet ready to write. Keep these samples for comparison with writing done later in the year.

(e) Extensions. Make a "community heroes" bulletin board. Try to arrange phone or in-person interviews with community heroes—fire fighters, police officers, rescue workers. Collect stories that they tell of heroic acts performed by themselves or their colleagues.

Activity 7: A Civil Rights Hero—Martin Luther King, Jr.

Groupings:
  Full group, teacher-directed
  Small group discussions
  Superhero profile chart
  Individual, duplicated copies of superhero profile
Materials:
  Books, films, filmstrips, or videos on the life of Martin Luther King, Jr., e.g., *Boy King.*
Procedures:

(a) A Real-life hero. Ask the students if they have ever heard of Martin Luther King, Jr., and have them share what they know about him. Ask the students who are familiar with King if they think he is a real-life hero. Ask them to explain their answers.

Explain to the class that they are going to learn more about Dr. Martin Luther King, Jr. Referring to the superhero profile chart and other lists of heroic characteristics that you've compiled, ask students which characteristics a real-life hero would have. As they study about the life of Martin Luther King, Jr., they should note characteristics that fit on the chart.

Select one or more films, filmstrips, or videos about Martin Luther King, Jr., to share with the class.

The first time through, show the film with sound-narration. Ask the students to write down key words to remind them of events that occurred in King's life.

Discuss the key events depicted in the film. Ask students who have written down key words to stand at the front of the room with the words written in magic marker on cards so that all can see. Have the class tell the students standing at the front of the room how to rearrange themselves so that the events on the cards are in chronological order from left to right.

Show the film again, this time without sound. Have students hold up key words when the events occur to which the cards refer. Ask different student volunteers to narrate portions of the film.

After the film, divide the class into small groups and give each group a superhero profile chart. Ask the group to work together to fill in the relevant categories with information about Dr. King.

Bring the groups back together, and have students explain what groups have discussed in order to fill in the superhero profile chart on chart paper or overhead transparency. Discuss what characteristics about King make us consider him a hero, what his "superpowers" were (e.g., speaking and writing ability, charisma, commitment to his cause, courage).

Have students use information on the chart to dictate a narrative about King as you write it on chart paper or on the board.

(b) *Assessment/evaluation.* Listen to students' contributions to full and small group discussions. Note how well students remember facts about King's life, how well they express information that they know, and how well they put information into chronological order.

(c) *Extensions.* If someone in your community or class has worked in the civil rights area or has special knowledge of Dr. King, invite him or her to share this expertise with the class. (This could also be done for other real-life heroes from other countries.)

Have the students use the superhero profile as an outline for their own narratives about King. Have them generate time lines of major events in King's life.

Discuss other civil rights movements, e.g., Cesar Chavez and the farm workers' movement. Encourage students to read about these movements and to report to the class on their findings. Have students research and write about other real-life heroes whom they admire.

Display books on civil rights movements in the class library.

Assign each student one key word, and ask the student to expand the word into a paragraph about that event in Dr. King's life.

Activity 8: "I Have a Dream"—A Hero's Speech

Groupings:
    Full group, teacher-directed
    Small writing support groups
Materials:
    Taped selections from several famous speeches, e.g., King's "I Have a Dream"; Patrick Henry's "Give Me Liberty or Give Me Death"; Abraham Lincoln's Gettysburg Address; John F. Kennedy's Inaugural Address; Winston Churchill's "We Will Never Surrender"
    Audiotaping or videotaping equipment
Procedures:

(a) *Listening to speeches.* Introduce the activity by giving students short quotes from several famous speeches. Have the students try to identify the speaker and related events. Ask the students why they think these speeches were so memorable.

Discuss devices used by speechmakers, such as metaphor ("I have a dream"); dramatic, unusual phrasing ("Four score and seven years ago"; "We have nothing to fear but fear itself"); contrasts or opposites ("Give me liberty or give me death!"; "Ask not what your country can do for you; but ask what you can do for your country"); vocalizations and intonations; gestures; etc.

Explain that the speeches will be part of a learning center activity, and introduce the activity (see Activity 12).

(b) *Writing and delivering speeches.* Later on, after all of the students have completed the learning center activity, discuss with them things that they would like to make better in the world. Ask them to write a speech as if they were a hero who would solve that problem.

Have the students use the writing process and writing support groups to improve the speeches.

Have students rehearse the completed speeches. Videotape the rehearsals, and give students the opportunity to see themselves on tape. Help the students to observe specific things that they are doing right and specific ways in which they might improve aspects of their speaking.

(c) *Assessment/evaluation.* Watch the videotapes of the speeches to assess pronunciation problems and problems with expression, ease in public speaking, etc.

Ask the students to restate excerpts from the famous speeches in their own words in order to check comprehension.

(d) *Extensions* Have students go to the library to find other memorable speeches.

Encourage students to memorize a favorite part of a famous speech to recite to the class.

Activity 9: HomeFUN—Heroes from Native Cultures

Groupings:
Student and older family member dyads
Procedures:

(a) *Heroes from Home* With the students, revise the superheroes profile chart to make a hero profile chart.

Duplicate the revised chart, and send it home with students, requesting them to ask family members about a famous real-life hero from the family's or ancestors' country of origin.

Adjust explanations and expectations according to students' proficiency. Some may bring back the chart filled out in their native language; some may write only a few key words in English; others may write in complete English sentences.

Have students share what they have learned about the hero from their country of origin by telling the story, reading it, or directing several peers to act it out.

(b) *Assessment/evaluation.* Use a checklist of speaking skills to evaluate students' presentations. Include on the list common pronunciation errors for second language speakers such as sound substitutions, omissions of plurals, or incorrect verb agreement. Also include such speaking skills as pace, clarity, expressiveness, and use of gestures. Provide students with individual feedback, orally or in writing.

(c) *Extensions.* Encourage students who are interested in so doing to revise and publish their accounts of heroes from their native countries.

Activity 10: Heroes and Superheroes Learning Center

(a) Where is Spidey?—communication game.

Grouping:
   Dyads
Materials:
   Cardboard screen to block vision between two students facing one another
   2 identical maps
   5 pairs of identical cutout superhero figures
Procedures:
   Two students sit facing one another with a cardboard screen blocking their view. Before each student is a map.
   Student A places the figures at different locations on the map.
   Student B must determine where the figures are located, and place his/her figures in the same places on his/her map. In order to do this, student B may ask only questions that can be answered by "yes" or "no" and cannot use the name of the superhero figure.
   Students time how long it takes student B to place the figures correctly.
   When student B thinks that all the figures are placed correctly, he/she asks student A to check them. If they are not all correct, a one-minute penalty is added to the time and the game continues until they are all correct. Students then switch roles and play again.
   Student A checks student B's placement, thus giving feedback on the effectiveness of the questions. In order to let the teacher know that they have completed the activities, and to give some idea of how well they were communicating, students record their times on a chart at the learning center.

(b) Sequencing heroic adventures.

Grouping:
   Individual
Materials:
   Sets of pictures/written narratives showing sequences in myths, superheroes' adventures, real heroes' lives (all individuals that students have studied and discussed in class), varied to match different students' abilities, and ranked by number according to difficulty.
Procedures:
   Individual students begin with the easiest set of pictures/narratives. They study the cards and place them in the correct order. They may consult reference books in the learning center and chart stories, time lines, and profiles around the classroom.
   When the student thinks that the cards have been sequenced correctly, he/she turns the cards over to check. Cards are numbered on the back.

The student continues until the card sets become too difficult. Then the student records the scores on a checklist at the learning center.

(c) Listening to speeches.

Groupings:
   Individuals or dyads
Materials:
   Excerpts from famous speeches, in print and recorded, e.g.,
      Lincoln's Gettysburg Address
      Washington's Farewell
      King's "I Have a Dream"
      Kennedy's Inaugural Address
      Patrick Henry's "Give Me Liberty"
      Roosevelt's "We Have Nothing to Fear"
      Churchill's "We Will Never Surrender"
   Record player, cassette recorder, or VCR
   Dictionaries, thesauruses, historical dictionaries (e.g., *American Heritage Dictionary, Oxford English Dictionary*), translation dictionaries from students' native languages
   Index cards
Procedures:
   Review skills needed for the activity: using the dictionary and thesaurus, defining figures of speech and speechmaking devices.
   Rehearse the learning center procedures by choosing a selection and doing the exercises with the whole class.
   Have students listen to tapes at the learning center over the course of the unit, changing the tapes when a given speech has been heard by everyone.
   Have students select a favorite passage. They should then look up any unfamiliar words in the passage and write the word and a translation, an English definition, and their initials on an index card. The cards should be left in the learning center for future participants, who should select words that have not already been defined by a previous student.
   Have students look for figures of speech in the selected passage. Are there examples of metaphor, simile, personification? Do the speakers use contrasts, dramatic phrasing, pauses, gestures (for speeches on video)?
   Leave a checklist at the learning center for students to mark after they have completed activities.
   The student continues until the card sets become too difficult. Then the student records the scores on a checklist at the learning center.
   The teacher may check the cards at center to see the level of words students chose to learn, and use the word cards in future vocabulary activities and games.

(d) Interpreting supergraphs.

Groupings:

Groups of 2 or 3 students

Materials:

Graphs of information obtained in Activity 3 or similar graphs (see examples in Figure B-5)

Duplicated questions about graphs

Writing materials

Procedures:

Have groups work together to answer questions about graphs. When they have completed questions, they may check their answers on the answer sheet.

After students have answered questions and checked answers, they are to think of one new question that can be answered by the graphs to leave at the learning center for future groups. They may add the new answer to the answer sheet.

Students may return to the activity to answer questions that have been left by other students.

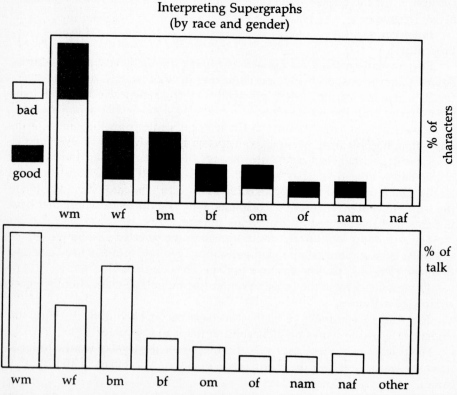

Figure 5.5: Superhero Cartoon Graphics

(e) Designing a supervehicle.

Groupings:

Groups of 2 to 4 students

Materials:

Pictures of simple machines in science texts, science magazines, and encyclopedias for reference

Junk! (foil, cardboard tubes and boxes, construction paper, tape, glue, jar lids for wheels, straws, dowels (Ask students to bring these supplies from home.)

Procedures:

Review study of simple machines.

Ask small groups to design and create a supervehicle for the superheroes they created in Activity 4.

Students are to incorporate at least three simple machines into the creation and must write a brief description of how these machines operate.

After all vehicles are complete, groups may present their vehicles and descriptions to the class.

Part C: Supercelebration

Activity 11: Refreshments: Hero Sandwiches, Superhero Cake

Groupings:
Small groups with parent volunteer assistants
Materials:
Cake and frosting ingredients (mix, eggs, oil, powdered su~~g~~ ., butter, milk, food coloring) and utensils (bowl, mixer, scraper, cake pans, cake plate)
Hero sandwich ingredients (unsliced loaf of bread, sliced sandwich meats, sliced cheeses, tomato, lettuce, dressing) and utensils (knives, serving platter)
Procedures:

(a) *Cooking terms and tools.* Explain to students that they are going to help make refreshments for their supercelebration, to which they are inviting family and school friends. At the celebration, they will share what they've learned and done during the unit.

Divide the class into small groups of bakers, frosters, and sandwich makers. Groups may work with parent volunters at different times during the day, or, if you have enough volunteers, all at the same time.

Orient your volunteers to the language potential of the cooking activities. Ask them to help the students learn measurement terms and terms for cooking procedures, ingredients, and utensils. Make sure the volunteers understand that the *students* are to perform the preparations and actions and to talk about them as they do so.

(b) *Assessment/evaluation.* Listen to the students as they prepare the food, and take advantage of spontaneous language learning opportunities that arise.

How did the food taste? Did the students have fun cooking? Good things to eat and good fun are important objectives of this activity.

(c) *Extension.* Students may enjoy collecting recipes for dishes they have prepared at class and at home. Have them each contribute a recipe to a *Kid's Cookbook.*

Activity 12: Program—Speeches, Biographical Sketches, Comic Display

Groupings:
    Full group, the class plus visitors
    Dyads—a student guide and a visitor
Materials:
    All of the products of the "Heroes and Superheroes" unit: superhero profiles, hero profiles, *Marvelous Universe,* cartoon superhero tallies, charts, and graphs, superhero adventures, supervehicles, stories about superheroes from students' native cultures, school community heroes bulletin board
Procedures:

(a) Preparing to be hosts/hostesses. Two weeks before the celebration, review friendly letter format and have students each write two invitations, one to the student's family and one to a special guest from the school or community (include the persons students have interviewed). Revise and send the invitations.

Have students help you attractively display books, profiles, graphs, adventures, vehicles, etc.,

Before the celebration, rehearse host/hostess roles. Have students practice giving one another tours of the classroom, showing the accomplishments of the unit, and offering one another refreshments.

With the students, plan and rehearse a formal program in which each student has a role. Students may tell about the unit activities, read a story about a mythological hero, read aloud a comic adventure with illustrations on overhead or opaque projector, recite a memorized part of a famous speech, or recite an original speech.

(b) Assessment/evaluation. Watch how students perform in this new situation. How does their language use change when they are in front of the public? How well do students manage the social aspects of the situation?

(c) Extensions. If you have developed a superheroes database, have students demonstrate its operation for the visitors.

SUGGESTED RESOURCES FOR
HEROES AND SUPERHEROES

The American Spirit: 1776–1976 (Record). 1975. New York: London Records.

Bahree, P. 1983. *The Hindu world*. Morristown, NJ: Silver Burdett Company.

Barlow, G. 1966. *Latin American tales: From the Pampas to the pyramids of Mexico*. Chicago: Rand McNally & Company.

Benjamin, C. L. 1982. *Cartooning for kids*. New York: Thomas Y. Crowell.

Caplan, R. (Producer). 1974. *Legacy of a dream* (Film). Atlanta, GA: Martin Luther King Foundation.

Cummings, R. M. 1986. *Make your own comics for fun and profit*. New York: Walch.

d'Aulaire, I., & d'Aulaire, E. P. 1957. *Abraham Lincoln*. Garden City, NY: Doubleday & Company.

———. 1967. *Norse gods and giants*. Garden City, NY: Doubleday & Company.

Dawood, N. J. 1978. *Tales from the Arabian nights*. Garden City, NY: Doubleday & Company, Inc.

deKay, J. T. 1969. *Meet Martin Luther King, Jr.* New York: Random House.

Field, E. 1973. *Eskimo songs and stories*. Cambridge, MA: Dell Publishing Company.

Finlayson, I. 1980. *Winston Churchill*. London: Hamish Hamilton.

Floethe, L. L. 1967. *A thousand and one buddhas*. New York: Farrar, Straus & Giroux.

Franchere, R. 1970. *Cesar Chavez*. New York: Thomas Y. Crowell Company.

Fritz, J. 1975. *Where was Patrick Henry on the 29th of May?* New York: Coward, McCann & Geoghegan.

Gibson, M. (no date). *Gods, men & monsters from the Greek myths*. Great Britain: World Mythologies Series.

Great American: Martin Luther King, Jr. (Video). 1982. EBE.

Great American speeches, Volumes 1–4 (Record). 1969. New York: Caedmon Records.

Great British speeches, Vols. 1. 2. 3. and 4 (Record). 1975. New York: London Records.

Hoff, S. 1983. *The young cartoonist: The ABC's of cartooning*. New York: Stravon Educational Press.

John Fitzgerald Kennedy: A memorial album. (Record). 1963. New York: Premier Albums.

Junaluska, A. (Editor). *Great American Indian speeches*, Volumes 1 and 2 (Record). New York: Caedmon Records.

King, M. L. (Speaker). 1986. *Martin Luther King: I have a dream*. (Video). MPI Video.

McKissack, P. 1984. *Martin Luther King, Jr.: A man to remember*. Chicago: Children's Press.

Patterson, L. 1969. *Martin Luther King, Jr.: Man of peace*. Champaign, IL: Garrard Publishing Company.

Riordan, J. 1985. *Tales from the Arabian nights*. Chicago: Rand McNally & Company.

Shapiro, I. 1967. *Heroes in American folklore*. New York: Julian Messner.

Shapp, M., and Shapp, C. 1965. *Let's find out about John Fitzgerald Kennedy*. New York: Franklin Watts.

Smith, C. E. 1965. *The patriot plan* (Record). New York: Folkways.

Snyder, G. S. 1980. *Human rights*. New York: Franklin Watts.

Bibliography

Aaronson, E. 1978. *The jigsaw classroom* Beverly Hills, CA: Sage Publications.

A Language for life, report of the committee of inquiry appointed by the Secretary of State for Education and Science under the chairmanship of Sir Alan Bullock, F.B.A. 1975. London: HMSO.

Allen, V. L. (ed.). 1976. *Children as teachers: Theory and research on tutoring.* New York: Academic Press.

Allen, J. B. 1985. A three-level curriculum model for second-language education. *The Canadian Modern Language Review,* 40(1):23–43.

Applebee, A. N. 1978. *The child's concept of story.* Chicago, IL: University of Chicago Press.

Applebee, A. N. 1984. *Contexts for learning to write: Studies of secondary school instruction.* Norwood, NJ: Ablex Publishing Corporation.

Applebee, A. N., and Langer, J. A. (1983). Instructional scaffolding: Reading and writing as natural language activities. *Language Arts,* 60(2):168–75.

Appleton, N. 1983. *Cultural pluralism in education: Theoretical foundations.* New York: Longman.

Armbruster, B. B.; Osburn, J. H.; and Davison, A. L. 1985. Readability formulas may be dangerous to your textbooks. *Educational Leadership,* 42(7):18–20.

Arnow, B., and Byrd, P. 1986. Writing to policy/decision makers. *TESOL in Action,* 1(1):1–7.

Ashton-Warner, S. 1963. *Teacher.* New York: Bantam Books.

Ashworth, M. 1985. *Beyond methodology: Second language teaching and the community.* New York: Cambridge University Press.

Au, K. H. 1979. Using the experience-text-relationship method with minority children. *The Reading Teacher,* 32(6):677–79.

Au, K. H., and Jordan, C. 1981. Teaching reading to Hawaiian children: Finding a culturally appropriate solution. In H. Trueba, G. P. Guthrie, and K. H-P. Au (eds.), *Culture and the bilingual classroom; Studies in classroom and ethnography* (pp. 139–52). Rowley, MA: Newbury House Publishers.

Ausubel, D. P. 1963. *The psychology of meaningful verbal learning.* New York: Grune and Stratton, Inc.

Baker, G. C. 1983. *Planning and organizing for multicultural instruction.* Reading, MA: Addison-Wesley Publishing Company.

337

Barnes, D. 1976. *From communication to curriculum.* Hammondsworth, Middlesex, England: Penguin Books.

Barnes, D., and Todd, F. 1977. *Communication and learning in small groups.* London: Routledge & Kegan Paul.

Barth, J. S. 1972. *Open education and the American school.* New York: Schocken Books.

Barton, B. 1986. *Tell me another: Storytelling and reading aloud at home, at school and in the community.* Markham, Ontario, Canada: Pembroke Publishers.

Bassano, S. 1986. Helping learners adapt to unfamiliar methods. *ELT Journal,* 40(1):13–19.

Bates, J. 1984. Educational policies that support language development. *Theory into Practice,* 23(3):255–60.

Bauman, R. 1977. Linguistics, anthropology and verbal art: Toward a unified perspective, with a special discussion of children's folklore. In M. Saville-Troike (ed.), *Linguistics and anthropology (Georgetown University Round Table on Languages and Linguistics, 1977)* (pp. 13–36). Washington, DC: Georgetown University Press.

Bauman, R. 1982. Ethnography of children's folklore. In P. Gilmore and A. A. Glatthorn (eds.), *Children in and out of school: Ethnography and education* (pp. 172–86). Washington, DC: Center for Applied Linguistics.

Baynham, M. 1986. Bilingual folk stories in the ESL classroom. *ELT Journal,* 40(2):113–20.

Beane, J. A. et al. 1980. Synthesis of research on self-respect. *Educational Leadership,* 38, 84–87.

Becker, H. J. & Epstein J. L. 1982. Parent involvement: A survey of teacher practices. *The Elementary School Journal,* 83(2), 85–102.

Bellack, A. A.; Kliebard, H. M.; Hyman, R. T.; and Smith, F. L. 1966. *The language of the classroom.* New York: Teachers College Press.

Berger, E. H. 1981. *Parents as partners in education: The school and home and working together.* Toronto: The C.V. Mosby Company.

Bissex, G. L. 1980. *GYNS AT WRK: A child learns to write and read.* Cambridge, MA: Harvard University Press.

Bloom, B. 1956. *Taxonomy of educational objectives.* New York: Longman, Green.

Britton, J. 1970. *Language and learning.* London: Penguin Press.

Britton, J. T.; Burgess, N.; Martin, N.; McLeod, A. L.; and Rosen, H. 1975. *The development of writing abilities 11–18.* London: Macmillan Education.

Bronfenbrenner, U. (ed.) 1975. *Influences on human development.* Hinsdale, IL: Dryden Press.

Bronfenbrenner, U. 1975. Is early intervention effective? In U. Bronfenbrenner, (ed.), *Influences on human development.* Hinsdale, Il: Dryden Press.

Brooks, D. M. 1985. The first day of school. *Educational Leadership,* 42(8):76–78.

Brumfit, C. 1984. *Communicative methodology in language teaching: The roles of fluency and accuracy.* Cambridge: Cambridge University Press.

Brumfit, C. J.; and Johnson, K. (eds.). 1979. *The communicative approach to language teaching.* Oxford: Oxford University Press.

Bruner, J. 1975. Language as an instrument of thought. In A. Davies (ed.), *Problems of language and learning.* London: Heinemann Educational Books.

Buber, M. 1965. *Between man and man* (translated by R. G. Smith). New York: Macmillan Publishing Company.

Burke, M. 1986, Autumn. Immigration. *Canadian Social Trends (Statistics Canada)*, pp. 23–27.

Burt, M., and Dulay, H. 1981. Optimal language environments. In J. Alatis, H. B. Altman, and P. Alatis (eds.), *The Second language classroom: Directions for the 1980's* (pp. 175–92). New York: Oxford University Press.

Buscaglia, L. 1972. *Love.* New York: Fawcett Crest Books.

Bussis, A. M., and Chittenden, E. A. 1970. *Analysis of an approach to open education.* Princeton, NJ: Educational Testing Service.

Butterfield, R. A. 1983. The development and use of culturally appropriate curriculum for American Indian students. *Peabody Journal of Education,* 6(1):49–66.

Calkins, L. M. 1983. *Lessons from a child.* Exeter, NH: Heinemann Educational Books.

Calkins, L. M. 1986. *The art of teaching writing.* Portsmouth, NH: Heinemann Educational Books.

Cambourne, B. 1987. The turning tide: The move to whole-language approaches in education. Paper presented at the International ESL Conference, Hong Kong, October, 1987.

Canale, M., and Barker, G. 1986. How creative language teachers are using microcomputers. In I. Dutra (ed.), *TESOL Newsletter Supplement No. 3: CALL: Computer-Assisted Language Learning* (pp. 1–3).

Cantoni-Harvey, G. 1987. *Content-area language instruction: Approaches and strategies.* Reading, MA: Addison-Wesley Publishing Company.

Carrasco, R.; Vera, A.; and Cazden, C. B. 1985. Aspects of bilingual students' communicative competence in the classroom: A case study. In R. Duran (ed.), *Latino language and communicative behavior* (pp. 237–49). Norwood, NJ: Ablex Publishing Corporation.

Carrell, P. L. 1984. Schema theory and ESL reading: Classroom implications and applications. *Modern Language Journal,* 68(4):332–43.

Carrell, P. L. 1985. Facilitating ESL reading by teaching text structure. *TESOL Quarterly,* 19(4):727–52.

Carteledge, G., and Milburn, J. F. (eds.). 1980. *Teaching social skills to children: Innovative approaches.* New York: Pergamon Press.

Carthcart, R. W.; Strong, M. A.; and Wong-Fillmore, L. 1980. The social and linguistic behavior of good language learners. In C. A. Yorio, K. Perkins, and J. Schachter (eds.), *On TESOL '79: The learner in focus* (pp. 267–74). Washington, DC: Teachers of English to Speakers of Other Languages.

Cherry-Wilkinson, L. (ed.). 1982. *Communicating in the classroom.* New York: Academic Press.

Chud, G., and Fahlman, R. 1985. *Early childhood education for a multicultural society.* Vancouver: WEDGE, University of British Columbia.

Clark, E. V. 1973. What's in a word?: on the child's acquisition of semantics in his first language. In T. E. Moore (ed.), *Cognitive development and the acquisition of language* (pp. 65–110). New York: Academic Press.

Clark, R. M. 1983. *Family life and school achievement: Why poor black children succeed or fail.* Chicago: University of Chicago Press.

Clarke, M. A. 1987. Don't blame the system: Constraints on "whole language" reform. *Language Arts,* 64(4):384–96.

Clay, M. M. 1972. *Reading: The patterning of complex behavior.* Auckland, New Zealand: Heinemann Educational Books.

Clay, M. M. 1975. *What did I write?* Auckland, New Zealand: Heinemann Educational Books.

Cochran-Smith, M. 1984. *The making of a reader.* Norwood, NJ: Ablex Publishing Corporation.

Cohen, E. G. 1986. *Designing groupwork: Strategies for the heterogeneous classroom.* New York: Teachers College Press.

Cohen, P. A. and Kulik, J. A. 1981. Synthesis of research on the effects of tutoring. *Research Information System,* 39:227–29.

Coleman, J. S. 1985. Schools and the communities they serve. *Phi Delta Kappan,* 66(8), 527–532.

Combs, A. W. 1979. *Myths in education: Beliefs that hinder progress and their alternatives.* Boston: Allyn and Bacon.

Comer, J. P. 1986. Parental participation in the schools. *Phi Delta Kappan,* 67(6), 442–446.

Commission on Reading, National Academy of Education. 1985. *Becoming a nation of readers: The report of the commission on reading.* Champaign, IL: Center for the Study of Reading. University of Illinois. Boston: Allyn and Bacon.

Condon, J. C., and Yousef, F. 1975. *An introduction to intercultural communication.* Indianapolis, IN: Bobbs-Merrill.

Cook-Gumperz, J. 1977. Situated instructions: Language socialization of school age children. In S. Ervin-Tripp and C. Mitchell-Kernan (eds.), *Child discourse* (pp. 103–21). New York: Academic Press.

Cook-Gumperz, J. and Gumperz, J. J. 1981. From oral to written culture: The transition to literacy. In M. F. Whiteman (ed.), *Variation in writing: Functional and linguistic-cultural differences* (pp. 89–109). Hillsdale, N.J.: Lawrence Erlbaum Associates.

Cook-Gumperz, J. and Gumperz, J. J. 1976. Context in children's speech. In idem. (eds.), *Working papers on language context 46.* Berkeley: University of California, Language Behavior Research Laboratory.

Corwin, R.; Hein, G. E.; and Levin, D. 1976. Weaving curriculum webs: The structure of nonlinear curriculum. *Childhood Education,* 52(5):248–51.

Cramer, R. L., & Cramer, B. B. 1975. Writing by imitating language models. *Language Arts,* 52(7):1011–18.

Cross-cultural learning in K-12 schools: Foreign students as resources. 1982. Washington, DC: National Association for Foreign Student Affairs.

Cuban, L. 1982. Persistence of the inevitable: The teacher-centered classroom. *Education and Urban Society,* 15(1):26–41.

Cullinan, B. E. 1982. Books in the classroom. *Hornbook Magazine,* 62(1):108–10.

Cummins, J. 1981. The role of primary language development in promoting educational success for language minority students. *In Schooling and language minority students: A theoretical framework* (pp. 3–49). Los Angeles: Evaluation, Dissemination, and Assessment Center, California State University, Los Angeles.

Cummings, J. 1984. *Bilingualism and special education: Issues in assessment and pedagogy.* Clevedon, England: Multilingual Matters.

Curran, C. A. 1976. *Counseling-learning in second languages.* Apple River, IL: Apple River Press.

Davies, D. (ed.) 1981. *Communities and their schools.* New York: McGraw-Hill.

De Costa, S. B. 1984. Not all children are Anglo and middle-class: A practical beginning for the elementary teacher. *Theory into Practice,* 23(2):155–62.

DeFord, D. E. 1981. Literacy: Reading, writing and other essentials. *Language Arts,* 58(6):652–58.

dePaola, T. 1978. *Pancakes for breakfast.* New York: Harcourt Brace Jovanovich.

dePaulo, B. M. and Bonvillian, J. D. 1978. The effect of special characteristics of speech addressed to children. *Journal of Psycholinguistic Research,* 7(3):189–211.

Devine, J. 1981. Development patterns in native and nonnative reading acquisition. In S. Hudelson (ed.), *Learning to read in different languages* (pp. 103–14). Washington, DC: Center for Applied Linguistics.

Dewey, J. 1916. *Democracy and education.* New York: Macmillan Publishing Company.

Dixon, C., and Nessell, D. 1983. *The language experience approach to reading (and writing): LEA for ESL.* Hayward, CA: Alemany Press.

Doake, D. B. 1985. Reading-like behavior: Its role in learning to read. In A. Jagger and M. T. Smith-Burke (eds.), *Observing the language learner,* (pp. 82–98). Urbana, IL: National Council of Teachers of English.

Doake, D. B. 1979. Book experience and emergent reading behavior. Paper presented at the Preconference Institute, "Research on Written Language Development," International Reading Association Annual Convention, Atlanta, GA.

Donnan, C. S. 1985. Tackling world hunger in an elementary school. *Educational Leadership.* 43(4) 49–52.

Dulay, H., and Burt, M. 1974. A new perspective on the creative construction process in child second language acquisition. *Language Learning,* 24(2):253–78.

Dulay, H., and Burt, M. 1975. Creative construction in second language learning and teaching. In M. Burt and H. C. Dulay (eds.), *New directions in second language learning, teaching, and bilingual education.* Washington, D.C.: TESOL, 21–32.

Dulay, H.; Burt, M.; and Krashen, S. 1982. *Language two.* Oxford, Oxford University Press.

Dyson, A. H. 1981. Oral language: The rooting system for learning to write. *Language Arts,* 58(7):776–84.

Edelsky, C. 1983. Writing in a bilingual program: The relation of L1 and L2 texts. *TESOL Quarterly,* 16(2):211–28.

Edelsky, C. 1984. Is that writing—or are those marks just a figment of your curriculum? *Language Arts,* 61(1):24–32.

Edelsky, C. 1986. *Writing in a bilingual program. Había una vez.* Norwood, NJ: Ablex Publishing Corporation.

Edelsky, C.; Draper, K.; and Smith, K. 1983. Hookin' 'em in at the start of school in a "whole language" classroom. *Anthropology and Education Quarterly,* 14(4):257–81.

Edelsky, C. and Smith, K. 1984. Is that writing—or are those marks just a figment of your curriculum? *Language Arts,* 61(1):24–32.

Editorial Note. 1978. *National Elementary Principal,* 57(6):28–29.

Ehlers, H., & Crawford, D. 1983. Multicultural education and national unity. *The Educational Forum,* 47(3):263–287.

Elkind, D. 1981. *The hurried child: Growing up too fast too soon.* Reading, MA: Addison-Wesley Publishing Company.

Ellis, D. W., and Preston, F. W. 19. Enhancing beginning reading using wordless picture books in a cross-age tutoring program. *The Reading Teacher* 37(8), 692–710.

Emig, J. 1981. Non-magical thinking: Presenting writing developmentally in schools. In C. H. Frederikson and J. F. Dominic (eds.), *Writing: Process, development and communication* (pp. 21–30). Hillsdale, NJ: Lawrence Erlbaum Associates.

Emmer, E. T.; Evertson, C. M.; & Anderson, L. M. 1980. Effective classroom management at the beginning of the school year. *The Elementary School Journal,* 80(5):220–31.

Enright, D. S. 1982. Student language use in traditional and open bilingual classrooms. Unpublished doctoral dissertation. Stanford University.

Enright, D. S. 1983. The concept of experience in open education. Paper presented at the annual meeting of the American Educational Research Association, Montreal, Quebec, Canada.

Enright, D. S. (ed.) 1983. *From pancakes to puppets to poison ivy: The Garden Hills international summer school curriculum guide, Vol. 1.* Atlanta, GA: Georgia State University.

Enright, D. S. 1984. The organization of interaction in elementary classrooms. In J. Handscombe, R. A. Orem, and B. P. Taylor (eds.), *On TESOL '83: The question of control* (pp. 23–38). Washington, DC: Teachers of English to Speakers of Other Languages.

Enright, D. S., and McCloskey, M. L. (eds.) 1984. *From balloons to bubbles to banana bread: The Garden Hills International summer school curriculum guide, Vol. 2.* Atlanta, GA: Georgia State University.

Enright, D. S., and Gomez, B. 1985. PRO-ACT: Six Strategies for organizing peer interaction in elementary classrooms. *NABE Journal,* 9(3): 431–53.

Enright, D. S., and McCloskey, M. L. 1985. Yes talking!: Organizing the classroom environmenet to promote second language learning. *TESOL Quarterly,* 19(3):431–53.

Enright, D. S. 1986. "Use everything you have to teach English": Providing useful input to young language learners. In P. Rigg and D. S. Enright (eds.), *Children and ESL: Integrating perspectives* (pp. 115–62). Washington, DC: Teachers of English to Speakers of Other Languages.

Epstein, J. L. 1985. Home and school connections in schools of the future: Implications of research on parent involvement. *Peabody Journal of Education,* 62(2):18–41.

Erickson, F. 1984. What makes school ethnography "ethnographic"? *Anthropology and Education Quarterly,* 15(1):51–66.

Erickson, F., and Mohatt, G. 1982. Cultural organization of participation structures in two classrooms of Indian students. In G. Spindler (ed.), *Doing the ethnography of schooling: Educational anthropology in action* (pp. 132–74). New York: CBS Publishing.

Ervin-Tripp, S., and Mitchell-Kernan, C. 1977. *Child discourse.* New York: Academic Press.

Fagan, E. R.; Hassler, D. M.; and Szabo, M. 1981. Evaluation of questioning strategies in language arts instruction. *Research in the Teaching of English,* 15, 267–73.

Fantini, A. E. 1976. *Language acquisition of a bilingual child: A sociolinguistic perspective.* Brattleboro, VT: The Experiment Press.

Farmelo, M. 1987. The D.C. schools project. *TESOL Quarterly,* 21(3):578–82.

Feeley, J. A. 1979. A workshop tried and true: Language experience for bilinguals. *The Reading Teacher,* 33(1):25–27.

Feinberg, L. V. 1981–1982. Review of a review: Hunger of memory. *NABE Journal,* 6(2–3):115–16.

Ferreiro, E. 1986. The interplay between information and assimilation in beginning literacy. In W. H. Teale and E. Sulzby (eds.), *Emergent literacy: Writing and reading* (pp. 15–49). Norwood, NJ: Ablex Publishing Corporation.

Firestone, W. A. and Wilson, B. L. 1984. Culture of school is a key to more effective instruction. *NASSP Bulletin,* 68(476), 7–11.

Flanders, N. A. 1970. *Analyzing teaching behavior.* Reading, MA: Addison-Wesley Publishing Company.

French, L. A.; Lucariello, J.; Seidman, S.; and Nelson, K. 1984. The influence of discourse content and context on preschoolers' use of language. In L. Galda and A. D. Pellegrini (eds.), *Play, language and stories: The development of children's literate behavior* (pp. 1–27). Norwood, NJ: Ablex Publishing Corporation.

Gaies, S. J. 1979. Linguistic input in first and second language learning. In F. R. Eckman and A. J. Hastings (eds.), *Studies in first and second language acquisition* (pp. 186–93). Rowley, MA: Newbury House Publishers.

Galda, L. and Pellegrini, A. D. (eds.) 1984. *Play, language and stories: The development of children's literate behavior.* Norwood, NJ: Ablex Publishing Corporation.

Galloway, C. M.; Seltzer, M. C.; and Kerber, J. E. (eds.) 1984. Multicultural education. *Theory in Practice,* 23(3).

Garvey, C. 1977. *Play.* Cambridge, MA: Harvard University Press.

Gass, S. M., and Madden, C. G. (eds.), 1985. *Input in second language acquisition.* Rowley, MA: Newbury House Publishers.

Geller, L. G. 1985. *Wordplay and language learning for children.* Urbana, IL: National Council of Teachers of English.

Genesee, F. 1986. The baby and the bathwater, or what immersion has to say about bilingual education. *NABE Journal,* 10(3):227–51.

Genishi, C. S. 1976. Rules for code-switching in young Spanish-English speakers: An exploratory study of language socialization. Doctoral dissertation, University of California at Berkeley, Berkeley, CA.

Genishi, C., and Dyson, A. H. 1984. *Language Assessment in the Early Years.* Norwood, NJ: Ablex Publishing Corporation.

Gersten, R., and Woodward, J. 1985. A case for structured immersion. *Educational Leadership,* 43(1):75–78 and 85–86.

Gibbons, J. 1985. The silent period: An examination. *Language Learning,* 35(2):255–67.

Gilmore, P., and Glatthorn, A. A. (eds.) 1982. *Children in and out of school: Ethnography and education.* Washington, DC: Center for Applied Linguistics.

Glasser, W. 1969. *Schools without failure.* New York: Harper and Row.

Glatthorn, A. A. 1987. *Curriculum renewal.* Alexandria, VA: Association for Supervision and Curriculum Development.

Goelman, H.; Oberg, A. A.; and Smith, F. (eds.) 1984. *Awakening to literacy.* Exeter, N.H.: Heinemann Educational Books.

Goffman, E. 1963. *Stigma: Notes on the management of spoiled identity.* Englewood Cliffs, NJ: Prentice-Hall.

Gollasch, F. V. (ed.) 1982. *Language and literacy: The selected writings of Kenneth S. Goodman. Vol. 2: Reading, language and the classroom teacher.* London: Routledge & Kegan Paul.

Gomez, B. 1987. 'Friends gotta talk': An ethnographic study of behavioral patterns exhibited by young children in the process of acquiring English as a second language. Unpublished doctoral dissertation, Georgia State University, Atlanta, Georgia.

Goodlad, J. I. 1984. *A Place called school: Prospects for the future.* New York: McGraw-Hill Book Company.

Goodman, K. S. 1971. Children's language and experience: A place to begin. In H. Robinson (ed.), *Coordinating reading instruction.* Glenview, IL: Scott, Foresman and Company.

Goodman, K. S. 1977. Acquiring literacy is natural: Who skilled Cock Robin? *Theory into Practice,* 16(5):309–14.

Goodman, K. S. 1979. The Know-more and know-nothing movements in reading: A personal response. *Language Arts,* 56(6):657–63.

Goodman, K. S. 1985. Unity in reading. In H. Singer, and R. B. Ruddell (eds.), *Theoretical models and processes of reading (3d ed.)* (pp. 813–40). Newark, DE: International Reading Association.

Goodman, K. S. 1986a. *What's whole in whole language?* Portsmouth, NH: Heinemann Educational Books.

Goodman, K. S. 1986b. Basal readers: A call for action. *Language Arts,* 63(4):358–63.

Goodman, K., and Goodman, Y. 1983. Reading and writing relationships: Pragmatic functions. *Language Arts,* 60(5):590–99.

Goodman, K. S.; Goodman, Y.; and Flores, B. 1979. *Reading in the bilingual classroom: Literacy and biliteracy.* Washington, DC: National Association for Bilingual Education.

Goodman, Y. M. 1983. Beginning reading development: Strategies and principles. In R. P. Parker and F. A. Davis (eds.), *Developing literacy: Young children's use of language* (pp. 68–83) Newark, DE: International Reading Association.

Goodman, Y. M. 1986. Children coming to know literacy. In W. H. Teale and E. Sulzby (eds.), *Emergent literacy: Writing and reading* (pp. 1–14). Norwood, NJ: Ablex Publishing Corporation.

Goodman, Y., and Burke, C. 1972. *Reading miscue inventory.* New York: Macmillan Publishing Company.

Gordon, W. J. 1969. *Synectics: The development of creative capacity.* New York: Harper & Brothers.

Grant, C. A., and Sleeter, C. E. 1985. The literature on multicultural education: Review and analysis. *Educational Studies,* 37(2):97–118.

Grant, C. A.; Sleeter, C. E.; & Anderson, J. E. 1986. The literature on multicultural education: Review and analysis. *Educational Studies,* 12(1):47–71.

Graves, D. 1983. *Writing: Teachers and children at work.* Exeter, NH: Heinemann Educational Books.

Greene, M. 1986. Toward possibility: Expanding the range of literacy. *English Education,* 17(1):230–43.

Greenfield, P. M. 1984. A theory of the teacher in the learning activities of everyday life. In B. Rogoff and J. Lave (eds.), *Everyday cognition: Its development in social context* (pp. 117–38). Cambridge, MA: Harvard University Press.

Grow-Maienza, J. 1984. Issues of multiculturalism in native American education. Paper presented at the annual meeting of the American Educational Research Association. Chicago, IL.

Hakuta, K. 1986. *Mirror of language: The debate on bilingualism.* New York: Basic Books.

Hall, E. T. 1976. *Beyond culture.* Garden City, NY: Anchor Press/Doubleday.

Hall, M. A. 1970. *Teaching reading as a language experience.* Columbus, OH: Charles E. Merrill Publishing Company.

Hannah, G. G. 1982. *Classroom spaces and places.* Belmont, CA: Pitman Learning, Inc.

Hansen, D. A. Family-school articulations: The effects of interaction rule mismatch. *American Educational Research Journal,* 23(4), 643–659.

Harris, B. H. 1976. No labels, please! *Language Arts,* 53(8):906–16.

Harste, J. C., and Burke, C. L. 1977. A new hypothesis for reading teacher research: Both teaching and learning are theoretically based. In P. D. Pearson and J. Hansen (eds.), *Reading: Theory, research and practice* (pp. 32–40). Twenty-sixth yearbook of the National Reading Conference. Clemson, SC: National Reading Conference.

Harste, J. C.; Woodward, V.; and Burke, C. 1984. *Language stories and literacy lessons.* Portsmouth, NH: Heinemann Educational Books.

Hatch, E. M. 1983. *Psycholinguistics: A second language perspective.* Rowley, MA: Newbury House Publishers.

Hawkins, D. 1973. How to plan for spontaneity. In C. E. Silberman (ed.), *The open classroom reader* (pp. 486–503). New York: Random House.

Heath, S. B. 1982. What no bedtime story means: Narrative skills at home and school. *Language in Society*, 11, 49–76.

Heath, S. B. 1983. *Ways with words. Language, life and work in communities and classrooms.* Cambridge, Cambridge University Press.

Heath, S. B. 1985. Literacy or literate skills? Considerations for ESL/EFL Learners. In P. Larson, E. L. Judd, and D. S. Messerschmitt (eds.), *On TESOL '84: A brave new world for TESOL* (pp. 15–28). Washington, DC: Teachers of English to Speakers of Other Languages.

Heath, S. B., and Branscombe, A. 1985. Intelligent writing in an audience community: Teacher, students and researcher. In S. W. Freedman (ed.), *The acquisition of written language: Revision and response* (pp. 3–32). Norwood, NJ: Ablex Publishing Corporation.

Hodes, P. 1977. Oral reading of bilingual Yiddish/English children. Paper presented at the annual meeting of the International Reading Association, Miami, FL (ERIC Document –ED 137 731).

Hodes, P. 1981. Reading: A universal process. In S. Hudelson (ed.), *Learning to read in different languages* (pp. 27–31). Washington, DC: Center for Applied Linguistics.

Holdaway, D. 1972. *Independence in reading: A handbook on individualized procedures.* Auckland, New Zealand: Ashton Education.

Holdaway, D. 1979. *The foundations of literacy.* Sydney, Australia: Ashton Scholastic.

Honig, A. S. 1982. Research in review. Prosocial development in children. *Young Children,* 37(5):51–62.

Hoopes, D. S., and Pusch, M. D. 1979. Teaching strategies: The methods and techniques of cross-cultural training. In M. D. Pusch (ed.), *Multicultural education: A cross-cultural training approach.* (pp. 104–206) LaGrange Park, IL: Intercultural Networks.

Hough, R. A.; Nurss, J. R.; and Enright, D. S. 1986. Story reading with limited English speaking children in the regular classroom. *The Reading Teacher,* 39(6):510–14.

Hudelson, S. 1984. Kan yuret an rayt en Ingles: Children become literate in English as a second language. *TESOL Quarterly* 18(2):221–38.

Hudelson, S. (In press). Second language learners in "normal" classrooms. In C. Staab and S. Hudelson (eds.), *The power of talk.* Urbana, IL: National Council of Teachers of English.

Hudelson, S. 1986. ESL children's writing: What we've learned, what we're learning. In P. Rigg and D. S. Enright (eds.), *Children and ESL: Integrating perspectives* (pp. 23–54). Washington, DC: Teachers of English to Speakers of Other Languages.

Hudelson, S., and Barrera, R. 1985. Bilingual/second-language learners and reading. In L. Searfoss and J. Readance (eds.), *Helping children learn to read* (pp. 370–92). Englewood Cliffs, NJ: Prentice-Hall.

Jaggar, A., and Smith-Burke, M. T. (eds.). 1985. *Observing the language learner.* Newark, DE: International Reading Association.

Johnson, D. M. 1980. Peer tutoring, social interaction, and the acquisition of English as a second language by Spanish-speaking elementary school children. Unpublished dissertation, Stanford University.

Johnson, D. M. 1983. Natural language learning by design: A classroom experiment in social interaction and second language acquisition. *TESOL Quarterly,* 17(1):55–68.

Johnson, D. W.; Skon, L.; and Johnson, R. 1980. Effects of cooperative, competitive and individualistic conditions on children's problem-solving performance. *American Educational Research Journal,* 17(1):83–93.

Johnson, D. W., Johnson, R. T., Holubec, E. J., and Roy, P. 1984. *Circles of learning: Cooperation in the classroom.* Alexandria, VA: Association for Supervision and Curriculum Development.

Johnson, K., and Morrow, K. (eds.) 1981. *Communication in the classroom: Applications and methods for a communicative approach.* Essex, England: Longman.

Johnson, P. 1982. Effects on reading comprehension of building background knowledge. *TESOL Quarterly,* 16(4):503–16.

Jones, K. 1982. *Simulations in Language Teaching.* Cambridge, England: Cambridge University Press.

Jones, S., and Tetroe, J. 1987. Composing in a second language. In A. Matsuhashi (ed.), *Writing in real time: Modeling production processes* (pp. 34–57). Norwood, NJ: Ablex Publishing Corporation.

Jordan, C. 1983. Cultural differences in communication patterns: Classroom adaptations and translation strategies. In M. A. Clarke and J. Handscombe (eds.) *On TESOL '82: Pacific Perspectives on Language Learning and Teaching* (pp. 285–294). Washington, DC: Teachers of English to Speakers of Other Languages.

Jordan, C. 1985. Translating culture: From ethnographic information to educational program. *Anthropology & Education Quarterly,* 16:105–23.

Joyce, B., and Weil, M. 1972. *Models of teaching.* Englewood Cliffs, NJ: Prentice-Hall.

Kagan, S. 1986. Cooperative learning and sociocultural factors in schooling. In *Beyond language: Social and cultural factors in schooling language minority students* (pp. 231–98). Los Angeles, CA: Evaluation, Dissemination and Assessment Center, California State University.

Karp, W. 1985. Why Johnny can't think. *Harper's Magazine,* 270(1621):69–73.

Keller-Cohen, D. 1981. Input from the inside: The role of a child's prior linguistic experience in second language learning. In R. W. Andersen (ed.), *New dimensions in second language acquisition research* (pp. 95–103). Rowley, MA: Newbury House Publishers.

Kendall, F. E. 1983. *Diversity in the classroom: A multicultural approach to the education of young children.* New York: Teachers College Press.

Kierstead, J. 1986. How teachers manage individual and small-group work in active classrooms. *Educational Leadership,* 44(2):22–25.

King, M. L. 1984. Language and school success: Access to meaning. *Theory into practice,* 23(3):175–82.

Kirby, D., and Liner, T. 1981. *Inside out: Developmental strategies for teaching writing.* Montclair, NJ: Boynton/Cook.

Kohl, H. R. 1976. *On teaching.* New York: Schocken Books.

Krashen, S. D. 1981. Effective second language acquisition: Insights from research. In J. Alatis, H. B. Altman, and P. Alatis (eds.), *The second language classroom: Directions for the 1980's* (pp. 95–109). New York: Oxford University Press.

Krashen, S. D. 1982. *Principles and practices in second language acquisition.* Oxford: Pergamon Press.

Krashen, S. D., and Terrell, D. 1983. *The natural approach: Language acquisition in the classroom.* Hayward, CA: Alemany Press.

Kreeft, J. 1984. Dialogue writing—Bridge from talk to essay writing. *Language Arts,* 61(2):141–51.

Lampert, M. 1985. How do teachers manage to teach? Perspectives on problems in practice. *Harvard Educational Review,* 55(2):178–94.

Langer, J. A., and Applebee, A. N. 1984. Language, learning and interaction: A framework for improving the teaching of writing. In A. N. Applebee (ed.), *Contexts for learning to write: Studies of secondary school instruction* (pp. 169–81). Norwood, NJ: Ablex Publishing Corporation.

Larsen-Freeman, D. 1986. *Techniques and principles in language teaching.* New York: Oxford University Press.

Lauterbach, C. 1986. Young critics at large. *Atlanta Magazine,* April, pp. 98–99.

Lay-Dopyera, M., and Dopyera, J. 1987. *Becoming a teacher of young children, 3d ed.* New York: Random House.

Leichter, H. J. 1974. *The family as educator.* New York: Teachers College Press.

Lightfoot, S. L. 1978. *Worlds apart: Relationships between family and schools.* New York: Basic Books.

Lindfors, J. W. 1987. *Children's language and learning* (2d ed.). Englewood-Cliffs, NJ: Prentice-Hall.

Lindfors, J. W. 1983. Exploring in and through language. In M. A. Clarke and J. Handscombe (eds.), *On TESOL '82: Pacific perspectives on language learning and teaching* (pp. 143–55). Washington, DC: Teachers of English to Speakers of Other Languages.

Littlejohn, A. P. 1983. Increasing learner involvement in course management. *TESOL Quarterly,* 17(4):595–608.

Littlewood, W. 1981. *Communicative language teaching.* Cambridge: Cambridge University Press.

Lombana, J. H. 1983. *Home-school partnerships: Guidelines and strategies for educators.* New York: Grune and Stratton, Inc.

London, C. B., Molostoi, P. H. and Palmer, A. 1984. Collaboration of family, community, and school in a reconstructive approach to teaching and learning. *Journal of Negro Education,* 53(4), 455–463.

Long, M. H.; Adams, L.; McLean, M.; and Castaños, F. 1976. Doing things with words: Verbal interaction in lockstep and small group classroom situations. In R. Crymes and J. Fanselow (eds.), *On TESOL '76* (pp. 137–53). Washington, D.C.: Teachers of English to Speakers of Other Languages.

Long, M. H. 1981. Input, interaction and second language acquisition. In H. Winitz (ed.), *Native language and foreign language acquisition. Annals of the New York Academy of Science, No. 379* (pp. 250–78). New York: New York Academy of Sciences.

Long, M. H. 1983. Native-speaker/non-native speaker conversation in the second language classroom. In M. A. Clarke, and J. Handscombe (eds.), *On TESOL '82: Pacific perspectives on language learning and teaching* (pp. 207–25). Washington, DC: Teachers of English to Speakers of Other Languages.

Long, M. H., and Porter, P. A. 1985. Group work, interlanguage talk, and second language acquisition. *TESOL Quarterly,* 19(2):207–28.

Loughlin, C. E., and Suina, J. H. 1982. *The learning environment: An instructional strategy.* New York: Teachers College Press.

Lynch, J. 1986. *Multicultural education: Principles and practice.* London: Routledge & Kegan Paul.

Lyons, B. 1981. The PQP method of responding to writing. *English Journal,* 70(3), 42–43.

Macnamara, J. 1973. Nurseries, streets and classrooms: Some comparisons and deductions. *Modern Language Journal,* 57(5–6):250–54.

Majoribanks, K. 1979. *Families and their learning environments: An empirical analysis.* London: Routledge & Kegan Paul.

Maley, A., and Duff, A. 1978. *Drama techniques in language learning: A resource book of communication activities for language teachers.* Cambridge: Cambridge University Press.

Marland, M. 1977. *Language across the curriculum: The implementation of the Bullock Report in the secondary school.* London: Heinemann Educational Books.

McCloskey, M. L. (ed.) 1987. *Turn on units.* Atlanta, GA: State of Georgia Board of Education.

McCloskey, M. L., and Enright, D. S. 1985. *From rainbows to rhythms to runaway cookies: The Garden Hills international summer school curriculum guide, Vol. 3.* Atlanta, GA: Georgia State University.

McCloskey, M. L., and Nations, M. J. 1987. *English everywhere: An integrated English as a second language curriculum guide.* Atlanta, GA: Educo Press.

Mehan, H. 1979. *Learning lessons.* Cambridge, MA: Harvard University Press.

Michaelis, B., and Michaelis, D. 1977. *Learning through noncompetitive activities and play.* Palo Alto, CA: Learning Handbooks, Pitman Learning.

Milberg, A. 1976. *Street games.* New York: McGraw-Hill.

Moffett, J. 1968a. *A student-centered language arts curriculum, grades K-13: A handbook for teachers.* Boston: Houghton Mifflin Company.

Moffett, J. 1968b. *Teaching the universe of discourse.* Boston: Houghton Mifflin Company.

Mohan, B. A. 1986. *Language and content.* Reading, MA: Addison-Wesley Publishing Company.

Molnar, A. (ed.). 1985. *Current thought on curriculum.* Alexandria, Va.: Association for Supervision and Curriculum Development.

Moorman, C.; Dishon, D.; and O'Leary, P. W. 1984. Overview of cooperative learning: A strategy for effective teaching. In J. Reinhartz (ed.), *Perspectives on effective teaching and the cooperative classroom* (pp. 42–48). Washington, DC: National Education Association.

Morgan, A. L. 1983. Context: The web of meaning. *Language Arts,* 60(3):305–14.

Morgan, J., and Rinvolucri, M. 1983. *Once upon a time: Using stories in the language classroom.* London: Cambridge University Press.

Morin, K. D. 1986. The classroom teacher and curriculum developer: A sharing relationship. In K. K. Zumwalt (ed.), *Improving teaching* (pp. 149–68). Alexandria, VA: Association for Supervision and Curriculum Development.

Moss, J. F. 1984. *Focus units in literature: A handbook for elementary school teachers.* Urbana, IL: National Council of Teachers of English.

Munn, N. D. 1973. *Walbiri iconography.* Ithaca, NY: Cornell University Press.

Nelson, K., and Gruendel, J. 1979. "At morning it's lunchtime": A scriptal view of children's dialogues. *Discourse Processes,* 2(2):73–94.

Nessel, D. D., and Jones, M. B. 1981. *The language experience approach to reading: A handbook for teachers.* New York: Teachers College Press.

Newman, J. M. (ed.). 1985. *Whole language: Theory in use.* Portsmouth, NH: Heinemann Educational Books.

Ogbu, J. U. 1982a. Cultural discontinuities and schooling. *Anthropology and Education Quarterly,* 13:290–307.

Ogbu, J. U. 1982b. Societal forces as a context for ghetto children's school failure. In L. Feagans and D. C. Farran (eds.), *The language of children reared in poverty: Implications for evaluation and intervention* (pp. 118–37). New York: Academic Press.

Olson, D. R., and Torrance, N. 1981. Learning to meet the requirements of written text: Language development in the school years. In C. H. Frederiksen and J. F. Dominic (eds.), *Writing: Process, development and communication* (pp. 234–55). Hillsdale, NJ: Lawrence Erlbaum Associates.

Orlick, T. 1978. *The cooperative sports and games book: Challenge without competition.* New York: Pantheon.

Orlick, T. 1982. *The second cooperative sports and games book.* New York: Pantheon.

Ovando, C. J., and Collier, V. P. 1985. *Bilingual and ESL classrooms: Teaching in multicultural contexts.* New York: McGraw-Hill.

Oxford, R.; Pol, L.; Lopez, D.; Stupp, P.; Peng, S.; and Gendell, M. 1981. *Projections of non-English language background and limited English proficient persons in the United States to the year 2000.* Rosslyn, VA: InterAmerica Research Associates.

Page, L. G., and Smith, H. (eds.) 1985. *The Foxfire book of toys and games: Reminiscences and instructions from Appalachia.* New York: E. P. Dutton.

Papert, S. 1980. Mindstorms: Children, computers and powerful ideas. New York: Basic Books.

Park, B. 1982. The big book trend—A discussion with Don Holdaway. *Language Arts,* 54(8):815–21.

Parker, R. E. 1985. Small-group cooperative learning—Improving academic, social gains in the classroom. *NASSP Bulletin,* 69(479):48–55.

Parker, R. P. 1983. Schooling and the growth of mind. In R. P. Parker and F. A. Davis (eds.), *Developing literacy: Young children's use of language* (pp. 139–55). Newark, DE: International Reading Association.

Pasternak, M. G. 1979. *Helping kids learn multi-cultural concepts.* Champaign, IL: Research Press.

Peck, S. 1978. Child-child discourse in second language acquisition. In E. M. Hatch (ed.), *Second language acquisition: A book of readings* (pp. 383–400). Rowley, MA: Newbury House Publishers.

Pellowski, A. 1984. *The story vine: A source book of unusual and easy-to-tell stories from around the world.* New York: Collier Books.

Philips, S. U. 1972. Participant structures and communicative competence: Warm Springs children in community and classroom. In C. B. Cazden, V. J. John, and D. Hymes (eds.), *Functions of language in the classroom* (pp. 370–94). New York: Teachers College Press.

Philips, S. U. 1983. *The invisible culture: Communication in classroom and community on the Warm Springs Indian Reservation.* New York: Longman.

Piper, D. 1986. Language growth in the multiethnic classroom. *Language Arts,* 63(1):23–36.

Prizzi, E., and Hoffman, J. 1985. *Reading around the world: Functional reading fun.* Belmont, CA: David S. Lake Publishers.

Prizzi, E., and Hoffman, J. 1985. *Reading everyday stuff: Functional reading fun.* Belmont, CA: David S. Lake Publishers.

Rich, D. 1985. Helping parents help their children learn. *Educational Leadership,* 42(7), 80.

Rich, S. V. (1985). Restoring power to teachers: The impact of "whole language." *Language Arts,* 2(7):717–24.

Richards, J. C., and Rodgers, T. S. 1986. *Approaches and methods in language teaching.* Cambridge: Cambridge University Press.

Rigg, P. 1977. The miscue-ESL project. In H. D. Brown, C. Yorio, and R. Crymes (eds.), *Teaching and learning ESL: Trends in research and practice* (pp. 106–18). Washington, DC: Teachers of English to Speakers of Other Languages.

Rigg, P. 1981. Beginning to read in English the LEA way. In C. W. Twyford, W. Diehl and K. Feathers (eds.), *Reading English as a second language: Moving from theory* (pp. 81–90). Bloomington, IN: Indiana University, School of Education, Monographs in Teaching and Learning, 4.

Rigg, P. 1986. Reading in ESL: Learning from kids. In P. Rigg, and D. S. Enright (eds.), *Children and ESL: Integrating perspectives* (pp. 55–92). Washington, DC: Teachers of English to Speakers of Other Languages.

Rigg, P. & Enright, D. S. 1986. *Children and ESL: Integrating perspectives.* Washington, DC: Teachers of English to Speakers of Other Languages.

Rodriguez, R. 1982. *Hunger of memory: The education of Richard Rodriguez.* Boston: David Godine.

Rosenblatt, L. M. 1969. Toward a transactional theory of reading. *Journal of Reading Behavior,* 1:31–47.

Rosenblatt, L. M. 1983. The reading transaction: What for? In R. P. Parker, and F. A. Davis (eds.), *Developing literacy: Young children's use of language* (pp. 118–35). Newark, DE: International Reading Association.

Rowe, M. B. 1969. Science, soul and sanctions. *Science and Children,* 6(6):11–13.

Sanders, D. P. and Schwab, M. 1981. Schooling and the development of education. *Educational Forum,* 45, 265–289.

Santiago, R. L. 1985. Understanding bilingual education—or the sheep in wolf's clothing. *Educational Leadership,* 43(1), 79–83.

Sarason, S. B. 1982. *The culture of the school and the problem of change.* Boston: Allyn and Bacon.

Savignon, S. J. 1983. *Communicative competence: Theory and classroom practice.* Reading, MA: Addison-Wesley Publishing Company.

Saville-Troike, M. 1978. *A guide to culture in the classroom.* Washington, DC: National Clearinghouse for Bilingual Education.

Saville-Troike, M. 1980. Cross-cultural communication in the classroom. In J. E. Alatis (ed.), *Current issues in bilingual education* (pp. 348–55). Washington, DC: Georgetown University Press.

Saville-Troike, M. 1982. The development of bilingual and bicultural competence in young children. In L. G. Katz (ed.), *Current Topics in Early Childhood Education* (pp. 1–16). Norwood, NJ: Ablex Publishing Corporation.

Scarcella, R., and Higa, C. 1982. Input and age differences in second language acquisition. In S. D. Krashen, R. C. Scarcella and M. H. Long (eds.), *Child-Adult differences in second language acquisition* (pp. 175–201). Rowley, MA: Newbury House Publishers.

Scardamalia, M.; Bereiter, C.; and Fillion, B. 1981. *Writing for results: A sourcebook of consequential composing activities.* LaSalle, IL: Open Court Publishing Company.

Scheer, J., and Bileck, M. 1964. *Rain makes applesauce.* New York: Holiday House.

Schlossman, S. 1978. The politics of child psychology in the 1970s. 79(4), 788–808.

Schmidt, V. E., and McNeill, E. 1978. *Cultural awareness: A resource bibliography.* Washington, DC: National Association for the Education of Young Children.

Schmuck, R., and Schmuck, P. 1979. *Group processes in the classroom.* (2d ed.). Dubuque, IA: William C. Brown.

Searfoss, L., and Readance, J. (eds.) 1985. *Helping children learn to read.* Englewood Cliffs, NJ: Prentice-Hall.

Seelye, H. N. 1984. *Teaching culture: Strategies for intercultural communication.* Lincolnwood, IL: National Textbook Company.

Sharan, S. 1980. Cooperative learning in small groups: Recent methods and effects on achievement, attitudes and ethnic relations. *Review of Educational Research,* 50(2):241–71.

Sharan, S. 1984. *Cooperative learning in the classroom: Research in desegregated schools.* Hillsdale, NJ: Lawrence Erlbaum Associates.

Shatz, M. and Gelman, R. 1973. The development of communication skills: Modifications in the speech of young children as a function of listener. *Monographs of the Society for Research in Child Development,* 35 (5, Serial No. 152).

Sheehy, G. 1986. *Spirit of survival.* New York: William Morrow & Company.

Short, T. R., and Dickerson, B. 1980. *The newspaper: An alternative textbook.* Belmont, CA: David S. Lake Publishers.

Silberman, C. E. (ed.) 1973. *The open classroom reader.* New York: Random House.

Silverstein, S. 1974. *Where the sidewalk ends.* New York: Harper and Row.

Simmons, J. S., and Palmer, B. C. 1985. *Reading by doing: An introduction to effective reading.* Lincolnwood, IL: National Textbook Co.

Sirotnik, K. A. 1983. What you see is what you get: Consistency, persistency, and mediocrity in classrooms. *Harvard Educational Review,* 53(1):16–31.

Slavin, R. E. 1980. Cooperative learning. *Review of Educational Research,* 50(2):315–42.

Slavin, R. E. 1981. Synthesis of research on cooperative learning. *Educational Leadership,* 38(8):655–660.

Slavin, R. E. 1983a. *Cooperative learning.* New York: Longman.

Slavin, R. E. 1983b. *Student team learning: An overview and practical guide.* Washington, DC: National Education Association.

Slavin, R. E. 1983c. When does cooperative learning increase student achievement? *Psychological Bulletin,* 94(3):429–45.

Smith, C. A. 1982. *Promoting the social development of young children.* Palo Alto, CA: Mayfield.

Smith, C. A., and Foat, C. 1983. *Once upon a mind: Using children's literature for self-discovery.* Manhattan, KS Kansas State University.

Smith, E. J. and London, C. B. G. 1981. Overview: A union of school, community, and family. *Urban Education,* 16(3), 247–260.

Smith, F. 1971. *Understanding reading.* New York: Holt, Rinehart, & Winston.

Smith, F. 1984. The promise and threat of microcomputers for language learners. In J. Handscombe, R. A. Orem, and B. P. Taylor (eds.), *On TESOL '83: The question of control* (pp. 1–18). Washington, DC: Teachers of English to Speakers of Other Languages.

Smith, F. 1985. A metaphor for literacy: Creating worlds or shunting information? In D. R. Olson, N. Torrance, and A. Hildyard (eds.), *Literacy, language and learning* (pp. 195–213). Cambridge: Cambridge University Press.

Smith, F. 1985 *Reading without nonsense.* Second Edition. New York: Teachers College Press.

Snow, C. E. 1972. Mothers' speech to children learning language. *Child Development,* 43(2):549–65.

Snow, C. E. 1977. Mothers' speech research: From input to interaction. In C. E. Snow, and C. A. Ferguson (eds.), *Talking to children: Language input and acquisition* (pp. 31–49). Cambridge: Cambridge University Press.

Snow, C. E., and Ferguson, C. A. (eds.) 1977. *Talking to children: Language input and acquisition.* Cambridge: Cambridge University Press.

Sobel, J. 1983. *Everybody wins: 393 non-competitive games for young children.* New York: Walker.

Spindler, G. D. & Spindler, L. S. (eds.) 1981. Roger Halker and Schonhausen: From instrumental adaptation in an urbanizing German village. In G. D. Spindler (ed.), *Education and cultural process: Toward an anthropology of education.* New York: Holt, Rinehart & Winston.

Spindler, G. D. & Spindler, L. S. (eds.) 1987. *Interpretive ethnography of education: At home and abroad.* Hillsdale, NJ: Lawrence Erlbaum Associates.

Spolsky, B. 1979. The comparative study of first and second language acquisition. In F. R. Eckman and A. J. Hastings (eds.), *Studies in first and second language acquisition* (pp. 167–84). Rowley, MA: Newbury House Publishers.

Staton, J. 1981. Literacy as an interactive process. *The Linguistic Reporter,* 24(2):1–5.

Stauffer, R. G. 1970. *The language-experience approach to the teaching of reading.* New York: Harper & Row.

Stauffer, R. G. 1975. *Directing the reading-thinking process.* New York: Harper & Row.

Steffensen, M. S.; Joag-dev, C.; and Anderson, R. C. 1979. A cross-cultural perspective on reading comprehension. *Reading Research Quarterly,* 15:10–29.

Stegall, C. 1977. Nashery. *Language Arts,* 54(7):767–74.

Stevick, E. W. 1982. *Teaching and learning languages: A way and ways.* Cambridge: Cambridge University Press.

Stocking, S. H.; Arezzo, D.; and Leavitt, S. 1980. *Helping kids make friends.* Allen, TX: Argus Communications.

Strevens, P. 1983. Teachers of—what? A global look at the "E" of TESOL. In M. A. Clarke, and J. Handscombe (eds.), *On TESOL '82: Pacific perspectives on language learning and teaching.* Washington, DC: Teachers of English to Speakers of Other Languages.

Strong, M. 1983. Social styles and the second language acquisition of Spanish-speaking kindergartners. *TESOL Quarterly,* 17(2):241–58.

Sulzby, E. 1986. Writing and reading: Signs of oral and written language organization in the young child. In W. H. Teale, and E. Sulzby (eds.), *Emergent literacy: Writing and reading* (pp. 50–89). Norwood, NJ: Ablex Publishing Corporation.

Sutton-Smith, B. 1982. A performance theory of peer relations. In K. M. Borman (ed.), *The social life of children in a changing society* (pp. 65–77). Hillsdale, NJ: Lawrence Erlbaum Associates.

Swain, M. 1985. Communicative competence: Some roles of comprehensible input and comprehensible output in its development. In S. M. Gass and C. G. Madden (eds.), *Input in second language acquisition* (pp. 235–53). Rowley, MA: Newbury House Publishers.

Swift, J. N., and Gooding, C. T. 1983. Interaction of wait time feedback and questioning instruction on middle school science reading. *Journal of Research in Science Teaching*, 20(8):721–30.

Tafoya, T. 1983. Coyote in the classroom: The use of American-Indian oral tradition with young children. In O. N. Saracho, and B. Spodek (eds.), *Understanding the multicultural experience in early childhood education* (pp. 35–44). Washington, D.C.: National Association for the Education of Young Children.

Taylor, D. 1983. *Family literacy: Young children learning to read and write.* Exeter, NH: Heinemann Educational Books.

Taylor, N. E.; Blum, I. H.; and Logsdon, D. M. 1986. The development of written language awareness: Environmental aspects and program characteristics. *Reading Research Quarterly*, 21(2):132–49.

Teale, W. H., and Sulzby, E. (eds.) 1986. *Emergent literacy: Writing and reading.* Norwood, NJ: Ablex Publishing Corporation.

Temple, C., Nathan, W., and Burris, N. 1982. *The beginnings of writing.* Boston: Allyn and Bacon.

Terrell, T. D. 1982. A natural approach. In R. Blair (ed.), *Innovative approaches to language teaching* (pp. 160–73). Rowley, MA: Newbury House Publishers.

Tiedt, P. L., and Tiedt, I. M. 1979. *Multicultural teaching: A handbook of activities, information and resources.* Boston: Allyn & Bacon.

Tizard, B., and Hughes, M. 1984. *Young children learning.* London: Fontana Paperbacks.

Tizard, J., Schofield, W., and Hewison, J. 1982. Collaboration between teachers and parents in assisting children's reading. *British Journal of Educational Psychology*, 52(1):1–15.

Tobin, K. G. 1986. Effects of teacher wait time on discourse characteristics in mathematics and language arts classes. *American Educational Research Journal*, 23(2):191–200.

Toffler, A. 1970. *Future shock.* New York: Random House.

Tough, J. 1985. *Talk two: Children using English as a second language in primary schools.* London: Onyx Press.

Trelease, J. 1982. *The read-aloud handbook.* New York: Penguin Books.

Trueba, H. T.; Gutherie, G. P.; and Au, K. H. (eds.). 1981. *Culture and the bilingual classroom: Studies in classroom ethnography.* Rowley, MA: Newbury House Publishers.

Urzúa, C. 1985. How do you evaluate your own elementary program? Look to kids. In P. Larson, E. L. Judd, and D. S. Messerschmitt (eds.), *On TESOL '84: A brave new world for TESOL* (pp. 219–32). Washington, DC: Teachers of English to Speakers of Other Languages.

Van Allen, R. 1976. *Language experiences in communication.* Boston: Houghton Mifflin Company.

Van Allen, R., and Allen, C. 1976. *Language experience activities.* Boston: Houghton Mifflin Company.

Van Dongen, R. 1987. Children's narrative thought, at home and at school. *Language Arts,* 64(1):79–87.

Veatch, J.; Sawicki, F.; Elliott, G.; Barnette, E.; and Blakey, J. 1973. *Key words to reading: The language experience approach begins.* Columbus, OH: Charles E. Merrill Publishing Company.

Ventriglia, L. 1982. *Conversations of Miguel and Maria: How children learn a second language.* Reading, MA: Addison-Wesley Publishing Company.

Vygotsky, L. S. 1978. *Minds in society: The development of higher psychological processes.* Cambridge, MA: Harvard University Press.

Walberg, H. J., Paschal, R. A., and Weinstein, T. 1985. Homework's powerful effects on learning. *Educational Leadership,* 42(7):76–79.

Walters, K. and Gunderson, L. 1985. Effects of parent volunteers reading first language (L1) books to ESL students. *The Reading Teacher,* 39(1):66–69.

Watson, D. 1985. Watching and listening to children read. In A. Jaggar, and M. T. Smith-Burke (eds.), *Observing the Language Learner* (pp. 115–28). Newark, DE: International Reading Association.

Waynant, L., and Wilson, R. 1974. *Learning centers: A guide for effective use.* Paoli, PA: The Instructo Corporation.

Wells, C. G. 1974. Learning to code experience through language. *Journal of Child Language,* 1(1):243–69.

Wells, C. G. 1981. *Learning through interaction: The study of language development.* Cambridge, England: Cambridge University Press.

Wells, C. G. 1986. *The meaning makers: Children learning language and using language to learn.* Portsmouth, NH: Heinemann Educational Books.

Wells, C. G. 1987. Apprenticeship in Literacy. *Interchange,* 18(1–2):109–23.

Wells, C. G., and Robinson, W. P. 1982. The role of adult speech in language development. In C. Fraser, and K. R. Sherer (eds.), *Advances in the social psychology of language* (pp. 11–76). Cambridge, England: Cambridge University Press.

Wendelin, K. H., and Greenlaw, M. J. 1984. *Storybook classrooms: Using children's literature in the learning center.* Atlanta, GA: Humanics Limited.

Whitehead, R. J. 1975. *The early school years read aloud program* (Four Volumes, Fall, Winter, Spring, Summer). Homewood, IL: ETC Publications.

Widdowson, H. G. 1979. *Teaching language as communication.* Oxford: Oxford University Press.

Wigginton, E. 1985. *Sometimes a shining moment: The Foxfire experience.* Garden City, NY: Anchor Press/Doubleday.

Williams, L. R., and De Gaetano, Y. 1985. *A multicultural, bilingual approach to teaching young children.* Reading, MA: Addison-Wesley Publishing Company.

Wolf, D. 1985. Ways of telling: Text repertoires in elementary school children. *Journal of Education,* 167(1):71–85.

Wong-Fillmore, L. 1976. *The second time around: Cognitive and social strategies in second language acquisition.* Unpublished doctoral dissertation. Stanford University.

Wong-Fillmore, L. 1982. Instructional language as linguistic input: Second language learning in classrooms. In L. Cherry-Wilkinson (ed.), *Communicating in the classroom* (pp. 283–96). New York: Academic Press.

Wong-Fillmore, L. 1983. The language learner as an individual: Implications of research on individual differences for the ESL teacher. In M. A. Clarke, and J. Handscombe (eds.), *On TESOL '82: Pacific perspectives on language learning and teaching* (pp. 157–73). Washington, DC: Teachers of English to Speakers of Other Languages.

Wong-Fillmore, L. 1985. When does teacher talk work as input? In S. M. Gass & C. G. Madden (eds.), *Input in second language acquisition* (pp. 17–50). Rowley, MA: Newbury House.

Wong-Fillmore, L. 1986. Teaching bilingual learners. In M. C. Wittrock (ed.), *Handbook of research on teaching, (3d ed.)* (pp. 648–85). New York: Macmillan Publishing Company.

Wood, D.; Bruner, J. S.; and Ross, G. 1976. The role of tutoring in problem solving. *Journal of Child Psychology and Psychiatry,* 17(2):89–100.

Yalden, J. 1983. Chicken or egg? Communicative methodology or communicative syllabus design? In M. A. Clarke, and J. Handscombe (eds.), *On TESOL '82: Pacific Perspectives in Language Learning and Teaching* (pp. 235–42). Washington, D.C.: Teachers of English to Speakers of Other Languages.

Zeigler, N.; Larson, B.; and Byers, J. 1983. *Let the kids do it!* (Books 1 and 2). Belmont, CA: David S. Lake Publishers.

Index

AUTHOR INDEX

SUBJECT INDEX

**The Addison-Wesley Second Language
Professional Library Series**
Sandra J. Savignon
Consulting Editor

CANTONI-HARVEY, Gina
Content-Area Language Instruction

**CONNOR, Ulla and KAPLAN,
Robert**
Writing Across Languages: Analysis
of L2 Text

**CURTAIN, Helena Anderson
and PESOLA, Carol Ann**
Languages and Children—
Making the Match

DAMEN, Louise
Culture Learning: The Fifth
Dimension in the Language
Classroom

**DUBIN, Fraida, ESKEY, David and
GRABE, William**
Teaching Second Language Reading
for Academic Purposes

MOHAN, Bernard A.
Language and Content

PENFIELD, JOYCE
The Media: Catalysts for
Communicative Language Learning

SAVIGNON, Sandra J.
Communicative Competence:
Classroom Practice

**SAVIGNON, Sandra J. and BERNS,
Margie S.**
Initiatives in Communicative
Language Teaching Volumes I and II

SMITH, Stephen M.
The Theater Arts and the Teaching
of Second Languages

VENTRIGLIA, Linda
Conversations of Miguel and Maria

WALLERSTEIN, Nina
Language and Culture in Conflict